Building Character and Culture

To Fran
dear friend
and gifted
organizer.

Pat Duffy Hutcheon

Building Character and Culture

Pat Duffy Hutcheon

Westport, Connecticut
London

Library of Congress Cataloging-in-Publication Data

Hutcheon, Pat Duffy.
    Building character and culture / Pat Duffy Hutcheon.
      p. cm.
    Includes bibliographical references and index.
    ISBN 0–275–96381–0 (alk. paper).—ISBN 0–275–96469–8 (pbk. :
alk. paper)
    1. Socialization. 2. Character. 3. Moral education. I. Title.
HQ783.H88   1999
303.3'2—dc21   98–33617

British Library Cataloguing in Publication Data is available.

Library of Congress Catalog Card Number: 98–33617
ISBN: 0–275–96381–0
    0–275–96469–8 (pbk.)

First published in 1999

Praeger Publishers, 88 Post Road West, Westport, CT 06881
An imprint of Greenwood Publishing Group, Inc.

Printed in the United States of America

The paper used in this book complies with the
Permanent Paper Standard issued by the National
Information Standards Organization (Z39.48–1984).

10 9 8 7 6 5 4 3 2 1

Contents

Contents

Preface

I would like to thank all those people who have encouraged me in this project, since its conception a number of years ago when my long-simmering concern about the direction in which our culture was going began to mature into outright consternation. My appreciation goes especially to Dr. Erika Erdmann, publisher and editor of *Humankind Advancing*, for her unfailing enthusiasm and support. I also want to extend thanks to the Unitarian Church community of the Vancouver area for providing me with a venue for developing moral education guidelines and curricula, and to Fran Hodgkinson and Conrad Hadland for organizing and leading discussion groups that gave me feedback, from the perspective of the general reading public, on preliminary sketches of some of the key material. Theo Meijer, an instructor in the International Baccalaureate Program at Abbotsford, British Columbia, has also earned my sincere gratitude for editing the entire manuscript in its final stages. Al Cox, formerly of the Psychology Department of Langara College in Vancouver, deserves special mention as well, for his contributions to an early version of Appendix B.

This book has benefited greatly from the help of colleagues who read and commented on early drafts of the various chapters, providing me with invaluable criticism and suggestions for improvement. I would like to mention the following: Dr. James Alcock of the Department of Psychology at York University; Dr. Susan Crawford of the Department of Psychiatry at the University of Illinois at Chicago; Dr. Donald Fisher of the Faculty of Education at the University of British Columbia; Dr. Susan Haack of the Department of Philosophy at the University of Miami; Dr. Roger Herz-Fischler of the Department of Mathematics and Statistics at

Carleton University; Dr. John McTaggart of the Department of Sociology at King's University College, Edmonton; Dr. Nancy Milio of the School of Nursing at the University of North Carolina at Chapel Hill; Dr. William Norton of the Department of Geography at the University of Manitoba; Dr. Ernest Poser, formerly of the Departments of Psychology at the Universities of McGill and British Columbia; Dr. Christian Dieter Schunn and Dr. Beth Littleton of the Department of Psychology of George Mason University; and Dr. Douglas Stewart of the Faculty of Education at the University of Regina. The responsibility for final inclusions, interpretations and conclusions, however, is mine alone.

I would also like to thank the publishers of some of my own earlier works for permission to reprint certain short excerpts from the following chapter and essays: "Toward a Unified Social Science," in *Leaving the Cave: Evolutionary Naturalism in Social Scientific Thought* (Waterloo, ON: Wilfrid Laurier University Press, 1996), pp. 478–481; "A Humanist Perspective on Spirituality," *Humanist in Canada* (Spring, 1994): 5–8, 13; and "Is There a Dark Side to Multiculturalism?" *Humanist in Canada* (Summer, 1994): 26–29.

My heartfelt gratitude goes as well to Professor G. W. Bassett of the University of Queensland in Australia, who first encouraged me to pursue the idea of working toward an interdisciplinary consensus on socialization—the long-term project of which this book is but one essential step. And, finally, I want to express my appreciation to all the members of my family, particularly to my husband, Sandy, for his unfailing support and advice.

Introduction

This is a North American book, but only in the sense that most of the examples used are drawn from the American and Canadian scenes. The issues dealt with are universal. My conclusions and suggestions are equally relevant to all industrializing nations at this troubled point in human history. Thoughtful people everywhere seem to be sensing that their culture is in a destructive downward spiral, and that the situation is in some way contributing to a crisis of character in individuals. But there is so much confusion regarding the nature and sources of culture and character, and of the relationship between the two, that corrective action seems impossible. My purpose in writing this book was twofold. I wanted to persuade parents and ordinary concerned citizens that they should not despair, for we do have the means to improve our situation. Once we recognize that socialization is the critical key to both character and culture, we are in a position to begin to attack the problem. My second objective was to provide students and instructors in education, sociology and the helping professions with a readily understandable, interdisciplinary overview of the nature of the human socialization process, based on the findings of contemporary social science and interpreted from an evolutionary systems perspective.

I had become convinced of the impossibility of progress in the absence of a clear definition of the problem area in terms of some major unifying concept, preferably a concept already familiar to the community of scholars studying the relevant issues. The second necessary step, as I now see it, is to ensure that our clarifying concept is based upon those findings from the life and social sciences that have demonstrated reliability in enabling people to initiate and direct change. The completion of these initial steps should allow us to identify the directions for change implied by our conceptual clarification of the problem. Only after all this is done will it be possible to attempt the kind of workable, step-by-step reform demanded by the complexity and interactive nature of the process. Our current social scene is no place for massive programs based on grandiose visions. We *can* do better, but only if we rely on rigorously tested hypotheses and continuous monitoring of results to see whether we are in fact moving in the desired direction.

The social-psychological concept of socialization describes and explains the dynamic, adaptive, feedback process by which human beings acquire their beliefs and values in the context of *social interaction*. It is through this uniquely human process that new entrants join the ongoing community of thought and make their contributions to it. Socialization results in character and knowledge in the individual and an evolving culture (or civilization) for the group as a whole. If we are to learn anything about how and why people behave as they do—and how this behavior can be changed so as to make the world a better and safer and more sustainable place—we must comprehend the all-important role of socialization.

As an educator and sociologist, I have for some time felt an urge to put together in readily readable, essay form what I consider to be the most reliable conclusions currently available about this process. In attempting this small beginning, I make no claim to infallibility; nor would I even go so far as to maintain that my fellow professionals and I have access to a body of "hard scientific knowledge" on this subject—as yet. I believe, rather, that we are still in the "pre-scientific" stage of development: that stage which requires a focus on rigorous definition and precise communication among those who work in the area concerned. I see this book as a contribution to the necessary initial task of clarifying the problem. What follows is therefore not intended as gospel. It is merely the best judgment on the subject that I can make on the basis of a lifetime's study of socialization from the perspective of a number of relevant disciplines.

I also make no claim to value neutrality. In each of the ten chapters comprising *Building Character and Culture*, my intent has been to move from careful and informed analysis of present conditions to the implications for society flowing from that analysis; and then to argue with all the persuasion I can muster for a reasoned, informed and humanitarian assault on our self-created problems. This book is dedicated to the proposition that we need what the would-be social sciences have always sought: reliable facts resulting from the testing of hypotheses about the way social relations operate in the real world. If they are to be workable, conceptual tools of the type that I am hoping to clarify can only be derived from a model or frame of reference rooted in the most compel-

ble from the life and social sciences. It is the broad
olutionary systems model of human socialization
to present.

hat we can begin to shed light on the socialization
to grips with what it is that makes us distinctive
ll of the fascinating possibilities and limitations
need to recognize that human distinctiveness
nd culture-building propensities, and in the key
nnecting the two. This means that we can never
ing problems until we face up to our unique
he fact that humans learn both from the so-
re so crucially dependent for the contents of
from the physical environment that confronts
turn. It is our immersion in this interactive
ional and developmental change that defines
most complex of all the dynamic adaptive
tion.

chapters are intended to drive home this all-
important understanding. Chapter 1 examines the power of culture: that
humanly created environment which provides both energy and direction
for humanity. Culture is presented as a world of images and artifacts, of
ideas and customs, of shared memories of the past and visions of the
future. It is a world that shapes our characters as inevitably as the available supply of food, water and fresh air determines physical health. Human institutions form the framework of culture. They have their origins
in collective ways of doing things that have endured for countless millennia, along with the structures of social organization that gradually
developed to further their operation. They comprise the beliefs about the
nature of things in which these organizations are grounded, as well as
the ideals and goals which inspire and guide them. Ten apparently essential institutional functions are identified in this chapter—and their
probable evolutionary origin described. These include the family relationships involved in procreation and nurturing; the group's historical
record and the products of its artistic and scientific endeavors; its sacred
objects, rituals and symbolized ideals; its organized means of acquiring
and defending territory; its arrangements for providing order and security; its organizations for making and administering policy decisions;
its established customs for producing and distributing resources; and its
formal means of socializing the young. This cultural environment alters
the physical surroundings, just as the latter limit and control the direction taken by the culture. At the same time, in a complex, self-generating
interactive feedback process, the individual affects—and is affected by—
both worlds.

Chapter 2 deals with what it means to be human. It proceeds from the premise that if we are ever to understand what makes us different from the other animals, we must appreciate the ways in which we are similar. Once we do this, we realize that there is no need to look for essentially unknowable sources of the self-consciousness that engendered human-kind's transition into culture. We discover that there is available a per-fectly natural explanation based on the findings of archeology, evolutionary science and anthropology: one that recognizes the uniqueness of our species as a readily comprehensible result of the gradual evolution of the human capacity for *language*. Among the distinctively human characteristics made possible by language are the ability to imag-ine and create objects of art; to respect and marvel at the forces deter-mining our origin and destiny; to sense and remember regularities in experience and to seek to explain them; to idealize and value the objects of our love and to make moral judgments; and to transmit the results of these activities across the generations. All these things define us as hu-man. They are the capacities that make it possible for us to build from the sum of life experience our individual characters and collective cul-tures.

Evidence from the social and life sciences indicates that we have little choice but to accept the fact that the adult transmitters and carriers of culture have a compelling shaping effect on the character of the young. This occurs because the individual is a two-way conduit for socializa-tion—influencing others and being influenced by them in turn. The sig-nificance of this process stems from the fact that it is the chief source of individual learning and social change, and that biological evolution op-erates in tandem with the cultural at every juncture. Because socialization is the one factor in development amenable to human direction, those who function in a socializing capacity are incredibly potent in determin-ing the direction that a society takes. The role in this process of the family, mass media, peer group, school, place of worship and other com-munity organizations is too often inadvertent, unrecognized and un-planned. Nonetheless, as discussed in Chapter 3, these social entities determine the *context* in which the child learns as well as the *content* of the habits, ideals, beliefs and values acquired.

We have no hope of understanding how culture is assimilated if we do not have some idea of how children learn. It is a complex three-way process, due to the fact that maturation and socialization intersect and influence one another at every stage, in response to the demands of the physical environment. Caregivers need to be aware that, for newborn infants, every experience counts. Those little ego-driven seekers and im-itative sponges are, in fact, superbly efficient primitive scientists, geog-raphers, artists and recapitulators of the history of the species. From the moment of birth, their learning proceeds both systematically and devel-opmentally—by means of trial-and-error forays into their surroundings and through imitation of available models. Desirable role models are crucial, as is an environment rich in challenging stimuli and opportunities for the natural reinforcement of life-enhancing responses. Whether or not we wish it so, we are all models for our miniature artists in their self-creation, just as we all participate in the reinforcement of their behaviors, for good or ill. Every one of us is irrevocably enmeshed in the socializing-learning process; we cannot opt out any more than a fish can choose to leave the water. Chapter 4 demonstrates how we, as humans, are shaped by conditions in the present and, in our turn, contribute to the shaping of the future. It explains the process celebrated by the Roman poet Lucretius over two thousand years ago when he wrote: "Our lives we borrow from each other; and men, like runners, pass along the torch of life."

Chapter 5 asks, "Where does character come from?" The search for answers takes us into the sources of popular beliefs about whether or not people *learn* to be sinners or saints. Religious and philosophical world views that imply an ethical role for humans in the universe are contrasted to those defining us as powerless in this sense. The assumption here is that world views *matter*. They determine whether we see values as merely relative and subjective or whether we consider them a necessarily objective and collective concern: a concern rising out of the biological and social history of our species, the imperatives of group survival and our joint responsibility for the future. Our world views either predispose us to recognize an integral relationship between knowledge and morality—and between morality and art—or they encourage us to deny any connections among these key human pursuits. They determine whether we believe it is acceptable to use immoral means to achieve our goals; or whether we believe, instead, that every goal is shaped by the means employed to reach it, and that every end becomes the means to an end that beckons further on. Finally, our world views affect the way we approach the issue of character building: of how we can encourage and enhance the moral development of children and whether, in fact, we consider it necessary or possible at all.

Several chapters explore the problem from the perspective of the enveloping culture. Culture is viewed not as a seamless web but as the evolving product of a nesting system of social worlds within social worlds, each contributing to the shaping and control of the individuals who derive their ways of being from these surroundings. The all-enveloping culture of violence; the co-existing two-world cultures of poverty and affluence; the mutually incompatible cultures of pluralism and tribalism; the multi-layered culture of fantasy: all are explored along with their consequences for the socialization process and the survival of the social group.

The horrific consequences of five decades of a steadily accelerating deluge of media violence are identified in Chapter 6. Clearly discernible is the dark cultural whirlpool created by that deluge: a whirlpool threatening to engulf all who are exposed to it—regardless of age and family background. Chapter 7 focuses on socialization as it occurs at later stages of the human life cycle. It looks, as well, at the methods available for modern societies to re-incorporate drop-outs and to rehabilitate offenders. Readers should not be surprised to note that the same principles of learning operate throughout the socialization-learning process—whether the individuals involved are acquiring or relinquishing various adult roles, or whether they are in the process of replacing destructive behaviors and attitudes with a more socially beneficial and workable approach to life.

The thesis of Chapter 8 is that the culture of violence discussed in Chapter 6 feeds into a dysfunctional "culture of poverty" which is in many ways a distorted mirror of the prevailing "culture of affluence." Both subcultures tend to reinforce immediate self-gratification at the expense of concern for the welfare of the group over the long term. Both are inherently unstable: the culture of poverty because it destroys its young; and the culture of affluence because it is founded on two irreconcilable and unwarranted premises. One of these is the "conservative myth": a belief in the utopia of an unrestricted free market of goods and services in which the best inevitably rise to the top. The other is the "liberal myth" that universal entitlements, financed from a bottomless well of government funds, are the answer to social inequality. The chapter's conclusion is that the all-too-predictable result of this confusion is an increasingly stratified—but nominally egalitarian—society in which the school is asked to do the impossible in its role as an agent of social mobility.

In Chapter 9 we look at the culture of tribalism toward which modern democratic societies appear to be moving. A comparison with the culture of pluralism and with the situation in other parts of the world where tribalism has flourished would seem to indicate that we should be applying the brakes while there is yet time. History shows that the journey into tribalism is a notoriously one-way street. Although its proponents often wave the flag of pluralism, their route, in fact, leads elsewhere— away from the civic society that makes collective self-government possible. Too often the tribal dance has propelled true believers and skeptics alike into an anarchic wilderness of social fragmentation and intergroup conflict. One of the conclusions forced upon us by the information in this book is that uniqueness is a characteristic of *individuals*—not of ingroups defined by their so-called "racial" roots. The complexities of the interactive process of maturation and socialization allow for no other possibility.

We return to this process in Chapter 10 to examine some possible developmental causes of another serious problem plaguing modern democracies. This is the lack, in the public at large, of critical thinking and the corresponding capacity to make wise choices. Once again, it is a symptom of inappropriate or failed socialization. The prevailing culture of fantasy that results from this failure is identified as the source of our widespread gullibility and inclination to delusion. How many times have we wondered why it is that so many people are so readily satisfied with explanations that reveal nothing whatsoever about how a puzzling condition arose, nor how it can be remedied; and why more people today are committed to a belief in aliens than to the logic of scientific inquiry? Why do so many of us seem to desire, and even insist upon, responses that call not on readily ascertainable facts but on unknowable mystery and magic? Or conversely, why are some of the uniquely fortunate among us stimulated by an apparently "natural" curiosity to seek out answers that explain how things came to be the way they are, answers that serve to open up rather than to close off the inquiry process?

Chapter 10 presents the proposition that, because of our past history of socialization, a number of interpretive modes or what can be called "explainways" now co-exist in the broader culture. It suggests that youngsters are able to understand and benefit from different kinds of explanations at different levels of conceptual development—and that adults continue to apply these in varying circumstances, as their emotional needs dictate. These are thought to vary from the *magical* explainway typical of early childhood through the *tautological*, *projective*, and *ideological*—to the *conjectural* or cause-and-effect mode made possible by achievement of the "formal" or abstract level of reasoning. However, the conclusion here is that, as in the case of moral development, the corresponding level of conceptual reasoning is merely *necessary* for progression through these stages; it is not *sufficient* to guarantee success. The content of the culture and the socialization process by means of which it is transmitted and created are crucial.

A country with a culture in which a majority of the adult population has failed to acquire the habit of connecting cause to consequence in daily life, and of generalizing from observations and applying principles to experience, is a dangerous world in which to live. So, too, is a violence-prone society fragmented along class and tribal lines. It is time we realized that there are no short-sighted, self-serving ways to avoid "the tragedy of the commons," any more than there can exist a tribally gratifying pathway to a pluralist culture. By the same token, there are no magical or ideological shortcuts to the type of civic society where unique individuals would feel at home, and within which the socialization process could forge the kinds of character required for world citizenship. I am suggesting that there can be no solutions to our current problems if we continue to ignore the central role of socialization in the lives of all of us. The recurring theme of *Building Character and Culture* is that morally responsible, inquiring and creative contributors to the self-government essential for a humanly fulfilling process of cultural evolution do not come fully formed from the womb. They develop only gradually throughout a lifetime of adaptation to surrounding contingencies: contingencies that we dare not leave to chance.

CHAPTER 1

The Power of Culture

There is a dawning recognition among ordinary people that something is dreadfully wrong in modern industrial society. We are destroying our earthly home. Too many of our habitual behaviors contribute to the degradation of our physical surroundings and the disappearance of valuable forms of life. We are losing control of our lives. Too many people from all walks of life are abusing drugs. We are losing control of our cities. Too many of our streets have become dangerous places where predators lurk in the dark and pre-adolescents are encouraged to sell their unformed bodies in return for drugs. We are losing control of our offspring. Too many children prey on one another, with guns and knives. Too many babies are being born to unwed teen-aged mothers. We are losing the precious core of values necessary for keeping any society workable. Too many youngsters cheat and break the law without compunction. Too many of our news media make heroes of ruthless commercial exploiters and serial murderers. Too many of our political leaders and professional and business people have abandoned ethics.

In the face of all this it may seem trite to say that it all comes down to a matter of character, and how that character is formed, and to a matter of culture, and how that culture is formed. But it is true. Character and culture are what it is all about. Until we understand what it means to be a human being capable of acquiring a character and participating in and contributing to a culture, we will have no hope of solving the problems that are growing worse with every passing day.

Far more than we can ever know, culture is our destiny: the source of both the beliefs that inform us and the values that guide us. Two experiences recalled by two different officials with the Canadian International

Development Agency (CIDA) in two very different developing countries will serve to illustrate this. The first story tells of neighboring farmers in India. One has used Canadian-supplied fertilizer to vastly increase his yields, feed his family and invest in new equipment. The other has refused to adopt the new farming methods and remains in poverty. The reason? The second farmer believes in reincarnation. He is convinced that he is being punished for sins committed in a previous existence, and only by accepting his fate can he hope for a better life next time around. His particular belief system is a far more limiting prison than any imposed by genetic predisposition or external circumstance. The second story comes from the recollections of a teacher in Tanzania. For ten years he had experimented with growing improved varieties of corn in an area where, although it was the staple food, the plant matured so poorly that the people lived in semi-starvation. His corn consistently grew taller and produced more abundantly than any of the neighboring plots. Yet, in all those years, not one person ever asked him how this had come to be. The prison in this case was the magical conceptual world of essentially mysterious, arbitrary and unknowable forces imposed on every individual from birth by a culture preserved and transmitted through previous generations.

Some cultural beliefs have consequences in the real world that are appallingly destructive. Yet they are tolerated because they are defined as spiritual and therefore somehow assumed to be embedded in the nature of things, and thus above the laws devised by human beings. For example, in 1997 a member of the Ojibwa tribe in the province of Ontario in Canada was acquitted on a charge of manslaughter, in spite of irrefutable evidence that he had bludgeoned an innocent man to death. Why was the killer exonerated? The victim was reputed to have been a "bear-walker"—a powerful demon who uses sorcery to trigger fatal illnesses in people—and the "cultural hero" who had wielded the ceremonial walrus bone with such devastating effect had believed that he was merely performing a ritual defense of his people. The decision of the court has been praised by some academics as a long-overdue recognition of aboriginal culture.

A similar series of events occurred during 1996 and 1997 in Ghana, Nigeria, Ivory Coast and Senegal. Lynch mobs burned and beat to death a number of people accused of being sorcerers. Their crime? Genital thievery! They are believed to have used their powers to cause a man's penis to shrink or disappear by means of something as innocuous as a handshake. For people conditioned by their culture not to rely on evidence, it seems that not even one instance of a vanishing penis is required to set the scene for mob vengeance.

Industrialized societies can be similarly victimized by unquestioned cultural imperatives. One example is the way that we have unthinkingly created optimal conditions for the spread of AIDS in North America by jettisoning well-tested measures for containing infections while at the same time failing to discourage an explosion of drug abuse and sexual promiscuity in our inner cities. Culture is also implicated in the appalling inroads made by the AIDS epidemic in Africa during the past fifteen years. Since the 1980s the disease has battered most of central and east Africa—its deadly progress enhanced by the tyranny of a culture supporting polygamy and nurturing excessive reliance on denial and taboo. As of 1997, it was calculated that in the world at large, 16,000 people a day were being infected with the virus, with a large percentage of these new infections occurring in Africa. Since apartheid was ended in South Africa, the population in that country has begun to experience an exponential spread of the HIV virus, with the result that, by 1997, there were, proportionately, three times as many infected people there as in the United States. If present trends continue it is estimated that life expectancy in South Africa—which had been on the increase for some time—will fall from 63 to 40 years in one decade. A major reason for the absence of any effective official response to the problem is the resurgence of belief in ancestral spirits and "traditional" medicine. Even the highly schooled are putting their faith in witchdoctors who claim that they can effect cures by smearing secret herbal potions on the body.

Not all of the apparently obsolete beliefs and customs that endure are equally harmful in today's world, however. Many have simply outlived their usefulness. They now seem merely quaint and, at the worst, unnecessarily limiting to individual freedom of choice. Examples of the latter are dietary rules pursued by some of the major religions. One can readily surmise how these might have contributed to survival in past millennia. Another example may be the Chinese law, still extant in some countries, prohibiting the intermarriage of clan members who are identified according to a common family name. Considering what we now know about the harmfulness of inbreeding, it is easy to understand how these Confucian rules amounted to an "evolutionarily stable strategy" for the groups that followed them some 25 centuries ago. Today, however, when vast numbers of unrelated members of the population answer to the same surname, the old restrictions—obviously without relevance—can inflict real hardship on courting couples, and even on society.

THE TRIPLE HELIX

But, of course, we need not—and should not—accept without question such archaic cultural demands and constraints. For, just as they can cripple and imprison us, our beliefs and values and ways of being in the world have the potential to free us from much of the determinism otherwise imposed by biological predisposition and the imperatives of climate and geographical terrain. In order to better understand the complex interrelationships involved, we can think of genes, physical environment and culture as three strands in an incredibly complex "triple helix." All three contribute to the shaping of individuals as well as the societies they form. Any one of the three can become the decisive factor if, for any reason, contingency operates so as to precipitate a situation where that one strand overrides the other two.

The inheritance of a severe genetic defect sufficient to prevent learning is a case in point. The other two strands of the "triple helix" can be similarly overridden by a dominant world view so closed by ideological commitment, or so past-oriented, magical or authoritarian, that there is little opportunity for critical thinking or imagination. A destructive family setting during early childhood can cripple subsequent emotional and moral development, regardless of biological potential. Climatic conditions imposing severe limits on the availability of food and shelter can be ultra-determinative of both the customs that are possible and the genes that survive. For example, life in the Arctic regions was such that, however much incoming tribes may have differed ethnically upon arrival, the sheer exigencies of survival—combined with the low level of technology common to all of them—forced groups to make similar choices of lifestyle. Conversely, conditions that make group life so effortless and problem-free that little or no adaptive challenge is demanded by the surroundings can override all else, thus condemning the culture to remain at a primitive level. The aboriginal cultures of the Pacific islands and some areas in Africa could be examples of this.

The cultural geographer Carl Sauer offers a different interpretation, however, in his suggestion that Southeast Asia was a key area of early agricultural advance precisely *because* of its adequate resources combined with the leisure time made possible by a hospitable environment. This may have been true of the Fertile Crescent as well. Genetic analysis of the "founder crop" of einkorn wheat in 1997 has provided the first hard evidence that the practice of agriculture originated there, in southeastern Turkey's Karacadag Mountains, 10,000 years ago. The head start obtained by the peoples of this region is explained by Jared Diamond in his 1997 book *Guns, Germs and Steel: The Fates of Human Societies*. He cites the availability of singularly opportune environmental contingencies such as big-grained protein-rich cereals and small-brained, easy-to-tame mammals (such as sheep, pigs and horses) as contrasted to the conditions obtaining in Australia and Africa.

An instance of what can happen with the occurrence of a severe alteration of environmental circumstances has recently come to light. Scientists are unearthing evidence that a disturbance in the pattern and frequency of El Niño which occurred in the Andes Mountains of Peru over three thousand years ago suddenly posed new environmental opportunities and challenges for the inhabitants. Apparently, this crucial event precipitated the emergence of one of the most complex civilizations of all time.

Four of the other earliest advanced cultures probably came into being largely as a result of an expanding population's need to exploit the agricultural potential of fertile river valleys by harnessing the rivers into functioning irrigation systems. This seems to have been a major impetus for enormous technological advances and corresponding cultural spirals in the ancient civilizations that sprouted along the Indus River in India, the Nile River in Egypt, the Tigris-Euphrates River system in the Middle East and the Yellow River in China. Somewhat similarly, the accessibility of ocean travel no doubt had much to do with the explosion of complexity in the ancient Minoan civilization on the Greek island of Crete, and in the subsequent Mycenaean culture of the Achaeans.

For we now know that human beings have the capacity to be much more than merely carriers and transmitters of past traditions and myths. Although most of us are insufficiently aware of the fact, humans are also the creators of culture—if the conditions of life happen to encourage it— and therein lies the hope and promise of our species. Most of our current problems stem from the fact that so few are willing to accept the inevitable and awesome responsibility involved in this. Yet the evidence is incontrovertible that, as knowing and valuing animals, we forge the future with every choice we make. The course of human history is to a large extent directed by the evolution of scientific knowledge (itself a response to environmental challenges and opportunities such as those discussed above) and the technological innovations and social changes that follow in its wake. It is also shaped by the definitions of present and future as envisioned and communicated by artists and other interpreters of the social scene.

That said, however, it is essential to understand that no particular technology or institutional arrangement is wholly *determined* by the science and art currently prevailing in the culture. Art does indeed bring forth a variety of compelling and seductive models and images for humans to emulate, and the growth of scientific knowledge does provide a continuously expanding range of possibilities to explore, as well as the tools with which to do it. But, within the realm of what surrounding conditions and genetic predisposition make possible, it is the sum of individual habits and value choices that actually charts the future. At the same time, culture building is itself a two-way street. To a degree seldom appreciated, the habits and values driving our responses and decisions are conditioned by interaction with other people and by what is felt and seen and heard and read in the surroundings. As previously pointed out, culture operates as but one of the three strands of the "triple helix." It is affected by the current contents of the gene pool of humanity and by the current challenges of the physical environment—both of which are, in turn, being continuously altered by the effects of sociocultural change.

Given the physical terrain provided by these limiting and motivating factors, it is as if our art and science constitute the aesthetic and technological equipment for building the future road of an inextricably intertwined genetic-cultural co-evolution. All the while, however, *human values* are astride the driver's seat of the road-building machine: values which have their source in the very culture that is either continuously being forged by our artistic and scientific endeavors or frozen into anachronistic form by our mythologies. We are all contributors to—and joint enforcers of—the social norms and ideals of today and tomorrow; just as we are all the products of those established and perpetuated by our predecessors. This interactive process, which we call *socialization* or *enculturation*, is at the very root of the powerful cultural strand of the "triple helix." Unfortunately, it is as yet little understood by most of the humans who shape and are shaped by it.

What all this means is that both energy and direction for humanity are being provided continuously by that second environment which resulted from the evolutionary breakthrough into language: a humanly created world of images and artifacts, of ideas and customs and shared visions of the future. It is the environment of human culture, and it shapes, reinforces and limits our values just as significantly as our genetic legacy and the available food and water supply determine—for good or ill—our physical health.

THE INSTITUTIONAL FRAMEWORK OF CULTURE

This humanly created environment is the total way of life of a people. It comprises all those communal ways of doing things that have endured over the generations, along with the forms of social organization furthering their operation. It involves the knowledge in which these organizations are grounded and the group ideals and goals that inspire and direct them. We call these *institutions*. We can think of each one of these as an extremely complex adaptive system. Together, all of a society's institutions embody at least ten crucial functions necessary for the survival of any human group.

The major institutions established and participated in by the members of human society can be described as follows: (1) their family relationships and rules of behavior having to do with procreating and nurturing the young, ministering to the sick and elderly and the dead and dying; (2) their language and the history embedded in it; (3) the arts and the drawings, literature, music and other artifacts produced by those who seek both to communicate and to create; (4) their scientific knowledge and the technology following in its wake; (5) the sacred objects and rituals which they worship and pursue, along with the mores that determine appropriate behavior and the ideals to which the group as a whole aspires; (6) their organized means of acquiring and defending territory; (7) their arrangements for providing order and security within society; (8) their organizations for making and administering policy decisions; (9) their established customs for producing and distributing resources; and (10) their formal means of socialization—or ways of preparing new members for adult roles. These patterns and processes make up the all-encompassing institutional framework forming the environment of human culture. It is an environment that shapes its carriers and members just as surely and profoundly as do their physical surroundings.

THE EVOLUTION OF THE FAMILY

Among the earliest institutions is the one involving cooperative caring for the weak and vulnerable members of the clan or tribe, especially the elderly, pregnant females and helpless infants. No doubt it was this requirement that led to the evolution of the family as the most fundamental unit of human society. Evolutionary scientists tell us that the animal family resulted from an effective intersection of the primary bond uniting mother and child with the pair bond uniting male and female. The need to protect and nurture the young is so intimately related to biological survival for humans that, clearly, only those individuals so motivated would have produced offspring with any hope of surviving. Evolution would have selected out the others.

In fact, according to the anthropologist Wenda Travathon, successful childbirth itself would have necessitated care and concern on the part of one's fellow humans. As our primate ancestors became increasingly bipedal (some five million years ago) the associated changes in the female pelvis meant that infants could no longer be expelled from the birth canal in a front-facing position, as occurs in the case of monkeys and apes. Because of these changes, the mother became unable to guide the newborn out herself without risking severe damage to the infant's spine. Accordingly, she could not continue to "go it alone." Essential tasks surrounding childbirth began to require attendants. Only those groups that had found a workable way to ensure a safe birth under these altered conditions, as well as subsequent care and protection of their young, would have endured sufficiently long to have evolved a culture.

What scientists now recognize as the biological phenomenon of "kin selection" is probably at the root of all human social structures beyond the primary procreative unit. This is the behavioral pattern that results in the preservation of the genes of those who sacrifice themselves for the welfare of the group: a preservation that occurs through the survival of the children of their close relatives. The clan was a natural outgrowth of kin selection. It provided a uniquely favorable environment for those born within it, because of the lack of self-serving behavior on the part of many of its members. Because clan cooperation provided a secure situation for childrearing, it would have enhanced the chances for survival of the genes of those who practiced it. Thus, evolution came to favor a proclivity within individuals to behave in a self-sacrificing (or altruistic) manner.

An alternative (although not incompatible) explanation of such behavior is provided by P. L. Wagner's "geltung hypothesis." He discusses the probable evolutionary role of the human biological drive for acceptance by the group. Both theories demonstrate, in concrete, believable terms, the interplay of two strands of the "triple helix": the sociocultural and biological. The urge to care for other clan members who were temporarily vulnerable no doubt grew out of the institutionalization of all behaviors furthering the necessary functions of procreation and childrearing. In other words, by means of nothing more mysterious than the process of natural selection, clan cooperation became entrenched as an "evolutionarily stable strategy" for our primitive forebears—and those involved were poised for a take-off into culture.

Nevertheless, we need to be aware that what provides for evolutionary stability in one era can become counterproductive when circumstances change. The tribalism threatening to overwhelm the world today is but an obsolete manifestation of the very biological propensities that once ensured survival—wherever these have not been overlaid by an extended and more universal altruism that must be culturally acquired. The problems for humanity posed by the persistence of tribal proclivities in modern times are dealt with in detail in Chapter 9.

THE CULTURAL FUNCTION OF RELIGION

It is generally agreed that one of the earliest institutions of human culture was religion. Its evolution from the simplest forms of totemism to the concept of a single creative force personified by a God or Spirit symbolizing ultimate reality and worth is described in the following chapter. The role of religion in the evolution of the family has been traced by archeologists and anthropologists. Primitive clan rituals involving elderly and dying members seem to have been grounded in evolving religious convictions—particularly those having to do with ancestor worship and belief in afterlife. The earliest archeological evidence of this incipient cultural activity is at least 60,000 years old.

It is clear that ritualized religious faith has been a powerful shaper of individual values, attitudes and behavior in every cultural group in every time and place. The subconscious fear of total and irrevocable annihilation of the self is perhaps the deepest motivation for any human behavior, and it is the one tapped into most effectively by beliefs emphasizing rewards and punishments in an afterlife. The mythologizing function of religion was of great value in that, in the absence of reliable knowledge, it provided comprehensible explanations of an existence fraught with danger and with terrifying and seemingly unfathomable mystery. Every early culture had its creation story, along with its myths explaining the origin of human knowledge, fire, agriculture, and so on. The telling and teaching of these gave order and comfort to individuals, and group identity as well. In addition, the discipline, cohesion and continuity provided by the group-sanctioned leadership of the medicine man, guru or priest gave the tribe so blessed a distinct evolutionary advantage. In fact, it is doubtful that early humans could have survived without the comfort, meaning and rudimentary social organization provided by their religions.

THE INSTITUTIONALIZATION OF WAR

Anthropologists and evolutionary scientists generally conclude that another very early cultural institution was the military. Battling with neighbors competing for the same territory may have defined the very existence of wandering tribes of hunters and, subsequently, of pastoral groups. On the other hand, Barbara Ehrenreich argues, in her 1997 book (*Blood Rites: Origins and History of the Passions of War*), that the cultural artifact of war was heralded by the emergence of "man the hunter." She suggests that this occurred only after the decimation of the giant ungulates (easily hunted by the tribe as a whole): a change in the nature and availability of prey that led to the evolution of projectile weapons and a division of labor on the basis of gender. "Man the warrior" was the next step.

There is general agreement that the earliest enduring agricultural settlements were chiefly dependent on the labor of women; and that they were constantly under siege from marauding bands—especially after the settled groups had built up a surplus of food or other wealth by means of the authority of the religious leader. There is also considerable evidence that warfare was endemic in human culture throughout most of prehistory and history. In fact, all early societies—such as the city-state of Rome and its warring neighbors in the fifth century B.C.E.—were organized in terms of military values and leadership as well as by the high priests or other interpreters of the will of the gods.

Ironically, the needs of the military, to the present day, have been the single most powerful spur to scientific and technical invention, and thus to social change. From the invention of the horse-drawn chariot, the longbow, gunpowder, the aeroplane, the submarine, radar and the computer to the nuclear bomb and the Internet, we can trace a cumulative trail of radical shifts in social organization. These shifts affected all the other institutions, as well as the way in which people viewed their world. It is no wonder that the process of cultural evolution has sometimes taken strange and ethically unwarranted directions!

THE EVOLUTION OF THE RULE OF LAW

Many evolutionary theorists suspect that primitive systems of law grew out of the institutions of religion and the military. It is easy to envisage how religion would have provided the communal grounding and moral justification for general social discipline and, ultimately, for self-discipline as well. The requirements of invasion and defense would have necessitated a rigid, power-based group discipline imposed on individuals from above. On the other hand, the idea of a system of laws grounded in an authority stemming from some source other than sheer military might or political dominance is directly attributable to religion. The priest owed his power not to a threat of force but to the authority granted by the group of believers to his role as an intermediary between the gods and themselves. There are many historical examples of the process by which this authority gradually spread to large-scale religious organizations influencing and controlling human behavior over vast territories. In fact, it can be traced in the development of all of the great world religions. As early as the mid-nineteenth century a pioneering sociologist, Harriet Martineau, described examples of this process in her book on the Mid-eastern source of three great world religions: Judaism, Christianity and Islam.

The traditional religion-based form of the rule of law was undermined in Western Europe by King Henry VIII of England, when he successfully challenged the Catholic Church. Sir Thomas More was sufficiently far-sighted to warn of the danger posed for civilization by the destruction of the only institution standing between the people and arbitrary actions dictated by sheer force in the hands of politically powerful and unrestrained individuals. In taking this courageous stand it is possible that he was referring to the rule of law—not necessarily to the Catholic Church as such—but it just so happened that the church was then the only authoritative source of a trans-national system of law in that part of the world.

Enlightenment philosophers were responsible for the evolution of a non-supernaturally based system of laws to replace both those of the church and of divinely justified kings. These were laws originally thought to reside in nature and thereby to transcend the power of temporary rulers. However, pioneers of social science, such as Thomas Hobbes and David Hume, dissented from this position. They believed that—as with other aspects of culture—the source of law is nothing less than the entire experience of the human species throughout evolution. There is no moral or legal order in non-human nature, they said, in spite of the obvious fact that human morality and societal laws are rooted in, and have evolved out of, animal social behavior and instincts.

Unfortunately, the very concept of the rule of law has suffered grievous setbacks during the twentieth century. The vacuum left by the loss of consensus among earlier religions—and that of the subsequent Enlightenment—has not yet been filled by an effective, humanly inspired international system of law. Reports of the surveillance and bullying tactics of neighbors at the grassroots level in totalitarian countries provide telling illustrations of how attitudes and actions throughout a society can be subverted by unrestrained and arbitrary political power; and the behavior of crowds during riots in the cities of Western democracies is a chilling instance of a different kind of failure of the rule of law. Even more dismaying is the growing threat of terrorism and the power it gives to individuals and minorities who operate outside the commonly accepted universe of standards and rules. Their actions tear asunder the web of trust on which every functioning society depends. All this demonstrates how rapid is the breakdown of civilized behavior, once a general respect for an all-encompassing, culturally sanctioned authority has deteriorated. Where personal safety of the innocent is not guaranteed by the social system, some form of generalized terror inevitably ensues, and people then are forced to accommodate themselves as best they can to the rule of "might makes right."

We are beginning to recognize the fact that laws concerning contracts and property rights may be the single most crucial prerequisite for development in countries struggling to emerge into modernity and relative affluence. Only when ordinary citizens can trust that agreements will not be unilaterally terminated—or that their belongings will not be taken from them at the whim of someone with more power—will each invest the time and effort required for the society as a whole to prosper. In the absence of such guarantees, the majority of individuals will never learn to defer immediate gratification in order to achieve a better future. Perhaps more than any other one thing, it is this particular attitude which defines both the mature person and the civic society.

THE EVOLUTION OF GOVERNMENT AND THE ECONOMY

Government is another institution that grew out of religion, as well as from the needs of the military. Most anthropologists assume that the making and administering of policy for the group as a whole expanded gradually from these beginnings. Then, as the productive exploitation of the physical environment gained in importance, decisions concerning the production and distribution of goods and of necessary services became ever more essential. As with the political, economic matters were no doubt originally the responsibility of the religious leader—and concurrently, of the military required to protect and replenish the store of surplus goods. Gradually, the crucial functions of law and order, and of governing and managing the group's resources, became separated from the religious-military establishment. It has been argued by many scholars that this separation is what marked the onset of modern civilization.

THE INTERDEPENDENCE OF CULTURE AND PHYSICAL ENVIRONMENT

From the earliest stirrings of civilized life, economic choices and the habits and lifestyles growing out of these have changed the surroundings in very significant ways. Political, religious and military decisions have had similarly profound consequences for the landscape and other species of life dependent on it. Conversely, physical geography (a major defining aspect of the environmental strand of the "triple helix") has set limits on the cultural activities of particular human groups—especially the economic.

The story of the tragic fate of the great Andean civilization in the sixteenth century illustrates the power of cultural beliefs and values to shape the physical and social environments, as well as the actual course of history. Although the Spanish expeditionary force of 120 horsemen and 50 foot soldiers led by Francisco Pizarro in 1532 provided the precipitating contingency, scholars now think that the Incas capitulated readily to the little band of barbarous European marauders chiefly because of a cultural rot at the heart of their society. The real culprits were their own customs and myths: in particular, those customs which dictated an unsustainable relationship with the physical environmental and a mythology that operated as a destructive, self-fulfilling prophecy demanding continuous warfare and the blood sacrifice of the best and brightest of the young.

Another example of the complex interplay between the physical and cultural environment is what happened on Easter Island. A fertile physical setting was completely destroyed by the imperatives of religion and the military. Warring tribes competing for scarce land and lumber rendered these resources increasingly scarce by exploiting them ruthlessly in a desperate bid for supernatural sanction in battle. They sought to ensure the support of their gods by appeasing and rewarding them with ever-more-impressive stone objects of worship. The construction of these required the razing of the forests and the concentration of all resources on that one activity. As the trees disappeared the land and climate changed rapidly, rendering the island increasingly uninhabitable.

Other examples abound in the records of past and current history. In the third century B.C.E. a plant called satyrion was harvested to extinction only a few decades after the Greek philosopher Theophratus recommended it for the treatment of male impotence. Cattle, representing negotiable currency for certain East African tribes—and sacred forms of life for Hindus—expanded in numbers in those societies to the point where the land came under siege, and life and health were threatened. Forests in industrialized countries have been obliterated and rivers polluted to serve culturally induced needs for esoteric objects such as blown glass and bleached toilet tissue. Entire species are being eradicated today because of beliefs concerning the medical or aesthetic value of certain plant products or body parts. The pervasive marketing of Pepsi Cola in Mexico has radically altered the religious rituals of the Mayan peoples. They have gradually incorporated this bottled drink into their worship and this, in turn, feeds back profoundly deleterious effects on the surroundings and on the health of their children.

There is now considerable evidence indicating that exposure to lead in the environment is contributing significantly to delinquent behavior in relatively young boys. It has also been found that such early anti-social activity is the single most important predictor of adult criminality. Here we have a clear example of how a cultural change in the economy (the twentieth-century expansion in the use of the automobile and various lead-based substances) may have altered the physical environment to the extent of producing organic deficiencies in individuals which, in turn, may induce a tidal wave of altered behaviors. These behaviors may then contribute to a downward evolutionary spiral in the culture and perhaps indirectly in the gene pool. The "triple helix" in action! Something similar is thought to have happened in the last centuries of the Roman Empire as the lead pipes of the water systems adversely affected the organic functioning of individuals. The civilization became increasingly corrupt and decadent. The cultural roots of Rome's centuries-long fall are described tellingly by the second-century A.D. poet Lucan, in his great epic on the civil war that ended the Roman Republic—and subsequently by Gibbon in *The Decline and Fall of the Roman Empire*.

THE EFFECTS OF CULTURE ON THE GENE POOL

An example of the power of culture to affect biological evolution is the phenomenon of "color consciousness" among communities of African Americans and in the West Indies of post-colonial times. Light-skinned women have traditionally been considered a prize by men of African ancestry. Darker-skinned females with typical African features even today recall painful experiences of being referred to scornfully by males who, regardless of their own appearance, communicated their preference for light skin in numerous hurtful ways. Many tell of critical comments even within the home about their flat noses and thick lips from parents and aunts with similar features. This color hierarchy—a mirror image of the racism in the encompassing society—thus came to reflect the prevailing class structure as well, for the lighter the skin the more opportunities there were for advancement, and the more likely it was that one's offspring would have the opportunity to benefit from a good education. So the most attractive, able and ambitious of both sexes tended to look for partners with relatively light skin. There is no doubt that these cultural pressures had a cumulative effect on the composition of America's present-day underclass.

What is going on here? It appears that the culture of the prevailing literary, economic and political establishment—and of the opinion leaders in the media who promote its values—is so all-encompassing that it is accepted unknowingly even by its victims. In fact, culture is so powerful that those who benefit least from a particular set of dehumanizing or exploitative norms and ideas are often the most enthusiastic agents of their own oppression. Only after the 1960s—when the "Black is beautiful" movement and the Afro hair style came to be valued by the community as a whole—did the earlier cultural norms dictating standards of beauty begin to change direction in North America. A similar phenomenon is revealed in the popularity of eyelid operations among women of East-Asian descent, and the surge in cosmetic breast surgery among females in general, in spite of questions about the safety record of implants. The increase in diet-related illnesses among young girls is yet another costly by-product of culturally dictated standards of beauty with their obvious power to affect sexual selection—and the health and physical attributes of future generations as well.

A potentially devastating situation has arisen in many democracies today with the working out of modern libertarian values concerning female reproductive freedom, combined with the notion of unlimited rights to state support. Largely because of the abuses of Nazism, any reference to collective responsibility for the health of the human gene pool is frowned upon. At the same time, "human rights" have been defined in the broadest of terms, incorporating that of any woman to produce as many babies as she wishes and to be supported by society in her choice—regardless of whether she is intellectually, physically, financially or emotionally capable of caring for a child, and regardless of the extent to which she is destroying the brain of her unborn child with drugs and other forms of destructive behavior. This has meant that schools and other socializing and caring institutions are being overwhelmed by congenitally damaged and socially abused children, who, in their turn, go on to produce disproportionately large numbers of the same, in an exponentially accelerating downward spiral of biological-cultural evolution.

Related to this is yet another dismaying modern example of the effect of the interaction of cultural and biological evolution upon the physical environment, which has to do with the global population explosion. Our widespread and deeply rooted commitment to the unlimited freedom of the individual to procreate has persevered in conjunction with the improvement in health care and corresponding drastic decrease in infant mortality, along with increases in food supply made possible by scientific advances. This incompatible combination of tradition and science is now endangering the earth's forests, wildlife, soils, waters and ozone layer. It is true that some scientists point to the decline in fecundity in developed socioeconomic systems, and therefore predict the possibility of a stable population sometime in the twenty-first century. However, this is scarcely encouraging when we consider what will have happened by that time to the prospects for human civilization and for a healthy ecosystem.

The 1994 Jonathon Weiner book, *The Beak of the Finch*, shows how the behavior of humans is affecting the evolution of other forms of life on earth in increasingly deleterious ways. Weiner notes startling changes in animal and plant populations wrought by ongoing processes of natural selection, all of which should have been readily foreseeable. At least 27,000 species are now being lost every year, and we have yet to face up to the long-term harm that this entails for the earth's ecosystem. Widespread overuse and misuse of antibiotics and insecticides has encouraged the natural selection of ever more resistant varieties of disease-causing organisms and crop-destroying weeds. This presents us with the real possibility of devastating plagues against which we will grow increasingly powerless. If competing world views had not prevented the majority of our decision makers and consumers from understanding Darwinian theory, things might have been very different. We could have predicted the evolutionary consequences of those cultural demands which led to our thoughtless and inadvertent introduction of new organisms into established ecologies—and of our indiscriminate use of antibiotics and pesticides. Thus do the strands of the "triple helix" interact to shape our future!

UNDERSTANDING CULTURAL EVOLUTION

Evolutionary scientists have suggested that we should begin to think of units of culture similar to the genes which we now recognize as reproducers of vital aspects of the human genotype. In the case of culture, then, what can be identified as the smallest transmissible unit? Clearly, it has to be the simplest form of covert or overt behavior which can be passed along the generations. This means that the basic unit of culture is either a single idea (or belief) *capable of being communicated through language*, or a social custom requiring transmission by means of verbal description and direction, rather than resulting merely from imitation during the lifetime of an individual. Richard Dawkins recommends calling these "memes." Almost a century ago, the French sociologist Emile Durkheim suggested that the basic units of such transgenerational psychological and social behavior be referred to as, respectively, individual and collective "representations." Durkheim had inherited the term "representation" from Herbert Spencer who, in turn, had borrowed it from the early nineteenth-century philosopher Arthur Schopenhauer. Some time later, Julian Huxley introduced two terms for representing such symbolically reproducible behaviors at the psychological and social levels. These were "mentifacts" and "socifacts," which he proposed would correspond to those physically enduring cultural entities long known as "artifacts."

Regardless of what we choose to call the ultimate components of culture, this kind of thinking about its evolution would considerably clarify our understanding of the process. We can visualize ideas being joined together by thinkers to form systems of thought (analogous to skeletons in biological evolution), some of which are reformulated, expanded upon and made more accurate and workable as experience accumulates throughout the ages. Others are frozen into mythologies and ideologies with built-in resistance to correction and change. Individual behaviors become habits which, when modeled, articulated and pursued by groups, evolve into rituals. Over time, rituals solidify into customs that tend to assume a life of their own. That is, they become "objectively real" aspects of the culture in that they function as both cause and consequence of behavior. Similarly, new technical and aesthetic products (such as tools and objects of art) enter the cultural stream in enduring forms, replacing others judged by the members of society as less worthy, or less immediately titillating, as the case may be.

Although humans may long for the stability and certainty of a static way of life, nature guarantees that no culture can remain intact for long. Change is the only certainty, both in the universal culture of all humankind and in particular cultures or subcultures. Ongoing challenges from the physical environment, as well as the artistic and scientific endeavors of new generations, generate continuous change. Periodically, in an environment radically altered by technological innovation, beliefs and practices that no longer work for the good of the group are forsaken by their carriers, to be replaced by more effective responses. A study of cultural evolution throughout human history indicates that cultures have always either changed in order to allow their carriers to adapt to changing times, or else they have perished.

This suggests that culture, like the species creating and carrying it, must either evolve or die. As with biological evolution, change within a culture is not necessarily progressive. It can just as readily spiral downwards as upwards, in terms of possibilities for human fulfillment and the survival of life on earth. Cultural evolution differs from its physical counterpart in that what is acquired during an individual's lifetime does not enter the gene pool; it must, instead, be passed on in books and music and in the teachings of the elders. Individuals are not just passive carriers of chance arrangements of "memes"—as in the analogous case of genes. They are also creators and self-conscious accumulators of the creations of others. Characteristics are *acquired* during the lifetime of the individual and transmitted, in symbolic form, by cultural means. Each generation can stand on the shoulders of the generation that went before, in a cumulative process of change that is extremely rapid compared to biological evolution.

In cultural evolution, it is the *behaviors* of individuals and the values and habits determining these that matter. This gives individuals a power much greater than that which is associated with their merely reproductive role in biological evolution. On the other hand, it also makes the possibility of regressive evolutionary spirals in cultural evolution much greater than in the case of its biological counterpart. We can be destroyers or builders for those who follow us. New members enter society as barbarians—utterly bereft of culture. Unlike genes, "memes" of culture (such as religious belief systems and scientific theories) are not inherited biologically. They must be learned; and, like all aspects of culture, they tend to change over time in response to altered circumstances.

CHANGING PERSPECTIVES AND PRIORITIES

The Hellenic Greeks seem to have been the first to demand that their religious world views be framed so as to remain consistent with evolving explanations of observed regularities in nature. This made possible the earliest known beginnings of a formal science. However, evolutionary sources of the roots of that pursuit extend much further back in time. Informal scientific inquiry would have originated with the first human to wonder how something came to be, and to note which of the consequences of trial and error meanderings "worked" and which did not. It was dependent upon an ability to identify some sort of effective measure of reliability concerning claims about "the real." Similarly, advances in the arts required a degree of agreement on standards of excellence or quality where the nature of "the beautiful" was concerned. Dissonayake points out that not just any collection of stones on the beach or markings on the cave wall would have aroused admiration in the onlookers. Not just any arrangement was recognized as "special" in this sense.

It is therefore not surprising that early humans similarly sought a common scale of priorities concerning the nature of goodness. With the gradual evolution of religion, the sources and symbols of ultimate worth came to be envisioned as gods, or some alternative versions of the supernatural. This development was accompanied by a network of beliefs concerning appropriate behavior and ultimate rewards and punishments. Over the millennia, supernaturally based belief systems gradually emerged as powerful cultural sources and conditioners of the values and behaviors of the group—and these, in turn, functioned to determine the interaction of humans with other aspects of nature.

Eventually, with the expansion of knowledge through the centuries, people began to be aware of the extent of past human fallibility and gullibility around such issues. Many of the absolute answers concerning ethics that had been derived from traditional religions came to be called into question. Nonetheless, most people continued to believe that disagreement on the origin and justification of "the good" in no way detracts from the importance of the basic concept of ultimate worth. For example, a consensus began to develop among many of the world's people, around the time of the Renaissance in Europe, that one need not believe in the divine inspiration of the early Babylonian priesthood—or of Confucius or Moses or Jesus or Mohammed—in order to accept the significance and social utility of the Golden Rule and most of the Ten Commandments. In fact, many of the foremost social thinkers throughout history have agreed that the general human quest for moral guidance and ideal goals has always been based primarily on a belief in the significance of the task for survival of the human group, and on the possibility that some values are *universal*—if not unchallengeable and *absolute*.

This seems to have been the general consensus until modern times, that is. During the past three centuries a number of philosophies have propounded the idea that morality is innate within the individual—requiring only freedom from society's taboos; or, conversely, that it is merely relative to the particular culture or class—or even to the immediate situation in which one finds oneself. This has led to an unfortunate Western belief in personal sovereignty and, more recently, in cultural relativism. The former premise can be traced from the more libertarian of the post-Enlightenment thinkers, such as John Stuart Mill, to its apex in the philosophy of the twentieth-century existentialism of Heidegger and Sartre. It involves the notion that individuals are free to act *as if* their choices had no consequences for the universe of which they are a part. This is a profoundly anti-evolutionary as well as anti-religious belief. It may well be a belief that humankind can no longer afford.

The "postmodernist" premise of cultural relativism, which assigns total moral sovereignty to the ethnic clan or tribe, is open to the same criticism. Ironically, this newly popular perspective stems from an unacknowledged commitment to an ideology growing out of nineteenth-century group-based biological determinism, or "Social Darwinism": an ideology which ignored the potential function and power of human culture in general, in order to focus exclusively on the unchallengeable imperatives of the tribe. Both the libertarian and "postmodernist" perspectives appear to deny the very possibility of universal values applicable to all members of our species because of a shared humanity.

In spite of the power of the above cultural biases or ideologies, traditional religious justifications for a universal human moral quest are still valid for many of the earth's peoples. But we need not depend solely on these. Scientifically oriented thinkers conclude that those moral precepts and ethical traditions which have stood the test of time have probably done so because they *worked* for the human beings who lived in terms of them. They enabled those beings to live healthfully and peacefully in groups, to nourish offspring, to protect the weak and vulnerable among them and to achieve a measure of personal fulfillment. Both theists and non-theists might well agree that it may be dangerously reckless to abandon traditional codes and principles before we have something obviously more workable to put in their place.

The possibility of a new consensus on ethics is based on the premise that there is an alternative to the dilemma posed by the old dichotomy of absolute *versus* relative morality. We can learn to think, instead, in terms of *universal* values; that is, values which, although evolving, are applicable to all members of the species because of our shared humanity. In fact, there are many non-theological reasons for seeking such universal values and priorities. We have a common biological and evolutionary past and a common human need to live as social beings. First of all, this means that we inevitably share certain innate egocentric needs, aggressive drives and tribal propensities that—although essential to survival in earlier stages of evolution—must now be overlaid by civilized *cultural* imperatives if we are to continue to evolve. Second, it means that we share the need to live in social groups, and thus the need to develop workable rules to accomplish this.

There is a third imperative that is becoming increasingly difficult to ignore. Our species is obviously the most powerful aspect of nature and, as such, is uniquely responsible for the welfare of the planet Earth. We cannot choose *not* to accept this role. By the mere fact of our existence as the most self-conscious and knowledgeable part of nature, we as a species exercise a unique kind of joint sovereignty of power and responsibility. Every act of every person has a ripple effect impossible to measure. We *are* responsible, whether we like it or not. All this should attest to the need for universally applicable guideposts and readily correctable rules for living. The search for these, and their continuous evaluation and modeling, can be traced in the history of our race. This moral pursuit has always been a major cultural function both of religion and of its offspring, philosophy.

It follows that some sort of selection process by adult members of society is required, so that harmful ideas and practices are weeded out and only the most species-advantageous and fruitful are transmitted. Clearly, not all "memes" are equally ethical or fruitful; not all are worthy of preservation. Some may even have become maladaptive. That is, they no longer provide fulfillment for individuals or contribute to survival for the group. Some practices that worked in earlier, isolated settings are now so counterproductive that they threaten the very future of humanity as a whole. Advances in technology have made possible numerous responses so dehumanizing and anti-life that they simply cannot be allowed. Modern warfare is the most telling example of this, as is modern totalitarianism. Some "memes" are now so destructive to the species that we are justified in comparing them to viruses, or to those faulty genes that carry heritable diseases. The particularly virulent mix of mysticism and ethnic-fixation which we now know as twentieth-century tribalism is the most obvious of these. Belief in the unlimited sovereignty of the individual may be another. Others (such as "The Golden Rule" recommended by Confucius and the early Babylonians and subsequently taught by Jesus) may be so essential that a concerted effort must be made to inculcate them in all the world's children.

Once we understand that a culture is, in fact, a web of interacting, complex adaptive institutions, we can begin to identify more effective approaches to solving the problems faced by modern industrial societies. We can recognize that the direction of adaptation need no longer be merely a matter of mindless natural selection. Cultural evolution—unlike its biological counterpart—can be guided from within, but only to the extent that we possess and utilize reliable social-scientific knowledge of cause-effect relations. We can render our institutions "intelligent"; that is, capable of adapting constructively to changing external circumstances through the application of step-by-step social engineering in combination with rigorous evaluation of ongoing consequences. An example of this kind of thinking is the Ashoka Foundation, which trains and finances "social entrepreneurs" who design and lead in the implementation of adaptive institutional change in a number of countries throughout the world.

The point is that the *direction* of universal cultural change need not be left to chance. Modern societies need to recognize that the evolution of culture eons ago placed our species in a uniquely powerful role. As long as human beings had little grasp of the kind of knowledge that could enable them to control future consequences, they had little power to do either harm or good. They were, like other animals, shaped by evolution but relatively powerless to affect its progress. The ability to manipulate symbols changed all that. The first creative fruit of the symbol-using capacity was art, which memory and imagination had made possible, followed by the potential for moral choice that art engendered. But scientific knowledge was the true Pandora's Box. With that remarkable cultural tool humankind has become so powerful we can now retrace the genesis and history of the universe itself. We now possess the technological means to destroy all that we value in our earthly home, along with the sensitivity and very humanity of the people who inhabit it; or we can build a far less brutal and punishing world than we have ever known. The choice is ours to make.

REFERENCES

Asimov, Isaac. *Worlds in Genesis*. New York, NY: Doubleday, 1962.
———. *The March of the Millennia*. New York, NY: Walker and Co., 1991.
Dawkins, Richard. *The Blind Watchmaker*. New York, NY: W. W. Norton, 1986.
Diamond, Jared. *Guns, Germs and Steel: The Fates of Human Societies*. New York, NY: W. W. Norton, 1997.
Dissonayake, Ellen. *What Is Art For?* Seattle, WA: University of Washington Press, 1988.
———. *Homo Aestheticus: Where Art Comes from and Why*. Toronto, ON: Macmillan, 1992.
Durkheim, Emile. *The Elementary Forms of Religious Life*. Trans. Joseph Wood Swain. Glencoe, IL: The Free Press, 1915.
———. *The Division of Labor in Society*. Trans. George Simpson. Glencoe, IL: The Free Press, 1933.
Ehrenreich, Barbara. *Blood Rites: Origins and History of the Passions of War*. New York, NY: Metropolitan/Henry Holt, 1997.
Ewald, Paul. *Evolution of Infectious Disease*. New York, NY: Oxford University Press, 1994.
Fisher, Helen. *The Sex Contract: The Evolution of Human Behavior*. New York, NY: W. Morrow, 1982.
———. *Anatomy of Love: The Natural History of Monogamy, Adultery and Divorce*. New York, NY: W. W. Norton, 1992.
Fox, Robin. *The Challenge of Anthropology: Old Encounters and New Exclusions*. New Brunswick, NJ: Transaction Publishers, 1994.
Girard, Rene. *Violence and the Sacred*. Baltimore, MD: Johns Hopkins University, 1979.
Huxley, Julian. *Evolution in Action*. New York, NY: Harper and Brothers, 1957.
Martineau, Harriet. *Eastern Life, Past and Present*. Philadelphia, PA: Lea and Blanchard, 1848.
Murdock, George Peter. *Culture and Society*. Pittsburgh, PA: University of Pittsburgh Press, 1965.
Nesse, Randolph and Williams, George. *Why We Get Sick: The New Science of Darwinian Medicine*. New York, NY: Times Books, 1994.

Rue, Loyal. *By the Grace of Guile: The Role of Deception in Natural History and Human Affairs.* Oxford, UK: Oxford University Press, 1994.

Sauer, C. O. *Agricultural Origins and Dispersals.* New York, NY: American Geographical Society, 1952.

Sullivan, William. *The Secret of the Incas: Myth, Astronomy and the War against Time.* New York, NY: Crown Books, 1996.

Travathon, Wenda. *Human Birth: An Evolutionary Perspective.* New York, NY: Aldine de Gruyter, 1987.

Wagner, P.L. *Showing Off: The Geltung Hypothesis.* Austin, TX: University of Texas Press, 1996.

Weiner, Jonathon. *The Beak of the Finch: A Story of Evolution in Our Time.* New York, NY: Alfred A. Knopf, 1994.

Wilson, Edward O. *On Human Nature.* Cambridge, MA: Harvard University Press, 1978.

CHAPTER 2

Humans as Creators and Creatures of Culture

In the preceding chapter we discussed the power of human culture: that symbolic community of shared ideas and norms and artifacts and ideals surrounding and influencing all of us. The philosopher Karl Popper referred to it as World 3, as distinct from the World 1 of organic functioning which followed from the emergence of life, and the World 2 of the psychological level of systemic relations initiated by the manipulation of symbols and the resulting emergence of self-consciousness. A half-century earlier, the social psychologist George Herbert Mead arrived at similar conclusions concerning these two great transition points in evolution, and Julian Huxley subsequently developed a comprehensive theory explaining the dynamic, adaptive nature of the process in terms of the biology and social science of his day. Following these theorists, we can think of human culture as a complex, self-organizing, feedback system: the most all-encompassing of all the systems in the evolutionary hierarchy. In this chapter we will examine the significance of this for our understanding of what it means to be human.

Above all, to be human is to be a cultural being. It is culture that has made us unique in the world—perhaps in the universe. To be both a creator and creature of culture is to be capable of unimagined heights of greatness and unspeakable depths of depravity. To be human is to have the potential both for building magnificent civilizations and for destroying one's fellows in centuries of meaningless wars. It is to be burdened with the knowledge of a remarkable but sometimes shameful past—and with an awareness of our distinctive responsibility for creating an enduring future, for our own species as well as all those other living things whose welfare depends upon us. Perhaps it is time for us to ponder on how we came to acquire this awe-inspiring and potentially tragic role in the evolution of life, and on how we came to be so inappropriately and inadequately prepared for the task. What are the sources of the gullibility and aggressiveness and the inter-group hatreds and short-sighted selfishness that continue to cripple us, even as our technological advances render us ever more powerful? Can we achieve the kind of understanding of our propensities and potentialities that will allow us to use our power more wisely, or are we destined to follow the dinosaurs into oblivion? Are we capable of learning what we need to know in order to create the characters and cultures necessary for building a better world, or are we irrevocably limited—and perhaps even doomed—by our animal natures?

OUR ANIMAL ANCESTRY

Indeed, human beings share many attributes with the other animals, and those commonalities should be recognized and appreciated. The "lower" animals suffer pain as we do; like us they feel love and loyalty and loss. Like us they use all available means to exploit the physical environment for their survival needs. Like us, most of our fellow animal species have been, during their evolutionary history, both predator and prey (and it helps us to understand our continued propensity for war to realize that we are still linked—both genetically and socially—to these primeval states). Other animals also live in groups and bond with mates, sometimes for life. They expend great effort in seeking to nurture their young in warmth and safety. Many species have established ongoing societies; that is, their behavior is marked by the consistent patterning which we term *social*. Members communicate and cooperate with their fellows wherever there is a tendency for individual survival to be furthered by those practices. We now know that parrots, orangutans and dolphins learn from experience, apparently developing and retaining systems of intuitive belief or crude concepts that then function as guides to action. Jane Goodall has shown us that the higher apes make tools, use herbal medicines, and exhibit puzzle-solving behavior. In the face of all this, how, we might well ask, can human beings be considered unique?

A CRUCIAL EMERGENCE

The answer is that something of overwhelming importance occurred for our species somewhere along the evolutionary trail. Regardless of how we choose to explain the causes of this occurrence, we must unite in understanding its nature if we are ever to achieve rational and ethically based control of the character- and culture-building process. It is clear that evolution has produced in humankind certain capacities not yet present in any other form of life. These are (1) the ability to imagine and create objects of art; (2) the tendency to wonder about (and to revere) the forces or processes determining our origin and destiny; (3) the mental skills required not only to sense and become habituated to regularities in experience but to seek to explain them, and to be curious when remembered regularities do not occur as expected; (4) the capacity not only to *feel* love for another but to idealize the object of that love and the relationship involved; (5) the propensity to value or make judgments of worth and to strive for desired ends; and (6) the ability to transmit the products of all these imaginative and cognitive operations from generation to generation. Together, these capacities contributed to the emergence of a distinctively human *character* and *culture*. It is these that mark us off as human.

All had their source in one seminal evolutionary watershed that occurred eons after the evolution of life almost four billion years ago. As in the case of other crucial emergences in evolution, the transition threshold which propelled us into our uniquely human self-consciousness would have required a long build-up in terms of geological time. We know that the first hominid evolved approximately four million years ago, but that an ape-like body structure existed at least sixteen million years prior to that. The fossil record now shows that the first primitive members of our own *Homo* species evolved over two million years before the present era. At some indeterminate stage in this time-consuming, cumulative, complex adaptive process, humankind evolved symbolic language.

Evolutionary theorists have long referred to major watersheds in evolution, such as those of life and the symbolic breakthrough leading to human self-consciousness, as *emergences*. Although this concept was probably used first by Thomas Huxley, it was developed by George Herbert Mead and subsequently refined by Julian Huxley. It was considerably substantiated in 1969 by the work of Roger Sperry, the Nobel prize-winning neurological scientist. A 1995 book by another Nobel prize-winner, the physicist Murray Gell-Mann, shows how the concept has received added support from recent discoveries in physics concerning "transition thresholds" in non-linear, complex dynamic systems. (It is unfortunate that this phenomenon has been referred to, somewhat misleadingly, as "chaos"—a term denoting an "essential" disorder at the heart of physical existence which is quite unwarranted by the theory.)

Emergence is perceived within the evolutionary systems model as a function of the hierarchical nature of evolution. At each increasingly complex level of relations, some sort of breakthrough in organizational complexity is understood to have occurred: a breakthrough which evolutionary scientists explain in terms of a build-up of relatively small changes generated by the ongoing process of natural selection. Because of the nature of dynamic, self-organizing systems, it appears that, in such situations, a minute but key alteration in initial conditions can trigger a developmental spiral capable of sparking a major transition to a different order of functioning. The emergent system will be characterized by a new set of structural components governed by a new pattern of relations. These increasingly complex levels of relationship in nature can be traced from the quarks and electrons of physics through the activities of the atoms studied by chemistry and the genes of the biological level, to the organic interactions of physiology and the brain circuits of neuropsychology. From there they can be perceived in the environmentally stimulated responses and habits and the sensing-reasoning, self-conscious mental processes of the psychological level and, ultimately, from the social patterning of group behavior to the customs, ideas and ideals of the cultural level of interaction. Once emerged, the higher-level system seems to have the capacity to operate in a causal relationship to the lower-level processes. This is evidenced in the way that psychological states can affect neurological functioning, the way that repetitive chanting and group hypnosis can alter states of consciousness, and the way that peer-group pressures and culturally sanctioned ideologies can shape individual choices.

One of the significant implications of all this for social science is that some form of adaptive feedback from the consequences of action is likely to be the operative principle of change even at the most complex levels of relations, and we should be looking for behavioral and cultural equivalents of that process. Another is that, although our explanations must take account of all available tested knowledge in physics, biology and neuroscience, it is not appropriate to reduce them to the basic units of analysis operating at those simpler levels of interaction. In other words, we should not attempt to explain complex psychological and sociocultural activity solely in terms of genes or chemical reactions—and especially not in terms of neutrinos or the motions of planetary objects. A third implication of the concept of emergence is that we should expect society and culture to "cause" individuals to function in certain ways. We should not be surprised to find that collective rituals and social approbation and approval affect the behavior of individuals; nor should we be surprised to find that the culture created by humans in their symbol-using capacity does, in fact, feed back to influence their thoughts and actions. Finally, we can conclude from all this that the process of ongoing change in which humankind is immersed is an extremely complex one that can best be viewed as some form of genetic-cultural co-evolution.

THE EVOLUTION OF SELF-CONSCIOUSNESS

There is a consensus among evolutionary scientists that the crucial breakthrough into symbolic language which precipitated self-consciousness would have required a step beyond the routinely emitted vocal or bodily reaction common to all animals. It is thought to have been rooted in the *gesture*: a sound or signal emitted with the intent and power to evoke in the receiver the response being felt by the initiator. Although numerous species of social animals communicate the presence of "danger" or "food" by means of an instinctive sign language, the gesturing that emerged among advanced primates somehow became a more complex and powerful tool. An early stage of this capacity has been observed in pygmy chimpanzees, who arrange plants and branches on the trail to communicate the route they have taken. The upright, bi-pedal ancestors of the human species who had evolved this type of tool could, for the first time, empathize with other sentient beings and share events not immediately present. This represented a significant point of no return in that it opened the door to culture. It meant that, in the absence of the tiger, the responses of fear and awe ordinarily felt only in the tiger's presence could be experienced once more. And a hunter returning empty-handed from the hunt after a narrow escape from a tiger could communicate the event to those at the campfire.

Social psychologists, too, have long assumed that gestures—the crude beginnings of which are shared by all social animals—were the evolutionary roots of symbolic language. However, it has only recently been observed that humans everywhere seem to rely on similar sets of gestures for signaling distress, fear and happiness. For example, although there are indeed cultural differences in interpretation, all over the world people communicate by means of a hand to the throat, smiles, frowns, parental crooning, arms cradling the body, hands clapping, a furtive adjustment of one's clothing, raised fists, flinching with a hand upraised, and so on.

The symbols that evolved out of elementary gesturing behavior are both tools for distinguishing or making sense out of the chaos of experience and the means by which such continuously refined distinctions are communicated so that ever more varieties of experience can be shared. Scientists now agree that the organic foundation for the development of symbolic language was the ability to manipulate the tongue and chop up the single breath in subtle and complex ways, a combination no other species seems to have evolved. The evidence also suggests that, over countless millennia, the early human symbol-users acquired some sort of awareness of a boundary between the self and other selves, and between clan members and outsiders. Through the development of an increasingly sophisticated series of imitative sounds, facial expressions, actions and drawings, simple stories could be told and mistakes or successes could be noted. Thus, a sense of the past was slowly able to emerge in the participants and eventually, as the stories developed into planning sessions, a sense of the future as well. In this way, early humans—unlike other animals—gradually evolved the capacity to distinguish among past, present and future and between life and death. They learned to record the passage of time and the change of the seasons. They were increasingly able to communicate to others, around the campfire at night, the identities of more and less dangerous (and more and less appetizing) prey—and of the various families of predators in the vicinity. The process of making these distinctions among objects and events and places and times, as well as the process of acquiring common symbols to represent them, was continuous, interactive and ongoing, and required countless millennia for its fruition. Once acquired, it was the type of capacity that was readily passed along from one generation to the next, because those with proficiency in acquiring these skills would have been the most likely to survive to produce offspring.

It is generally agreed that, with the breakthrough into symbolic language heralded by the gesture (and the memory and imagination that language engendered) a new kind of world emerged for our primitive ancestors. Along with the physical surroundings with their powerful determining effects on biological evolution and individual behavior, a second level of environment entered the picture. Thereafter, the human tribes were to find themselves immersed in this cultural environment as overwhelmingly as in the physical. This humanly created world gradually began to function as effectively as did climate, geography and ecology to control and shape their behavior and yearnings. For the young child, the various rituals, taboos and customs concerning the hunt would have come to seem as real, and as inherent in the scheme of things, as the fury of the winter storms or the growl of the beast of prey.

HUMANS AS ARTISTS

Art could not have come about without the self-consciousness and historical awareness arising from the use of language. Scientists now agree that our aesthetic capacities must have evolved only very gradually, in tandem with the language that gave them birth. Innovative endeavors resulting in drawings depicting everyday experience probably emerged along with gestures and the first crude beginnings of spoken language. All these activities arose out of—and furthered—the ability to manipulate symbols.

It is easy to understand how the first language of early human primates took the form of crude drawings as well as simple gestures; and how, from the need for gesturing and drawing to explain the results of the hunt and to fire enthusiasm and courage for future hunts, play-acting was born. Music probably began early as well, in the mother's humming sounds. The soothing effect of crooning to babies has been found to be universal. It is the most likely precursor of music which, because of its symbolic aspect, no doubt contributed in turn to the ongoing cognitive development of individuals and the integration of the community. In fact, recent archeological evidence appears to indicate that the early Neanderthals—those ancient, failed competitors of *Homo sapiens*—created sound-emitting instruments from bones. It is likely that repetitious rhythm preceded symbols. Then, gradually, as words became the primary instruments of communication, stories and narration in the form of poetry and song gained ascendancy, and ever greater opportunity to expand imagination emerged through the memorization and elaboration of these.

From its very onset in the ability to manipulate symbols, the role of the arts in extending and amplifying individual experience would have been incredibly significant. Through the ongoing interrelationship of language and the arts, humans were able to move beyond the limits set by momentary private sensation and to live in an expanded world of vicarious experience. They could create symbols and rituals known only to their own group. These artifacts and activities then operated as means of bonding the group together and arousing the heights of emotion necessary for the hunt—or for successful defense or attack on predators and competing groups. Art would have functioned as a survival mechanism in other ways as well. By amplifying the "antennae" of humans it enabled them to feel and see and hear what others had felt and seen and heard, in other places and other times. They could even visualize possible future happenings.

All this was essential in moving our species to the next stage in human evolution: that in which the crucial aptitudes of empathy and imagination had fully emerged. It was a remarkable collective invention that must have come about gradually over a considerable time span. We do not know the exact details and timing of this remarkable occurrence, but no modern scientist would deny the fact that it happened. It was only through the acquisition of empathy and imagination that humankind could eventually manage to escape the prison of animal subjectivity and break through into a cultural world experienced by no other species.

HUMANS AS WORSHIPPERS

An inevitable accompaniment to this breakthrough would have been a sense of appreciation and wonder at the magnificence and mystery of that stream of life of which the individual formed a part. But it had a dark side as well. The emergence of self-consciousness, memory and imagination would have brought home to our early ancestors a terrifying realization: an awareness of the insignificance of the human person in the scheme of things, and of the universality and inevitability of death. Studies of pre-history and history indicate that this spurred the creation of all sorts of idealistic visions and rituals to ease the dread and pain associated with remembered loss of dear ones, and fear of what the future must hold for every living thing. Signs of this stage of cultural evolution have been found in the mid-Eastern caves of some of the earliest *Homo sapiens*.

Understandably, in a world of semi-isolated clans where little was known but much was feared, the most pervasive and enduring beliefs involved a yearning for a superhuman agency to provide care and guidance. Most fundamentally, the knowledge of inevitable death—engendered by empathy and imagination—would have acted as a spur to visions offering hope of otherworldly life. It is likely that the source of the religious impulse is this awareness of universal insignificance, and the yearning for some form of everlasting parental-type protection and the sense of supernatural purposefulness stemming from this. We have good reason to suspect that gradually, over the millennia, there evolved a cultural tendency to revere those beliefs and things and rituals that reassured humans of something beyond the mere individual life span: brutish and short as it inevitably was. It is probable that this is the way in which a variety of sacred reminders of the group's collective journey through space and time became firmly rooted in human culture.

To members of a vulnerable hunting society, those observable beings and forces of nature wielding the greatest power over their lives symbolized all that they feared and needed to propitiate. It is not surprising that, at some stage in evolution, the group's predators and prey in the surrounding area came to be recognized as the ultimate arbiters of life and death—and thereby to represent superhuman influences. Thus, the idea of the clan totem was born. Animals or objects in the surroundings were seen as blood relatives representing the family or clan, protecting it from harm and ensuring the satisfaction of its basic needs. We call this complex of beliefs and practices "totemism," and it is widely recognized by sociologists and anthropologists as the earliest form of religion.

Worship of the stars, sun, moon and earth no doubt developed in a similar fashion. Gradually, these immanent forces assumed human form in the imagination of many primitive believers. Their cultural world became peopled with demons, spirits, devils, ghosts, fairies and gods—all of whom had to be placated and bargained with in ways that were conscientiously taught and learned from childhood on. These fictional beings inspired such awe that countless images and stories were required to demonstrate and explain their origin and nature. Eventually, this humanly inspired environment became as real to the people experiencing it as the living beings and physical surroundings that they saw and felt.

Magical thinking was the norm for early peoples. This meant that human destiny was interpreted within primitive cultures in terms of pervasive nonmaterial influences—both malevolent and beneficent—which could be manipulated by humans using appropriate recipes or rituals. Among these influences, ghostly presences released from the bodies of dead ancestors were inevitably of prime concern. Belief in the perseverance of the disembodied breath or spirit of parents and grandparents was characteristic of social groups in the early stages of cultural development. It was probably the source of the concept of "soul" subsequently taught by the Hellenic Greek, Parmenides, and of ancient Asian doctrines and rituals involving ancestor worship.

By studying the evolution of human culture, we can see how, at each stage, people tried to satisfy their cravings for security and personal significance by explaining their joint origin and destiny in believable and comforting terms. A body of myths devoted to this purpose was developed and passed along the generations. These myths combined language, visual arts, music and dance, as well as the human experience of wonder and reverence. They were responses to the spiritual need for a unified sense of self and human destiny within some sort of larger picture: a need created by that uniquely human self-consciousness which in turn had resulted from the birth of language. However, although these integrating myths functioned compellingly as the first "knowledge," they did not always prove reliable as guides to experience. With the passage of time they were often revealed as having been based on false premises about nature, and on wishful fantasies and emotions.

At some point during the myth-making stage of cultural development, the concept of a hierarchy of gods made its appearance, each symbolizing a particular set of traits or virtues deemed valuable by the group. This marked another crucial advance, for it allowed *morality* to become a central focus of religion. From that point on, religious beliefs and strivings were two-pronged. In addition to providing a satisfying and comforting explanation of reality and the role of humankind within it, they defined ethical ideals and rules for living. This stage of religious evolution was achieved prior to the Bronze (or "Golden") Age in Ancient Greece and also during the fourth millennium B.C.E. in Egypt, Persia, India and China.

Eventually, in certain situations where tribal cohesion seemed threatened by fragmenting internal pressures, or by aggression from without, a unifying belief in one God began to gain ascendancy. This process is actually recorded in the Old Testament of the Jews, and it seems to have occurred in Central and South America as well. It was a revolutionary development, for it opened the way for the ethical principle of human solidarity as spelled out by the early Buddha and Confucius and, sub-sequently, by Christianity and Islam.

With the advance of the moral thrust within religion, however, its mythologizing function gradually gave way to new and more intellec-tually satisfying attempts to explain the nature of the universe and the human role within it. Human beings were discovering instruments more powerful than totems and spirits could ever be. They were learning to use new and more reliable approaches to knowing. They were beginning to think in terms of cause and effect in their attempts to make sense of their experience. As the concept of causality gained ground among the members of the tribe it was natural to apply it to the mystery surround-ing their own origin and role in the scheme of things. The concept of a First Cause and of a supernatural purpose and plan for humanity was a predictable outcome of this development—thus confirming and strength-ening the intuitive belief in an all-seeing and all-powerful God or spiri-tual force as the source of all.

Sometimes the new cause-and-effect thinking confirmed traditional myths. Often, however, it provided insights and evidence that contra-dicted the old answers. Resulting tensions fueled the search for better explanations and thus the tools for knowing continued to evolve, in tan-dem with the urge to worship.

HUMANS AS KNOWERS

We can surmise that, countless millennia before the emergence of lan-guage, animals operated within their environment by means of a sub-conscious form of "knowing." This has been referred to variously by psychologists and philosophers as animal knowledge or animal faith or intuition. It was probably crucial for the early hominid ancestors of the cave people (Homo habilis) who—about three million years ago—had learned to respond to experienced regularities in the habits of the hunted, and to shape simple tools from the rocks around them.

Eventually, some precursor of Homo sapiens (possibly the species named Homo antecessor, the fossils of which were discovered in 1997) began to use the arms and hands for communication. With the critical development of the gesture, the returning hunter was able to indicate in the absence of the prey how that particular animal had sounded and acted. Although we can never know at what precise point in evolution this came about, there is no doubt that it marked the onset of descriptive or historical knowledge—a major step beyond mere animal intuition. From then on, the group of hominids who had made the breakthrough were able to tell their comrades about previous occurrences; and, when lives depended on their accuracy, the truth or falsehood of such primitive descriptions would have been all-important. Only the communicated experience of others participating in the same or similar events could have provided testimony as to the veracity of the story teller in the cave at night. This meant that some crude method of checking up on the truthfulness of hunters' reports had to be generated, simply because to proceed otherwise would have been too costly in human lives. The development of that very symbol-using facility which made knowledge possible also encouraged the onset of the creative imagination which, for the first time in evolution, made lying an option for early humans—and self-delusion an ever-present danger. It is one of the many ironies of the human condition that language rendered factual or historical knowledge both feasible and necessary.

THE EVOLUTION OF SCIENCE

The first science probably had to do with ways of improving the hunt and thereby the survival of the group. Every discovery would have profoundly affected the ways in which members of the tribe felt and thought and behaved. In a similar fashion, the results of each cultural breakthrough would have changed the physical surroundings forever, so that the altered challenges from that quarter, in turn, influenced subsequent behavior. For example, the discovery—approximately 400,000 years ago—of how to control and make use of fire would have quite suddenly transformed the surrounding forests from a mysterious and terrifying obstacle into an economic resource, while greatly expanding the environment as a source of food. It would have revolutionized the role relationships of the members of the group as well, selecting those which best contributed to survival under the new conditions.

There is evidence that linguistic ability and the concept of number evolved in tandem in the primitive human—just as they develop in the child. Zoologists are now aware that some apes seem able to judge gross differences in quantity. However, the ability to designate observable variations in some verbal way, and ultimately to compare these and communicate them to others, was the crucial first step necessary for the beginnings of mathematics. It is a capacity that seems to have evolved only in the specific evolutionary branch that had become the human species. "Naming" was an essential prerequisite for the specifically human operation of "numbering."

It was this major advance in language use that, ultimately, made *scientific* knowledge possible. Science depended upon the development of logical thought, which amounted to a new way of coping with experience. Logical thought required something more than merely remembering and using gestures to recount and attest to a singular experience. It had to do with the ability to organize the chaos of immediate sensation into discrete events and objects, to sense relationships and differences among these, and to respond to new situations in terms of the remembered relationships. The new mental operation was the categorizing function.

This process of learning to order experience into conceptual bins (and to assign sounds to these) must have occurred gradually, over hundreds of thousands of years. We know that it originated in the animal nervous system long before the actual emergence of language in the human primate, and the subsequent evolution of what we can term "historical" knowledge. It probably had its *conscious* beginning in the simple recognition by early cave people (and common in other animals) that some creatures are dangerous; and it would have spiraled from there. For example, all members of the clan might gradually have made the connection that beings that kill and eat smaller creatures will kill and eat humans also. Eventually, names would have been devised for these and warnings issued and recounted.

No doubt it was this sort of behavior that ultimately produced those habitual responses to signs of danger which constitute the intuitive roots of both deductive and inductive (or inferential) reasoning. A hunter, coming upon a lion eating a smaller animal, would respond instantly, without any conscious thought whatsoever, by sensing personal danger and retreating from the scene. If he were in a group he would pass a warning to the other hunters by gestures, and ultimately, by language. Those who did not learn to run from the flesh-eating animal would not have lived to hunt another day—or to reproduce. In a similar vein, it would not have required many experiences of deadly snakebite for the members of an entire clan to relate the agony that followed to the characteristics of a particular category of snake. The process of moving from sensing and responding to regularities in immediate experience to deriving conscious generalizations about them—and of applying the generalizations to new experiences and communicating these to children—would have evolved only with great difficulty. The evolution of this capacity, as well as the ability of the cave people to classify and order whatever they encountered in the environment, probably required many millennia. For a long time humans would not have *thought* the words of warning concerning dangerous animals in the vicinity. But those who survived contact with such predators were establishing the habit of appropriate and immediate response, just as did their fellow social animals. The consciousness of it would have come much later, with the logical concepts and the language to express them evolving together.

What is significant is that once logical thought emerged in a few fortunate individuals, it would have spiraled in an accumulative genetic- and cultural-evolutionary process, for those inheriting the capacity would have been able to take another giant step away from the prison of momentary sensation. They would have been capable of performing mental operations in two directions. They could move imaginatively from unconscious responses to specific experienced consequences of action, through the gradually acquired intuition of a regularity, to a consciously recognized category representing this. ("I have seen this animal stalking or attacking other animals; it must be dangerous for me too.") They could also move from a general principle or abstract category ("Dangerous animals are the ones that prey on other animals.") to a description of a specific case of it that would have to hold if the first principle were true. ("This animal that I have just seen attacking another is dangerous.") The hunter would be justified in his conclusion even though he had never been attacked by the particular animal. In fact, his still largely intuitive reasoning abilities would help him to anticipate and thus *avoid* an attack, rather than merely to learn from the experience if he happened to survive it.

These complex intellectual capacities would have contributed to the differential survival of the individuals who used them to the best advantage; in turn, their offspring no doubt survived in disproportionately large numbers. We now know that, in time, these capacities led inexorably to an entirely new way of knowing: what came to be called scientific inquiry. Science is the most powerful form of mental operation ever developed by humanity. "*If* you see certain signs," some generation of elders probably began to say, "*then* there will be tigers in the vicinity. And *if* you use this weapon in this particular way, *then* you will kill the tiger before he kills you." Like the factual and logical statement, this type of "if-then" proposition differs from unreasoning compulsions to act (whether instinctive or acquired) and from rudimentary memory traces of previous experience—all of which are characteristic of other animals as well.

When experienced by humans, the unconsciously arrived-at, private compulsions which precede the scientific approach are called intuitive beliefs or opinions. In the absence of the necessary facts they can be useful guides to action, for their source is the same experience of regularities that leads to scientific hypotheses. But intuitions are not knowledge, and their reliability can never approach that of science, for *knowledge requires language*. Only by encasing private beliefs in language did humans become able to share them and make them part of the public domain where they could be checked and verified by others. As people gradually became more scientific in their approach to knowing, logic played an increasingly crucial role in defining the concepts and variables to be measured, and in predicting results. Finally, in the early Hellenistic Greek era, Aristotle's formalization of familiar logical operations marked an important breakthrough. His "syllogism" provided the critical conceptual tool for distinguishing those predictions that made sense from those that did not.

Predictions were, of course, what the new form of knowing was all about. What we have come to call science differed from the descriptive and definitional forms on which it was based, in that it was conjectural. This means that it implied some sort of disciplined activity on the part of the knower that could be repeated by other knowers. Building on the previously evolved ability to signal, categorize, describe and check facts and to draw logical inferences, science finally emerged as humankind's most powerful tool for predicting probable outcomes of present action.

Scientific knowledge is based on the same kind of publicly verified facts that are the goal of history, and it relies on logical thought for the framing of its conjectures or hypotheses. But it goes further than either of its predecessors and necessary components. Historical knowledge is a public confirmation of what has occurred—of the facts as attested to by observers. And the logical conclusions of definitional or tautological knowledge define what can be assumed to be the case *if the first premise were indeed in accordance with the facts*. It is a way of exploring all the possibilities inherent in a given factual situation. Science, on the other hand, utilizes both these essential forms of knowledge plus something more. It involves a factual statement of initial conditions *plus* a statement of the probable consequences of specific changes to these conditions.

The issue of whether or not the experienced effects have happened as predicted is a matter of historical, or objectively verifiable, fact. However, what distinguishes science from both descriptive history and tautological definition is that a precise *action* is proposed and a precise *result* of the action is hypothesized and subsequently observed and confirmed (or found wanting) by means of a public process of some kind.

Another way of saying all this is that scientific knowledge begins and ends with the publicly confirmed data of experience, while being directed and propelled into the future by logic. After witnessing an accidental flame sparked by the shaping of an arrowhead, a hunter might have taken the first step toward scientific inquiry by trying to make the event happen again. If the trial was successful, he might have concluded that *if* two flints are struck together in a certain way, *then* a fire will start. The next step would have been to communicate his guess to others. In order to convince them of the strange occurrence, he would have had to gather witnesses to a further test. His friends would have been all too aware that people are gullible and easily led astray by wishful thinking. If, indeed, the public attempt to replicate the event had failed, our hunter's fire-making hypothesis would have been cast aside. In some such manner early proto-scientists learned that if one is to approach an objective reading of what actually happened in any trial-and-error situation, it is necessary for the individuals involved to share and compare what they saw or heard or felt or smelled or tasted. That is, historical or factual knowledge is required.

Again, language is critical here. It is the vehicle by which only humans of all the animal species have found an escape from the confines of subjectivity. Through the clear and concise use of language human beings learned to achieve a degree of objectivity about what had taken place. That is, they acquired the capacity to construct a version of the event or object with which all witnesses could agree and which, as closely as possible, accorded with the truth. The truth is what actually happened; however, humans can never guarantee that they know it with absolute completeness or certainty. But they *can* be confident that the more precise they are in the recording and checking of facts, the closer they will come to their goal. Nevertheless, human knowledge of the truth will always be partial and subject to new and more accurate information coming to light, for those seeking historical knowledge can never achieve perfect objectivity. They can only try to approach it as closely as possible. This means that we can never *prove* definitively the absolute truth of any historical claim.

On the other hand, humans *have* developed a decisive means of distinguishing among scientific hypotheses or theories. It is the test of survival. The very use of such hypotheses requires continuous testing—and they are always expressed in a form that leaves no doubt as to whether or not they have been refuted. This means that only the fit (or the unrefuted) survive. Thomas Hobbes referred to science as the control of consequences. Two centuries later Poincaré described it as a rule of action that succeeds. If the early hunter's strategy had failed to kill the predator as predicted, both he and his crude scientific hypothesis would have died. In less perilous situations—such as the discovery of how to start a fire—only the hypothesis would have been exterminated while the hunter lived on to test another one. When early humans learned that there were ways to test hypotheses without actually putting their lives on the line, they had made a great leap forward in distinguishing what "works" from that which does not, and thus controlling the consequences of their actions. The experiment (in thought or action) was born. Because scientific knowledge is thus constantly open to revision in the light of experience, it tends to accumulate and to become increasingly reliable over time. It works more and more effectively. Like the culture for which it provides the leading edge, the factual content of science is constantly evolving.

Whereas humans have had to be satisfied with an inevitably imperfect *verification* of the truth of historical statements, in the case of scientific propositions they discovered that there is indeed a decisive test of reliability—if not of truth. It is the evolutionary ability to survive repeated attempts at *falsification*. Whereas humans found historical knowledge to be necessary because it was their only available means of understanding and learning from the past and present, they learned to value scientific knowledge for a different reason. They discovered that it allowed them the possibility of a degree of control over their future. We now realize that science is the most powerful instrument ever invented by human beings. Of descriptive fact or history we ask, "To what extent can we count on its being *true*?"; and we question the *validity* of the inferences or implications drawn from factual knowledge concerning the regularities symbolized by these concepts. But of the findings of science we ask, "To what extent are they presumed to be *reliable*?" The truth is what happened. Validity is what would follow logically from a premise concerning some assumed state of the system. It helps us identify a predictable result, *given* our knowledge of the past and present circumstances. Reliability, on the other hand, deals with the future. It is about what will work *to make something happen*. Of all the animals, only humans can build objective knowledge of all these things.

HUMANS AND THE CONCEPT OF LOVE

It is probable that all social animals sense closeness to certain members of their group. In fact, the instinct for imprinting is inherited by many, and subsequent bonding is probably built upon that. We are aware of the capacity of pets to establish deep ties of affection, just as human infants do. Still, there is something unique in the way that our species approaches the *idea* of love. We have evolved a capacity not only to experience affection and to develop bonds of belonging, but to *idealize* the objects of our love. Humans, unlike other animals, can expand upon the experienced emotion of love and separate it conceptually from familial affection and lust. It is this idealization of love, and its use as a foundation and justification for all human relationships, that is distinctively human. When our primate ancestors acquired the ability to idealize a loved one—or to personify "the good" in the form of human-like gods representing specific virtues—this involved something more than merely the bonding common to all animals.

HUMANS AS VALUERS

Humans are distinctive in another important way as well. Gradually, with the evolution of knowledge, there emerged the possibility of *choice* for individuals. The stories told by the elders, and the plans envisaged, provided a variety of imagined opportunities and fates previously not available to consciousness in the absence of direct experience. With the skills of memory, art and language, and the instruments of knowledge, a child could learn about tigers long before encountering them, and could prepare a number of strategies ahead of time. When the moment came to act, the hunter could judge the probable effectiveness of known tools and methods. He could even choose not to use them at all that day. Gradually the concept of "better," "best" and "least desirable" would have begun to buttress the intuitive preferences previously felt but never consciously acknowledged.

Valuing, like knowing, has its source in the sensations experienced by all animals. The infant human *feels* that the mother's milk, and the warmth of her breast, are good. All subsequent values are built on these early feelings of satiation, comfort and security. When we say that cave people came to value small animals as food, we mean that they enjoyed the response of their bodies to that food. Pleasurable feelings, and the urge to prolong them, are the elementary roots of the valuing process. Clearly, we share these roots with other animal species. However, when we include the notion of values as the idealized objects of love and reverence, we have something distinctively human. For example, when we say that cave people revered their animal totems and rituals and myths we mean that, in addition to sensing the immediate presence of these things, the very act of remembering and visualizing them aroused emotions of warmth and safety and joy.

But the evolution of the human valuing process did not end there. Ultimately, it came to involve judging the best means of prolonging or repeating enjoyable experiences, and of expanding them or bringing them to fruition over the long term. This level of valuing was not possible until reasoning and advanced knowing entered the picture. Once these intellectual instruments had evolved they provided the means for achieving valued outcomes—or culminations of experience. The successful valuer was the one who was informed about the current situation and the choices available, and was able to predict the most likely consequences of these choices in terms of whether they would aid or prevent achievement of the desired end. This required all three of the ways of knowing discussed earlier. These were: (1) an objective observing and weighing of the facts, such as significant past and current history and traditions that have stood the test of time; (2) logical thinking—or the ability to categorize in terms of both quantity and observable qualities; to derive conclusions and generalize; to identify and apply principles; to order priorities and to make connections between cause and effect; and (3) a grasp of the relevant "if-then" type of knowledge, along with a willingness to learn from the test of experience.

With this magnificent achievement, and the potential for controlling the consequences of their actions that it provided, human beings became distinctive in a truly significant sense. They had evolved into the only creatures in the known universe with the capacity not only to affect the evolutionary process but to provide moral direction for its course.

What does it mean, then, to be a creator and creature of culture? It involves more than a recognition that, once we have entered the stream of life, there is no erasing our impact on the current. It means that, as the most powerful form of life in all of evolution, we cannot escape responsibility for the very *survival* of that current. In the words of the philosopher George Santayana, "Hell is set in the bond. . . . Nothing that has ever occurred can be annulled. That is what eternal damnation means" (Santayana 1986: 167). For better or for worse, the fact of genetic-social co-evolution implies that the human race is now largely in control. To abdicate the responsibility to provide moral direction to the course of cultural evolution is itself a moral choice. This brings us to the critical role in this entire process of *socialization* (termed enculturation by anthropologists), and the particular form of it that we know as education.

THE CULTURAL FUNCTION OF EDUCATION

The institution of education is closely related to that of procreation and the nurture of infants. Education involves the preparation of the young for membership in the human group, whenever it is assigned to specific people and pursued with specific objectives in mind and by specific means. It is the deliberately planned aspect of the more comprehensive process known as *socialization*. This process is the means by which people acquire the habits, intuitions, attitudes, standards, values, concepts and beliefs of their species in general—and of their immediate subculture in particular. It provides for that all-encompassing humanization without which members of our species are incapable of functioning in civilized society. It is only through this process that children are enabled to "take in" the *memes* of the human group and, ultimately, to refine and improve them; or, where necessary, to select and discard them. Indeed, one way of describing our human conscience is "the society within." Another crucial by-product of what will be referred to throughout this book as socialization is empathy, or sensitivity to the feelings of other living beings. In the absence of these attributes, human beings become merely a uniquely dangerous form of animal.

Socialization is in many ways similar to the physical care and feeding of the child. In fact, the two processes are inextricably linked. In both cases three different kinds of problems can arise. We can have malnutrition, starvation or a poisoning of the inputs required for growth. In both cases development can be stunted, halted or grievously warped and crippled. We are all aware of the tragic results of deficient nourishment. Unfortunately, however, modern society is blinded by a general lack of understanding of what a faulty socialization process can do to children. Few of us make the connection between the lack of empathy and conscience that turns humans into psycho- or sociopaths and deficiencies in the socialization process. This failure of comprehension prevents us from realizing the significance of the *content* of the culture assimilated by children. An obviously polluted water and food supply would alarm us and we would act at once to identify and deal with the polluters. But we do not even recognize the concept of cultural pollution—much less the gravity of the problem.

We can begin by understanding that the child whose precious learning years are squandered watching and participating in televised or computerized violence is no less threatened than the one exposed to poisoned food and water. In the latter case, the failure of the child's early caregivers, and the pollution of the physical surroundings, are readily seen and decried—albeit not always easily remedied. In the parallel situation, we are so blissfully ignorant of the crucial nature and necessity of socialization that we actively encourage the destruction of our vital spiritual lifeline and cry "censorship" whenever anyone questions the right of reckless and self-serving individuals to pollute at will.

Evidence of the increasing distortion and failure of human socialization will force us sooner or later to recognize the shaping impact of culture. Our evolving power to create culture—first through the psychologically based habits and social routines that evolve into customs, and then through the arts and, ultimately, science—is inevitably accompanied by other powers. We now have the opportunity to apply universal ethical principles to a democratic process of selecting the most *constructive* of cultural attributes and discarding the obviously destructive ones. But with that power we have, as well, the capacity to corrupt and pollute that cultural fountain from which all who would be human must necessarily drink. As the geographer P. E. James said, we humans "have brought into being mountains of hate, rivers of inflexible tradition, oceans of ignorance" (James 1964: 2). And we are all potential victims when the process goes so wrong, for who is capable of questioning the direction of the paths traversed and the taste of the water drunk since childhood?

The power to corrupt human culture is, in fact, the power to destroy the social/moral (or spiritual) aspect of all humanity. Indications of approaching disaster may finally force a reluctant and overdue recognition of the need to make value judgments concerning matters of priority and ultimate worth. Thoughtful and concerned people everywhere are beginning to realize that as humans we cannot continue to abdicate the power we wield over the lives that follow ours. They are beginning to suspect that, as the joint creators of the world's universal culture, we are *necessarily* responsible for the values and beliefs that in turn control the future course of all life on earth.

REFERENCES

Asimov, Isaac. *Science Past—Science Future*. New York, NY: Doubleday, 1975.
Cole, Stephen. *Making Science: Between Nature and Society*. Cambridge, MA: Harvard University Press, 1992.

Dawkins, Richard. *River Out of Eden: A Darwinian View of Life*. New York, NY: Basic Books, 1995.

Degler, Karl N. *In Search of Human Nature: The Decline and Revival of Darwinism in American Social Thought*. New York, NY: Oxford University Press, 1991.

Dennett, Daniel C. *Darwin's Dangerous Idea: Evolution and the Meaning of Life*. New York, NY: Simon and Schuster, 1995.

Erdmann, Erika and Stower, David. *Beyond a World Divided: Human Values in the Brain-Mind Science of Roger Sperry*. Boston, MA: Shambhala, 1991.

Fox, Robin. *Conjectures and Confrontations: Science, Evolution, Social Concern*. New Brunswick, NJ: Transaction Publishers, 1997.

Gell-Mann, Murray. *The Quark and the Jaguar: Adventures in the Simple and the Complex*. New York, NY: W. H. Freeman, 1995.

Gribbin, Mary and John Gribbin. *Being Human: Putting People in an Evolutionary Perspective*. London, UK: J. M. Dent, 1993.

Haack, Susan. *Evidence and Inquiry: Towards Reconstruction in Epistemology*. Oxford, UK: Blackwell Publishers, 1993.

Huxley, Thomas. *Evidence as to Man's Place in Nature*. London, UK: Williams and Norgate, 1863.

James, P. E. *One World Divided*. 2nd ed. Toronto, ON: Xerox College Publishing, 1964.

Mayr, Ernst. *This Is Biology: The Science of the Living World*. Cambridge, MA: Harvard University Press, 1997.

McCrone, John. *The Ape That Spoke: Language and the Evolution of the Mind*. London, UK: Macmillan, 1990.

———. *The Myth of Irrationality: The Science of the Mind from Plato to Star Trek*. London, UK: Macmillan, 1993.

Mead, George Herbert. *Mind, Self and Society*, ed. Charles W. Morris. Chicago, IL: University of Chicago Press, 1934.

Midgley, Mary. *Beast and Man: The Roots of Human Nature*. Ithaca, NY: Cornell University Press, 1978.

Piaget, Jean. *Behavior and Evolution*. Trans. D. Nicholson-Smith. New York, NY: Pantheon, 1978.

Popper, Karl. *Objective Knowledge: An Evolutionary Approach*. Rev. ed. Oxford, UK: Clarendon Press, 1979. (First pub. 1972.)

Popper, Karl and Eccles, John C. *The Self and Its Brain: An Argument for Interactionism*. London, UK: Springer International, 1977.

Santayana, George. *People and Places*, ed. Wm. G. Holzberger and Hermann J. Saltkaamp, Jr. Cambridge, MA: The MIT Press, 1986.

Searle, John. *The Mystery of Consciousness*. New York, NY: The Free Press, 1997.

Singer, Irving. *The Pursuit of Love*. Baltimore, MD: Johns Hopkins University Press, 1994.

Sperry, Roger. "Bridging Science and Values: A Unifying View of Mind and Brain." *American Psychologist* 32 (1977): 237–245.

Vygotsky, L. S. *Thought and Language*. Cambridge, MA: MIT Press, 1962.

CHAPTER 3

Agents of Socialization

It is easy to recognize the potency of socialization when we view it as something esoteric occurring among strangers in some far-off place or time. The conceptual enclosures erected by foreigners, and into which their children are forced in the context of social interaction, are readily identifiable and easy to criticize. But in the case of our own culture—and the network of socialization in which we have swum, like fish in water, since birth—it tends to be a different story. In this chapter, then, we will try to bring the process home.

One of the cultural tunnels impeding our understanding here is a peculiarly Western and a particularly enduring one. It is the ideology of the free-floating, internally sufficient individual—requiring only freedom from outside interference and from the imposition of society's beliefs and values: an individual maturing from an innately implanted seed into an autonomous self. But the problem with this model is that it contradicts all that we have learned in the life and social sciences since the onset of the Enlightenment. It ignores the fact that humans are, above all, social beings: the products of a complex mix of genetic predisposition, organic maturation, and the social interaction that both engenders and contains the socialization process. Any real comprehension of this crucial process, then, requires that we attempt to free ourselves from the power exerted by the crippling myth of romantic individualism which our culture inherited from as far back as Tacitus and, more recently, from Rousseau, Kant and others.

To begin with, it may be enlightening to apply the perspective developed in the previous chapters to the process by which we acquire our beliefs and values. We can think of the learning individual as a complex dynamic feedback system operating within an environment of complex adaptive systems—both physical and sociocultural. The sum of the responses of those around us constitutes a socialization process that encourages our adaptation to the evolving web of the human community. At the same time, our adaptive actions are contributing to that ongoing evolution. By a process akin to natural selection, socialization implants within us the culture that makes us human, just as it provides the means by which we extend that common humanity to those who follow after us. Through socialization, all that we have known becomes part of us, and we become a part of all that we have known. Depending on what is being learned in the context of this encompassing social interaction, the process serves either to sustain or rot the social fabric. By our example and the feedback we provide for the behaviors of others—no less than by our procreative activities—we sow the seeds of generations yet to come.

It is worth repeating, however, that at no time does the process of inculcating values and beliefs in the growing child occur in isolation. It is one of *two* remarkable sources of ongoing change that, together, are responsible for the development of culture and the accumulation of organic alterations within the human species. These operate interactively in the incredibly complex adaptive process of genetic-cultural co-evolution described in the previous chapters. One is biological evolution, with its vehicle of natural selection which selects out, or discards, those genes within the species favoring *organic forms* (phenotypes) that fail to adapt to new environmental challenges. The other is socialization—likewise a process of inducing adaptive change but, in this case, in the *beliefs and habits of individuals*. The two processes affect and feed on one another, for the human socializers of each generation form part of the general environment (both physical and cultural) which operates inevitably in a selective capacity for human organisms as well as their behaviors—and thereby, for both species and culture.

For the most part, human agents of socialization operate unknowingly. They influence which types of individuals and segments of society will give birth and to how many offspring, whether or not the group will be able to ensure the security and health of the pregnant females and helpless children, and which mating behaviors will be reinforced or discouraged and discarded. We could even imagine a culture interdicting red hair, left-handedness or color-blindness which could, theoretically, make the attribute disappear from the gene pool given sufficient time. Responses of individuals and customs of the collective—both of which are inevitably products of a mix of the genetic and social—would be even easier to eradicate if the social deterrents (or environmental pressures) were consistently applied. In a parallel process within this complex "triple helix," genetic factors determine the degree to which the group's members will possess the potential to make use of those inputs from the environment—whether social or physical—that provide the necessary fuel for mental and organic growth. In other words, both biology and physical surroundings function to establish the boundaries within which the river of culture ebbs and flows—propelled along by its currents of socialization.

As the previous chapters implied, the socialization process is crucial to the building of character and culture. It is therefore imperative that the public in general begin to comprehend it. It is not surprising that few are aware of how the process works, for even social scientists have tended either to ignore it or to deal with it in a grossly oversimplified fashion. We are going to have to begin by viewing socialization as much more than merely a one-way process by which children are deliberately trained or indoctrinated within the family or school for relatively unchanging adult roles. Even though we are accustomed to thinking of it as coincident with *education*, we need to understand that socialization involves a great deal more than what is consciously intended and conscientiously taught. It is a social process of system adaptation which is incredibly complex because it is both ongoing throughout life and intertwined with biological maturation. It is also reciprocal in that it inevitably affects all participants, and it is often unplanned and unrecognized by the influencer and influenced alike. It tends to spiral in the direction of its launching because of feedback from "significant others." Finally, it is necessary for anyone seeking to understand the nature of human development to be aware that socialization is shaped by the broader sociocultural milieu as well as by the primary group; and that it is a process powerfully affecting the total web of human learning from birth to death.

Socialization is a product of the *social interaction* in which all of us participate. Other people in the environment mediate the individual's experience of reality—whether physical or cultural. There is always and inevitably an ongoing exchange between the individual and social group, and the consequence of that exchange for the participating persons is socialization. To exist as a social being is to be forever enmeshed in some form of social interaction—in addition to the inevitable transactions with one's physical surroundings. The individual shapes society just as society shapes the individual. This means that the relationship involved in socialization is not one of simple linear causality but is instead that of a complex feedback mechanism occurring in a system setting. A baby affects the attitudes and behaviors of other family members (including older siblings) at the same time that their early influence shapes the newcomer in irrevocable ways. One child with severe problems can transform the culture of an entire classroom while it is in the process of assimilating him or her.

The individual learner can also be viewed from this evolutionary systems perspective. The developing child is indeed an evolving adaptive system of responses and values—a character in the process of formation. In fact, it is helpful to think of socialization as an ongoing activity of system change involving the entire stream of individual and group experience. The process can be fully understood only in conjunction with individual learning and human development in general, as these occur within a context of interaction. All the agencies of socialization are, in turn, systems of social interaction, and the most basic of these systems is the family.

THE FAMILY AS AGENT

Few would underestimate the role in human socialization performed by the primary unit responsible for nurturing the child during the early years of life. However, if we think that parents simply transmit values to their children in a consciously planned way, we are underestimating the significance of the family. It is true that most of the early research on the problem focused on attempts to correlate specific childrearing practices with children's subsequent attitudes and behavior. However, a modern and more fruitful approach involves conceptualizing the family as a functioning unit. It now seems clear that it is the *values* behind childrearing practices—and the *interactive context* in which they are encountered—that are important, rather than the nature of specific modes and techniques of childrearing. What counts is the totality of cues and response patterns to which children are exposed over time and in a variety of situations within the intimate setting of the family.

The family is a good place for us to begin because it is a relatively simple and informal type of social organization. We can think of organizations as social tools by which humans build and transmit their cultures: tools defined by the positions assumed and the roles performed within them, in collective attempts to carry out specific cultural functions. They, too, are dynamic adaptive systems affected by, and responding to, the activities of every member. The more formal the organization the more rigidly defined are the positions, the more specialized and prescribed are the role behaviors, the less subject to interpretation are the objectives, and the more all-encompassing and precisely defined before-the-fact—and less subject to individual discretion—are the rules. Throughout history the organization of the family has tended to be relatively informal and open to change in structure and function, except for the fact that it is limited to people joined by kinship and/or some similarly enduring approximation of a marriage bond.

There is an abundance of evidence available concerning specific aspects of family organization, such as its structure and the manner of its functioning. Families have been classified and assessed on the basis of (1) size, as in number of children; (2) whether they represent the nuclear birth-family, the traditional extended family, the modern "blended" family, the single-parent family, the "common law" family, or some version of a "same sex" partnership; and (3) the degree to which the family is functional or dysfunctional in terms of its key cultural roles.

It is easy to see how it is that the family's primary functions—those of procreation and the nurture and socialization of children, protection of its weak and vulnerable members, and provision of a secure and emotionally supportive retreat from the broader social milieu—are key to the survival of any society and the preservation of any culture. One's initial role in a family is ascribed rather than achieved; it is the first to be learned and the basis of all others. It is here that children are exposed to their first experience of social roles: who does what in caring for family members, keeping the household functioning, providing essentials and maintaining order. It is here that children acquire an intuitive sense of their own gender and of what behavior is sex-appropriate and what is not. It is within the family that they are stimulated to become confident inquirers into their surroundings and to seek out answers to puzzling situations; or, conversely, it is here that they assimilate a fear of change, a desire for certainty and a distrust of curiosity. Here they can experience the world as a secure and happy place or they can come to feel like cornered rats in a maze with the smell of danger everywhere, and no place to hide. They learn to perceive the sorts of "selves" they are and can ever hope to be. Within the family they develop the crucial capacities of language and thought. It is here that they achieve a sense of their intrinsic value or unworthiness and—providing conditions are right— an empathy for other "selves."

In addition, every day of their early childhood these little sponges are being exposed to selected segments of the broader culture as these are filtered through the family: segments related to the particular family's own position in that complex adaptive web of occupational and interest groups and various age cohorts comprising the surrounding society. Regardless of the intentions of the primary socializers, such factors as social class, ethnic background, family religion and the degree and nature of parental involvement in the work force can set severe limits on—or significantly expand—the nature and range of experience available to the children involved. Finally, there is the intentional socialization pursued by the family at every turn. It seems, however, that this type of within-family education, however decisive it can be in the childhood years, is effective into adolescence only to the degree that the youths in question maintain a loving respect for their parents. When this is not the case (for whatever reason) adolescents may reject everything they think their parents stand for.

Many studies have documented the disastrous effects on child development of the total absence of a supportive family during the vital formative years. We have abundant evidence that social/moral development—as well as emotional and intellectual—can be stultified and crippled for life by the wrong experiences at critical times. We have learned that early bonding with at least one caring adult is a necessity for normal development. Appropriate stimulation is similarly essential, especially for the acquisition of language. Research conducted with newborn kittens has shown how an environment lacking in normal inputs and challenges can have disastrous effects on neurological development. It seems that for all animals (humans included) there is a window of opportunity for building the synapses that pass signals from neuron to neuron in the brain. If the family fails to provide a situation conducive to normal development in early childhood, it is probable that the individuals thus deprived will grow up intellectually and emotionally crippled, somewhat like kittens who have been permanently blinded, or perceptually distorted, by having their eyes covered for the first few days of life. There are similarly significant findings indicating that even in the case of rats, appropriate early experience may be crucial to normal development. It appears that those baby rats that are frequently licked and groomed by the mother have a lower secretion of the hormones related to stress—and exhibit more exploring behavior—than do offspring that are relatively neglected.

People who seek to downplay the influence of early family socialization on child development often cite great differences in the personalities and characters of children raised within the same family. No knowledgeable social scientist would claim that biological propensities and limitations—inevitably inherited in varying combinations by different siblings—are unimportant. But these critics tend to ignore the fact that the specific socializing experience also varies for different offspring. No two children, even within one tightly knit family, are exposed to exactly the same social interaction. Even identical twins raised together can develop in different directions because one happens to assume the dominant role at an early stage while the other follows submissively. There is much evidence that firstborns differ from their siblings in important ways, and are similar to "only children" in their approach to life. Also, the economic situation or the health of the parents may have altered drastically by the time the youngest child in a large family is born; or the older siblings may have evolved a system of social relationships vastly removed from what had obtained in previous years. For many reasons "only children"—as well as "firstborns" and "lastborns"—can be socialized quite differently from middle children in large families.

To complicate matters further, chance operates throughout the process, so that one unforeseen incident can start the socialization and resulting developmental process spiraling in quite unpredictable directions. For example, a previously confident and precocious child at a critical stage in language development, who undergoes a traumatic experience, can suddenly begin to stutter and to exhibit a pattern of extreme shyness and anxiety—all of which will then profoundly affect subsequent relationships. When journalists flying into isolated communities in Alaska and the Yukon look for children to photograph they tend to select those who have been boldest in approaching them and asking for money. This practice, although well-intentioned, is rewarding the children who beg from strangers. Even one such experience can set them on a self-destroying road from which turning back is very difficult. These are only two examples that demonstrate the countless ways in which chance plays a crucial role in socialization. There are many stories of vulnerable children encountering committed and caring teachers—or sadistic ones—or particularly influential friends—or an early and inappropriate sexual experience—at decisive turning points. Even the failure to learn to read at the optimal stage can alter the entire subsequent socialization of the child in quite devastating ways.

To recognize that the family context is a potent and decisive setting for socialization is not to say that the presence of the *birth family* is essential to normal development, nor that any family, no matter how bad, is better than none at all. Indeed, because of the very fact of its potency and the irreversibility of its effects, the family has the potential for being the most destructive of all the agencies of socialization. For example, there is now considerable evidence to suggest that very young children who are exposed to a pattern of abuse—or who witness cruelty to other people or animals—may permanently lose their capacity for empathy. A mid-1990s survey indicates that almost 5 percent of American children encounter physical violence in the home—and that almost 2 percent are victims of sexual abuse. In Canada in 1994, the homicide rate for children below the age of one was more than twice the rate for the adult population. A Statistics Canada long-term study reported in 1996 that the chance of being crippled by poor language development is doubled for pre-schoolers from dysfunctional families. All this should make us wary of viewing the family as a panacea for society's ills. Those members of the helping professions who are committed to keeping families intact at all costs should be aware that the family, like all powerful agents of socialization, is a two-edged sword.

THE FALTERING FAMILY

Two types of change have been occurring within the family during recent decades, both of which have weakened it considerably as a constructive agent of socialization. One involves a shrinking of its overall function within society; the other has to do with a disintegration of its structure. With increasing industrialization and automation, the family has lost many of the multiple tasks which it had performed in the past. It now assumes fewer aspects of the educational, religious, political and economic roles for society than did traditional families in rural settings. For example, most families no longer *produce* as a unit; they merely *consume*—and even that is done in a fragmented way. Family members seldom sit down to eat together, and few children today are taught to cook, clean house, mend, sew, or plant and preserve fruits and vegetables. Even the more general socializing role of the family has been undermined by the competition of television and by the partial assumption of that task by various social agencies such as daycare facilities and nursery schools. Where structure is concerned, ever fewer roles are enduring within the family. Grandparents have become less significant for two reasons: the increased mobility of their adult offspring, which has often separated the generations geographically; and the relative independence—both financial and emotional—of the older generation in recent decades. Other former members of the extended family, such as uncles, aunts and cousins, are even more likely to be absent for similar reasons. Clan no longer performs a significant childrearing role in the modern industrialized world. It is possible that the increase in "common-law" families is contributing to this as well. This category of family grew by 28 percent in Canada during the 1991–1996 census period.

The most significant change in structure, however, has to do with the missing father. Although it is true that there are single-father families as well, these made up only 7.3 percent of Canadian families in 1996, and one would expect about the same proportion to hold in other industrialized nations. On the other hand, according to a 1996 Statistics Canada study, the father was absent for one in six children in Canada. The proportion of children living in such families increased by 60 percent during the 1980s. The number of unwed mothers giving birth has increased by 50 percent in North America since 1980. In the United States in the late 1990s, 70 percent of all black children were being raised in lone-mother families. This reflects an astounding revolution in the family's role as an agent of socialization.

Until the 1980s and 1990s, much of the research on the effects of marital disintegration and one-parent households indicated that the children of fractured families were better off than the products of intact but unhappy marriages. However, there has now been time for longer-term follow-up studies, and the results are increasingly worrisome. The divorce culture and the unwed-mother culture of North America, and much of the industrialized world, can now be seen to have been purchased at a massive cost, and the price is being measured in the twisted lives of children. It is becoming clear that the traditional role of fathers—

to protect and provide for and guide the children—cannot be performed adequately by an overworked or poverty-stricken or negligent mother, and is but poorly played by the state. In the United States, 85 percent of all poor children live in lone-mother homes. The 1996 Statistics Canada study mentioned previously found that the incidence of emotional and other problems almost doubles for children of single mothers, as compared to those from other forms of families, with 56 percent of such children being poor, as compared to 13 percent of those in two-parent families.

Recent American findings concerning the role of fathers in family socialization (including a 1997 study commissioned by the federal Education Department) provide compelling support for this conclusion, and can be summarized as follows: both boys and girls appear to suffer long-term negative cognitive, linguistic, emotional and behavioral effects from the absence of a supportive father—especially during the first five years of life. An even more dismaying trend is revealed by the growing body of evidence concerning the complicity of stepfathers and live-in boyfriends in the abuse and murder of children.

Other areas of concern have to do with dysfunctional families in general—whether the father is present or not. Members of such families usually have difficulty in communicating, and with giving and receiving affection, resolving problems, protecting children from harmful influences and experiences, and controlling anti-social behavior. Response patterns or norms evolve in all social systems and it is all too easy for destructive ways of behaving to become firmly entrenched within families. Sometimes a mother fails to bond emotionally with an infant and an unhealthy pattern of overcompensation can occur—or a pattern of rejection obvious enough to be discerned by all the children and even exploited by a competitive sibling. Parental favoritism, or failure to deal wisely with sibling rivalry, can be devastating. Conflicts between parents—especially around the question of disciplining children—can have disastrous consequences. Exposure to desensitizing experiences, either vicarious or interpersonal, can destroy character. The abuse of children by older siblings, parents or other adult members of the household—or failure to provide a minimal level of physical or emotional security or of basic nutrition—are so obviously harmful that one would hesitate to mention them if they had not become so sadly prevalent. What all this adds up to is that, because family socialization is so crucial, cumulative, potent and irrevocable, whenever it is either absent or destructive in nature the harm done to both character and culture is almost too appalling to contemplate.

The dysfunctional family setting has become so prevalent and so disastrous for so many children that efforts to deal with the situation are beginning to be made in some jurisdictions. A program in Hawaii called

"Hawaii Healthy Start" is one such. It began as a federally funded pilot project on the island of Oahu in 1985 and was extended to the state's seven main islands in 1989. As of mid-1997, the program's goal of turning potentially bad parents into good ones was being achieved to a surprising extent, as indicated by an astounding drop in cases of child abuse. This success is attributed to the early identification of new mothers with risk factors, and to an insistence that the parents concerned attend parenting courses.

THE MASS MEDIA AS SOURCES OF SOCIALIZATION

In most societies today children are not very old when they are first exposed to socializing influences from beyond the family. In fact, for a number of the very young, the mean streets in a city ghetto may be their primary home for much of the day. For countless others, television is the main baby sitter for hours at a time. From an organizational standpoint, the mass media seem to represent an incongruous mix of the formal and informal. Although they can be viewed individually as formally organized, independently operated entities, together they function in a largely unplanned way as the foremost transmitter of modern "mass" culture. The collective power of this agent is due to the intrusive and all-pervasive nature of the technology carrying its messages and the virtually uncontrolled, corporate nature of the organizations involved. As with all economic enterprises, the mass media are primarily market-driven. However, in this case, the market is being continuously created by the product in an adaptive feedback cycle with the potential for producing a rapid downward spiral in civilization. This danger is due to the fact that the media, as they currently operate, encourage the packaging of culture merely as a saleable commodity: one that is shaped by the need to titillate and capture an audience through the reinforcement of the most elemental of emotional responses. It is largely due to this "massification" of culture that the network of corporations operating the media has emerged as the second-most-potent socializing agency of our times, even replacing the family in its significance for the lives of many children. It is therefore not surprising that, for the past 25 years, its impact on beliefs, attitudes and behaviors has been studied intensively.

According to Marshall McLuhan, an early authority on the impact of television, "the medium is the message." Nevertheless, most researchers have found it informative to distinguish between the effects of the medium itself and the content and values conveyed to the viewer, although the significance of the interrelationships involved is generally recognized. Many of the *medium effects* observed are likely to have long-term, indirect consequences for socialization. These have to do with a considerable diminution of time devoted to reading, interacting with friends, imaginative play, thinking, writing, engaging in sports and other outdoor activity; as well as of time spent in sleeping, eating together as a family and just generally interacting with parents, siblings and friends. A consequent decrease in imagination and creativity has been documented. Other effects likely to have similarly long-term significance for habits and values include noticeable changes in emotional response patterns involving startling increases in defensiveness and aggressive behavior, a growing passivity interspersed with periods of overexcitement and disturbed sleep with frequent nightmares. A disproportionately high rate of injury has also been documented among children who are heavy viewers of television. Overriding all of these has been the indirect effect of a marked loss of sensitivity or empathy for others and of compassion for suffering.

When it comes to the *messages* carried by the media, there is often a vast gap between what was intended by the creator of a program and what is actually conveyed to children at varying stages of their intellectual/moral development. It is the messages *as assimilated by the learner*— as well as the powerful images communicated by television and the movies—that shape role expectations, value systems and world views. The bulk of the research to date shows that the direction of this shaping is, more often than not, corrupting and destructive.

Most researchers conclude it is in the slow accumulation of all the above effects that the media are likely to have the most telling influence on character. They agree that these effects have been sought by no one and are still anticipated and recognized by very few. Nonetheless, they are being brought about every day by exposure within the normal childhood environment to a steady diet of the type of program that both feeds and creates socially destructive attitudes and values: programs depicting disregard for the law and for the rights and feelings of others, along with violence as a routine response to problems. In light of all this, any intended moral of the plot—such as "the good guys win in the end"—is singularly ineffective. Moreover, a 1996 study of American programming indicates that even that traditional ending has largely been jettisoned. Researchers from four universities found that characters who commit violent crimes now go unpunished in almost three television programs out of every four.

A telling example of the power of a consistent media message is the change in the attitudes of American children and youth toward drug use which occurred from 1992 to 1998. During the years immediately preceding that period, even the president and Majority House Leader were shown on television as reaching for popularity among youthful voters by implicitly condoning pot smoking. The pushing of drugs by cult figures in the entertainment world had proceeded apace. Meanwhile, where media-carried drug education was concerned, "Just say no" directives had been superseded by subtly seductive "How to use drugs responsibly" messages. The result? Reported drug use by teens more than doubled during the brief time period in question, while the number of American children experimenting with drugs grew by 50 percent from 1993 to 1998.

By no means are all media messages and images harmful. In the hands of responsible producers and artists, along with wise teachers and parents, television has proven to be a superbly efficient conveyor of information and an effective educational tool. But it is a tragic indication of our lack of understanding of the crucial role of socialization in human development that we have failed to establish as a priority the harnessing of this powerful Trojan Horse in our midst to culturally constructive ends.

THE PEER GOUP

Although the peer group provides the most intimate and enduring relationship outside the family, we probably know less about it than about any other agent of socialization. This is no doubt because it varies considerably according to the age of the children concerned, and because of the informal nature of its organization. It varies, for different age groupings, in its capacity to maintain a stable structure and membership, shape behavior and beliefs, either reject or conform to familial and cultural norms, and exert control over its members. One important consistency, however, is the linkage of the peer group to the mass media—notably the movies and television. At any particular time, the language used, the clothing favored and the behaviors either rewarded or censured by the group members are almost mirror images of whatever is being popularized by the media. It is almost as if the peer group operates as the consolidator and reinforcer of media-projected world views at the level of face-to-face interaction. Another consistency across groups—closely related to the previous one—is the "herd" mentality that the phenomenon encourages.

Until about the age of eighteen months, children tend to interact most freely with objects and adults. After that there is a steady increase in their direct involvement with friends and in their ability to integrate toys and peers in their play, until social play begins to predominate after the age of two. Socializing with peers at this stage involves learning to share toys and to avoid hurting others. It appears to be crucial for developing empathy and an intuitive concept of justice—both of which are prerequisites for moral development. The source of authority is still outside the group, and peer pressures have little meaning for pre-schoolers. Although television is beginning to intrude more and more at this level, it tends to operate mainly as a *substitute* for these necessary socializing activities rather than as an energizing partner of the peer group.

A few years later, the same children are likely to be involved in loose peer structures in the neighborhood and school. These demonstrate the beginnings of an internal hierarchy of prestige and power. For most of them, the group is only gradually becoming an important source of non-adult approval and acceptance, and a new source of authority in competition with that of the family and teachers. For some (often those who are least successful in the broader arena of school and community) it will ultimately evolve into their major vehicle for achieving prestige and power and self-esteem.

This does not mean that the consequence of peer group influence at this stage is primarily negative; far from it. Elementary-school children need the give and take of social interaction with their peers in order to develop an understanding of how rules operate to establish and maintain fair play, and so that they can learn to cooperate and to be both leaders and followers in group situations. In numerous ways the peer group is a valuable socializer. It is the only cultural institution in which developing youngsters are central and relatively equal, and their concerns are supreme. It provides a sense of security and "belongingness" in the world outside the family, and it enables children to loosen the emotional bonds that tie them to their parents. Because informal peer relations are relatively free of society's institutionalized role-expectations, the members are forced to develop their own rules of conduct.

Peer interaction is crucial in providing role-playing practice in which members learn to sustain a constant "presentation of self" in the face of a variety of responses. It is a relatively safe place for role rehearsals— including that of the gender role. In this way children are confirmed in the intuitive sense of self which is gradually developing. The peer group also provides a context for testing both old and new rules. Like the unconscious role playing, this rule-making and rule-testing process is essential for moral development. In stable societies with homogenous cultures the rules established are not usually in conflict with those of the home and school; in fact, they serve to enforce prevailing norms and values. However, in periods of rapid social change, all this can backfire, with destructive peer group influences at this stage igniting the spiraling process mentioned earlier in the context of the family.

In the case of many boys, something of importance happens around the age of nine to eleven. The peer group appears to solidify and take on the characteristics of a gang. For girls this has been less the case, although the situation appears to be changing. Pairing off in giggling, gossiping twosomes has been more the norm for them. However, the peer group—in a relatively amorphous form—becomes increasingly significant as the setting for discussing taboo subjects, for learning new fashions and trends, for expanding social horizons, and for achieving independence from parents and other authorities. Where some boys are concerned, however (and, increasingly, girls as well), the pre-adolescent gang stage can be a harbinger of serious trouble to come. The marauding groups of knife- and gun-wielding schoolyard bullies, "shaking down" or "taxing" the more vulnerable students and terrorizing the entire community; the vicious outlaw gangs fighting over territory in the inner cities, doing obeisance to the god of rap and snuffing out the lives of those who "diss" them: all have their roots in the social processes described above.

The brutalization of the teenage peer group (both female and male) increased exponentially during the 1990s. It has been marked by the development of a casual acceptance of violence as a way of life: one which, although actually practiced only by the minority, is increasingly tolerated and unchallenged by the terrorized majority. It is no accident that over half of the North American teenagers surveyed in recent years admitted to having been victimized in school. If the only source of power, prestige, privilege and self-worth for a large number of individuals comes to be their own intimate cohort and the entertainment media—and if the values and behaviors modeled by those media are destructive to morality and the social order at large—we can expect to lose generation after generation to the barbaric standards of the totalitarian peer group.

THE SPORTS INDUSTRY AND THE PROMISCUOUS BULLY AS MASCULINE IDOL

A prime example of the socializing power of the totalitarian peer group is what is occurring within certain sectors of the professional sports establishment today—especially in hockey. It is something quite sinister in its implications—and there are signs that its roots go back to the neighborhood teams or training regimes in which talented youngsters begin their early socialization into the sport in question. A euphemism for the activity is "building team spirit," but what goes on may not be as harmless as the term implies. It has become the custom in North America for newcomers to team sports to be forced to go through an abusive initiation which is planned and dominated by the team's "veterans." Increasingly, coaches and others who should be responsible for the moral welfare of the youngsters in their care are looking the other way—if not actively encouraging a type of amoral herd behavior deliberately aimed at humiliating the new team entrants. Children are thus led to understand that the very authorities and sports heroes whom they have revered—and who are in control of their futures—are now telling them that it is okay to degrade and abuse outsiders, and even those team members temporarily below them in the hierarchies of power. The subtle, overriding message is that all the traditional rules about human decency and respect for the dignity of persons no longer hold, once one has "made the grade"—or been accepted by the wielders of power.

Understandably, the shock of the hazing experience for many children is such that their conscience is wiped clean of previous perceptions and expectations concerning right and wrong, and their empathy for the feelings of others begins to erode. They are launched on their way to becoming moral zombies. People are to be used *by* the team, and to be sacrificed *for* the team. The team is all. This is the age-old call of the tribe, of the peer-group totalitarianism to which pre-adolescent and adolescent boys are, by nature, grievously prone. What makes it so sinister in this instance is that it is being manipulated by adults in the guise of something as innocuous-sounding as "team spirit." What parent could possibly object?

The result of all this is a crippling of moral development—particularly so in the case of those who are identified early as potential stars. These youths learn that they can use other people (especially females) for their own self-gratification without any concern for the other's welfare, and without any adverse consequences rebounding on them. They are rendered unfit socializers of oncoming generations. At the same time, they are given society's approval as cultural icons: an approval that allows them, during the course of their lifetimes, to contribute to the creation of a cultural climate where widespread abuse of power is tolerated and even admired. This pattern of behavior and the way of life it produces is not confined to sports. It is sadly characteristic of many other "closed" organizations such as the military, boarding schools and penal institutions. One of the predictable consequences of such a climate is a rise in the number of reports of sexual abuse and generally barbaric behavior, and an increasing acceptance of these norms in the public arena and even the justice system.

THE FASHION INDUSTRY AND THE EMACIATED CHILD-VICTIM AS FEMININE IDOL

A similarly worrisome manifestation of the totalitarian, media-inspired peer group is the reigning fashion ideal influencing pre-adolescent and teenaged females of the 1990s. Early in the decade, popular magazines and fashion shows began to feature weird, pouty, made-up child-faces staring from wraith-like, unformed bodies: bodies gyrating and slouching in sexually suggestive stances while sporting slinky and transparent articles of clothing. By the end of the 1990s the new category of "tween" had taken hold, and even toddlers were being taught to gyrate erotically and peer seductively through mascara-laden lashes, while dancing along with the Spice Girls on television and modeling age-inappropriate, revealing clothes. All this operates as a perverted but compelling form of socialization: one that is perhaps not unrelated to that occurring in the sports industry. The two processes may well be symbiotic, in that the ideal role being imposed on girl-children by the media—and those commercial interests with the money to control them—is the mirror opposite of the bully-boy image being projected by the destructive aspects of team sports. Young males are equally receptive to the fashion industry's subtle communication concerning the female role.

One could imagine no more resounding turnaround for the womens' liberation movement of the past several decades than the picture of the willing child-victim into which young girls are being shaped through the messages bombarding them from all directions. In countless ways, society is reaping the tragic effects of this destructive version of peer socialization. Even the most secure of families is no match for the totalitarian peer group, as several incidents reported in 1997 have demonstrated. A loving, supportive home prevented neither a girl in Britain nor another in Quebec from committing suicide because of their perception of being overweight and undesirable in the eyes of the group. The combination of these personal attributes with a culturally marginalized family setting can create the most perilous situation of all, as was shown by the fate of a plump and socially awkward female on Vancouver Island in 1997. The unfortunate 14-year-old daughter of immigrants from India (who were also Jehovah's Witnesses) was so desperate to be accepted by her peers that she joined a group of vicious girls bent on brutally beating and murdering her—all because she didn't "fit in."

The same pernicious message is affecting older women as well, as they struggle to alter their bodies by any means available, in order to wear the lingerie-like, high-style clothing that signifies success. It is not surprising that anorexia and bulimia have become the prevailing female disorders; and that pedophilia is rampant.

THE SCHOOL

By no means are all of the community inputs to the socialization process uncontrolled and relatively informal. On the contrary, many are educational in nature and deliberately planned with specific learning objectives in view, and with resources organized in the service of those objectives. Human beings seem always to have recognized that the socialization of the young is too crucial for the welfare and survival of the group to be left to chance alone. Plato was one of the earliest thinkers who spelled out a program to accomplish this. He sought a rational (albeit authoritarian) approach to the process by substituting explicit control and direction for the mix of traditional belief that was being passed on without critical examination and evaluation in the Greece of his day. Nineteenth-century social scientists such as Emile Durkheim maintained that the educational objective must always be to develop in the young those physical skills and intellectual and moral states necessary to keep society functioning. John Dewey, the American philosopher, wrote that education is the primary means by which the values that any society cherishes, and the goals it wishes to realize, are brought home to the thought of the individual.

The responsibility of the school to provide young people with necessary knowledge and skills is well recognized. Appropriate education facilitates the ongoing structuring of basic cognitive capacity as well. New evidence demonstrating the effect of the environment on intelligence has been collected by Professor James Flynn of the University of Otago in Dunedin, New Zealand, and by Professor Ulrich Neisser of Cornell University of Ithaca, New York. They found that scores on IQ tests are improving in industrialized nations around the world while, at the same time, student *achievement* scores are slipping. This indicates that, although cognitive skills in children are being increasingly honed by the availability of advanced technology—both within the school and without—the socializers responsible for building the vital knowledge base and conceptual framework required for interpreting experience are somehow failing in their task.

SOURCES OF CONFLICT IN EDUCATION

The fault may not lie with the teacher. The problem may be in the system within which teaching and learning occur. There is always a complex of organizations involved in educating the young, and the nature and extent of this has differed greatly across cultures and historical eras. Nevertheless, educational mechanisms of some sort have been present wherever humans were aware of having produced a culture and were capable of feeling concern for the survival of the group. These mechanisms have varied from the witchdoctor of the primitive tribe to the vast and complicated school and university systems of today. Over time many have sought to expand the function of formal schooling to include concerns of the broader world setting as well as the perceived needs of the tribe or nation—and the conflict between these two objectives is still largely unresolved. A related conflicting imperative can derive from the fact that the educational goals of the family, in a pluralistic and rapidly changing cultural setting, may be very different from those of a public school system required to serve the needs of society. Other conflicts besetting the school in modern times involve the seemingly infinite expansion and incompatibility of the demands made upon it by various interest groups, and the nature and desirability of its role as a vehicle of social mobility.

Finally, one of the most serious sources of confusion has to do with conflicting perspectives of the child as learner and individual. An obsolete but still prevalent view sees the welfare of the individual as separate from—and in essential conflict with—the welfare of society, so that if the one is pursued by the school the other must be sacrificed. According to this view, if children's self-esteem is to be strengthened and their needs met, they must be showered with affection and ego-enhancing experiences and left alone to follow their own interests at their own pace. Any "imposition" of cultural values must be avoided. Rights are emphasized while responsibilities tend to be overlooked. Conversely, where society's interests are considered uppermost, children are seen primarily as trainees for adult work roles and the activities involved in responsible citizenship. This misguided either/or position turns the entire educational enterprise into an ineffective battleground of contending ideologies. Once human beings are perceived within an evolutionary systems framework, however, the door is open for children to be understood as characters in formation *and* as potential participating members of society—as well as the creators, carriers and creatures of culture.

There is an unfortunate tendency on the part of many professional educators in modern democracies to treat children *as if they were already responsible adults* capable of functioning in a democratic setting—rather than as unformed learners who must *acquire* these attributes. This is at the root of much of the breakdown of authority that is rendering education virtually impossible in many schools. The problem is worsened considerably by the inappropriate and incompatible expectations of numerous ethnic and religious subcultures, as well as by the defensive "ingroup" professionalism of the beleaguered teachers. All of these activities badly cripple the school in its necessary function of integrating diverse groups and individuals into the society. Leaders of totalitarian polities and emerging nations have shown themselves to be well aware of the school's significance as a potentially powerful—and socially controllable—shaper of values and beliefs. It is time that democracies recognize how they have allowed their schools to be rendered ineffective and even counterproductive in their task of socializing children for responsible participatory citizenship.

In addition to these serious conflicts over objectives there is fundamental disagreement in North America concerning the role of the teacher. For example, a startlingly large proportion of the population seems unaware of the socializing power of the instructor role in an educational establishment. A few years ago, Canadians witnessed an outpouring of media support for the continued tenure of a college instructor in Toronto who had written articles in praise of pedophilia and had been openly moonlighting as a male prostitute. "What a teacher does in his spare time is no-one's business but his own!" was the message. Absent from the discussion was any recognition of the fact that this teacher was being perceived by his students in terms of his whole "self" with all its values and beliefs: a self immeasurably empowered with the cloak of authority granted him by the society which entrusted its very future to his care. Every hour of his teaching life, he was presenting that powerful persona to the unsophisticated and often gullible youngsters trapped in his classroom, and dependent on him for their grades and future prospects.

Other sources of conflict have to do with the content of the curriculum, methods of teaching, and issues of administrative control and classroom discipline. At every level of the enterprise, procedures for selecting, organizing and evaluating content and teaching techniques tend to be influenced more by ideology than by a systematic or scientific approach. Furthermore (again mainly because of ideology), discipline within the school at all levels has become so confused and non-directive that many high schools in North America are now extremely dangerous and morally destructive places to be.

What we recognize as discipline problems are usually rooted in an inability to comprehend that the school and classroom are functioning social systems. As teachers, administrators and parents, we need to understand that every social system inevitably produces a unique climate of interaction as well as particular cultural norms and group perceptions of what is possible and what is desirable—and what the limits of tolerance must necessarily be. If the teachers and principals do not maintain a climate conducive to learning by controlling the experience available to the learners in appropriate ways, others will exert that control and the learning will proceed apace—but in ways quite different from those envisioned by the educators. It will not occur in directions determined by some romantic vision of the individual's all-wise creative blossoming. Those other players in the school social system who will immediately take over are the students who already control the most powerful and rebellious of the ongoing peer structures. A current result of this type of neglect of responsibility on the part of educators is revealed in the report of a 1997 study commissioned by the National Center on Addiction and Substance Abuse at Columbia University. It was found that American adolescents were considerably more likely to be exposed to the sale of illegal drugs *within* their school than without. Like nature, peer groups abhor a vacuum—especially when the vacuum represents the absence of authoritative leadership at the helm of a floundering, "democratically" operated ship of education.

At the level of the high school there are usually a number of contending peer groups vying for power within the system. The offspring of relatively affluent professionals will tend to be guided somewhat more by family-imposed career imperatives, and may form their own academically inclined groupings. Team sports will claim the time of many of the physically favored children of those families who have been sufficiently caring and affluent to devote the time required for shepherding them through extra-curricular activities during their formative years. But for all too many of the less fortunate, the educational system will have provided only a uniquely concentrated and inescapable supplement to their character-destroying experience in the surrounding neighborhood. It has to be said that, with the unwitting connivance of well-meaning ideological educators, the North American high-school system, in general, has become part of the problem. All too many schools are now operating primarily as protected social systems in which a media-shaped totalitarian teenage subculture can flourish almost unimpeded by external authority of any kind—intimidating and warping all but the most stubborn and independent of the youngsters who pass through it.

There is a pressing need for a more systematic approach to educational matters, along with a cultural consensus on goals. Concerned parents and educators are becoming aware of the corresponding need for increased independence for individual schools within the public system in terms of *methodology* and *governance*. This would allow for rigorous comparative studies to be carried out on different teaching techniques and modes of socialization; that is, on the ways in which the total pattern of social interaction involved in learning is organized and encouraged to operate within the classroom and school. An important side effect of moving in this direction would be a long-overdue acceptance by teachers and administrators of their role as the sole authorities responsible for controlling the social system in their charge in the service of clearly defined social ends. However, it is very possible that the "charter school" and "voucher" movements, as currently defined, could be harmful to society in the long run. Increased independence within the system can only be beneficial if the program is designed in experimental terms with *educational*—as opposed to *ideological*—ends in view.

This implies the need for *less*—rather than *more*—variation in terms of overall educational objectives and core curriculum content than is presently the case. Nothing useful can be learned about teaching methods unless there is a commonality from district to district and school to school both in what is to be taught at each stage of the child's development and in the precise learning outcomes expected for each level. It is also necessary to maintain the representative nature of the student population in these experimental schools. This requires that applicants be randomly selected from all those choosing any particular school, with no ethnic or religious or economic or special-skill requirements for entry. Only measures such as these would ensure the scientific integrity of the enterprise as well as prevent irrelevant discrimination and segregation on the basis of non-educational factors.

Agreement on overall sociocultural goals for schooling is the first imperative. Another is recognition of the teacher's inevitable role as a moral model. The character-building and enculturating function of this powerful socializing institution is too important for us to allow it to be squandered and corrupted through our ignorance of the process and our confusion over values

THE WORSHIP COMMUNITY AS SOCIALIZER

In Western society, the church (or temple or synagogue) has been steadily declining in terms of its overall impact on the culture, in spite of the fact that *religiosity*—in the form of generalized mystical belief and proclamations of piety—is becoming all-pervasive. Whether one concludes that this is good or bad depends on one's assessment of the nature, purpose and consequences of traditional religious socialization, and on how the process is conceptualized and carried out. Where religious teaching is focused on inculcating unchallengeable faith in a reality defined in supernatural rather than scientific terms, there is considerable evidence to indicate a strong *negative* correlation between degree of doctrinal orthodoxy achieved and degree of intellectual autonomy. On the other hand, when such socialization emphasizes ethical issues rather than adherence to abstract belief structures, children in religious communities have demonstrated relatively high levels of emotional stability and academic achievement. This would seem to indicate that organized religion as a source of socialization is offering something of significance that is unrelated to its specific theological message. It may be that what is in short supply in the modern urban society is the *social* function of a close and caring community for emotional support, the celebration of life's passages and the moral guidance of the young. If the church or its equivalent provides these things without burdening the child with beliefs which contradict the findings of science, its influence should be applauded.

Religion can have further, and more indirect, effects on socialization. Among the more harmful of these is the fostering of a provincial and authoritarian (and even paranoid) view of the world. The Waco incident in the United States is but one example of the lengths to which some fanatics can go. Religious indoctrination can also contribute to the perpetuation of competing, ethnically based territorial claims along with inter-tribal hatreds and historical grievances; or, conversely, universalist religions can provide an effective means of transcending tribal boundaries. Also, there is often a large network of sports activities and clubs offering leisure-time pursuits made available to the community through the work of religious organizations. To the extent that the latter are in-clusive rather than exclusive and are not used for proselytizing purposes, they are likely to contribute positively to the total socialization being undergone by the children fortunate enough to take part in them.

THE SOCIALIZING FUNCTION OF GOVERNMENT

Government at all levels has a significant, but seldom recognized, so-cializing role. Elected leaders are invariably role models—whether or not they accept the responsibility that goes with the position. Their com-ments and personal choices on any social issue carry considerable ethical weight. Another aspect of their work is crucial to the socialization proc-ess as well. The programs that they put in place function inevitably as feedback systems in the general social environment, rewarding and thereby multiplying certain behaviors over others—and altering values in the process. Many of the most well-meaning of these are the most misguided in that they are based on some form of "the honor system": one that relies on the individuals concerned to forego an obvious im-mediate benefit in favor of some longer-term or broader social goal. Ex-amples are transit systems in which riders are expected to purchase tickets in the absence of watchful gatekeepers and drivers; and govern-ment crop-insurance programs requiring only the farmer's word as to the crop-yield. These types of programs have been shown over and over again to be devastating to character, for the dishonest emerge as clever "winners" while the honest lose out and are made to feel stupid and, in certain circumstances, even guilty for not going along with their peers.

Another example is government-sponsored gambling. This is favored by many politicians because it provides them with a relatively cost-free pool of funds without having to levy unpopular taxes. However, the practice communicates several immoral messages—not the least being that it is acceptable to take advantage of the poorest and most vulnerable of society's members. A deeper, and even more dangerous, message is that one's future depends on a whim of fate rather than on diligence and good planning. All these examples serve to demonstrate that, regardless of objectives, it is the incentives and disincentives built into any govern-ment program that will determine the direction in which it moves the culture. Sadly, a pervasive lack of understanding of the functioning of dynamic feedback systems in the social setting prevents most planners and administrators from recognizing the predictable consequences of their ideologically driven projects.

OTHER SOCIALIZING AGENCIES IN THE COMMUNITY

Formally organized youth groups such as the Scouts—as well as sports associations of all kinds—can be important sources of education. In order for this to be the case they must be controlled so that the reigning neighborhood peer-group values and norms do not prevail. If the leaders are successful in this, such groups can develop self-discipline and help to reinforce the values and habits considered necessary and desirable for society in general.

Little attention has been paid, even by those who work within them, to the socializing function of the law courts and police in modern societies. This is unfortunate, because it is a function that is essential and unavoidable. The law is one of humankind's universal institutions, and those who assume careers within it are responsible not only for imposing its standards but for helping to instill the values required for making it work. The most basic of these are the concepts of justice and respect for the rule of law. If society's officially designated agents of social control are not merely to institute blind obedience, but to stimulate the principled behavior and climate of trust without which no society can endure, they must understand their own role in modeling legal norms and reinforcing them in the population at large. Lawyers who connive with their clients to undermine the spirit of the law; socially irresponsible or sexist judges; bullying police officers and prison guards; jury members who render verdicts that destroy the peoples' faith in the system: all are subverting their crucial cultural role.

What is common to all the above activities is that socialization is taking place, and that the participants are usually quite unconscious of the fact. In summing up what we have learned about the process, we could say that socialization is both universal and undergoing constant re-invention by those involved. It is the means by which human society has created and continues to re-create its culture. This occurs in response to the ever-present challenges and changes in the environment, and through the innovative efforts and value choices of its individual members. Society is both defined by, and ultimately dependent upon, the characters produced by its culture. And it is those characters—with their resulting social interaction and the socialization that it furthers—which, in turn, determine the continuing effectiveness of the culture and the direction of its ongoing evolution.

REFERENCES

Banton, Michael., ed. *Socialization: The Approach from Social Anthropology*. London, UK: Tavistock, 1970.

Berns, Roberta. *Child, Family, Community: Socialization and Support*. Fort Worth, TX: Harcourt Brace, 1989.

Bibby, Reginald and Posteriski, D. *Teen Trends: A Nation in Motion*. Toronto, ON: Stoddard, 1992.

Cherry, Andrew L., Jr. *The Socializing Instincts: Individual, Family-Social Bonds*. Westport, CT: Praeger, 1994.

Coleman, John. *The School Years: Current Issues in the Socialization of Young People.* New York, NY: Routledge, 1992.

Danziger, K., ed. *Readings in Child Socialization.* Sydney, Australia: Pergamon Press, 1970.

Dewey, John. *Experience and Education.* New York, NY: Collier Books, 1938.

Eisenberg, Nancy and Mussen, Paul Henry. *The Roots of Prosocial Behavior in Children.* New York, NY: Cambridge University Press, 1989.

Fraczek, Adam, and Zumkley, Horst., eds. *Socialization and Aggression.* New York, NY: Springer-Verlag, 1992.

Handel, Gerald. *Childhood Socialization.* New York, NY: Aldine de Gruyter, 1988.

Hutcheon, Pat Duffy. *Socialization: Toward Interdisciplinary Consensus.* Unpublished Ph.D. Dissertation, University of Queensland, Australia, 1976.

Levine, Robert A. "Culture, Personality and Socialization: An Evolutionary View." In *Handbook of Socialization Theory and Research*, ed. David A. Goslin. Chicago, IL: Rand McNally, 1969, pp. 503–541.

McGurk, Harry. *Childhood Social Development: Contemporary Perspectives.* Hillsdale, NJ: Lawrence Erlbaum Associates, 1992.

Neisser, Ulrich. *The Rising Curve: Long-Term Gains in IQ and Related Measures.* New York, NY: American Psychological Association, 1998.

CHAPTER 4

How Children Learn

Two pictures in the morning paper haunt the viewer. One shows the smiling face of a child—eyes trusting, innocent—the face of a little boy who seems eager to embrace the whole world. The other visage is that of a young man. The features are twisted into a cynical grimace, the eyes cunning and glittering with a mixture of despair and cruelty. The shock is not so much in the appearance of this man beneath the caption of "Serial Child-murderer Condemned to Life Behind Bars" as in the fact that the two photographs are of the same person. A question twists and turns like a knife in the memory and cannot be easily dismissed. What could have happened to that laughing child in the course of those two brief decades to have brought him, and his blameless little victims, to this tragic end? The easy answer is that he was born that way—destined to be a monster—in spite of the evidence to the contrary in that innocent, eager face. But it simply will not do. From the religious perspective, no Creator could be so intentionally evil; and from the viewpoint of the most rigid of genetic determinists, such poisonous genes would never have allowed for the reproduction of their individual carriers or survival of the groups that housed them. So the answer has to lie elsewhere—possibly in the type of congenital deficit in the adrenalin metabolism sometimes found to be associated with psychopathology or, even more likely, in the murky and disturbing reaches of those 20 years of experience.

Above all, humans are learning animals. More than any other species, we are born with the potential to develop in degree and detail only partly determined by genetic programming. The beliefs and attitudes and behaviors that come to define us as persons are not inborn. Although our "hard-wired" instincts and emotions are powerful in early child-hood, they need not decree what we eventually become; they provide merely an initial bundle of predispositions and simple coping responses. Only rarely are they the defining factors. It is now generally believed that genetic makeup does indeed shape *temperament* to the degree that it strongly influences the initial direction in which the child develops. Also, there is good evidence for the conclusion that intellectual and ar-tistic *potential* is inherited. However, genes actually determine very little about our eventual effectiveness as people and (except in extreme cases of chemically related psychopathology) nothing whatsoever about our "goodness" or "badness." No child is "hard-wired" for murder. In the vast majority of cases, anti-social propensities can be inhibited and over-laid by appropriate socialization. Generally, it is safe to say that it is *what happens to us* from the moment of conception that weighs most heavily on all aspects of human development: moral, emotional, intellectual and even physical. To an extent not generally appreciated or understood, the complex adaptive process defined in the previous chapter as *socialization* takes over, builds upon and re-fashions the programming inherited in our genes. Our grandmothers were wiser than we realized when they admonished parents and teachers that, as the twig is bent, so grows the tree. We should have listened better.

Compared to other animals, humans are incompletely programmed before birth and therefore relatively open to environmental influences. With the emergence of language, and the self-consciousness and gener-ational transmission of learned capacities that language made possible, a second revolution in potential occurred for our species. The process of environmental programming snowballed and the significant period for learning began to extend through childhood and beyond. It is this ex-tension, and the flexibility and plasticity thus provided—rather than the mere 1.4 percent of genetic difference separating us from our chimpanzee cousins—that explains the great leap forward taken by humanity.

This means that human beings are far more vulnerable to influences from the social and physical environment than is the case for other an-imals; and we are without the finely tuned instincts that keep animal behavior generally predictable and non-destructive to self and group. More easily than the young of other primates, children can be stunted and deformed physically by the wrong nutrition and treatment. Simi-larly, what they become as *persons* is, in large part, attributable to the nature of their contacts with the social and cultural environment. Char-acter is shaped by the habits and values assimilated and the beliefs about the nature of reality acquired through experience from birth onward. As we learned in the preceding chapter, the chief source of that critical early experience is the interaction of key people in a child's surroundings: the ideals and values personified by those "agents of socialization." What matters are the images and messages which they either communicate or allow to be conveyed by other means; the knowledge and reinforcement their responses provide; and the way in which these responses either encourage or block inquiry.

From an intellectual and moral viewpoint, then, a newborn infant has everything to learn. For the first few years at least, children are the most efficient learning machines ever thrown up by evolution. Just as healthful nutrition during those years is vital to the growing organism, so too is appropriate socialization crucial for emotional, moral and intellectual development. As we saw in the preceding chapter, what those daunting little learning mechanisms take in during the early childhood period largely shapes them, for better or for worse, for the rest of their lives.

This is not to claim that later life experience is insignificant. People learn continuously, from birth to death. However, the *rate* slows down considerably in adolescence and throughout adulthood; and the snowballing effect of early learning sets patterns that are difficult to change. We often refer to spirals in the evolution of species. In a similar fashion we can think of positive-feedback loops in learning for the individual: spirals that render a turnabout in direction increasingly difficult and unlikely. Another way of explaining this is that the crucial, experientially based extensions of the organic synaptic connections in the brain—those responsible for building the basic conceptual framework or response pattern which shapes subsequent learning—are established early. This pattern can be explained as our internally organized, experience-based intuitions about reality—what we call our "gut feelings" when they make it into consciousness—along with the language encasing and encoding these. It is grounded in the brain's neural circuits or synaptic connections which are subsequently built upon and refined during the early establishment of conditioned reflexes, or habitual behavior. Just as a trail through the woods selected by pioneers often becomes the highway of succeeding generations, the child's adaptive conceptual system acts as a sieve selecting out those messages or images that do not fit into its evolving organization. Environmental inputs that are totally meaningless in terms of one's current (but largely subconsciously held) operating model are simply not taken in. It is said that our child murderer had become a schoolyard bully by the time he was in elementary school, and that the teachers failed to prevent him from terrorizing his peers. Again, we come back to—"As the twig is bent . . . !"

HOW THE LEARNING PROCESS WORKS

The analogy of digestion is an apt one for learning. It is worth emphasizing that physical growth and intellectual, emotional and social/moral development are not different in nature. In both cases, the source of nutrition is the surroundings: the physical environment in the one (kitchen, garden, neighborhood, city streets, countryside, etc.) and the family, ethnic and national culture in the other. In both, the child's immediate family or caregivers are the first adults through which environmental stimuli (food and physical care—or human role-modeling activity and other behaviors evoking responses from the child) are made available and readily assimilated. This is why the family, or its surrogate, is the initial and most vital agency of socialization.

At every step the two parallel processes involved in childrearing (maturation and socialization) intersect and affect each other, with socialization inevitably in the controlling role. Even what and how babies are fed and clothed, as well as the routines of diaper changing and toilet training, are culturally determined—whether at the family, ethnic, national or international level. In fact, cultural influences go even farther back. They can affect the number, freedom from inherited disability and even gender of those fetuses carried to full term. (We need only be reminded of the vulnerability of prostitutes to HIV—or of the subcultural pressures on affluent professional women to postpone childbearing—or those many influences causing females in poverty-stricken developing countries to reject, or be unable to obtain, birth control technologies—or the pressures on women in China and India to abort female fetuses.) Cultural influences can affect whether or not the birth mother is to be the major caregiver, whether her bodily parts have been intentionally damaged in rituals such as female circumcision, and the degree to which she has been exposed since pre-adolescence to venereal disease or drugs. Cultural imperatives (or the social interaction communicating these) can also influence the degree to which newborns begin life lacking basic nutrients and the strength to respond to inputs from their surroundings. They can also determine whether or not children have been damaged congenitally by the previous behavior of either parent.

During early childhood, the culturally determined socialization process shapes eating and sleeping habits, as well as the amount and nature of exercise available to children and their exposure to stimulating play. Optimal development—social, emotional and moral as well as intellectual—is dependent not only on challenging physical surroundings; it also requires a social setting free from the threat of abuse, terrifying images and messages, and obstacles to free-ranging curiosity. It is all too obvious that we cannot separate out the influences of the genes—and of physical versus cultural environments—on early childhood learning. Regardless of that, however, the conclusions of the preceding chapter point to the necessity for recognizing the inevitability and crucial importance of the complex programming effected by the human socialization process. Clearly, we need to acknowledge that, of all the factors determining development, it is the one most amenable to rational and ethical influences. We need to be aware that, except in extremely rare instances, it can limit and override even deeply rooted biological propensities. Above all, if we are ever to achieve control of the vital content and direction of socialization, we need to understand the process of learning induced by it.

IN THE BEGINNING

The first step, therefore, is to be clear about how humans learn—whether that learning results from socialization or occurs through direct encounters with the physical surroundings. So let us begin at the beginning of life. It is not easy to imagine the world of experience encountered by a newborn infant. The child is born equipped with the established networks of synaptic pathways in the brain that make elementary forms of consciousness possible. Equipped as well with propensities for sucking, grasping and crying—and for responding with more or less intensity to stimuli—the infant strives for impact on a strange and overwhelming environment. Crowding in from every direction is a chaos of meaningless sound, blurred moving images, odors and textures. Some evoke good feelings; others, bad. Sounds and movements within the infant's hearing and sight are imitated naturally and effortlessly, as when the crying of one baby in the hospital nursery sets off the entire population. (In fact, it has been observed that all animals are born with this capacity.)

Gradually, regularities are sensed, connecting sensations of satiation and warmth with certain stimuli from without. Within the infant's nervous system these comforting inputs also come to be associated with previously aimless activities. If crying and squirming bring attention and bodily comforts, then those behaviors will recur periodically, signaling a growing control by the necessarily self-serving little being over strange and initially meaningless surroundings. If reaching and grasping result in pleasurable sensations, then such forays into the environment will be repeated—and the urge to explore will grow apace.

The forming of such synaptic connections has to do with the identification of regularities in the feedback from the learner's operations on the surroundings. It is analogous to the child organizing incoming experience into crude conceptual "bins" that give them meaning (although we must be aware that little consensus exists as to whether these are constructed as entities such as modules located in any one area of the brain). Gradually, one among the large movable objects that come and go and emit characteristic sounds is connected to the satiation of hunger and to warm and dry surroundings. Thus, a consciousness of "mother" slowly builds and others follow and multiply with every passing day.

Findings in cognitive neuroscience now indicate that learning proceeds during the child's first year at a rate unparalleled in all of nature, with progress during the next two years scarcely slowing in pace. In fact, it has been discovered that the essential neurological underpinnings for general reasoning—and especially for linguistic capacity—are largely established by the age of one, and that successful development requires consistent and intensive encounters with the spoken language. In fact, some recent research suggests that incipient language skills appear in infants within two days of birth. Other scientists suspect that language may be imprinted in a certain area of the child's brain during the initial "symbolic" stage of development in a way that does not happen in later years. Although there is as yet no agreement here, it appears that the synaptic web responsible for the activity of the self-organizing system of the infant brain relies, to a previously unsuspected extent, upon an incoming flow of sensory stimulation—especially that signaled by eye contact and the sounds of words. It is a process that, while inspiring great awe and respect, implies the gravest of responsibility for caregivers.

Although earlier attempts to document the observable results of this complex internal adaptive functioning have tended to be expressed in a variety of terminologies, the literature on the subject now indicates an emerging consensus on at least four fundamental features of the learning process. First, we have the techniques utilized by the learner, which can be described simply as (a) *trial-and-error* forays into the environment and (b) *imitation*—involving a (usually) unconscious copying of the behaviors of others. Second, there are two powerful principles that shed light on how these techniques function together to produce learning, from the simplest acquired response to the most complex restructuring of the conceptual system. These are (a) the *principle of reflex (or classical) conditioning* by which secondary signals in the environment assume the function of the original organic ones, and (b) the *principle of operant conditioning* by which those trials or imitative behaviors which evoke pleasurable responses are subsequently repeated while those not so reinforced are either forgotten or avoided.

Third, we now have compelling evidence from cognitive neuroscience that learning is *systematic*. Murray Gell-Mann picks up on this as he explains, in his 1995 book, *The Quark and the Jaguar*, how both the learning individual and the evolving species are "complex adaptive systems" undergoing change by means of similar feedback mechanisms. In the process, the child develops an expanding system of synaptic connections from incoming experience. We can picture learners as being engaged in a mapping enterprise during which the regularities among new inputs are recognized and organized by the brain within an ongoing internal system of cognitive rules or response patterns. The most readily assimilated of these inputs are the ones that make sense within the current state of the system. At the same time, those stimuli that do not quite fit tend to activate curiosity and further exploration as an attempt is made to accommodate them to (or render them meaningful within) the current map. Another way of saying this is that the child is engaged in a primitive form of *hypothesis formation* involving a largely subconscious process of trial and error—or the testing and rejecting of those guesses that are refuted by experience. All this implies a fourth characteristic. Learning proceeds *developmentally*; that is, new responses, habits and concepts build upon, refine and expand what has been learned before.

It seems reasonable to conclude from all this that the rules or response patterns thus acquired by the learner during social/moral and intellectual growth operate *effectively* as guides to subsequent action only to the extent that they reflect connections and regularities actually obtaining in the surroundings. The growing child is both an integral aspect and an intellectual product of the encompassing physical and social environment. The logical connections established in the learner's mental apparatus through experience within nature are therefore bound to reflect relations in that same nature. This is why many scientists studying child development feel justified in assuming a parallelism between the structures of human reason and the order of nature. It is why it makes no sense to speak of freedom from the "limitations" of reason; and it is why it is probable that harmony with nature, to the degree that it is attainable, can be achieved only through applying—rather than decrying—our organically and experientially constructed logic.

CHILDREN AS PRIMITIVE SCIENTISTS

Newborn infants are driven into acting upon their surroundings by innate biological urges (rooted in neural reflexes) to seek out food and comfort and thus to strive for control of the circumstances on which their lives depend. It is these urges that fuel initial trial-and-error behavior. Babies squirm and cry and grasp and suckle until something happens to bring about satisfaction of their basic need for sustenance. The process of activity on their part—followed by appropriate caregiving response— is repeated as long as satisfaction follows. In other words, behaviors are either selected or eliminated by their consequences on the basis of whether these are positively or negatively *reinforced* by environmental feedback. In this way, rewarded activity soon becomes habitual. These first habits, built upon innate instincts for self-preservation, set the stage for all subsequent learning. Almost immediately, an additional spur to intellectual growth begins to operate. Any sensation of lack of fit between experientially induced habitual expectation and the actual environmental response produces tension in our voracious little learner. This fuels the curiosity which propels children into an exploration of their surroundings. It amounts to a drive fully as powerful as are those for food and warmth.

On the other hand, when the behavior resulting from these urges brings no consistent response, the process of intellectual development breaks down. Generally speaking, neither humans nor other animals persist in "trials" that bring no gainful results. A psychologist who studied the children of Rumania's notorious orphanages noted that, in an entire roomful of these victims of neglect, two hours would pass without a single sound from the wakeful, staring little faces. Mental retardation of varying severity has been documented among children who were adopted by people from other countries. Much will be learned by the degree and rate of catching-up evidenced by those now installed in secure, stimulating homes.

Some preliminary data are now in. Professor Mary Carlson of Harvard Medical School conducted a controlled survey of 60 infants in one of the orphanages. She found that, by the age of three, children in the control group who had been left to the devices of the institution were operating at about half the intellectual level of the members of the experimental group who had been stimulated and cuddled on a regular basis. However, both groups were found to have abnormally low levels of cortisol: a condition usually indicating depression in adults. This is worrisome in that long-term depression is likely to interfere with the urge to explore that fuels the learning process.

This finding may have implications for institutionalized daycare. In late 1997 the U.S. National Institute of Child Health and Human Development released a long-term study of 1,364 children of diverse backgrounds from ten states. Their conclusion was that early placement in daycare provides "significant prediction" of relatively poor mother-child interaction as well as reduced cognitive and linguistic development. It would be enlightening to know whether trial-and-error activity is also low in these children.

This is important because, in normal circumstances, such behavior is accompanied by intellectual growth in the rewarded direction, rather than merely aimlessly repetitive activity. In other words, repeating that which "works" and abandoning that which fails to give satisfaction is the means by which feedback furthers the internal system-change known as learning. This is why we can say that from birth onwards children tend naturally to operate according to the scientific method. It is also why we can say that they build their own internal systems of tested knowledge—whether we prefer to call these experience-based intuitions or response patterns or habits or cognitive structures.

CHILDREN AS GEOGRAPHERS IN A FOREIGN LAND

The environment poses challenges that propel the newborn infant outward in simple exploratory movements. Stimuli evoking sensations of warmth, discomfort or satisfaction connect from without. Sound and movement initiate responses. Hunger and the need for warmth and security and control of impinging circumstances drive from within. From touching and handling things in the environment there is built up an intuition of "object permanence." The child begins to realize that the rattle beneath the pillow—or the parent who leaves the crib—is not gone forever. This particular concept is an essential basis for mapping strange surroundings and is established only gradually. No explorer can function effectively without it. Eventually, it results in the understanding that objects do not gain or diminish in quantity, weight, area or volume at will—or because certain aspects of their appearance (such as form and shape) happen to change. This requires an ability to coordinate different perspectives and to compensate mentally for alterations in the various dimensions of an observed object. The child learns that when water is poured from a short, wide glass into a high, narrow one it does not magically increase in amount. All these intuitions—or response patterns instilled through the manipulation of the physical environment—add up to the concept of "the conservation of matter." To children it represents the gradual embedding of an implicit belief in the existence and permanence in space of real objects beyond the confines of their own bodies. This crucial concept serves as both the ground on which the primitive geographer stands and the major instrument applicable to the task at hand.

Thus armed with a developing confidence in the permanence of most objects in the immediate surroundings, the child is equipped to begin the conquest of space. The activity involved in crawling about the room (and subsequently exploring the territory on walker, foot and tricycle) establishes an intuitive awareness of location in space and of distance and direction—and of reversals of these. Eventually, this action establishes in the body's neural circuits the ability to orient objects in space and to connect cause and effect in their movements. The child no longer blames the wall for reaching out and striking, nor the table for getting in the way. Eventually, the same child begins to acquire the skill of returning to a starting place—either by taking a shortcut or by reversing the exact route originally taken.

Associated with all this is the capacity to classify objects into groups of increasing abstraction and inclusiveness on the basis of a number of observable qualities and dimensions. The adaptive process of abstraction is of two kinds: empirical and reflexive. In the first case, the child begins to categorize the *qualities* of the encountered objects: their weight, volume, texture and size. No longer is every warm fuzzy thing a "dog." Some move and emit sound and some do not; some—whether toys or pets—come to be recognized as "cats," and so on and on. Second, in the case of reflexive abstraction, the *effects of the child's actions on the objects* are the source of the developing intuition. Shapes can be matched in a wooden jigsaw puzzle. Blocks can be arranged in groups according to color and shape and can be ordered in a series from larger to smaller. Comparisons between two handfuls of candy can be made on the basis of quantity. Candies can be removed and added to the handful once again. They can be shared fairly with friends by dividing the store evenly. All these kinds of learnings are involved in the growth of intelligence. They are immediately and automatically reinforced, for they carry their own reward for the child in the shape of power to operate successfully within the surroundings.

CHILDREN AS RECAPITULATORS OF CULTURAL EVOLUTION

Just as it is to a certain extent true that "phylogeny recapitulates ontogeny" (in that the developing fetus seems to go through many of the stages of biological evolution), there is also a sense in which we can say that individual intellectual development recapitulates cultural evolution. For example, there is a striking similarity between the course of the child's development of a workable concept of time and that reflected in the evolution of physics. Scientists have discovered two internal time-keepers, the roots of which seem to be established in the genes. The most familiar is the circadian clock controlling organic functions such as hormone production, digestion and sleep. The second is a sort of "stop-watch" within the brain that calculates the duration of brief time intervals between observations and actions. It is surmised that the latter evolved in all animals as a necessary response to—and means of—hunting prey, just as did the genetic basis for comprehending relations in space. These "hard-wired" timekeepers provide the foundation for the subsequent development of an experientially induced intuition of operational time.

This way of registering and comparing the passage of time comes later to children than does a comprehension of spatial relations. Before time is grasped operationally, at about the age of seven, it is understood only in localized terms. Duration is confused with the specific path traversed and velocity is tied up with overtaking another object in space, regardless of whether the two began at the same place and moment. In other words, no matter how the child dawdles on the way home, if the usual path is followed the time involved is felt to be the same as when every step is covered at a run. This is why, when young children are given a large "head start" in a race, they have no awareness of not having won unless someone actually overtakes them. Saving one's candies for tomorrow has little meaning for them.

Early humans probably saw time very similarly. To a large extent they would have lived in the present moment. The specific concept of velocity as separate from concrete events in space was only possible for them when a mobile standard of duration such as the regular swinging of a pendulum, or the movement of a shadow across a sundial, was introduced as a measure. By those means "lived" intervals between events had finally been rendered comparable. Even in Newtonian mechanics space and time were still treated as absolutes, with velocity being viewed as a relationship between them. Jean Piaget has explained how all that is involved in the measure of time anywhere on earth is "simultaneity": the intuition that, when two objects begin and stop moving in the same instant, the one which has gone the farthest has moved the fastest. Once humans tried to measure time-like events in outer space, however, they were confronted with a condition of non-simultaneity. Both the measurer and the measured are constantly moving relative to each other, with gravity posing a degree of interference in the process. Einstein's theory of relativity simply extended to the case of the velocity of light, the basic principle underlying our species' cultural evolution of a workable concept of time.

In all this, the primary mechanism of learning is trial and error on the part of the learner—just as it remains at the root of the hypothesizing and testing procedures of the mature scientist intent on building knowledge in a systematic and formally rigorous way. And the principle of learning is similar in both cases. It is a principle so simple and obvious that one can only marvel that it is still not universally recognized and practiced. It is called the "principle of reinforcement."

THE DEVELOPMENTAL ROLE OF REINFORCEMENT

In order to comprehend the power of the principle, we merely need to accept the proposition that humans, like other animals, are equipped with instinctive urges to control their environment. They are driven to (1) gratify the need for sustenance and procreation; (2) control the circumstances impinging on them; (3) avoid danger and discomfort; and (4) seek the approval and support of their fellows. We should also recognize that these inherited reflexes are built upon and conditioned by the feedback inherent in everything experienced from the moment of birth, if not before. The fact of conditioning as the key vehicle of individual adaptation to changing surroundings is now as firmly established by science as it was long ago by common sense. A recent breakthrough in the treatment of childhood autism brings this home in a telling way. In spite of the fact that autism is thought to have a strong genetic component, and therefore to be singularly resistant to environmental effects, a new approach emphasizing intensive behavior-modification therapy is proving remarkably effective. This treatment was pioneered by Dr. Ivar Lovass of the University of California at Los Angeles.

Behavior-modification therapies, unlike those derived from psychoanalytical models, have been found to work in a wide variety of the most difficult of re-socializing tasks. Like the great expansion of programmed learning made possible by the new computer programs, they are based on the simple principle of reinforcement. The path of desired behavioral change is broken down into minute steps, with each attempt at navigating these either strengthened or discouraged by its result. In layman's terms, what this key learning principle means is that speech or activity which is rewarded is repeated. That is, the conditioned behavior has been reinforced by whatever issued from it—from its effects or contingent conditions or feedback from the surroundings. To put it even more simply, children learn from the *consequences* of their actions.

This fundamental principle underlying all learning, like natural selection at the organic level, is so omnipresent that we often fail to recognize it. It is typically misunderstood because people are not clear about what can actually constitute a reward (or positive reinforcement) for vastly different personalities in a variety of situations. Most of us are similarly unable to recognize and apply the opposite of reward in the learning process; that is, the removal of reinforcing contingencies. Our cultures have taught us to rely instead on the age-old technique of punishment when we wish to deter undesirable actions. However, the problem with punishment in the raising of children is that, although it does indeed change behavior, it often does so in unpredictable ways and by leaving a trail of unfortunate and unplanned learnings in its wake. Guilt and self-hatred, or resentment, guile and a habit of bullying can be the real-life consequences of the punishment too often administered arbitrarily by angry parents. The enveloping physical and social environment doles out sufficient negative consequences if children are allowed to experience and learn from the less life-threatening of these—rather than protected from the effects that their actions have brought down upon them. Above all, this broader environment has the benefit of consistency of response. When caregivers substitute artificial—and often arbitrarily administered—punishments for the natural feedback inherent in the situation, the learning process can go sadly awry.

In the past, a large portion of this necessary negative feedback comprised pressures from the community at large. Socially unacceptable behavior was followed by openly expressed disapprobation (and even subsequent avoidance or ostracism) on the part of the entire neighborhood. Children quickly learned that there were "rules" in the social world that could not be transgressed without hurtful consequences, any more than one could safely challenge the law of gravity. Today, with the relative isolation of the family, it is doubly necessary for caregivers to structure the conditions of learning to allow for negative consequences of a child's rule-breaking actions to flow back immediately in some recognizable form. Above all, it is necessary to ensure that the child does not experience a feeling of enhanced control and thus positive reinforcement of the behavior.

Our little primitive, like all scientists, is rewarded most of all by experiencing increased power over the environment: power to wring from it the sustenance so necessary to the survival of the growing organism. The infant's cries are a desperate and effective survival strategy necessarily directed at inducing the mother to bend to its will. Crying noises are repeated—along with the sucking and grasping motions mimicking actions associated with the sensation of the mother's warmth—only to the degree that they do, in fact, result in satisfaction and relief from discomfort. There is nothing so sad as a neglected child lying silent and powerless in an unresponsive world. Almost as dismaying, however, are the little victims of overly attentive and permissive parents. Too often, such children learn to view all other living beings as slaves or objects to be manipulated for their gratification.

The demands of biological evolution have ensured that all animals experience satisfaction from the power to influence their surroundings. Throughout the countless millennia that shaped our species, those individuals who did not acquire a modicum of such power would not have survived to reproduce. It is important to keep this in mind in any consideration of the reinforcement principle. The concept of reward must always be interpreted in terms of this kind of power. Behavior that results in consequences satisfying or rewarding to the individual in the above sense are reinforced, and thus repeated. Those responses not so rewarded (the "errors" in the primitive experimental, or adaptive, process) tend to fade away, to be replaced by other "trials."

The principle of reinforcement in individual development is analogous to the principle of natural selection in biological evolution. Rewarded behaviors survive in the repertoire of the developing child while those not so reinforced gradually disappear. Behaviors followed by effects that do not enhance the child's internal sense of control are not *experienced* as rewarding, even though they may seem so to the outside observer. This is why it is sometimes difficult to understand why particular children fail to respond to what the teacher or parent has defined as a reward.

An example of this kind of confusion is the array of eating problems now common among children in affluent societies. In the course of the "trial" of refusing to eat, the child begins to experience a consequence of immeasurable worth to every little power-seeking primitive scientist. That consequence is the undivided attention and concern of every other person at the table. The child senses a power to manipulate *people* rather than aspects of the physical surroundings. It is the immediately gratifying experience of power that our child murderer may have enjoyed very early in the context of controlling the people in his caregiving or play environment. In the less extreme case of the indulged child, the power thus experienced is far more heady than the ability to maneuver the food on one's plate or the need to satisfy an urge at the pit of the stomach—which is often catered to a little later at any rate, for what parent can stand to see a child starve? Once children learn that any particular behavior can transform them into the focus of worried or admiring attention, or can make adults jump to do their bidding, instances of that behavior will multiply and a "bad habit" will soon be firmly implanted.

Teachers often encounter similar problems with disruptive children in the classroom. They either do not know, or forget, the simplest of teaching/learning rules. We get the behaviors we reward; or, better yet, those rewarded by the unimpeded responses of the physical and social environment. Behaviors not so reinforced gradually fade away. The embattled teacher might well respond, "But I am *punishing* that boy's bad actions—not rewarding them!" However, the first question to ask about the boy in question is "What is he really after? What response is bolstering his feeling of power over his surroundings, and feeding his need for ever more power?" Punishment may be experienced as a small price to pay for the power being ceded to him by all concerned: power to divert the attention of his peers from the teacher's goals; power to divert the teacher's attention from the legitimate needs of all the other pupils; power, even, to alter the plans of the entire school and of his busy parents who, eventually, must be involved; or, power to make those parents suffer, as they have made him suffer in the past. In the end, the teacher's punishment, by making the problem pupil a martyred hero to his peers, might turn out to be the greatest reward of all!

An appropriate response would, on the contrary, be aimed initially at rendering the child powerless to affect the learning situation of his classmates. At the same time the teacher would endeavor to reinforce different and desired responses. Swift and silent removal from the situation, accompanied by a studied refusal to acknowledge anything but acceptable conduct, is the first requirement in such situations. At one stroke this does away with the major source of reinforcement for the undesirable behaviors. The next step is to provide an opportunity for the little would-be outlaw to experience the sensation of enhanced control accompanying a new insight into the way things work in that *nature* of which he is an integral part. For example, the phonetic key to reading and the concept of number are tools of unparalleled power for the young child. Once experienced, the power of a new skill or a piece of new knowledge about the nature of things provides the greatest reward of all.

It is not only in the family and school that the principle of reinforcement is neglected. Modern society is full of examples of the institutionalized rewarding of undesirable behavior. Perhaps the most insidious form of this is the cultural conditioning of addictive behaviors such as smoking, drug-use and gambling. Indeed, addiction presents us with an "ideal-type" example of the principle of reinforcement operating in a self-destructive way. The initial trial evokes a rush of powerful emotive forces from the lower cortex region which we share with all animals: an uninhibited response in the form of profound relaxation, or sexual arousal, or sensations of heightened excitement, power or greed. The behavior initiating these feeling states is fed by the anticipation of their repetition as well as by the experience of the actual reward—occasional though that may be in the case of gambling. The resulting habits, although readily formed in these circumstances, are extremely difficult to alter or eradicate. Furthermore, they are vastly encouraged by any reduction of the social stigma traditionally associated with them. For example, government-operated gambling outlets, as well as institutionalized support of art works depicting graphic violence and brutalized sex, operate as powerful cultural reinforcers of the addictions in question, just as laws against lighting up in public places have an inhibiting effect on smoking.

Less obvious examples of the effectiveness of reinforcement abound in modern society. We wonder why we have a rising crime rate when more media attention and financial rewards accompany destructive behavior than that which is deemed socially desirable. We wonder why our politicians are increasingly wont to bribe voters with promises of unlimited expenditures and tax cuts, when we continue to vote chiefly for those who do just that. We wonder why so many abuse the welfare and unemployment insurance systems, when the benefits doled out to the abusers often turn out to be greater than those available to the working poor. We wonder why we are being deluged with television and movie violence when we increasingly favor, with our time and consumption dollars, the purveyors of this type of entertainment.

Inevitably, as the previous examples indicate, one of the most destructive results of our failure to apply this principle at both the personal and institutional levels is the effect on our children. The consequences that would logically follow from their actions are distorted or removed by misguided adult responses. Furthermore, all the corrupting adult habits produced by social-policy errors comprise the cultural mix from which our youngsters copy their own behavior. Children are imitators *par excellence*, and the most effective socialization in any society is the unintended kind occurring by means of unconscious modeling.

CHILDREN AS PRIMITIVE ARTISTS

The principle of reinforcement applies as well to a second powerful mechanism of learning operating concurrently with trial and error in the developing child. That mechanism is imitation. It is the incredible effectiveness of imitation that accounts for much of the rapidity of early childhood learning—and its apparent creative precociousness. Children, like the young of other species, are spongelike in their capacity to soak up the sounds, images, attitudes and actions in their environment and to reproduce them with an eery exactness and rapidity. In the case of the human child, the acquisition of symbolic ability results in a continuous creative activity of astounding proportions—seldom adequately recognized because the products are not seen as innovations within the culture at large. For the child, however, the act of imitating is profoundly innovative.

All art must originate with personal experience, and in some sense must involve imitation or reproduction of that experience. Primitive art is exactly that. Like early humans acting out the details of the hunt or drawing these on the walls of the cave, the three-year-old with an imaginary guitar—demonstrating the exact bodily expressions of a popular media personality—is the most creative of stage performers. So, too, is the infant smiling back at surrounding faces; the young television watcher shouting "Bang Bang" and aggressively attacking nearby companions; and the little singer trilling out the sounds of birds and the barking of dogs. Soon all these creations become habitual if reinforced by their social and physical consequences. Having lost their spontaneity, they become part of the learner's unconsciously held repertoire of behaviors. At that point they are difficult to eradicate or change.

Among the most dismaying of public discussions are those in which people argue about whether or not television characters or sports figures or teachers or religious leaders *should* be role models for children and youth. The fact is that we have no choice in the matter. We are *all* role models for those developing characters who are exposed—especially in culturally favored settings—to the images and messages we emit and the behaviors we exhibit. As in the case of conscious recall, children's intuitive reproductions reflect an organizing of memory within the brain's synaptic system or, to put it in other terms, a recording of previously coordinated responses to the environment. This means that the source of even the most elaborate of such imitations is those symbolic or real people in the children's surroundings who have been rendered significant by love and habituation—or by proximity, authority, notoriety or cultural bias.

Role models are a crucial source of learning in childhood. A society ignores the messages conveyed by them at its peril. They are powerful molders of attitudes, values and beliefs, molders that have operated throughout the centuries with or without the awareness of those concerned. Role models are singularly potent sources of either moral guidance or corruption because they provide avenues for the growing intellect that involve neither coercion nor obviously structured teaching. Human beings are particularly susceptible to the influence of admired cultural icons—whether these are fictional characters, famous sports figures, favorite teachers or movie and television stars. Sadly, most of the "heroes" encountered by children in modern industrial society set examples of violence, greed, promiscuous sex, egoism and irresponsibility. Yet it is from this appalling assortment of idols that we expect our little imitators to create their characters.

Like all artists, children learn to organize their mirrored experiences in a variety of ways, and the responses may emerge as very sophisticated combinations of what their senses had earlier taken in. That is, it is not always easy to identify a single, direct source of the reflected or remembered behavior. This means that, with children's reproductions of current experience—and even more so in the case of past events—memories seldom reflect the circumstances as observed by participating adults. Usually, the source of children's imitative behavior is social. As mentioned in previous chapters, it is thought that the first complex and coherent imitative act was the gesture which, in its turn, laid the foundation for language. To understand this we need only recall the universality of body language characteristically communicating fear, sorrow, anger and joy in humans. Imitation is fundamental to the social aspects of being human. It is a necessary source of the ability to "take the role of the other": an ability which involves, as well, the cognitive capacity to assume a variety of perspectives. It is also at the root of the empathy (or ability to imagine what the other is feeling) which is one aspect of artistic innovation. All this, in turn, contributes to the child's emerging self-concept as well as to the human capacity for morality; and the behaviors reflecting these spiritual or moral achievements are reinforced by the approval of loved or admired adults.

Gradually, from the consciousness of self thus formed, there evolves a conscience—initially a dimly perceived awareness of right and wrong—as modeled and reinforced by "significant others." Ultimately, the result is a mature character, recognizable in terms of a more or less consistent set of habits and an integrated value system. That is to say, this is the way the process works *if* the role models have been appropriately inspiring.

SOURCES OF PERSONALITY

Personality is somewhat different, and perhaps more closely associated with temperament. Some people appear to be happily responsive, placid or tractable by nature; others seem to be born stubborn, or overly anxious, excitable and nervous. There is considerable evidence that basic temperament may be inherited. Newborns exhibit an identifiable pattern of response to stimuli. Some respond rapidly and extremely to the slightest cue: others are sluggish and almost oblivious in their reactions to environmental challenges, while the majority are somewhere in between. Such initial propensities are important because of the snowballing effect initiated by the responses of caregivers. Sanguine, responsive babies attract pleasant and frequent attentions from all and sundry, while anxious squallers make seemingly endless demands on exhausted and increasingly short-tempered parents, and tend to be avoided by their older siblings and relatives. The two types of babies soon come to live in vastly different social worlds and are propelled in increasingly opposite directions by their contrasting experiences. Well-known conceptualizations of personality types—such as the "introvert-extrovert," the "inner-directed versus outer-directed" and the "choleric, sanguine, phlegmatic, melancholic" continuum—can probably all be explained simply in these terms. However, we must always be aware that, even though a certain initial propensity may have been programmed in the genes, subsequent reinforcing and inhibiting experience is likely to play a role—albeit much less in the case of personality than where character is concerned.

GENDER AND SEX

Two of the most important components of personality are grounded in our biologically based gender and sex. These would seem to be singularly invulnerable to socialization, but we now know that early imprinting, imitation, and trial-and-error function here as well. Although the genes determine the physical aspects of gender, as well as the onset, intensity and developmental aspects of the sex drive and fundamental gender identity, the characteristics of the social *role* assigned to each gender—and possibly even sexual *orientation*—may be quite different matters.

The child *learns* what it means to behave as a girl or a boy—both in a universally acceptable social sense and according to variously defined and culturally ascribed sex roles. Although it is likely that the intuitions by which the child comes to *feel* either female or male have an organic base, early social reinforcement affects the strength of their subsequent establishment. The social source of these intuitions is largely adult role modeling: usually an unplanned and unacknowledged activity accompanied by a similarly unplanned social reinforcement of appropriate behaviors. Toys and imitative play are extremely significant in this process as well—both in the personally necessary and organically rooted establishment of a specific gender identity and in the culturally variable, but inevitable, implanting of a more or less rigid set of sex-role expectations.

However, development does not always occur according to expectations. Children born with ambiguous sex organs, for example, have sometimes been steered by early surgery in a gender direction that subsequently conflicted with instinctive urges and feelings. There are also many documented instances of sexual disorientation in other species caused by genetic anomalies or by animals maturing in unusual circumstances. An example of the latter is the case of one of the first condors raised in captivity by conservationists working to save the species from extinction. Initially, this particular condor was subjected to an environment containing no others of his own kind. In early adulthood he would attempt to copulate with familiar structures in his pen, while manifesting no interest whatsoever in the female condors presented for mating. It required a consistent program of re-conditioning—with the help of a particularly patient female bird—for the captive condor to turn into a committed species-appropriate heterosexual. Konrad Lorernz once produced findings of similar significance, when he managed, through conditioning, to divert the sexual arousal of a female rook to himself and away from male rooks.

The issue of sexual orientation is a particularly sensitive one because of the history of abusive discrimination against homosexuality common to most cultures. It is made more difficult by the fact that, at the present time, we simply do not know whether or not—or to what degree—there exists a *genetic* predisposition to be sexually aroused by members of one's own sex. Some recent studies, as well as the persistence of homosexuality throughout human history, would seem to indicate this. Conversely, the fact of extremely wide variations in incidence across cultures and historical eras supports the proposition that homosexuality is at least to some extent culturally determined. Also, it is not easy to see how it could have been evolutionarily advantageous. On the other hand, there is the possibility—implied by modern theories of kin selection—that a number of non-reproducing adults within a clan may have contributed to the survival of a sibling's offspring, and thus to the survival of the genes of the non-procreators. In fact, Edward O. Wilson, the Harvard sociobiologist, has suggested that homosexuals may be the carriers of some of humankind's earliest innate altruistic impulses.

It remains the case, however, that in spite of numerous attempts to locate a gene for homosexuality—and a rash of (as yet) non-replicated studies purporting to have located organic differences between hetero-

and homosexual males—we still lack scientifically convincing evidence for a biological source of that particular pattern of response. This is consistent with the fact that we have no such evidence for the exclusive biological determination of *any* complex behavioral pattern in humans. It is possible that the environment plays an indirect role, causing congenital changes to the fetus. Research on rats has indicated that stress suffered by pregnant females can influence the sexual orientation of their male offspring. The most plausible explanation for both the persistence and variable occurrence of the phenomenon may be that, although certain people are born with some type of predisposition inclining them in that direction, the particular manifestation which we identify as homosexuality is considerably affected by contingent circumstances. It may emerge as a result of the reinforcement (and thus the selection) of trial-and-error or imitative behavior at a critical stage of a child's sexual development.

This interpretation does not mean that people *choose* to be homosexually inclined (although many with that propensity do indeed make conscious choices whether or not to *engage* in sexual activity). Only those who have no understanding of how socialization works would ever associate learned behavior with conscious choosing. We do not choose to speak our mother tongue; nor do we consciously select our habits, or the values, beliefs and attitudes that shape eventual choices in any arena of behavior. But, nevertheless, all these things are learned from the situations to which we are (often unwittingly) exposed. There are well-replicated research findings demonstrating how even grown men can be conditioned to be sexually aroused by the sight of a boot. Obviously, the object and circumstance of an adolescent's first sexual experience will be crucial in this particular aspect of socialization into adult roles. However, once that programming has occurred (be it "hard-wired" in the genes or "soft-wired" by experience), the effect on the individual is the same. The result is the present adult "self" with its own characteristic sexual orientation: a "self" worthy of acceptance and respect by society.

From a scientific perspective, then, the question of the heritability of sexual orientation is still open. In the current state of our knowledge we can only hypothesize that, while a minority among us may indeed inherit a propensity toward homosexuality, this is likely to be manifested in vastly different ways in different cultural settings. It is also possible that such urges could be overlaid and inhibited, or reinforced and enhanced, by socialization. This would explain the historical evidence suggesting that the actual incidence of homosexual behavior within populations has tended to wax and wane over the generations and across cultures, according to the nature of institutional arrangements for socializing the young, and the degree to which same-gender sex was condoned and celebrated—or merely tolerated, or discouraged—by the culture.

DIRECTING THE LEARNING PROCESS

We gain little by attempting to determine the precise proportion of any complex behavior due to genetic programming as distinct from learning—whether the subject is sexual preference, intelligence or aggression. The interactive, genetic-cultural system setting in which all attitudes and beliefs emerge and all habits develop precludes the possibility of success in this. We can only surmise that the *roots* of sexual and emotional propensities as well as certain intellectual and artistic capacities are innate. That said, we know that experience, and the learning engendered by it, plays a powerful role in determining all human attributes—including advanced sensorimotor skills, reasoning abilities, and the capacity for wise judgment. In fact, we are now aware that environmental influences begin to affect learning not merely at birth, but from the moment of conception. For example, congenitally acquired disease, or the effects of parental drug use, can impose lifelong crippling. On the more positive side, neurological scientists have discovered that exposure of unborn rats to complex classical music improves spatial-temporal capacities. This is consistent with previous findings concerning learning in humans. All this forces us to entertain the possibility that the concept of education may be of relevance not only for parents during the pre-natal period, but for their fetuses as well.

Once birth occurs, the learning process accelerates. As in the case of the cultural evolution of the species as a whole, the child develops the crucial habits and concepts described in this chapter chiefly in response to the demands of the environment.

As was pointed out in the preceding chapter, education involves structuring that environment with a particular objective in mind. In general terms, the educational goal is to bring long-term consequences into the learner's purview. It is to utilize the child's developing empathy, imagination and reason to make the prospect of distant "goods" function as reinforcements, in place of immediate rewards. This is inevitably a slow, cumulative process, in which it is necessary during the early stages to develop the tools of knowledge by dividing every task into minute steps and providing for positive feedback in the form of the experience of immediate empowerment at every step. Ultimately, however, education is about the capacity to defer instant gratification and to make wise choices by applying time-tested ethical principles to the predictable future effects of current actions—for society as well as oneself.

Throughout history, the effectiveness of human learning has allowed our species to wield great power, for better and for worse. Only by understanding the systematic and developmental nature of the process—and the principle of reinforcement directing its key operations of imitation and trial and error—can parents and teachers hope to do a better job of guiding it. The current generation, by abdicating its responsibility to monitor the experience of the young, can leave as a heritage a population of young people desensitized by direct and vicarious experience of violence and devoid of concern for the welfare of the group. Alternatively, we can attempt, in our role as socializers, to structure the learning process more wisely, with the aim of developing in all children the type of humane character that will ensure a better culture in the future.

REFERENCES

Baldwin, A. L. *Theories of Child Development*. New York, NY: Wiley, 1967.

Baskwell, Jane. *Connections: A Child's Natural Learning Tool*. Richmond Hill, ON: Scholastic, 1990.

Bell, Beverly F. *Children's Science, Constructivism and Learning in Science*. Geelong, Australia: Deakin University Press, 1993.

Bernhard, J. Gary. *Primates in the Classroom: An Evolutionary Perspective on Children's Education*. Amherst, MA: University of Massachusetts Press, 1988.

Berry, J.W. and Dasen, Pierre, eds. *Culture and Cognition*. London, UK: Methuen, 1974.

Bruner, Jerome S., ed. *Studies in Cognitive Growth*. New York, NY: Wiley, 1966.

Coloroso, Barbara. *Kids Are Worth It: Giving Your Child the Gift of Inner Discipline*. Toronto, ON: Somerville House, 1994.

Gagne, Robert M. *Studies of Learning: Fifty Years of Research*. Tallahassee, FL: Learning Systems Institute, Florida State University, 1989.

Gell-Mann, Murray. *The Quark and the Jaguar: Adventures in the Simple and the Complex*. New York, NY: W. H. Freeman, 1995.

Gesell, Arnold. *Child Development*. New York, NY: Harper, 1948.

Hutcheon, Pat Duffy. *A Sociology of Canadian Education*. Toronto, ON: Van Nostrand Reinhold (Nelson of Canada), 1975.

Kagan, Jerome, ed. *Cognitive Development*. San Diego, CA: Harcourt Brace Jovanovich, 1990.

Lloyd, Barbara and Duveen, Gerard. *Gender Identities and Education: The Impact of Starting School*. New York, NY: St. Martin's Press, 1992.

Millar, Thomas P. *The Omnipotent Child: How to Mold, Strengthen and Perfect the Developing Child*. Vancouver, BC: Palmer Press, 1994.

Piaget, Jean. *The Organs of Intelligence in the Child*. 2nd ed. London, UK: Routledge and Kegan Paul, 1953.

———. "The Theory of Stages in Development." In *Measurement and Piaget*, ed. D. K. Green et al. New York, NY: McGraw Hill, 1971, pp. 1–11.

Pinker, Steven. *How the Mind Works*. New York, NY: W. W. Norton, 1997.

Reimann, Peter and Spade, Hans. *Learning in Humans and Machines: Towards an Interdisciplinary Learning Science*. New York, NY: Pergamon, 1995.

Seligman, Martin. *What You Can Change and What You Can't*. New York, NY: Alfred A. Knopf, 1994.

Skinner, B. F. *Contingencies of Reinforcement*. Englewood Cliffs, NJ: Prentice-Hall, 1969.

———. *A Matter of Consequences*. New York, NY: Alfred A. Knopf, 1983.

Zentall, Thomas R. and Galef, Bennett G. *Social Learning: Psychological and Biological Perspectives*. Hillsdale, NJ: Lawrence Erlbaum Associates, 1988.

CHAPTER 5

Where Does Character Come From?

The most important of all the products of childhood learning is character; and a good measure of the success of any society is how well the task of character building is being performed. In recent years there have been disturbing signs that modern societies are not doing well in this regard. Pollsters routinely inform us of a virtual sea change in the values of youth, and of business leaders and ordinary working people. The message conveyed by their findings is a cause for serious worry about what may be happening to the level of trust in one another that is the prerequisite of any workable society. Numerous surveys indicate that a majority of people expect others to be dishonest. Others report that the percentage of teens who indicate that honesty is "very important" is dropping year by year, and that more than 50 percent of students admit that they would cheat on exams if they thought they would not be caught. The same has been shown to hold true for their adult mentors, where cheating on taxes and certain other minor violations of the law are concerned. Political leaders are regularly caught out in unethical escapades that only narrowly pass the tests of legality, while stretching to the limit their own much-heralded conflict-of-interest guidelines.

What are we witnessing here? Many dismayed commentators have concluded that we are facing a crisis of character. If this is indeed so, it is imperative that we understand something about the nature and sources of that essential attribute. The philosopher Mary Midgley justifies concern with character on biological as well as philosophical grounds. She equates a solid, continuous character with emotional stability, and argues that such a disposition was necessary to our evolutionary survival as a species and is a prerequisite, as well, for effective functioning of the individual. John Dewey claimed that underlying a strong character is an integrated set of sound habits: what we refer to when we say that we "know what this person would do in particular circumstances." When most people speak of a weakness of character, however, they usually mean something more than the instability of emotions and habits which does, indeed, seem to be a feature of it. What is typically included is the absence of a deeply entrenched awareness of the difference between good and evil, coupled with the moral courage to make choices and to act consistently in terms of that awareness. In the end, most of us would agree that what character amounts to is an identifiable value system reflecting good old-fashioned morality—honesty, responsibility, respect for the law, concern for others—or common human decency. However, when it comes to the question of where all this comes from, and how we can go about ensuring its development, we seem to encounter more confusion than consensus.

How do human beings become moral? Are intuitions and beliefs about "the good" different in some essential way from intuitions and beliefs about "the real"? Apparently, most of us think so. In spite of understanding, in a general way, that children learn about the real world from the totality of their experience, we still persist in believing something quite different where morality is concerned. Many people feel intuitively that, because being moral is associated with spirituality, it must have a suprasensual, transcendental source. They imagine that this aspect of our nature is implanted in the psyche in some sort of unknowable and irreversible way—perhaps as a reflection of a universal cosmic law. Others think that character, for good or ill, is determined by the genes. Both premises lead to the conclusion that we are impotent to change ourselves or others, either for better or worse. We are easily convinced that fate or Providence, in the form of nature or God—rather than a reasoned and conscientious desire for individual fulfillment, group viability and the survival of life—is the determinant where values are concerned.

Why is this so? Such a position is in no way warranted by modern religion. In fact, in many ways it seems anti-religious, because it implies that moral teachings and strivings are irrelevant. It also contradicts the findings of modern evolutionary science. We appear to be suffering from a widespread ignorance of evolution that feeds into the old Social Darwinist propensity to believe in a character somehow fixed in the genes. It is true that most modern evolutionists would agree with Matt Ridley when he makes the claim, in his 1997 book *The Origins of Virtue*, that humans have evolved an instinct for cooperation. However, there is a crucial difference between accepting the premise that the *roots* of morality (like those of reason and other complex human attributes) are to be found in our animal instincts, and leaping to the conclusion that we are born with virtuous characters intact. Ridley, who maintains that there is no general "will to virtue," would no doubt agree. In fact, even where the biological origins of altruism are concerned, the story is not simple.

Edward O. Wilson has gone to some length to explain the difference between the "hard-wired" variety of altruism and the "soft-wired" or reciprocal variety acquired through appropriate experience. He suggests that the former can be explained by the theory of "kin selection." It is manifested not only in pair bonding and parent-child bonding, but in the self-sacrificing behavior of siblings whose genes are carried on by those children of the brothers and sisters whom they protect—even though they may not themselves reproduce. Wilson points out that it is the underlying emotional bond of kinship, powerfully manifested in vir-tually all human societies, which evolves through the genes. But our genetically based altruism can backfire for the human species. Wilson notes the irony involved in the fact that this underlying "unselfish" emo-tion is responsible for the nepotism and tribalism at the root of so many wars throughout history. On the other hand, the "selfish" reciprocal and learned form of altruism—based on awareness that helping others works best for oneself and one's family in the long run—is what we need to promote through character education if we are to build a better future.

Modern evolutionary theorists can now help us to understand how humans have evolved into the only organisms on the planet with the capacity to acquire a conscience; how we are alone among animals in having the potential to develop a sense of right and wrong in the ab-stract. Their work is contributing to a growing awareness that the very direction of cultural evolution is determined by the process through which human choices produce the consequences that feed back to rein-force or discourage subsequent behavior. In spite of all this, however, the pessimistic and/or permissive stance on morality continues to per-vade our culture, with all of its destructive consequences.

THE BELIEFS THAT GUIDE OR BLIND US

The reason for the endurance of fatalism on moral issues is not difficult to find. Albert Schweitzer explained how it has been encouraged throughout history by a number of influential philosophical systems and religions. On the other hand, many philosophies and religious traditions have supported the very opposite conclusion. In fact, most religious peo-ple today would probably join social scientists in arguing that the notion that values or virtues cannot be "taught" (in the sense of being acquired through appropriate experience) is both unwarranted and likely to have devastating consequences for humankind.

It so happens that there exists not just one, but at least *two* sets of premises about this issue: both deeply embedded in human culture. The sources of these premises are "world views." A world view is a comprehensive interpretation of the cosmos from which individuals derive the meaning of life. Every world view implies a certain role for humans within the universe. Some of these have assigned to humans a distinctively *moral* role. This means that they define individuals as having the capacity for either good or evil, and thereby possessing the power to influence the thought and action of others and to alter the world in either desirable or undesirable ways. Early Buddhism and Confucianism upheld this view, and thus the necessity for moral teachings. In Classical Greece, the Sophists were moralists in these terms, as were the later Epicureans and Stoics. The Hindu belief in reincarnation could be interpreted as an encouragement of good behavior (although there is much in the Vedantist world view in which Hinduism is rooted that seems to imply a pessimistic fatalism). Ancient Judaism was essentially an ethics-based religion, as were primitive Christianity and early Islam. Most of the later offshoots of these movements carried on this emphasis on the necessity of *learning* to live the good life. For instance, we have Roman Catholicism, with its concept of "original sin" and tradition of "good works" within monasticism; and modern evangelical Protestantism with its concept of the Devil ever ready to exert an evil influence on the immature child if this is not countered by moral teachings. We also have the example of the ethical emphasis within Sikhism and the Baha'i faith. The philosophy of utilitarianism, coming out of the Enlightenment, and subsequently the pragmatism of John Dewey and George Herbert Mead, also spelled out a powerful moral role for humankind.

A second set of world views defines humans as powerless in this sense; that is, they imply that individual choices are irrelevant in the ultimate scheme of things. All animistic and primarily mystical religions belong to this category, as do those picturing the world in terms of transcendent forces of good and evil locked in eternal combat—with humans merely helpless victims of a cosmic process. Zoroastrianism is an example of the latter. Included in this category are religions encouraging a distrust and abhorrence of life, coupled with utopian visions of a hereafter. We can also include here the Platonic tradition of Ancient Greece with its ideal realm of "essential" value; certain aspects of Hinduism in India and Taoism in China; some versions of Protestant Christianity (such as Calvinism with its concept of predestination); the romanticism of Rousseau; the Marxist theory of morality as merely the reflection of class interests (and of individuals as either pawns or midwives of inexorable historical laws); and modern existentialism which tends to view individuals as sovereign, free-floating entities within a meaningless void.

The beliefs of human beings regarding the possibility for individual morality are not simply abstractions having no impact on the real world. They *matter* in that they determine how we approach the issue of how to inculcate desirable values in children; or whether, in fact, we consider

it necessary at all. If we believe that individual choices have no significance for the moral order (and *vice versa*)—or that morality is implanted
in infants at birth and requires only an unrestricted natural unfolding—
then we will not be concerned about the condition of the cultural environment or with the process of moral development. We will simply sit
back and let nature take its course, or expend our energy in attempts to
propitiate the arbitrary and often malicious spirits that exert control.
Some of the more evangelical among us may feel compelled to apply
labels such as the "damned" versus the "saved," while the more liberal
may use terms like "materialistic," as opposed to "spiritual" to distinguish the bad from the good.

But none of this will prevent, or even decelerate, what appears to some
observers as a worldwide descent into anarchy and violence. It is long
past time to free ourselves from all non-ethical belief systems: those implying the impossibility or irrelevance of individual moral choice. Evidence of the very real power of humankind, not only to create but to
destroy, demands that we jettison all world views encouraging a denial
of human responsibility for the future. This means that many "conventional wisdoms" will have to go. It means that liberal admirers of Rousseau must overcome their reluctance to "impose" values on their
children. It means that the existential followers of Nietzsche and Sartre
must stop dreaming of a moral autonomy operating with no consequences for others. It means that both right-wing and anarchistic libertarians must stop shouting accusations of censorship whenever attempts
are made to clean up the cultural environment to which our children are
exposed. It means that socialists must become critical of Marxism, and
any other theory based on the concept of a historical dialectic. It means
that modern transcendentalists, pantheists, mystics and animists must
stop assuming some sort of "natural moral order" external to humans
which is accessible directly through intuition and meditation—or by
communicating with spirits; and it means that conservative theological
and biological determinists must stop believing in an obsolete doctrine
of inherited (or "revealed") character long invalidated by science.

An effective attack on our problems also requires that we go beyond
attempts to discuss the current moral crisis in terms of dichotomies such
as "materialistic" versus "spiritual" values; or of a "state of grace" versus "self-centeredness." These definitions usually amount to mere labeling or name-calling, and lead nowhere. "Materialism" is always seen as
the motivation driving others—never us. Self-centeredness can be perceived similarly. What appears to be meant by both expressions can be
better understood as infantile egocentrism, along with the inability to
defer gratification, and the uninhibited desire for power over others. All
these are the natural characteristics of the immature child; however,
when exhibited by adults they are indicators of a lack of moral devel-

opment. If, indeed, large numbers of our population are growing up as spiritual (i.e., social/moral) cripples, then simply giving their condition a name will not turn things around. Surely it is time, rather, to assess the *socialization process* currently shaping them and the *cultural environment* feeding the process.

BUT HOW CAN WE KNOW WHAT IS GOOD?

If learning to be moral is not only possible but imperative for humans, what criteria can we use to select the contents and processes of appropriate socialization? That is, how can we determine what is morally good? Classical character education, based largely on Aristotelian principles, taught that individuals *know* how to be virtuous but simply lack the will and disposition to accomplish it. Civics, which was routinely taught in the classrooms of the past, was based on the assumption that the prerequisites for good citizenship and personal morality are at least compatible, if not the same, and fairly obvious. But both of these earlier positions would seem to beg the question of the ultimate origin of, and criteria for, values.

There are two legitimate sources for answers to this important question. The foundation for all valuing is the *empathy* furthered within the growing child by the socialization process. Without empathy the moral development so basic to character formation would be impossible. Some people argue that the roots of a capacity to feel anything at all for others is innate, and lacking from birth in a minority of instances. Childhood autism may be a case where the capacity has been short-circuited in some way. However, the probability of an infant being totally crippled genetically where empathy is concerned is quite remote. In general it is safe to say that sociopathic monsters and saints alike are made—not born!

At the most elementary level, then, we look to our human capacities for feeling, imagining, remembering and reasoning (or making connections among the sensations and images created by these capacities) and to the acquired ability to assess all this from the perspective of others. We judge a particular act as good because it is likely to make us, and our fellows, feel good—not just for the moment, but for tomorrow and beyond. However, although feelings can be said to operate as an ultimate experiential check on morality, they are not sufficient. Unfortunately, the goal of personal happiness is not, in itself, a reliable guide to moral behavior. The reason is that it is seldom possible for the individual, especially the child or adolescent, to predict which choice is likely to produce the most good feeling—even in a personal sense—over the long term. This is because human beings are enmeshed in a system of social interaction. Other people will necessarily be affected by the behaviors of each of us, just as their behaviors will have an impact on us. If it is not easy to apply our memory, imagination and reason to the task of predicting the long-term consequences of any choice in our own lives, it is doubly difficult to make reliable assessments of the feeling states aroused in the social group as a whole by the chain of consequences flowing from our projected action. Yet that is precisely what is required of us. For, as Marcus Aurelius said so long ago, "That which is not good for the beehive cannot be good for the bee."

Another source of guidance as to the nature of the good is tradition. Which precepts or virtues or principles for living have allowed human groups to survive and prosper throughout history? These traditional sources are usually exemplified in the persons of great ethical leaders or teachers (many of whom have been considered divine) and in their teachings, which are usually expressed as sacred codes. Ultimately, the concept of God or Divinity throughout the ages has symbolized humanity's noblest and most universal ideals. However, new realities emerge as science expands possibilities, and these present new moral challenges to be faced by human beings. From time to time we are made painfully aware that traditional answers are no longer sufficient or even workable in radically altered circumstances; and that the current ethical leaders assigned the task of re-interpretation and re-application may not necessarily be wise or trustworthy. Where, then, can fallible human beings look for *certain* guidance?

The honest answer to all this is that we must learn not to expect certainty in morality—anymore than we can expect it in knowledge. We adults striving for the wisdom to aid our children in developing character must do the best we can, using those sources available to us for guidance. Perhaps a comparison between valuing and *knowing* (as distinct from merely "believing") will be helpful here. Only those private beliefs that are amenable to some sort of disciplined, replicable public checking process—and have thus far survived these tests—can be considered to constitute our civilization's reliable knowledge. The factual knowledge that is sufficiently dependable for us to place our trust in it must therefore rest ultimately on the human ability to sense and remember images and sensations, and to organize them into communicable language so as to share them and render them testable in some sense. So too must morality have its organic origin in the innate capacities of the senses. What is relevant in the latter case are sensations of pain and pleasure, and the desire to prevent the first and to prolong the second— over the long term and the widest possible range of relationships.

This does not mean that morality is therefore relativistic, or a merely subjective matter. In fact, above all it is a *social* concern, experienced by all of us, for the actions inspired by individual moral choices produce consequences felt by the entire collective. Thus, morality, like knowledge, is *necessarily* objective. A further comparison with the process of knowing is enlightening here. As with the good, the ultimate test of what is real is the evidence of the senses. However, that perceived sensation represents merely the initiation and final check on each brick in the knowledge-building process. We all know that human perception is fraught with pitfalls. Language, intelligence and imagination are the necessary means by which immediate experiences are precisely communicated and checked with others, connections among them identified, defined and explained, and the *explanations* for these connections subjected to public testing as to their reliability and workability. Only then do we consider the product, or item of knowledge, to be an effective guide to action. The same approach can be applied to valuing.

Every living organism seeks to act so as to maintain a valued response. Memory and language, and the imagination and empathy that these advanced capacities generate in humans, make possible the representation of present "felt" values in abstract ideals. This is one of the aspects of the uniquely human "idealizing" function discussed in previous chapters. The urge to prolong immediate pleasure evolves gradually, for learning humans, into the goal of ensuring continued survival and achieving fulfillment for one's family and fellows along with oneself— and for the future as well as the present. Ideals such as benevolence, compassion, justice, respect for life and for human dignity symbolize these yearnings. Once formulated, these ideals imply rules and standards which operate as powerful directives for future behavior, thereby assuming an objective reality loaded with causal potential.

Tradition represents the institutionalization of those ideals, codes of conduct and ethical principles that have worked for the benefit of the social group and its members throughout history. As with the theories organizing our bodies of knowledge, the test of these moral rules is the consequence of living by them, over time, as assessed by the behaviors and feelings which they initiate and maintain in the population of the world at large. We are aware that, in the case of scientific knowledge, an established theory is given up only very reluctantly. It is relinquished only after the appearance of numerous unexplained anomalies in the experience it predicts, and then only when a more comprehensive and effective theory has appeared to replace it. Similarly, custom provides us with built-in resistance to changes in those traditional mores that have stood the test of time.

KNOWLEDGE AND THE PROBLEM OF MEANS AND ENDS

Perhaps the most harmful philosophies of the past two centuries have involved the notion that it is possible to separate means from ends. All of the historicist ideologies that arose out of Hegelianism, as well as certain militant fundamentalist versions of dualistic religion, subscribe in one form or another to this belief. They imply that, if we have access to some sort of revealed knowledge indicating that our end-in-view is an "absolute good," then we are justified in using immoral means in our attempts to achieve it. Some modern philosophies, influenced by phenomenology and existentialism, are based on the premise that cause and effect do not operate in the realm of values. The social theorist Max Weber, apparently beginning from this premise, claimed that one simply cannot think in terms of means and ends (or cause and effect) when making moral judgments.

But this approach is inherently dangerous for humanity. Apart from the obvious problems connected with the reliability of revelation—whether religious or political—there is a wealth of experience to demonstrate that moral desires and ideals not connected to effective action accomplish nothing fruitful. History teaches that they lead, instead, to disillusionment and cynicism; and means that initiate a stream of events propelling an individual in directions unrelated, or even contradictory, to intended goals can be spiritually destructive. Most moral philosophers have long understood that there is an inevitable continuity of means and ends. This position has perhaps been spelled out most clearly by the pragmatists. John Dewey explained how it is that each end becomes the means to an end that beckons further on. Thus, means, to be effective, must be shaped by the end we seek, and the end must be logically and knowledgeably predictable in terms of the means. Twentieth-century communists are among the many who have found, to their sorrow, that to proceed otherwise is to find the end distorted and forever lost. They discovered that their chosen paths led elsewhere, and the journey itself shaped the travelers' values and turned them into different people.

This brings us back once more to the all-important role of knowledge, or *reliable* beliefs, in predicting the likely consequences of our choices and in identifying the best means for achieving our goals. The only way we have of judging the effectiveness of those means selected to reach our valued ends—and, ultimately, the worth of our ideals as well—is the very same method humans have devised for the testing of knowledge claims. That is, we must learn to employ our human tools of reason, feeling and perception in a disciplined public process of observing, weighing and analyzing the evidence of experience. Means proposed as solutions to our social problems must be judged as to their moral and logical consistency with the desired goals, and then continuously evaluated under controlled conditions in terms of their consequences—*not* according to the intentions of their proposers. Do they move us toward our goals at an acceptable cost in terms of scarce resources and adverse side effects for the social fabric and the earth's ecology? Just as knowledge-building requires a shared, public testing process so, too, our means of establishing values worth living by must be a collective responsibility. As with knowledge, an intelligent approach discourages irreversible, large-scale innovation in matters of morality. We do not recklessly throw out any part of our accumulation of reliable explanations of facts. Nor should we too impulsively abandon the virtues that have been found to work throughout the history of the human race.

THE RELATIONSHIP BETWEEN MORALITY AND ART

As in the case of knowledge and morality, there is a close connection between moral and aesthetic sensibilities in humans. Just as meaning and value do not reside in a reality external to experience, neither does the quality of excellence sought by artists. It is humans, in general and over time, who attribute quality to a work of art as a result of the responses evoked by it within them. Those artistic products said to possess lasting quality are appreciated as such because of the consistency of the response aroused in those who experience them. These responses may take the form of feelings of fulfillment; or the experience of *déjà vu*; or heightened understanding of the universal human condition; or possibly an empathy so intense that the viewer or listener or reader has the sensation of re-living the artist's representation of experience. To the degree that the writer or performer or visual artist has succeeded in accomplishing this end, for people of diverse times and cultures, the work is judged to possess quality. Subjective relativism and elitist authoritarianism are no more valid in judgments of aesthetic quality than in those concerning knowledge or morality.

There is another connection between art and morality that is often overlooked. Students of moral development agree that, without empathy, morality is impossible. The literary, musical and visual arts perform a crucial function in providing the opportunity for vicarious experience of a depth and breadth of suffering and joy not likely to be acquired from private experience in the course of only one lifetime. They can initiate an intensification and enrichment of the range of available experience that sensitizes people to the potential consequences of their choices for the lives of others. Without this, moral choices lack the essential criterion of concern for something beyond immediate personal gratification.

There is a down side to this interaction between morality and the arts. Although morality can be enhanced by creative productions of high quality, it is vulnerable to corruption by decadent art and literature. Morality is manifested in the culture in terms of worthy and satisfying relationships—along with those ideal personalities, rituals and symbols representing society's loftiest aspirations. The arts, on the other hand, are embodied in artifacts which lend themselves readily to commerce and thus may be immediately and widely dispersed over time and space. Objects of art, whether of excellent, mediocre or atrocious quality, enter the universal cultural milieu this way and remain indefinitely. Today they are communicated to every corner of the globe by mass media fueled by a self-serving tendency to create, and then to feed, a variety of destructive psychological addictions. This means that the most violent and *desensitizing* of these "creative" products are often the most widely dispersed. These objects then begin to constitute a large part of the culture from which children and youth extract their values and ideals and rules for living. This is analogous to the process by which irresponsible corporations or individuals employ advanced technology in ways that pollute the air or drinking water of entire populations.

Knowledge and the arts are related to morality in yet another way. All three, at their best, can be said to embody and represent universal standards, whether of truth, beauty or virtue. Objective knowledge, be it historical or scientific, is built up by means of a worldwide public sharing and checking process. Although such knowledge does not purport to communicate *absolute truth*—and therefore remains open to change on the basis of evidence—it aims at *universal validity and reliability*. There is good reason to assume that this applies to the arts as well. For example, it has long been suspected that there are identifiable rhythms, combinations of sound and visual patterns that are uniquely capable of evoking pleasurable responses in humans from all cultural backgrounds. Tentative scientific findings now suggest the existence of universal standards of facial beauty, having to do with symmetry. Other studies have documented a correlation between the brain-wave activity associated with relaxation and listening to certain types of music.

Where morality is concerned, we have moved a long way from the simplistic moral relativism of the early twentieth century. It now seems clear that earlier anthropologists were failing to distinguish between those core values necessary for the functioning of any human group and the variable norms represented in culturally diverse customs. They were focusing on the exotic and particular and overlooking what was universal. There are three obvious reasons why we are justified in predicating the present existence and future necessity of a core of universally applicable values. In the first place, all humans share virtually the same evolutionary legacy, and therefore certain drives that must be satisfied and others that require restraint—along with a common need for fulfillment and survival. In fact, some social psychologists suggest that even the roots of a sense of justice may be biological, and related to aesthetic urges, in that justice (like beauty) is associated with an innate attraction to symmetry. Second, humans are social beings and the long-term survival of the group is a prerequisite for individual survival. Some behaviors and beliefs must be furthered, and others discouraged, if any group is to work at all. Third, the power of humans to create new realities, and to alter and destroy others, is such that it is now imperative for humankind to develop moral guidelines at the universal level.

BECOMING MORALLY MATURE

All this drives home the need to understand how children acquire moral habits and build their values. This is an important process that cannot be left to chance. We are aware that interaction with the *physical* environment provides children with the opportunity to absorb the connections and limitations in the inorganic realm—and thereby to achieve crucial concepts such as the conservation of matter. So, too, must children's *cultural* surroundings encourage them to experience social boundaries, to assimilate rules of conduct, and to develop the empathy and habits that make social life workable and rewarding.

The major conclusion of studies in moral development is that the process is contingent upon intellectual development. However, it does not occur simply as a by-product of either physical or mental maturation, nor does it proceed in stages corresponding to those which seem to characterize advances in cognition. Although a certain level of intellectual development is *necessary* for the accompanying advance in moral functioning, intellectual development in itself is not *sufficient* for morality. Appropriate nurturing, moral and otherwise, is essential. The relationship is a three-way one with physical maturation and socialization operating as crucial contributing factors. (Another example of the "triple helix"!) This means that, at each increasingly complex level of mental functioning, a corresponding level of moral functioning is possible *given* the appropriate experiences. Nothing is guaranteed, however. Moral habits and virtues must be planned for and painstakingly inculcated through modeling; and by carefully structuring the child's experience so as to reinforce desirable responses and thus encourage the formation of moral habits. At the same time, the socialization process organized for the purpose must not provide experiences, or employ practices, that are beyond the child's ability to comprehend.

Those responsible for children's morality would do well, therefore, to understand how children develop intellectually so that they can gauge what is possible at every age. Child developmentalists identify a four-stage process of conceptual development (or four recognizable phases of a continuous process) and cross-cultural research has shown these to be characteristic of all humans. Jean Piaget called them the *sensorimotor*, the *pre-operational*, the *concrete-operational* and the *formal-operational*—although other theorists have employed different terminology. Without going into the complexities of these, it is worth emphasizing that the developing child does indeed seem to move in a stage-like progression of understanding, and that the sequence of these has been found to be invariant across cultures. However, there is compelling evidence that many people, in cultural settings that do not provide intellectually demanding experience, never achieve the most advanced stage of conceptualization. It seems that, although the *pattern* of development is the same for humans everywhere, the *rate* varies considerably from person to person and from culture to culture—as does the *extent* or level achieved by adulthood.

That said, we can talk about the approximate or average age at which children in industrially advanced societies achieve each of the four levels of mental functioning—keeping in mind that any particular child can be far above or below the norm for her chronological age. We can also make some inferences about what kind of social experience is likely to further moral development at each level; and we can begin to understand why certain other experiences are likely to be devastating to the achievement of morality at each stage of intellectual development.

The *sensorimotor* stage extends from infancy to about the age of two, and includes the child's first sensory responses to—and trial-and-error sensorimotor manipulations of—the surroundings. The behavior of infants and toddlers is initially shaped by impulse and, almost immediately, by habit as well. They only gradually come to sense that movements are causal, and to recognize dimensions in the surrounding space as well as the separate identity of surrounding objects. The establishment of desirable motor habits is all-important here, for rules as such cannot be learned by infants and toddlers. A rule is merely a unique event for them, not transferrable, mentally, to other settings. For the most part, "telling" is fruitless. On the other hand, consistent positive reinforcement of desired behavior is imperative. Moral education, here, is about the development of appropriate habits and the inculcation of an intuitive sense of "good" and "bad."

At about the age of two the child moves into the *pre-operational* stage of cognitive functioning. This is the period of spontaneous and differentiated emotional responses during which children begin to establish the limits—first of the self, and then of the physical and social world. They still have no concept of time other than an intuition controlled by movement through positions in space. This stage also marks the construction of language upon the sensorimotor base—through imitation and imagery and, finally, the use of symbols. This is the function that makes representation of thought possible, although even the simplest of logical operations are still out of reach. Thinking remains largely in terms of a progression of images. At this stage (sometimes described as "egocentrism") notions of right and wrong are rapidly assimilated and deeply rooted. If this does not occur at this particular time in the child's life it will be extremely difficult, if not impossible, to compensate for the resulting deficiencies in conscience in later years. Television is a powerful socializing influence here, as suggestion and modeling produce instantaneous leaps in imitation and learning—in directions either good or bad—and these occur at an astounding rate.

During the *pre-operational* stage of cognitive development children learn to emulate, in idiosyncratic ways, the rule-following behavior of others. In this way rules can be learned, although they are regarded by most pre-school children as sacred and untouchable, and as an unchangeable aspect of a reality accessible only to adults. Punishment following transgression is similarly seen as immutable and part of the natural order. Children are very open to acquiring the habit of obedience to authority at this time. Without such a habit, it will be difficult to establish, at some later date, the necessary virtue of respect for law. A mildly authoritarian approach to the teaching of morality would seem to be essential here, although punishment is not.

At this *pre-operational* level of cognitive functioning, a concern with "moral reasoning" is inappropriate. *Explaining* to children why certain behaviors are not allowed is futile and may even be harmful, for the reasons being provided are likely to be beyond their grasp. Children of this age have difficulty connecting cause to consequence, and it may well be counterproductive to attempt to provide them with complex justifications for moral rules. Instead, this is the time in the child's life when consistent reinforcement of desirable moral habits and appropriate behaviors and attitudes by significant others is particularly essential. It is during this period that what is sometimes called a "moral disposition" must be developed.

Pre-schoolers of this age tend to have trouble functioning in any cooperative context and require consistent encouragement in this direction. Because of their natural egocentrism, their own feelings are interpreted as having absolute value while the feelings of others do not exist for them. The cry of "mine! mine!" is familiar to all parents and nursery-school teachers. Only gradually, in response to appropriate experiences, is self-centeredness diminished to the extent that children can become *empathetic*; and only gradually do they develop the capacity to transfer rules of conduct from particular situations and authority figures to life in general.

Because *pre-operational* children can make no clear distinction between fantasy and reality they are extremely vulnerable to images presented on television. As a result, they may have their impressions of the world irrevocably distorted by that powerful medium. The typical pre-schooler cannot relate images and modeled behaviors to the context within which they are presented. Consequently, what they take from media presentations tends to be quite different from what may have been intended by the artists involved in the production. Needless to say, all children's programming should be carefully analyzed with this in mind.

One of the crucial tasks of moral education during the later phase of the *pre-operational* stage and the beginning of the *concrete-operational* one is to ensure that children build up a sound concept of reality as distinct from the imaginary. From the age of three most children are capable of understanding what "pretend" means so long as they are made aware that it applies in a specific instance. No legend or myth expressing fictional and fantastic events (whether religious or secular in content) should ever be presented without a reminder of its non-accordance with the reality actually encountered in the everyday world. Nor should young children be introduced to abstract concepts concerning religion or any other subject: concepts having no grounding in their own concrete experience. Such presentations encourage a non-questioning acceptance of "truths" which, by the very abstract quality that distinguishes them, cannot be checked against the child's everyday experience. This all-too-common type of socialization can cripple the capacity for critical thinking before it has had a chance to form.

Another necessary task at this time is to move children gradually from the relatively authoritarian mode required to instill the habit of obedience to social rules in the direction of a more cooperative mode. By about the age of seven most are mentally equipped to work and play cooperatively and to accept the responsibility of following the rules. These social/moral capacities have become possible because average children of that age are able to perform concrete mental operations: that is, internalized actions that are *reversible* (like adding and subtracting) and *transitive* (like knowing that if A is less than B, and B is less than C, then C is greater than A). This means that they have mastered classes, relations and number. These involve the comparative notion that is necessary for sequencing—for understanding that a series of objects differing in size or number can be viewed from largest to smallest and *vice versa*; and that groups can be formed on the basis of a number of attributes or dimensions. This marks the onset of logical reasoning, an ability to assume a variety of perspectives in space, and a sense of time as duration.

The *concrete-operational* stage in mental development also heralds a capacity for empathy and perspective in social relations, and the ability to follow a story line or plot and to derive a lesson from it. The all-important attribute of empathy is a good example of the intricate relationship between cognitive and moral functioning. Empathizing with others requires not only sympathetic *feelings*. It involves, as well, the cognitive ability to assume different perspectives; to project oneself—in the imagination—into the emotional "space" of the other. It is this essential capacity to assume the perspective of the other person that also allows the child to understand the function of rules: one of the crucial achievements making cooperation and compromise fully possible.

However, although cause and consequence in behavior can now be sensed intuitively, connections are made only in concrete terms and for the present moment. This is the time when it is necessary to acquaint children with pay-offs for virtuous acts by immediate reinforcement in the form of social approbation and the experience of enhanced effectiveness. It is also the time to present virtuous heroes as models to live by: men and women whose lives and actions exemplify the virtues of benevolence, honesty, responsibility and respect for human dignity that make social life possible and personally gratifying. And, because one's peers become the most powerful agents of socialization at this time, much attention needs to be given to the operative mores of the group. As this is the age when gangs begin to form, it is imperative that all the influences shaping the values of the peer group be subjected to wise adult control. The impact of television, computer games and home videos is especially significant for children at this stage of development because these media are the major sources of the powerful pressures for conformity exerted by the peer group.

The *formal operational* stage begins at about the age of eleven for children of average intelligence—if previous socialization has been adequate. Here the child's distinctive personality and character become relatively fixed. Here, too, we find the emergence of an ability to handle abstract ideas. It is only at this age that complex concepts, removed from their concrete reference points, can be presented without doing harm. It is only now that implications can be deduced from premises, generalizations can be inferred from experience and general principles can be applied to concrete situations. In fact, it is only in senior high school that class discussions of moral issues and exercises in moral reasoning can be employed fruitfully and constructively. Although the practice of connecting cause to effect in resolving disagreements with one's fellows should have been encouraged during the preceding stage, it is usually not until late adolescence that arguments can be built up step-by-step in an increasingly logical manner. For the average teenager, it has finally become possible for logical contradictions to be recognized and avoided. Ideals and future goals can be formulated and theories designed and tested in terms of consequences. Ideas can be separated from the person expressing them, and assessed on their merits. Thought itself can be mastered.

At this stage of cognitive development young people are learning how reason combines both logic and value to become instrumental in the making of wise choices. The source of this powerful capability is their own experience—providing, of course, that their previous socialization has made available the appropriate kind of interaction with other people and things. The person who has successfully assimilated the basic virtues necessary for compassionate and effective group living (such as kindness, trustworthiness and respect for human dignity) will now be prepared not only to aspire to worthy ideals and goals but to identify and apply the ethical principles derived from them to the everyday problems of life. Reason and knowledge will indicate the paths to be followed and will supply, as well, a means of assessing progress and learning from mistakes. To the extent that moral maturity has been achieved, one's conscience now has the capacity to operate as an inner standard bearer and the source of a self-discipline requiring no external constraints. The Golden Rule can now be fully comprehended and accepted as a universal moral principle.

Increasingly, however, the socialization to which today's teenagers and younger children are being exposed is moving them relentlessly in a direction far from the desirable goal described above. Things are going very wrong for many of them. The turn-of-the-century French sociologist Emile Durkheim developed a concept called "anomie" which provides an apt causal explanation for the condition in which all too many young people in industrialized societies find themselves today. He began with the proposition that human desires are, by their very nature, insatiable unless in some way constrained by a force transcending the individual. Only the collective (itself created in the course of history by previous members) can establish sanctions, rules and goals for current members. It is these *moral* patterns in the culture that give meaning and value to existence, Durkheim said, and it is these that are the source of virtuous habits. Without them, society disintegrates. The result is that people suffer "anomie": a condition of insufficient or failed socialization which, at the extreme, becomes the amorality of the sociopath. Simply put, there is too little of society in them, and too much of sheer animal lust for momentary pleasure. In the absence of the self-discipline and conscience that come from "the society within," any imposed discipline becomes unbearable. "A thirst arises for novelties, unfamiliar pleasures, nameless sensations, all of which lose their savor once known" (Durkheim 1951: 256). The person in question is unable to endure any frustration of impulse driven by "felt need." The "road rage" so common today is an example of this. Too rapid a pace of social change is the usual cause of this affliction, especially when accompanied by loss of traditional religious beliefs and rites, with no accompanying development of a broader social morality to fill the vacuum.

The prevalence of signs of "anomie" throughout modern societies means that we are producing increasing numbers of dysfunctional and dangerous adults. The following chapter will show how the commercial interests and programmers controlling our mass media are contributing to this situation, and to the disruption of character development that inevitably results.

REFERENCES

Bennett, William J. *The Book of Virtues: A Treasury of Great Moral Stories*. New York, NY: Simon and Schuster, 1993.

de Waal, Frans. *Good Natured: The Origins of Right and Wrong in Humans*. Cambridge, MA: Harvard University Press, 1996.

Dewey, John. *A Common Faith*. New Haven, CT: Yale University Press, 1934.

Durkheim, Emile. *Suicide*. Trans. John A. Spaulding and George Simpson. Glencoe, IL: The Free Press, 1951.

Fox, Robin. *The Search for Society: Quest for a Biosocial Science and Morality*. New Brunswick, NJ: Rutgers University Press, 1989.

Hutcheon, Pat Duffy. "Value Theory: Toward Conceptual Clarification." *The British Journal of Sociology*, 23, 2 (1972): 172–187.

———. "Toward a Unified Social Science." In *Leaving the Cave: Evolutionary Naturalism in Social-Scientific Thought*. Waterloo, ON: Wilfrid Laurier University Press, 1996, pp. 478–481.

Huxley, Julian. *Knowledge, Morality and Destiny*. New York, NY: Mentor Books, 1957.

Kupperman, Joel. *Character*. Oxford, UK: Oxford University Press, 1991.

Leach, Penelope. *What Our Society Must Do—And Is Not Doing—For Our Children Today*. New York, NY: Alfred A. Knopf, 1994.

Lumsden, Charles J. and Wilson, Edward O. *Promethean Fire: Reflections on the Origins of Mind*. Cambridge, MA: Harvard University Press, 1983.

Midgley, Mary. *Wickedness: A Philosophical Essay*. London, UK: Ark Paperbacks, 1984.

———. *The Ethical Primate: Humans, Freedom and Morality*. London, UK: Routledge, 1994.

Murdock, Iris. *The Sovereignty of Good*. London, UK: Routledge and Kegan Paul, 1970.

Peters, Suzanne. *Exploring Canadian Values: Foundations for Well-Being*. Rev. ed. Ottawa, ON: Canadian Policy Research Network, 1995.

Piaget, Jean. *The Moral Judgment of the Child*. London, UK: Routledge and Kegan Paul, 1950.

Ridley, Matt. *Origins of Virtue: Human Instincts and the Evolution of Cooperation*. New York, NY: Viking Press, 1997.

Schulman, Michael and Mekler, Eva. *Bringing up a Moral Child: Teaching Your Child to Be Kind, Just and Responsible*. New York, NY: Main Street/Doubleday, 1994.

Schweitzer, Albert. *Civilization and Ethics*. London, UK: Adam and Charles Black, 1949. (First pub. 1923.)

Skinner, B. F. *Walden Two*. New York, NY: Macmillan, 1976.

Spencer, Herbert. *The Principles of Ethics*. London, UK: Williams and Norgate, 1904.

World Values Surveys. *A Call to Civil Society: Why Democracy Needs Moral Truths*. New York, NY: Institute for American Values, 1998.

Note: See also Appendix A in this book.

CHAPTER 6

The Culture of Violence: Creating the Monsters among Us

There is a story about a group of men who saw a number of drowning people floating down the river. After pulling out the dead and dying for several hours, one of the men said, "Isn't it about time that someone went up river and stopped these people from falling in?" There is a lesson in this for humans as builders of culture and character. It is extremely difficult to undo, during later stages of learning, the harm brought about by faulty early childhood socialization. It is far better to examine what is causing the problems in the first place, and to attempt to rectify the situation. Many social scientists are now suggesting that, rather than directing ever more of our resources toward incarceration and punishment, it might be wiser to focus on preventing the *creation* of anti-social drop-outs and criminals.

Perhaps we can begin by recognizing that the greatest tragedy of our times is the failure of the most influential of our agencies of socialization—the electronic media—to perform what one would expect to have been their prime mandate: the type of character building described in the preceding chapter. Even more ominous is the fact that the compelling power of this institution has functioned, instead, to push the culture into anti-social pathways. Many thoughtful people today are aware of a dark sense of tragedy and foreboding for the future of industrialized society, due largely to feelings of helplessness and frustration in the face of a tide of media-fueled violence that apparently cannot be stemmed. Like the plagues of old it seems to be taking everything in its path. A glance at the programs featured in prime time is sufficient to drive home the frightening realization that what is being conveyed by television is a virtual virus of violence that promotes, more than anything else, the cultural equivalent of the basic DNA instruction: "Duplicate me! Duplicate me!"

It is now almost a truism to say that our children are being addicted to violence. However, we are only belatedly accepting the fact that they are being socialized, as well, into a premature, perverted and abusive sexuality. This is tantamount to acknowledging that the virus of dehumanization is in the very air they breathe and every source of the water they must drink. If the corporations operating the electronic media had hired social scientists to show them how to create a generation of barbarians, they would have embarked on a path no different from the one so obliviously followed for the past 40 years. The result of all this should come as no surprise to anyone who understands how reinforcement works. As the late television journalist Fred Friendly once said, "How can we expect TV to do well when there is so much more money to be made by doing badly?"

Violence is now being propagated (albeit unwittingly, for the most part) within the family setting almost from infancy on. It is being modeled and reinforced by the peer group, school and almost every entertainment facility to which the child is exposed. In fact, if there is one thing in which modern technological societies excel, *when unimpeded by wise human direction*, it is the provision of means and opportunities for an effective socialization into violence. In our hearts most of us know what is happening. Nevertheless, we persist in denying the evidence surrounding us in the vain hope that it will go away. One common form of denial is the "It was ever thus!" approach. Another seeks a reason in the wrath of God, while others blame human conspiracy on the part of those in the opposing ideological camp. But for once statistics and personal experience and common sense all point relentlessly to the same conclusion. Something quite terrible and unique in human history is happening and it is human beings who are both the victims and the culprits. With no conscious intent on the part of anyone, we are using the most powerful instrument of socialization ever invented to build a culture of violence.

SIGNS OF THE TIMES

This conclusion may appear to be refuted by the fact that *adult* violent-crime rates in North America have begun to move lower since 1995. However, this is a predictable decrease correlated with changes both in the demographic makeup of the population and in policing and sentencing policies, as well as with the introduction of programs for keeping inner-city neighborhoods free of graffiti and broken windows. Also pertinent is the remarkable increase in successful trauma treatment in the emergency departments of hospitals, which has resulted in a reduction in the number of documented homicides. Nevertheless, this change for the better must be viewed in the context of a sixfold growth in violent crime in Canada since 1963, and an even greater increase for the same period in the United States. It must be considered, as well, in full awareness that, when we control for population decreases in the relevant age group, the opposite trend still holds for children and adolescents. Although the United States is often considered the most violent country in the developed world, it is not alone: in fact, a 1998 survey conducted by the Canadian Center for Justice Statistics reported that victimization rates for a recent year were highest in Australia, New Zealand, Canada and the United States in that order.

Throughout North America the violent crime rate for youths remains untenable. In many American cities approximately half the murders in a typical year involve victims or assailants eighteen years of age or younger. If current trends continue, the number of teenagers convicted of murder in the United States will spiral to 5,000 annually by 2005. From 1970 to 1996 the number of cities reporting active youth gangs increased eightfold. The murder rate among younger teenagers more than doubled in the seven years from 1986 to 1993, and, for every violent death among these children more than a hundred were wounded. A nation-wide American study found that two-thirds of all teenagers could name friends who had been harmed through deliberate acts of violence in the previous ten months.

By the late 1990s, firearms were being used in three-fourths of American teen homicides—twice the figure for the mid-1980s. Forty percent of those between fourteen and seventeen years of age were acquainted with someone who had been shot during the past few years. From 1985 to 1993, homicides committed by American males aged eighteen to twenty-four increased by 65 percent, while the comparable increase for fourteen- to seventeen-year-olds was 165 percent. With the advent of the crack culture, the number of teen homicides in many American cities is now doubling every two years.

In Canada the basic pattern is similar. In one year in the early 1990s there was a sixfold increase in violent–youth crime in the country as a whole. While it is true that the youth *homicide* rate decreased by approximately 25 percent from 1977 to 1996, this reversal was accompanied by a drastic increase in overall violent crime. In fact, the violent-crime rate for youth doubled from 1985 to 1995. During that period there was a more than 100 percent per capita increase in the total number of such charges; youth offenses involving robbery with a weapon increased threefold; the per capita rate of weapons offenses of all types doubled; the rate of assaults causing harm increased by more than 90 percent. Accompanying this was an appalling increase in drug abuse by young people—and, consequently, in drug-related robbery. In one Canadian city, experimentation with crack and speed by teenagers quadrupled in the two years preceding 1995, while twice as many reported the use of cannabis and LSD. Overall, young offenders accounted for approximately 25 percent of all persons charged with criminal offenses, while the twelve-to-seventeen age group in question represented less than 10 percent of the population. The total number of sexual-assault offenses among this age group was up by over 50 percent.

This last figure is one of many indicators of a worrying deterioration in the treatment of females by males. During one school year, over a thousand children in Minneapolis were suspended or expelled on charges related to sexual harassment. Teachers of sex-education programs say that boys routinely name as their male idols O.J. Simpson, Mike Tyson and a well-known serial killer-rapist. Harassing and violent behavior toward girls is now being reported as early as grade two, with its incidence increasing throughout the elementary school grades. For example, in July of 1996 three boys aged from nine to thirteen were charged with gang-raping a seven-year-old girl in Peoria, Illinois. From 1984 to 1991 the rate of violent sexual assault in Canada rose by 98 percent, and the number of women killed through family violence in the past decade in the United States is equal to all the troops killed in Viet Nam.

Females are not merely victims. In the decade between 1983 and 1993, the number of young females charged with violent crimes more than quadrupled in Canada. From 1986 to 1993 in the province of British Columbia, assault charges against teenage girls increased by 250 percent as compared to a rise of 118 percent for teenage boys during the same period. Teenaged girls are now over three times more likely than adult women to be involved in crime. Several cases reported in the summer of 1996 illustrate this trend. A twelve-year-old girl in Texas brutally murdered a child of two. Another twelve-year-old in California poisoned her teacher. A sixteen-year-old was indicted for killing a younger boy merely because he had spent the twenty-five dollars her gang had given him to purchase pot for them.

Young children are increasingly at risk, accounting for 60 percent of those abused in sexual assault cases in Canada. Most major North American cities report a 10 to 15 percent annual increase in the number of confirmed cases of child abuse. As the end of the millennium approaches, American children are being killed by gunfire at the rate of two a day. Even more ominous, children are becoming perpetrators as well. In Britain, in 1996, a five-year-old was accused of 30 assaults on other children and adults. A British school headmaster who was attempting to protect a student from a juvenile gang was stabbed to death on school property. In 1996 the American National Education Association estimated that 100,000 children bring a gun to school every day. Another survey found that 12 percent of youths claimed that they had to carry a gun in order to protect themselves. During 1997, one in ten American schools was involved in violence. In March of 1998, four children and a teacher were shot to death in a schoolyard in a small town in Arkansas by two pre-adolescent boys dressed in camouflage and armed with an arsenal of weapons—the third such incident in a few months. Two months later an equally horrendous and deadly incident occurred in Oregon.

Particularly worrisome is the increasing *banality* of the violence committed by children and youth. A judge in Chicago sentenced to youth prison two young boys who, at the age of ten and eleven, had dropped a five-year-old from the window of a high-rise because he refused to steal candy for them. A six-year-old girl in California knifed a seven-year-old in the back during a quarrel over a Barbie doll. Another six-year-old in the same state kicked in the head of a four-month-old baby who happened to be sleeping in the room which the child had entered for the purpose of stealing a tricycle. A teenager in Texas murdered a boy who honked his horn at him. A Brooklyn girl killed an acquaintance in an argument over a boyfriend. It is becoming commonplace for school-yard fights to end, not merely in the nose bleeds of past eras, but in death.

A generation ago we were appalled at the increasing incidence of the brutalization of children. Now we are being forced to witness the abuse and killing of children *by children*. A few decades ago we began to fear for our children. Now some of us live in fear *of* our children. To claim that this is abundantly predictable, in the face of the corruption and degradation of our culture during the interim, is not to excuse it. It is merely to recognize that diseases of the human spirit, if not caught and treated at their source, are no less infectious and destructive to humanity than are those more readily identified as organic illnesses.

It is time that we asked why our children—in the relatively brief span of two generations—have begun to behave like brutal barbarians. The answer is blatantly obvious: we need only re-read William Golding's *Lord of the Flies*. In the absence of the kind of informed judgment and moral guideposts discussed in previous chapters, adults have unthinkingly abdicated responsibility for socializing the coming generation. In fact, many have themselves been brutalized during childhood, or have become parents while still irresponsible youngsters. Those institutions that formerly functioned as major agencies of socialization have been weakened or superseded by new and powerful influences in the cultural environment. In general, it appears that the roles of the family and of formally designated agencies, such as the school and religious and community organizations, have been corrupted and diminished in relative terms. At the same time, the media and their offshoot, the media-inspired and media-shaped peer group, have gained remarkably in their power to shape values and behavior.

THE PERVASIVE PRESENCE OF THE ELECTRONIC MEDIA

From infancy onwards, television is now the single most influential socializer in modern urban society. It is an increasingly violent one, increasingly global and increasingly aimed at a youthful audience. Recent content analyses of programs indicate that the period of the day in which the most violence is aired is from 6:00 P.M. to 7:00 P.M. on weekdays and before 6:00 P.M. on weekends. Productions originating in the United States are by far the worst culprits, incorporating almost twice as many violent incidents per hour as those produced elsewhere. This fact becomes even more worrisome when we realize that American television programming is exported all over the world.

Whereas in the past a strong family was able to guarantee a protective enclave during the child's formative years, this is no longer possible. The family's ramparts have been broached irretrievably by television and the video recorder. Sometimes a specific family unit manages to keep the destructive effects of the media at bay for a little while. Still, the battle will be lost on the broader front, for children attend daycare or nursery school (and later, school and Scouts) and play with friends and visit neighboring homes. The violence propagated by television is an inevitable aspect of all these settings. Even the most lovingly and carefully raised child will have to emerge eventually from the cocoon to become either a terrified onlooker, or the victim or victimizer, in the media-corrupted culture that allows for no other role. More often, however, the adult members of the family unit itself have been so desensitized to violence that they are oblivious to what is occurring for the children in their care. These are the young parents who blithely say, "I watched anything I wanted to and it didn't hurt me!"

Sometimes it takes a child to drive home the message of what we have done to our culture. A sex-educator tells of a grade five boy who listened intently while she was discussing sexual intercourse as it occurs between a male and female. Then he asked her, "But what I want to know is, why do you always have to tie them up and beat them first?"

The anecdotes are legion, and have been coming in for at least three decades. This time span means that the early victims of media socialization are now feeding their own creative products into media programs. They are also raising children. Perhaps this accounts for the emergence of even more ominous trends. A new species of violent cartoon strip is now being distributed. For example, "Mother Goose and Grim" informs us that Rudolph the Reindeer just needs to "blow away" Prancer in order to resolve old hurts. Children's programs are filled with horrific, mind-numbing acts of violence. Cartoon characters threaten to kill one another, using supposedly comical language such as "I'll have to crush you like bugs!", "Time to go squishy-squishy!" and "I'll incinerate you. You'll just be smears of soot!"

We now have serial-killer board games that reward players with plastic baby tokens for killing victims (such as an old woman with a bag of groceries). We have millions of collector cards being sold to children featuring mass murderers and their gruesome exploits. We have murder games being played in group settings and proposed unthinkingly by teachers and club leaders. We have video games the object of which is to "blow away" opponents, whose demolition is signaled by puffs of smoke and dripping blood. We have publishers such as Paladin Press of Colorado, which brought out *Hit Man: A Technical Manual for Independent Contractors* (referred to by a lawyer for the family of one of the murder victims of a dedicated reader as a "blueprint for murder") along with *Twenty-one Techniques of Silent Killing, How to Dispose of a Dead Body*, and *The Ancient Art of Strangulation*. We have advertising of a violent and degrading nature now available to viewing children all day long. Due to the pervasiveness and immunity to control of the home video, teenagers can watch dehumanizing sexual activities anywhere at any time. To feed the rapidly growing market produced by all these means of addicting young people to violence, we now see a rash of movies with no other conceivable purpose than to titillate and shock, and to actively incite gratuitous brutality. Recently, the viewing public has been introduced to a new and particularly disturbing movie phenomenon: the deliberate use of violence to provoke laughter. Hacking people to pieces and blowing them apart is now being depicted as sophisticated and humorous!

We are witnessing an ever more widespread distribution of violent rap albums, accompanied by a social epidemic of commitment to these by children, as well as the idolization of rap heroes. In the summer of 1996 the rock band "Slayer" (whose albums include "Show no Mercy," "Hell Awaits," and "Reign in Blood") was accused of inspiring the rape, torture and fatal stabbing of a fifteen-year-old girl in Los Angeles. The titles of popular rap songs are particularly revealing. One piece is called "Back Off Bitch." Others such as "Another Body Murdered" and "Come Die with Me," are apt reflections of the cultural directives within.

A uniquely chilling new form of societal child abuse is "Cybersex"—interactive television and realistic video games that allow people (including children) to act out their sexual fantasies. Here children are not merely viewing violent pornography, but are being encouraged to become *active participants in it!* And, finally, we have the Internet: our new communications medium with its open access to hate literature and frighteningly powerful potential for uncontrolled and abusive socialization of all those technologically precocious children with access to it.

Nothing to worry about? Merely the usual kid stuff that they will grow out of? Just who do we think we are kidding? Those who still refuse to be concerned should ask themselves how much of this sort of culturally induced brutalization of the young can any society endure? And should we really be pursuing a policy of institutional reinforcement of the process? For example, should governments be subsidizing self-styled artists who gain money and notoriety by producing multi-media depictions of men copulating with children; of women being tortured and abused; of animals being grotesquely butchered?

BUT IS IT REALLY A PROBLEM?

In spite of all of the above, many continue to support a policy of non-interference. One of the most popular beliefs is that media portrayals of violence are only entertainment and, as such, have no real impact on values and behavior. It is said that the mass media merely reflect our violent culture. A common claim is that, if violent drama and visual art are to be curtailed, then we must stop all coverage of such events in newscasts. We are also told that those who deplore the production of violent entertainment are merely desiring to hide from reality. This argument often concludes with a reminder that the world has always been a violent place and children should learn this early rather than late.

Some even seek to convince us that violence is cathartic; that viewing it provides a harmless outlet for inhibitions. It prevents anger from being bottled up, they say, to explode unpredictably in destructive ways. Others claim that it is uniquely creative as well as inherently entertaining and pleasurable to watch. A famous movie director tells us that he loves violence. "There should be no question of how far is too far. Why should *creativity* be trampled on by officious bureaucrats and certain prudish members of the public?" he asks.

After all, we are reminded, it is parents alone who are responsible. Why don't they just shut off the television? In fact, so goes this argument, the *family* is actually at the root of the problem of societal violence. Junior beats people up because he sees Mommy being beaten by Daddy, who was himself beaten by his parents. Others lay the blame on *poverty*. Junior knifes his playmates because he is hungry and resents their owning things that he has never been able to possess. We should concentrate on putting more resources into family therapy—or into programs for eliminating poverty—rather than wasting our energies dealing with media violence, say the proponents of this position. Only after society has been rendered utopian in all other senses, they imply, do we have any right to hone in on the role of the media.

Some critics even accuse us of insulting youngsters in our paternalistic efforts to protect them. They often refer to their own early ability to discriminate as well as to that of their similarly all-wise children. They remind us of studies showing that teenagers, when asked, assure us that they have never been even remotely affected by viewing violent programs—that they have always been able to distinguish readily between reality and fiction. When confronted with the mass of rapidly accumulating evidence supporting the claim that exposure to violent images and messages both influences attitudes and values and creates violent response patterns, these people question the validity and reliability of the findings. They complain that the research designs are flawed and the methodology suspect. They conclude that the connection between media viewing and behavior has not been conclusively and *absolutely* proven for any particular case.

The most popular argument against interference is the *laissez-faire* philosophical one. Any attempt to curtail media violence is defined as *censorship* and, according to the libertarian stance, there can be no justification for limiting the right to free expression. Social libertarians tend to apply this principle not just to *ideas* (as was the original intent of bills of rights) but to all possible depictions of obscenity and brutality—no matter how degrading or extreme or how vulnerable the potential audience. They maintain that any attempt to control media violence would be "the thin edge of the wedge." We would be launched on the notorious "slippery slope" and thus inevitably propelled into the censoring of all the great literary classics.

Are concerned parents, sociologists and social psychologists merely crying wolf, then, or being deliberately mischievous? For there are numerous warnings being sounded by people who would seem to be qualified by experience and training to understand the way that children acquire their values and norms. Indeed there are good reasons why knowledgeable people view the prevalent pattern of media offerings as problematic. Those most commonly cited by researchers are as follows: (1) it is continuously addicting new generations to violence as a necessary feature of entertainment; (2) it glamorizes violence; (3) it validates violence as a means of problem solving; (4) it teaches that violence brings rewards; (5) it presents violence that is gratuitous—not in any way integral to the plot and in a context that is seldom clear to children; (6) it prematurely destroys the innocence of childhood by exposing children to detailed, graphic portrayals of brutal acts that they would otherwise seldom, if ever, witness; (7) it desensitizes children to the suffering of others and is thus destructive of the empathy necessary for morality; (8) it routinely features guns in the hands of virtually everyone, transforming what should be perceived as an aberration into an acceptable norm; (9) no attempt is made inform viewers of the permanent and tragic con-

sequences of violent actions; (10) because of its pervasiveness in programming, it promotes, in viewers of all ages, exaggerated fears of
becoming a victim of violence; and (11) even in circumstances where the
use of violence might possibly be justifiable, it is inevitably presented in
excessive amounts.

All this would not be so dismaying if media violence were something
to which few children are exposed in their formative years; or if those
who watch it do so sparingly. Studies show this is not the case. In Britain,
the average child has witnessed 18,000 media murders by the age of
eighteen, while the comparable figure for the United States is much
higher. By the time most Canadian children have reached that age, they
will have spent 3,000 more hours in front of television than in a classroom. Because of all of the above, many people now conclude that media
violence is a form of pollution of the global cultural environment likely
to corrupt the whole of humanity if not stemmed at its source.

But what about the arguments of those who oppose any form of intervention? The most convincing response to each and every one is that
it flies in the face of common sense. Moreover, all of these arguments
either contradict, or reveal ignorance of, the most basic principles of science—as well as a growing body of compelling evidence. They also rely
on denial of the most fundamental of our social-scientific understandings
about how human beings acquire the attitudes and values that drive
behavior.

THE TRIVIALIZATION AND TRASHING OF CULTURE

Perhaps we should deal with the arguments against action on this
issue one by one. We can begin by stating the obvious. Only ignorance
or dishonesty could prompt the comment that because a particular media
portrayal is intended as entertainment it will therefore not be influential
in shaping values and behavior. Even the most surface acquaintance with
the concept of socialization—or the slightest exposure to the way children learn—would ensure that one would never write off *any* experience
as insignificant to that all-encompassing process. In fact, people of all
ages remember best and are affected the most by what they perceive as
entertaining rather than boring. Why else would advertisers expend so
much effort on catchy "sound bites"? Why else would marketers seek
out the most entertaining of commercials and teachers try to make their
classes exciting?

How do we respond to young people who maintain that the violence
they watch has no effect on them? Certainly not with surprise. Not even
the most sophisticated and objective of us is capable of identifying *any*
of the precise cultural influences that have cumulatively shaped our values and beliefs. It is equivalent to remembering the specific Halloween

candies that contributed to the unsightly bulge of flab on a middle-aged stomach.

What about the claim that the mass media merely *reflect* the violent culture; that they do not *create* it? But of course they do both. As we learned in previous chapters, cultural evolution is a dynamic feedback process. Individuals—notably artists and scientists and, especially, those with access to the mass media—contribute their creations to the stream of culture from which all must drink and consequently be shaped as "selves." And, in turn, the actions and expressed ideas of these "selves" affect all with whom they come in contact. Only gross ignorance of the power of culture—and of the interactive nature of culture building, socialization and psycho-social development—could cause anyone to believe otherwise. An obvious example of the role of television in the process is the way in which messages originally intended merely to increase product sales have become part of our entire cultural fabric. We need only think of "Marlboro Country" and "the Pepsi generation" to understand this. The toys around any family Christmas tree are obvious indicators of what is going on, as are the patterns of play and the language of the schoolyard. The fact that annual lists of the most popular names for newborns invariably reflect the relative popularity of soap operas rather than authentic community heroes should tell us something. In countless ways television and Hollywood have come to provide the major common base defining us as cultural beings. In the process they have managed to prostitute the symbols of our deepest values—those telling us who we are, and where we have come from—and make of them all merely items of consumption. Friendship and active social involvement are replaced by an artificial community that freezes the isolated viewer into a passive relationship to soap-opera figures, sports heroes, television evangelists, violent cops and robbers, and rock and rap stars.

The recent wholesale move into "trash TV" is singularly disquieting. Talk-show hosts have discovered they can attract huge viewing audiences simply by exploiting vulnerable and gullible people and by implicating them in doing violence to their own human dignity. George Gerbner, Professor Emeritus in Communications at the University of Pennsylvania, is particularly damning of these demeaning travesties of entertainment. He notes that, because they are so cheap to produce, they are likely to spread like wildfire. However, they represent only the latest fad in the wholesale destruction of all barriers between the "public" and the "private." The consequences of this for the human spirit are frightening to contemplate.

The claim that the media merely reflect the culture can be challenged as well. What a twisted mirror they do, in fact, present! A number of studies have demonstrated the degree to which they actually distort reality. For example, three-quarters of all starring roles in television and the movies are male and almost the same proportion of major characters have sex outside of marriage. Hardly typical! Until recently, African Americans seldom held leading romantic roles. To this day, few mixed-racial marriages are ever shown. In a similar vein, surveys indicate that, since 1990, movie images of cigarette smoking by leading characters have once again become far more common than what the actual trends warrant. Finally, about 8,000 media murders are witnessed by the average child during the elementary school years, while less than 1 percent of this age group would ever see such an event in real life—even in our violent times. These are only a few of the numerous examples of the mass media's gross distortion of the current social scene.

SO WHAT'S NEWS?

Next we come to the response that equates gratuitous celebrations of imagined violence with news coverage, and concludes that if the one is censored the other must be also. It is true that those who select items for newscasts are increasingly tempted to cater to the tastes of an audience now sadly addicted to violence—and in doing this they are becoming part of the problem. But the provision of necessary information about horrific events is not the same thing as dwelling on the most gruesome details of these to the exclusion of other equally significant news. Over half of the portrayals of brutality could be cut from news reports simply by applying minimal standards of decency and good taste and by making the selection process more representative of what is actually occurring throughout the world. *Selection*, not *censorship*, is the issue here.

THE MYTH OF VIOLENCE AS NORMAL AND FRUITFUL

To say that because violence is now the norm we should be endeavoring to socialize children into it at an early age is to give up on civilization. The notion that children should not be protected from the violence in modern culture is similarly perverse. Humans throughout the evolution of the species have always tried their best to protect their tender and helpless offspring from needless exposure to danger—whether to their physical or psychological well-being. Even Attila the Hun and Genghis Khan recognized that imperative. Humankind would not have evolved successfully otherwise. Those individuals who now demand the opposite would not themselves be sufficiently sound and capable of conducting their specious arguments if society had failed to provide a modicum of safety for them during their own formative years.

The proposition that exposure to violence is cathartic was never supported by evidence, and has been compellingly refuted by numerous studies since it was first popularized. The argument that violence is creative is derived from a perverted form of existentialism and depends upon a definition of creativity which no civilized community would countenance. In fact, history teaches us that violence is creative in one way only—as an uncontrollable begetter of ever more offspring in its own disastrous image!

THE PROBLEM OF POVERTY AND THE FALTERING FAMILY

Placing the blame and sole responsibility on the family is a fruitless pursuit. Simply asking parents why they don't shut down the television is like saying, "Just turn off the smog if you don't want to breathe it!" or "Don't turn on the tap if you think the water isn't safe!" Citing the family as the root of the problem is to misunderstand the changing role and current vulnerability and helplessness of that institution. People resorting to this argument are caught on the horns of a dilemma. They seem to be defining the family as all-good and all-powerful, and not to be interfered with in its socializing task, *while at the same time* concluding that it alone is the source of most of the violence in society. We need to inquire about what actually goes on within specific family systems of interaction. If indeed fathers and stepfathers are more violent toward wives and children than in the past, what are the cultural influences reinforcing this altered behavior? Are parents the *only* socializing agents with powerful influence during the child's early years? And how many of our most vulnerable children are safely ensconced in the bosom of a wise, strong and caring family anyway?

In Chapter 3 we discussed how technological and social changes during the twentieth century have stripped the family of many of the key functions that had contributed to its strength in former times. For instance, it is no longer an economic unit with all members, including children, both contributing to and benefiting from its productive activities. Its economic role is now chiefly that of marketing target, with the mass media defining and directing the rate and content of its consumption. Similarly, the family is no longer solely responsible for protecting and maintaining society's most vulnerable members. Because it is now impossible to count on women as readily accessible unpaid labor, the entire context of the family has altered drastically. For most of the day there is no one home. Full-time professional homemakers of either sex are in short supply. Even less available are members on the consuming end of the family equation who are willing and able to offer an appropriate share of their externally derived income to those who might be convinced that the role of serving the family is a sufficiently rewarding way to spend one's life.

Thus, of necessity, the care of the sick, the handicapped and the old has been moved to other venues. The nurturing and socializing of the young is rapidly being taken over by public organizations as well. During the week most young families use the home merely as a place to sleep and prepare for another day of life out in the "real world." Any necessary drudgery is shared, at least to some extent, by adult family members and must be done quickly and efficiently. Little responsibility is given to the children because teaching children to perform tasks capably requires time and consistent attention: both of which are in short supply in busy single-parent or two-worker households. For the same reason, there is little help available for those children who are having trouble in school; in fact, there is seldom any opportunity to recognize the need for such help. Passive entertainment is what this type of perennially exhausted family wants, and that is what television and the computer and home video provide in easy abundance.

Poverty plays an important role here as well, because poor families tend to be isolated from alternatives to the media such as community-provided leisure-time organizations and extra-curricular educational activities. At the same time, poor families are the most vulnerable to the socialization occurring on the mean streets in which they tend to be located. A disproportionate number of poor families have only one perennially harassed and exhausted parent, rather than two, so that television must be relied on as baby sitter and educator even more than is the norm. The "V-chip," designed to enable concerned and knowledgeable parents to block out offensive programs, will not help the children of the faltering family.

At best then, modern families tend to be oblivious and vulnerable and are thus prime victims for the socialization of the media. At worst, they may succumb to the pressures of life and the brutalizing influences of their entertainment sources—and evolve accordingly into abusive and destructive entities. In either case, the problems they face and, in turn, create for the next generation can only be exacerbated by their exposure to media violence. To argue that nothing need be done about that until we rescue the poor, and resolve the problems of the faltering family, is misguided at best and, at worst, represents an excuse for doing nothing. It is like declaring that we should not bother to mend an open sewer until we can afford to rebuild and upgrade the entire system.

In fact, no compelling evidence has ever been found for a direct causal relationship between a situation of poverty and social violence. During the deep, ten-year Depression of the 1930s, there was relatively little violence. The same can be said of the poverty stricken in many developing countries throughout the world. Being poor does not, in itself, make people violent. On the other hand, it does make them more *susceptible* and *vulnerable* to violent influences and to the impact of violent events; and, wherever a welfare-dependent way of life has emerged, and is transmitted from generation to generation, we have the likelihood of a degrading form of ongoing socialization. Most important, however, we might consider whether putting the problem of violence on hold until we resolve the issue of social inequality is an *effective* strategy. It would appear to be more feasible to attack the most direct and obvious perpetrators of the damage first or, at the very least, to work on all fronts concurrently.

THE MAKING OF A TEENAGER

Another reason for the current ineffectiveness of the family as a protective bulwark against television-inspired violence is the rise of a conflicting source of values and norms of behavior. It is that creature of the mass media which we introduced in Chapter 3, known as the teenaged peer group. One of the consequences of the coming of the affluent society of the postwar years was the creation of the category of "teenager." For the first time in history, the child physically capable of sharing the adult work load was no longer required to assume it. By coincidence, the non-print media became a powerful force for socialization at that very moment in our social evolution. A new category in human development was born—one that was cultural rather than biological. The high school became the social context for the new teenage grouping. Concurrently, the formal educational objectives of that organization were increasingly superseded by the informal objectives of the peer group. Both family and school gradually lost much of their socializing power to this new and powerful agent. During the same period, the peer group began to operate more and more as the filter and servant of the mass media. From then on it was the media, rather than the family or school, that defined the good and the appropriate for those youths who found themselves drifting between the dependent roles of childhood and the increasingly postponed world of adult responsibility. At the same time, because personal identity in a period of rapid change came to depend more and more on acceptance by one's peers (and it was only one's peers who could be cognizant of media-inspired "truths"), the peer group assumed an absolute and total power such as the diverse and unfocused influences of home and school could seldom achieve in a pluralist society.

The victims of the totalitarian peer group are the last to recognize its power and personal impact. The very notion that one can learn anything useful by asking people whether or not they have been influenced by what they have been exposed to since birth, through movies, television and friends, would be laughable if the consequences of such misguided beliefs were not so tragic. We do not consciously *choose* to be shaped by our experience; we just are. We are not aware that it is happening; it just is. Despite claims to the contrary, teenagers can have no clear memory of the moment at which they acquired the ability to distinguish precisely between fantasy and reality—assuming they have indeed accomplished this—nor of the effects of *context* on the operation of this capacity. In fact, asking an individual's opinion on this matter is like asking a fish if it has been in any way affected by the water in which it has swum all its life.

However, the extremity of the situation is now such that we are witnessing a growing realization, even on the part of the general population, of the harmful influence of media violence. A recent poll of British schoolchildren shows that 84 percent acknowledge the adverse effects of television viewing on their own behavior. Another poll indicates that a full 80 percent of Americans now recognize the destructive impact of violent media messages upon their society. Legislators are beginning to speak out and, now, with the advent of the "V-chip," media moguls are taking notice. The tide may be about to turn.

A QUESTION OF EVIDENCE

The quality of the research documenting a connection between media viewing and violent behavior is often attacked by those in favor of the status quo. They maintain that the linkage has not been proven *conclusively* in the case of any specific violent act on the part of a specific individual. This is the same type of argument that has been mounted for years against the evidence concerning the dangers of smoking. The accumulation of compelling evidence is similar in both cases, as is the weight of common sense. An annotated bibliography of relevant studies on the effects of media violence is to be found in Appendix B. Almost 4,000 studies on the effects of the media on socialization have been conducted since the 1950s, including at least 85 major surveys. The overwhelming majority of these found a link between aggression and the viewing of media portrayals of brutality. Every major mental health organization in the United States and Canada has identified television violence as a factor in anti-social behavior. To deny it is equivalent to denying the connection between *smoking and lung cancer, education and learning,* and *sex and procreation.*

As to the quality of the research involved, studies indicate that the more rigorous the research design the *stronger* is the evidence that media violence increases aggression among viewers; and as to the demand for *conclusive proof,* we should be aware that there can be no such thing where science is concerned. Legitimate science makes no claims of certainty; it predicts probabilities. What matters is the compelling nature of the evidence, and the fact that the hypothesis of a causal connection has survived attempts to refute it by research efforts acceptable to the scientific community.

Documented trends, anecdotal evidence and personal observation corroborate the mass of findings from follow-up studies and experimental research and are often more convincing to the average person. We know, for example, that gun sales in the United States go up in tandem with increases in the scale and frequency of television violence. We know that epidemics of suicide follow emphasis on the subject by the mass media— especially the romanticizing of suicidal rock stars. Police report that fads in crime vary according to the types of violence portrayed in movies and television—often imitating the latter in horrific detail.

Newspaper accounts revealed that one of the ten-year-old torturers of two-year-old Jamie Bolger in Liverpool had unsupervised access to violent crime and porn videos on weekends at his father's place. The toddler's last hours of life bore a chilling resemblance to *Child's Play 3*: a movie that the young killer's father had rented at that precise time. This accords with the well-known fact that many criminals doing time in jail recount how they got their ideas and methods from movies. For example, a murderer in Vancouver admitted to having watched *The Silence of the Lambs* shortly before he brutally attacked a prostitute and amputated her sex organs. A disturbed Canadian fourteen-year-old took the horror film *Warlock* to heart to the extent of killing a seven-year-old acquaintance and attempting to drink the boiled fat from his victim—believing this would enable him to fly. A double slaying and an abduction of a thirteen-year-old girl in a prairie town bears a striking resemblance to a television movie called *Murder in the Heartland*. A Canadian fifteen-year-old, who apparently murdered his entire family for no reason other than that he resented being asked to do chores, had been viewing *The Terminator* the preceding evening. He was known to be an addict of violent television. A number of young children throughout North America have died of strangulation while attempting to imitate a televised enactment of the process.

An admitted serial killer in upstate New York claimed to have been inspired by the movie *Robocop* when he attacked his first victim, cutting her throat and slitting her open from chest to stomach. "I done exactly what I seen in the movie!" he reported, indicating that he was a more efficient learner than many of our modern social libertarians. A mother in Maryland told of how her twelve-year-old boy persuaded his younger brother and a friend to help him rob a bank exactly as he had seen it done in the movie *Point Break*. Two university students in Spain bludgeoned a middle-aged street sweeper to death in the course of playing a fantasy board game, the rules of which required that they seek women and children as victims during the evening. In the daytime they were to attack only "weak, chubby, and elderly" men. Soon after the previously mentioned "Slayer" albums became popular, teachers in a North American city noticed that twelve-year-old girls were commonly being called "whores" and "bitches" on the school playgrounds. This soon came to be followed by "bitch fights" among organized gangs of girls. A five-year-old boy in Ohio started a fire that killed his younger sister after watching the MTV cartoon characters Beavis and Butt-head set several objects on fire and proclaim, "Fire is cool!". Many pre-schoolers who watched *Power Rangers* twice a day on television were observed habitually imitating the actions of the characters during their free play in other settings.

CENSORSHIP OR RATIONAL SELECTION?

The libertarian argument that every person must be free to choose her or his own "poison" applies only in an imaginary world where the individual's actions have no consequences for others—or for the social fabric as a whole. However, in the real-life biological and social arena out of which all must forge their beings, none can claim the absolute right to act *as if* reality were otherwise. The claim that any attempt to control media violence would lead inevitably to the censoring of great literary classics is scarcely worthy of response. Civilized behavior has always and everywhere involved and required the establishment of culturally defined limits. All morality and all systems of law are based on this premise and process. To claim that it is impossible to distinguish between gratuitous portrayals, and sick celebrations, of violence and those references to violent incidents that are necessary to the narrative is to reject the very possibility of literary standards.

Both the evolutionary systems model and the premises of most religions imply that freedom as an abstraction is a dangerous slogan. Freedom for anyone with the power to pursue any ends by any means has seldom been considered an unquestioned good. Value judgments must always be rendered by human societies on permissible means and ends. Humans attempting to form and preserve societies have always established limits beyond which their tolerance for socially destructive deviance would not extend. No social group could survive without such limits. For each society, the boundaries marking the limits of cultural tolerance expand and contract over time like a great social heartbeat, as the consequences of past limitations and extensions of tolerance are fed back and collectively experienced. The system adapts by extending these boundaries gradually until, at some point, the cost to the most vulnerable members becomes too obvious and irreparable, and begins to affect the more vocal and powerful majority as well. Then, typically, the boundaries contract—often convulsively and extremely—sometimes even to the extent that creativity and the impulse for all social change are severely curtailed.

But it is not always possible for the contracting beat of the great pulse to occur on time. Societies have been known to self-destruct. There have been cases where the unrestricted personal freedom of powerful elites became a license to harm others and where their behavior, in turn, resulted in widespread cultural decadence. This can happen whenever the group has ignored two social imperatives that are no less firmly grounded in the nature of things than are the physical laws of gravity. One is the requirement of a safe, nurturing environment for the relatively lengthy period of human childhood: a necessity for the continued evolution of the species. The second is the law of reinforcing consequences driving all self-organizing, dynamic systems: a principle of change that causes the choices of individuals to initiate irrevocable ripples of effects throughout the entire network of society. There is no family so educated, so affluent or so influential that it can keep those ripples out. When the cultural stream has been polluted with the virulent virus of violence there is no place to hide.

The danger is no longer only to the most vulnerable ones: to the children of the poor or to the children of those who have been previously rendered violent and desensitized. To paraphrase the words of Arthur Miller in *All My Sons*, they are all vulnerable now and we are all accountable for all of them. They are *all* our children, for they are the joint carriers of human culture and thus our only hope for the future.

REFERENCES

Annotated Bibliography. Ottawa, ON: National Clearing House on Family Violence, 1993.

Artz, Sibylle. *Sex, Power and the Violent School Girl*. Victoria, BC: Trifolium, 1997.

Blevings, Shirley. "Beat the Bad Rap." *The Vancouver Sun*, May 14, 1994, pp. D12–13.

Canadian Center for Justice Statistics. *Youth Court Statistics, 1994–95*. Ottawa, ON: Statistics Canada, 1996.

————. *A Graphical Overview of Crime and the Administration of Justice in Canada*. Ottawa, ON: Statistics Canada, 1996 and 1998.

Golding, William. *Lord of the Flies*. London, UK: Faber and Faber, 1954.

Grossman, Dave. *On Killing: The Psychological Cost of Learning to Kill in War and Society*. Boston, MA: Little Brown, 1995.

Hutcheon, Pat Duffy. "Suffer the Little Children." *Unitarian Universalist World* (March, 1986): 1; (April, 1986): 5.

Sanders, Barry. *A Is for Ox: Violence, Electronic Media, and the Silencing of the Written Word*. New York, NY: Pantheon Books, 1994.

Signorielli, Nancy and Gerbner, George. *Violence and Terror in the Mass Media*. Westport, CT: Greenwood Press, 1988.

Tester, Keith. *Media, Culture and Morality*. New York, NY: Routledge, 1994.

U.S. Department of Justice and Bureau of Justice Statistics. *National Crime Surveys, 1986–1991*. Ann Arbor, MI: Inter-university Consortium for Political and Social Research, 1992.

Note: See also Appendix B.

CHAPTER 7

Second Stages and Second Chances: Socialization in Later Life

In Chapter 3 we emphasized the importance of childhood socialization in determining the kind of people we become as adults. But that is not the entire story. Individuals, if given the opportunity, continue learning and changing until death. Although it is true that the habits and values acquired in the early years are crucial because they set the stage for subsequent development, there is obviously a good deal more to human socialization. There are second stages to the process and, for slow or recalcitrant learners, there are second chances too.

A distinctive form of socialization begins to function at the early adult stage in a person's life. In addition to the life skills and social attitudes acquired unconsciously at younger ages, people in their late "teens" start to search out new ways of responding in a more or less self-guided socializing process. In spite of the fact that previously attained values, interests and abilities establish limits and determine general direction, young adults are increasingly able to search out new learning experiences for themselves—either through more selective reading and viewing or by choosing their own avenues for social interaction. They can begin to take control of their own lives. Attendance at a post-secondary institution is a rich opportunity for this. Often these newly challenging adventures contribute to mature development in a variety of ways. Previously pampered children can learn to clean up their own messes and take control of their spending. They can learn to compromise with similarly omnipotent egos—and to share. They can encounter on a first-hand basis the family-generated values of a diverse group of friends and, perhaps for the first time, begin to acknowledge and assess their own subcultural heritage in terms of these.

Socialization, as it occurs in this second phase, is often described in more formal terms as *the total process that shapes the functioning of adult roles within society*. These roles determine (1) the way authority and power relations are conducted within the social group; (2) the way people participate in the function of producing, distributing, exchanging and consuming goods and services; and (3) the nature of adult male and female relationships. This means that, ultimately, adult socialization determines the operation of a society's institutions as well as the content of the values that guide those institutions.

ACQUIRING SOCIAL ROLES

The lay person might well be somewhat confused about what social scientists mean by "roles." For instance, one might ask if a "role" is simply the "position" one attains within an organization—as defined by the official job requirements—or whether it is how one relates to others every day of one's life in a myriad of informal situations. And does it depend upon what others expect one to do or on what one actually *does* from day to day? Many other questions require clear answers. Are social roles a universal and largely unintentional aspect of human interaction or are they typically assumed and dropped at will? Where do a society's roles come from? How are they learned? What are the components of a role? Do social roles ever undergo change and if so, how? Do we all operate within more than one role in childhood? In adult life? If so, can our roles be in conflict? How do people acquire and discard their roles? Do individuals change the roles they take on or do prescribed roles shape the individuals who assume them? Or both? Do we "play" social roles—putting them on or off like masks or parts in theatrical performances—or do we "live" them quite unknowingly? In what precise way do the behaviors and expectations surrounding social roles affect the institutions of a culture such as the family, government and economy?

It may be helpful to begin by looking at a relatively small and informal social system—one whose members are initially unfamiliar with one another—so that we can assume no previous patterns of social interaction. A hiking group formed in response to a newspaper advertisement might do. Let us suppose a group of strangers has gathered together in this way. Almost at once, certain things will begin to happen. The person who advertised might immediately move to take charge; or someone else with previous hiking experience might come forward with information about where the group could go for the first hike. One of these will likely offer to lead the hike or to organize the planning of hikes. This person will not necessarily be the one with the most knowledge of the terrain. However, it is probable that the would-be leader will possess a certain mix of attributes. He or she will be a confident hiker, will feel comfortable making suggestions to others and accepting responsibility, and will enjoy planning and organizing activities and communicating ideas. Subsequent *acceptance* by the group involves something more, however. The persons who gradually emerge as informal leaders will be the ones whose personalities, *as well as* their more obvious qualifications, make following their guidance an attractive prospect for the membership. Above all, they will have to demonstrate the capacity to forge the group into a workable and sustainable unit.

Other roles in addition to that of leader will eventually emerge as the group interacts in the process of pursuing their hiking experience. These may include the story-teller or joker; the comforter or healer; the natural-history educator; the song-leader or musician—or the one who raises the spirits of the group when the going gets tough. Someone might become unofficial party planner, or problem solver, or conciliator, or disciplinarian or even the group's political haranguer, absent-minded forgetter, complainer or gossip. As these habitual behaviors become recognizable the participating members come to expect them, to react so as either to reinforce or discourage them, and to make plans in terms of them; and the group as a whole takes on a coloration shaped by these expected responses *plus* expectations of how the others will respond to them in turn. The members evolve rules that work for them, as well as standards of acceptable behavior and generally unacknowledged (but subtly operating) limits of tolerance. Over the years they will gradually produce their own unique subculture, complete with an awareness of group history and in-group jokes and references.

In such informal organizations change is likely to be ongoing, for the entry of even one new member can alter the entire system of social interaction. For a while the position of newcomer is the only one available to the latest arrival, but soon he or she will forge a unique personal role influenced by the behavior manifested in the new group setting, and the responses of others to it.

One of the attractions of the above type of informal group is the opportunity it affords for a temporary shedding of one's other roles. For example, a woman who previously has been defined chiefly in terms of her successful professional husband can forge her own quite different role as a competent hiker. Of course, she cannot really relinquish her other roles. Like every new member of the hiking club, she arrives at the scene already laden with social roles shaped by previous socialization. One of the earliest acquired would have been that of gender. For example, adult female hikers will come to the group with firmly fixed notions and self-definitions having to do with being female in the larger society. We discussed in Chapter 4 how gender and sex roles are, to a considerable extent, learned in the context of social interaction almost from birth. One of the women who has a history of caring and assuming responsibility may take on a nurturing role for the club. She may become the matriarch of the group. Another may become the group flirt. Another may all too readily assume the role of victim here just as she has done elsewhere.

Still another may come burdened by a single all-purpose "drop-out" role. She may have never held a steady job anywhere, or looked after parents or raised children, or made any contribution of note to the welfare of others. In fact, she may seldom have functioned in society in any capacity other than that of "receiver" of the goods and services earned by others. In the club she may avoid taking her turn at leading hikes, working on trails, bringing her share of food to potluck dinners. The role she spins by this behavior will gradually become fully as recognizable and predictable as that of the matriarch—or that of the macho womanizer, or the tireless competitor, or the berry-picking laggard, or the "independent spirit" who resents being led.

But what about all the other settings in which the adult hiker interacts? A member of the hiking group assumes that role only a few times a month. For the rest of the time she may be, at one and the same time, a wife, mother, sister, grandmother or daughter in the bosom of her family; a teacher or administrator at the neighborhood school; a candidate for political office; an investor in company stocks; a member of the strata council in her condo development, and a voter in elections at all levels of the nation's political system. Her precise "role set" will be different from that of any of her hiking companions, even though theirs are likely to be similarly complex. It is important to understand that a "role set" is not a set of different "selves" designed in a calculating way for portrayal in each circumstance. For the normal person, it is the one "self" (or personality and character)—created out of biological propensity in conjunction with the totality of experience from conception on—that responds in a uniquely characteristic way to each new situation, and that is inevitably somewhat altered by each step of the process. However, some "selves" are less integrated than others even in the case of mentally healthy people, and inner conflicts may be manifested in relatively unpredictable responses to varying experiences.

Another problem is that some of these acquired roles may come into conflict. The club might be going out on a Saturday when our hiker has to attend meetings, or on a Sunday when her career goals and personal values demand that she be in attendance at church. Her role of daughter and caregiver for an elderly mother may allow her insufficient energy and opportunity to play with her grandchildren or to entertain her husband's business associates. Her work role in an educational establishment could make demands that contradict those associated with her role as the mother of a student in the same system. Her role in politics could come into conflict with her role as an investor in business enterprises over which she might exert political influence, or whose prospects might be affected by her political decisions. She may feel that her role demands are pulling her "self" in a maze of incompatible directions.

She has acquired all these roles in a variety of ways. She more or less created her own unique role in the hiking club. She was born into the role of female, as well as into the additional ascriptions associated with being daughter and sister. Certain expectations of how she would interact in these roles would have been present in the family at her birth. They may have been reflections of what her parents perceived as appropriate in the ethnic community of their ancestry—or in their religious tradition or social stratum. The more stable and inward-looking the subculture the more traditional and authoritarian her family is likely to have been; and the more uniform and resistant to change will be their familial role prescriptions.

Her role as wife is likely to have been somewhat less firmly ascribed—especially where the larger culture is undergoing rapid transition, as is the case in most industrializing societies. This situation presents another source of role conflict, however, in that the expectations of the partners in a modern marriage may be incompatible, depending on their familial subcultures and education. The wife may be engaged in a deliberate attempt to forge a new set of expectations for her role as spouse and working mother, while the husband may have contrasting expectations from his own early socialization: expectations which he subconsciously accepts as unchangeable aspects of reality even though, at the intellectual level, he expresses agreement with his wife.

None of these "role sets" occurs in a vacuum. They arise out of, are dependent on and in turn contribute to, the entire web of social interaction in which the individual has her being. Social roles are universal in human societies and often unrecognized by those who live them. Even in the most authoritarian of settings they tend to be reciprocal rather than merely unilaterally assigned and adopted. They are to some extent multiple even in the simplest preliterate societies and increasingly so as technology develops, with its resulting *division of labor*. Every role incorporates three major components: the *position* as spelled out for the incumbent ahead of time and as recognized by relevant others; the actual *performance* of the individual while occupying the position; and the *subjective expectations* inevitably held by all those involved, concerning how the incumbent should behave and how they should respond to that behavior. All of these aspects are in a continuous state of evolution—much more so in flexible, open societies than in traditional, closed ones. To summarize, we could say that role learning is an intricate process of continuing innovation: a process involving both unconscious conditioning and the active negotiating or weighing of costs and rewards in terms of the individual's values and knowledge and the demands and expectations of others.

It is the role relationships characteristic of human societies that comprise and sustain the institutional structures found in all cultures. For example, to begin to understand the institution of government we need to recognize the roles involved—such as that of the voter and candidate for office—and how these are achieved and evolve over time. It helps to know the formal positions in which people operate; positions like that of Party organizer, Prime Minister or President, Majority or Minority House Leader or Leader of the Opposition, Secretaries or Ministers of the Cabinet, and Speaker of the House. We also need to be aware of the actual performance of the incumbents of these positions and of how their behaviors affect the expectations of all of us regarding their roles. It is out of this amorphous reality (now most commonly communicated by portrayals on television) that the totality of a population's "role expectations" emerge and take root in the perceptions of all of us.

PREPARING FOR ECONOMIC ROLES

Some scholars use the term "economic socialization" to refer to the comprehensive process by which people acquire the roles of producer, distributor and consumer of goods and services. The necessity to educate for the role of consumer has usually been overlooked, with disastrous consequences in today's media-dominated world. The result is that socialization into this all-important role has come to involve mainly being on the receiving end of a steady barrage of commercials.

Perhaps the most important aspect of economic socialization involves those general attitudes and expectations required for making a living—commonly referred to as the "work ethic." This is important because one of the most significant aspects of the second stage of life is occupational choice; and one's willingness to accept responsibility and strive for excellence can be critical here. However, chance may be at least as significant as attitude in determining work roles. This is because, even though individual preference and demonstrated competence can *appear* to be directing the process at this stage, social class and ethnicity are important influences on the possibilities perceived, degree of choice available and opportunity to prepare for an occupation once a choice has been made. It is always necessary to be aware of the shaping effect of subcultural membership, as well as the decisive impact of sheer chance.

None of this detracts from the fact that—regardless of the individual's "luck of the draw" at birth—for most people, occupational concerns tend to take over in the second wave of socialization. The reason is that the most important institution into which adults have to become integrated in any society is the world of work. The need to make a living of some kind forces certain roles on everyone. Even the lack of a job imposes a role: that of drop-out—or welfare recipient or dependent or hustler. The potential worker needs to learn a very specific set of attitudes, abilities and habits. Work is the principal normal link between families as consumers and the economic system in general. Without it one is condemned to the perpetual role of outsider and loser.

In traditional societies, where sons followed the occupations of their fathers and daughters learned the duties of their gender at their mother's knee, preparation for the world of work was much more controlled and effective than is the case today. Entrepreneurs now often describe themselves as self-made, in that they received little formal training in the producing of goods and services. On-the-job apprenticeships are scarce and unduly difficult to obtain. Managers, trained in schools of commerce and administration, are often parachuted into businesses without knowing anything about the commodities being produced or retailed.

There are a number of reasons why the formal process of socialization for work roles in modern societies may be inadequate and ineffective. When technology and the social organization involved in its use are undergoing rapid change, a person may have several different jobs during a working life. Also, in such transitional or revolutionary periods, it is often the case that instructors in post-secondary educational institutions can become sadly out of touch with the needs of workers in "the real world." In areas less directly influenced by workplace technology, similar problems may arise from the occurrence of fundamental alterations of behaviors and values in society at large—the consequences of which have not yet been adequately recognized within the protected enclaves of professional schools and academia. Problems may result as well from scientific findings in areas beyond the expertise of those responsible for planning and implementing the training or socialization.

Those fortunate enough to be able to choose an occupation requiring relatively lengthy and sustained preparation will experience, along with their programmed acquisition of skills and knowledge, what is known as "professional socialization." This is intended to prepare people for work roles requiring special expertise. Along with the achievement of the official objectives, however, the prolonged period of necessary training can result in a movement toward a homogenization of attitudes and values concerning the anticipated work role. When this happens, there is no guarantee that the process will work to the advantage of the future consumer of professional services. For one thing, it has been observed that during professional socialization the total social value attached to the position—and the relative size of the rewards presumably owed it by society—increase perceptibly in the views of the candidates. A number of other debatable beliefs and values may be implanted as well. The process occurs in subtle ways over the course of the training period, often with the use of derisive jokes and laughter aimed at dissidents.

Medical students or nurses in training usually experience a socialization into a certain type of tough-mindedness about the suffering and death of patients. Hospital interns tend to develop increased status consciousness in relation to other members of the health profession as well as patients. Student teachers adopt the prevailing ideologies involving methods of teaching language and reading and approaches to curriculum and discipline. Would-be social workers and student ministers and priests may become more and more comfortable with the imagery and assumptions of the Jung cult, or of some other ideological model, regardless of their efficacy in practice. The examples, drawn from research findings over the years, are legion.

SOCIALIZATION IN THE WORKPLACE

The workplace has been found to be one of the most basic agencies of socialization within contemporary society. The group with whom one works on a daily basis exerts considerable power to affect one's attitudes and actions. In the process of induction into the work-group, approved ways of behaving and thinking may be assimilated by means of scarcely perceptible cues. Over time, workplace socialization amounts to a process of rewarding conformity to the norms of the group or of the occupation as a whole. It operates through the ongoing reinforcement of appropriate behavior—often by means of subtly communicated promises of career rewards and veiled threats of punishment.

A problem can develop when the routines and values imposed by the immediate work environment conflict radically with the expectations or moral principles of individual workers. In certain cases, preparation for the role may have been inadequate, outdated or otherwise inappropriate; or the individual may simply find herself unsuited to the actual tasks involved, or uncomfortable with the attitudes of fellow workers. It is sometimes possible for an innovative, sensitive and determined worker to reshape the role of administrator or doctor or lawyer so that it accords more with her own personality and abilities—and with whatever room she has to maneuver within the complexity of her personal store of multiple roles.

A more serious situation arises when the norms of the employees conflict with the objectives of the organization within which the group operates—or with the necessary function of the occupation as a whole within society. In the building trades, for example, we might have a situation where the workers have evolved a culture in which the regular use of marijuana and a habit of late-night partying has become the norm. This could have a disastrous effect on the quality of the work performed, with the result being the discovery of life-threatening and costly flaws in high-rise buildings and perhaps a few notorious accidents involving loss of life. The consequences over the long term for the companies employing the workers—and eventually for the reputation of the entire building industry—could be incalculable. Or, a similar result might occur where shady cost-cutting and time-reducing practices have been encouraged by the company's incentive system—all with the aim of enlarging short-term profits. Yet another example is the work situation as it has been described in certain tightly unionized enterprises, where a new worker soon discovers that the group finds ways to punish the "eager beaver" who finishes tasks quickly, arrives for work early and is willing to work extra hours without overtime pay in order to solve problems created by others.

We can find instances of this sort of thing in the professional arena as well. The professional associations of doctors, lawyers and priests can operate so as to provide cover for those guilty of sexual harassment or malpractice. In some academic settings the rewarding of self-promoting and people-manipulating skills at the expense of good teaching and scholarship can result in a situation where the relevant organizations are populated and controlled by many people whose ethics and abilities would be scorned by most businessmen. Students and youthful job candidates entering such establishments soon learn what they must do and what they must avoid doing if they are to have any hope of ultimate career success; and they quickly become aware that these strictures have little to do with personal integrity and rigorous scholarship in the relevant field of study. The predictable result of this perverted form of professional socialization is a widespread vacuum of moral leadership in the culture at large and consequent loss of societal trust in our professional elites.

SEX IN THE WORKPLACE

No discussion of socialization in the workplace can be complete without a look at the effects of sexual politics on workers of both genders. In the past the situation was fairly clear. Males held almost all of the top positions and consequently the power to exploit people lower in the hierarchy: the female secretarial and technical staff in business enterprises and the various categories of assistants and junior people in other types of workplaces. There have been changes in the past decades, however, with the occurrence of a marked increase in the proportion of women in executive positions. For example, by 1997, women accounted for almost 50 percent of all jobs in the Canadian federal bureaucracy and received approximately 57 percent of all promotions. Nonetheless, even in that most propitious setting, 87 percent of all the lower-paying jobs were still held by women, as compared to only 23 percent of executive positions. One could be sanguine about the prospect of the mere passage of time taking care of the problem in the corporate and professional world in general, if it were not for the results of research such as that conducted jointly by the Conference Board of Canada and Catalyst USA in 1997. This study found that the stereotyping of females by males continues to be the single most powerful obstacle to advancement by women.

Clearly, a long-established situation of inequality cannot be corrected overnight. However, within Western societies at least, it now seems that socialization is operating to minimize gender differences rather than to maximize them. Now the person who uses sexuality to forge ahead in a career is almost as likely to be a woman as a man, and the game is played on a more equal basis than was previously the norm. But the game continues, with as many losers as winners, and what is learned about sex roles and work roles in the process affects both the operation of the organization and the society it serves.

THE WORKPLACE AS A SOCIAL ORGANIZATION

Most people spend their working lives in organizations, whether within a loose network of positions with roles of more or less equal privilege and power, or in some form of large, hierarchically ordered business corporation or administrative arm of government. Organizations are ubiquitous in that they provide the skeletons for the institutions of a culture. The adaptability of the organization to the challenges thrown up by the environment determines to a large extent the nature and degree of the culture's continuing evolution. Indeed, organizational adaptation is, in some ways, both the vehicle and expression of that evolution. Openness to change depends on the degree to which the attitudes and behavior of the incumbents render their organization capable of benefiting from feedback, as well as from scientific knowledge and the technology produced by it.

However, organizational change is constructive for society only if it is inspired and led by a decision-making process directed by humane values as well as cause-and-effect thinking. Sometimes the products of certain organizations can generate a reinforcement loop causing an evolutionary spiral with the potential for great harm. One example of this is the way the electronic media propagate violent imagery, which then both fuels and feeds on an accelerating addictive demand from the consuming public. Another is the tendency for the providers of key technology (such as high-tech computer software) to monopolize the market simply because, as one particular company increasingly dominates the field, consumers will benefit accordingly by installing its products rather than those of competing firms. Initially, this sort of "evolutionary arms race" may be advantageous to society, because the ferocity of the competition results in an explosion of technological discoveries and relatively low prices. As the winner succeeds in driving out all other contenders, however, research tends to stagnate and prices tend to go up.

BUREAUCRATIZATION AS AN IMPEDIMENT TO ORGANIZATIONAL CHANGE

A particular form of workplace socialization is characteristic of bureaucracies such as those involved in government, large corporations and universities. This type of organization is defined by: (1) a chain of command with positions related to official differences in status and power; (2) a profusion of rules and detailed paperwork; (3) top-down communication in terms of written requests and memos with little opportunity for the accurate bottom-up feedback so crucial for honest evaluation; (4) consequent top-down evaluation based on criteria irrelevant to task performance (such as ability to flatter one's superior); (5) an isolation of authority from responsibility, resulting in a lack of accountability at all levels; and (6) a pervasive reluctance to make difficult decisions, plus varying amounts of confusion regarding the actual decision-making process and who is to be held responsible for implementation and assessment of consequences. This makes any objective testing of either the *efficiency* or the *effectiveness* of the organization very difficult.

Adding to the problems created by the inner workings of bureaucracies is the fact that the actual *output* of individuals within large formal organizations is often impossible to observe and measure. Consequently, tenure and seniority are emphasized and rewarded at the expense of performance. This creates a tendency for employees to be promoted routinely until they reach at least one step above their competence level, at which point their resulting insecurity drives them to hire only people who are likely to be even less competent. The inevitable consequence of this is a downward spiral in the level of ability throughout the organization.

The way the workplace incentive-system operates in bureaucratic organizations is another source of problems. Members tend to conclude that it is safer to simply follow the *letter* of the established rules in all instances—regardless of their *intent*—than to use one's personal discretion. Wherever evaluation of performance is a complex and demanding undertaking, something more readily identifiable like numbers of publications, or *adhering to the process*, or buttressing the ego of one's superior, can become all-important. Workers quickly learn that it is not in their career interests to make decisions unless they are sufficiently "covered" by a paper trail identifying the exact input and authority of every participant so that they are able to disclaim personal responsibility.

An all-too-predictable result of all this is what we call "goal substitution." This usually takes one of two common forms. The first occurs when the needs of the members for personal power and job security motivate them to view the rules as ultimate ends in themselves—regardless of whether those rules are furthering or hindering achievement of the original objectives or social function of the organization. Another common form of goal substitution is the unacknowledged and often unconscious replacement of the goals of the institution with a more immediate end: the perceived self-interest of the employee.

One of the most obvious examples of goal substitution is that which occurs when managers of large corporations are encouraged by the reward system to define the success of the organization in terms of the annual profit margin—rather than by more meaningful goals associated with longer-term customer satisfaction and the type of general operating effectiveness that requires a committed and experienced work force. Another is the emergence of powerful interest groups who come to define the welfare and goals of the organization in terms of their own job security and self-aggrandizement. Although business corporations are prone to this as well, it is in those government bureaucracies established to administer social, medical and educational programs that the tendency reaches full fruition. It is relatively easy to convince the recipients of services that their immediate needs coincide with the insatiable demand of the providers for more funds, regardless of whether or not the program requires re-assessment or updating. The very real need for continuous evaluation of results, and for the ongoing reform of strategies, structure and short-term objectives that would follow from this, tends to fall by the wayside. The more vocal of the internal groups focus their energies and the resources of their organizations, instead, on activities aimed at influencing the budgetary decisions of politicians, managers and the voting public in the direction of their own perceived self-interest.

Associated with this is another common form of goal substitution reinforced by bureaucratic organization: one to which welfare and psychiatric agencies and schools are particularly prone. Those whose jobs depend on either the provision of therapy, financial aid for the temporarily unemployed or remedial education may find their own future security hinging on the continuation—rather than successful conclusion—of the program. This can generate a feedback cycle by which the success of the intervention is measured not in terms of a decrease in needy clients, but by the expansion of their numbers and their long-term retention. This predictable process partially accounts for the tendency for recipients of between-job government aid to make welfare a way of life;

for psychiatric patients to become addicted to their therapy sessions; for remedial education students to somehow never quite be freed from the need for the remedy; and for those assigned to ESL (English as a Second Language) classes to remain in the program throughout their school lives.

This sort of thing contributes mightily to what is no doubt the most crippling consequence of bureaucratization: an inability to respond to changing circumstances and challenges—or even to learn from experience. In the work atmosphere typical of a bureaucracy it is simply not acceptable to admit to a mistake. One would expect that some opportunity for experimentation, with the inevitability of occasional illuminating errors, is a necessary aspect of doing a job well. But if the system rewards short-term gain and smoothness of operation over all else, anyone who interferes with this for any reason will tend to be seen as an obstruction—regardless of the potential significance of the person's contribution for the long-term goals of the enterprise. This "don't rock the boat" and "cover your behind" mentality is reinforced at all levels. One's immediate colleagues tend to close ranks as well to guard against anything likely to attract undesirable attention from above. All this encourages the evolution of a culture in which people are discouraged from acknowledging mistakes and learning from them, and then making the necessary changes.

Above all, employees learn that the most dangerous decision possible is to report any infraction of rules or even potentially serious error by someone in authority over them. It is always enlightening to observe what actually happens to the "whistle blower" in a bureaucratic organization. There is a powerful unwritten law against this, probably because the very first step in such a process requires breaking the most sacred bureaucratic rule of all: not to go over the head of one's immediate superior. The problem is amplified by the fact that, in most situations, the culprit is likely to be that very same authority figure. This almost ensures that, regardless of the severity of the reported misdemeanor, when the smoke clears the person who pays the highest price in career terms is usually the one who made a difficult but ethical decision in the interests of the institution and the society it serves.

The cumulative result of all this is that the organization is rendered incapable of adjusting to feedback, either from within or without. Bureaucracies tend to rigidify and become maladaptive in an evolutionary sense. This causes them to operate as obstacles to needed improvements in the society they are supposed to serve, rather than as the self-regulating vehicles of collective intelligence that are required for cultural adaptation in changing circumstances.

RELINQUISHING ROLES

Not only do people take on new roles, they give them up as well. One of the important functions of rites of passage is to legitimize and celebrate those watersheds in life when people are expected either to assume or relinquish socially significant roles. In the past we have tended to do a better job of marking the former than the latter. However, the coming-of-age step for adolescents is now becoming increasingly blurred and postponed, and some unfortunate consequences of this are showing up. As more and more people choose to live in common-law and same-sex partnerships, rituals surrounding the mutual commitment required for marriage are losing their cultural meaning and their power as well. At the other end of life, retirement and death have long been problems considered best ignored by many groups in the industrialized world. However, as the "boomers" reach old age we will likely see much more being made of graduating to "empty-nest" status and retirement from formal employment. We might benefit by learning from anthropology and history of the general human need to make the process of giving up roles a less traumatic and more fully natural one—including that final total role relinquishment represented by death.

RESOCIALIZING "DROP-OUTS"

The term "re-education" has been made unpopular by the uses to which it has been put in totalitarian countries, but that is precisely what this process is about. We are referring to a carefully planned structuring of experience, with specific learning outcomes in view, for those whose early socialization failed them. People can change. We are all being continuously altered, for good or bad, with every day's experience. The preceding chapters have described how developmental socialization can go tragically awry. When this happens everybody pays the price. Because the social cost in terms of human lives and suffering is so high, all societies have evolved some means for resocializing misfits, drop-outs and rule-breakers. It is as if, by certain organized efforts, the community tries a second time to bring people to the minimal standards of the civic society.

What is being dealt with here does not apply to one large category of citizens who may require re-education. These are the people with either physical or mental incapacities requiring therapy and rehabilitation, who are neither drop-outs nor offenders. In fact, their greatest need is usually for them to find a way to contribute to the group at large. They are the many worthy members of society who require certain treatments or specially altered circumstances to enable them to function effectively. For our purposes we will except these, and focus, instead, on adults whose problems are primarily due to faulty socialization and are therefore likely to be correctable in the same terms.

In most of the latter instances, what may be required initially is "de-socialization." The individuals concerned have developed values and be-haviors contrary to those required to keep the social web intact. These are the people who have become welfare dependent to the degree that they are, in fact, long-term non-contributors to society. Simply put, they have learned that it is socially acceptable to take from the common pool of resources without assuming any responsibility for doing their share to keep that pool healthy and intact. Their only real participation in the institutions of the containing culture is as recipients of welfare and var-ious forms of social aid. For many, the situation has occurred through no fault of their own. This is not about assigning blame; it is about the possibility of changing behaviors and values in a direction deemed nec-essary for the health of individual self-concepts and the welfare of so-ciety.

It may seem trite and even lacking in compassion to say that able-bodied, welfare-dependent drop-outs need to be re-educated in order to develop the skills and attitudes required for getting and keeping a job. But, for all too many, it is precisely because their previous socialization has rendered them unable or unwilling to carve out a role as a worker with something of recognizable social value to offer that they are in their current situation. Three objections are often raised to the argument for a deliberate and all-inclusive program of resocialization in these cases. The first is that it is every person's human right not to work if the conditions of employment are not to one's liking. The second is that social value is undefinable except perhaps long after the fact, and the single mother raising her one or two children—or the self-styled artist droning on the street corner or fashioning graffiti on walls and sidewalks—may be pro-viding something of immeasurable value to humanity in the long run. The third is that many of the people involved are not drop-outs but "throw aways": a situation requiring a vastly different cure. The first two arguments hold only in very limited circumstances, and are totally dependent on the generosity of those who provide the means of liveli-hood for the total group. The right not to work for one's keep is no more sacred than is the right not to support with one's own labors those who refuse to work. (In fact, the story of "The Little Red Hen" drove this lesson home to countless previous generations of children.) Similarly, the right to lifetime support by society merely for maintaining one or two children in the circumstances of one's choosing is very much conditional on the probability that children so socialized will become whole human beings and good citizens or, conversely, are likely to have been congen-itally damaged or abused by the mother or her male friends and subsequently to become wards of the state. It is also related to the ethical issue of overpopulation in general.

The third argument carries a good deal more weight. If a society and economy is so arranged that the bulk of the resources or rewards available go to a minority of the well-placed and powerful—to the point where there is insufficient income available to provide adequate funding for those of society's tasks which usually fall to its least schooled and most vulnerable citizens—then we cannot say that a position of joblessness is in any way related to the attitude or lifestyle of the unemployed. We must look elsewhere for the causes and remedies. In this case it could be argued that the resocialization should be applied at the *top* of the socioeconomic hierarchy while, at the same time, the arm of the state is deployed in the most effective ways possible to restrain the demands, and redistribute a share of the spoils, of those who are receiving much more than their fair share—whether these individuals operate in the role of professionals, managers, investors or fortuitously placed unionized workers. This problem will be discussed in Chapter 8. What is relevant in the present context, however, is the degree to which the unfortunates concerned *have succumbed* to the lifestyle into which they were so cruelly propelled and subsequently trapped.

If we choose the route of resocialization for all who have either willingly or unwittingly assimilated the values and attitudes of the dropout, a number of approaches are possible. The prerequisite is a safe and more or less self-contained community with an environment in which all responses are contingent upon the individual's own behavior. Two additional conditions are necessary. First, the learners require the opportunity to make self-paced series of interconnected discoveries and to experience at once the consequences of each action. This is the principle underlying all effective learning. The second requirement is that their experience be carefully planned to ensure that they come to view their own progress from the perspectives of all those with whom they interact. In other words, it is necessary that they receive appropriate reinforcing feedback immediately and that it comes from their social as well as their physical surroundings.

The obvious conclusion from this is that the goals of welfare programs can be met if *and only if* both the amount and duration of all financial support is contingent on the behavior of the recipient. This demands a learning situation where the individual's actions affect others in the same position; and where these interacting people have an opportunity to respond in a natural way to one another in the process of accomplishing the tasks necessary for group maintenance. A program providing membership in an initially closed and protected community, and rewarding contributions to the communal setting, is clearly essential. Well-supervised group homes designed specifically for resocialization would seem to be mandatory, except in those cases where there is an extended family ready and willing to take over. It is imperative that the social alienation of drop-outs, and their vulnerability to exploitation on the street, be dealt with as a precondition for welfare. And if welfare is not to become a way of life, it is equally imperative that socially productive work of some kind be provided by the government for those who have been appropriately prepared for the challenge and opportunity. No progress toward responsible citizenship can be expected without these essential steps.

It requires little reflection to realize that most modern industrialized societies have unknowingly, and usually with the best of intentions, done the precise opposite. To begin with, the widespread failure of the schools to develop basic literacy, and foster the work ethic, functions as both cause and consequence of the problem. A 1996 study conducted by the American National Association of Manufacturers found that almost 60 percent of employers reported serious deficiencies in the majority of their employees in simple mathematics and in reading and writing skills. It was further claimed that over 60 percent routinely failed to arrive at work on time and to remain working throughout the day.

For those who lose their jobs, or never make it into the work force in the first place, the situation is even worse. The incentive systems established for people trapped in a dependent situation generally operate in socially and spiritually destructive, rather than constructive, ways. Welfare payments are doled out in monthly packages that are too often flushed into the cesspool of inner-city drug dealers, back-street predators and saloon keepers in one single, riotous day. Rebellious adolescents are rewarded for leaving home rather than submitting to parental guidance. Single mothers on welfare are encouraged to set up establishments on their own at the taxpayers' expense rather than putting pressure on the father for maintenance. They are also discouraged by the current incentive system from living with an extended family, or in communal circumstances which would allow them to cooperate in caring for children and doing the housework or, alternatively, bringing home wages for sharing with those of their group who have chosen to remain in the home and take responsibility for the maintenance of the household. Able-bodied men are encouraged, by the ready availability of alternative family support, to avoid their responsibilities as fathers and spouses and to cheat the government at every opportunity. In these alienated circumstances the type of community surveillance which traditionally provided protection for the children is frighteningly absent. A socially destructive cycle of welfare dependency and child abuse is thus reinforced in people of both genders. All this is done in the name of kindness and respect for the rights of those who are either not psychologically equipped for working or do not choose to participate in the low-wage job market.

It would seem that we have been sadly misguided in our professed concern for the human rights of the less fortunate. No citizen desires the right to be crippled by deficient schooling and a destructive incentive system and thus rendered unfit to function as a productive member of society. One might argue that the foremost inalienable right shared by all of us is to participate in the joint task of making society function for the good of all. It is the right to make our personal contribution to the social web of life. No society can work if people are given rights without corresponding capacities to exercise them, and without corresponding responsibilities. Nor can society *bestow* self-esteem. People can only *earn* it by exerting and experiencing the power of their own abilities. In fact, there is nothing so corrupting to the self-concept as being forever on the receiving end of the sympathy and charity of others. Blaming individuals for their situation when those in power have stacked the cards against the possibility of constructive resocialization is likewise corrupting to all concerned.

RESOCIALIZING OFFENDERS

In the case of those who break the law it is similarly fruitless to assign blame. Determining causal connections and insisting on the acceptance of personal responsibility, however, are different issues and must be taken seriously. When a crime is committed, the general citizenry have three responsibilities to the social system whose precious, life-sustaining web of trust has been broken. The first of these is to achieve a general communal sense that justice has been done and that retribution has been achieved. This is far more essential to the integrity and integration of the system as a whole than is generally recognized—especially by professionals whose training has been too narrowly focused on individual inner needs and motivations, and insufficiently grounded in sociology and evolutionary science. The second priority is to ensure that society is protected from any further depredation by the person in question, or by others who might be influenced by observing a lack of negative consequences for criminal behavior. The third is to rehabilitate the offender. Our success or failure in any one of these feeds back to affect the possibility for resocializing those already guilty of criminal behavior, as well as the effectiveness of developmental socialization for the population at large.

As for the first priority, in order for the community to feel satisfied that justice has been served, two requirements must be met. Offenders must be apprehended with a certain amount of dispatch, and there must be a punishment meted out that is generally perceived to fit the crime. Whether its roots are genetic or experiential, a sense of retributive justice seems to be one of the most basic of human aptitudes or drives. It is very possible that sociocultural evolution could not have occurred without confidence on the part of the group's members that those who violated the rules and thus rendered the collective vulnerable—either to the vengeance of the gods or to natural forces and watchful enemies—would be dealt with appropriately.

In addition, wherever the system operated so as to warrant it, the deterrence value of this assurance throughout the history of the species was no doubt incalculable. Those who today maintain that deterrence does not work are really making one or all of the following three claims. They are saying either (1) that the threatened punishment is actually imposed so seldom and so unpredictably that it has, in fact, lost all deterrence value; or (2) that human beings are incapable of learning from vicarious experience; or (3) that humans are similarly incapable of anticipating the probable consequences of their actions. Most knowledgeable commentators would agree with the first statement, and the public in general is usually supportive of measures aimed at devoting the kind of resources to law enforcement that would correct the situation.

The latter two claims are less readily justified. They would seem to reveal a confused and bleak view of human nature, as well as an uninformed and unsubstantiated one. Crimes of passion are the typical examples used for this argument. Like the abuse of alcohol and drugs, passion is perceived as an essentially uncontrollable instigator of behavior and thus an excuse for inhumane and anti-social acts—and the ultimate proof that deterrence cannot work. But social psychologists tell us that learning to sublimate our baser instincts and emotional drives is an integral part of general emotional and intellectual development; a process dependent at every turn on experiencing, either directly or vicariously, the consequences of one's choices.

If deterrence does not work, then all efforts at educating and civilizing young people cannot work, for all are based on the premise that humans are capable of learning not only from direct consequences, but from connections envisioned in the imagination concerning the future impacts of current actions on self and others. Of course, deterrence works to prevent socially destructive behavior—*if* negative follow-ups are predictable and consistently applied. In a similar way, the positive reinforcement of destructive behavior causes it to multiply when the perpetrators are perceived to have been rewarded for their crimes.

Nevertheless, it may be that some forms of aggressiveness are biologically based. In those restricted situations deterrence—or, for that matter, any type of resocialization—is not likely to succeed. Recent studies indicate the possibility of a genetic source of violence in the case of certain experimental animals. Scientists working with mice that exhibit grossly deviant behavior, marked by seemingly uncontrollable rage, have discovered that the absence of a gene normally providing nitric oxide to the body may be the cause of the problem. If this holds for humans, compensatory treatment by means of medication should be quite simple for the relatively small proportion of violent criminals whose genes are found to be deficient in this way. However, the possible existence of this condition in a few people in no way detracts from the validity and efficacy of the general approach outlined above.

The second most crucial of the necessary functions of the institution of the rule of law is the protection of society. If the social group is to continue to exist, these first two prerequisites must take precedence over concerns about the welfare of the offender. Society can survive without any particular individual, but no individual can survive in the absence of society. Because of this, the rights of all the actual and potential victims of the one who has broken the social bond must always have clear priority over the rights of the guilty person. At the moment the crime was committed, the offender forfeited all those rights that had been created and guaranteed for individuals by society; rights dependent on a reciprocal relationship of responsibility and trust.

This does not mean that prison officials should be given a license to treat prisoners inhumanely. It is doubly necessary that respect for human dignity—often lacking in people guilty of brutal crimes—be taught consistently by the example of those wielding power throughout the period of confinement. In fact, to proceed otherwise would prevent the achievement of the third objective of the justice system—re-education or rehabilitation. The right to have one's basic human dignity respected is not, however, the same as general civil rights. There is so much confusion over this matter that it requires detailed treatment. Appeals for improved conditions in prisons that rest on the principle of prisoners' civil rights are misguided. By definition, convicted offenders have foregone their rights of citizenship for the period of their incarceration. An understanding of this would allow for the planning of prison experience in the light of one purpose only: the need for resocialization. In the end, of course, the right of the individual to become a self-fulfilled and productive member of society is the most important human right of all—and the one without which all other rights are meaningless.

Once we are clear on the *objective* of the prison experience, where the offender is concerned, it will be possible to focus more intelligently than is presently the case on the *means* by which this desired societal end can be achieved. The spelling-out of specific learning outcomes indicative of the underlying values and attitudes necessary for responsible citizenship is the first step. The second step is the identification of a practical, graduated program for achieving these outcomes, complete with designated means for conducting ongoing evaluation in terms of observed behavioral change, rather than self-serving posturing and promises. The third step involves the structuring of work programs with specific incentives designed to reinforce behavior and attitudes in the direction implied by the program's specific objectives and long-term goals. These are not likely to be too different from the qualities listed in the Guidelines for Moral Education provided in Appendix A. In the case of adult offenders, the instilling of certain specific virtues might well take precedence over all else, for their absence lies at the root of most of the problems of serious deviance. They include the aforementioned respect for human dignity, as well as respect for the rule of law, empathy, responsibility, honesty and the self-discipline required to defer instant gratification and persevere at difficult or boring tasks. Resocialization would be made easier if all prison sentences for violent crimes were indeterminate, with satisfactory completion subject to objective evidence of progress in the attainment of these essential attributes of character.

NONVIOLENT OFFENDERS

In the case of those who have been found guilty of *nonviolent* crimes, it is quite possible that prison is not the answer. The cost of incarceration—in human as well as economic terms—may simply be too great. The type of social climate necessary for resocializing violent criminals may be too different from the situation likely to be effective for other types of offenders. Much to be preferred are alternative forms of punishment and deterrence—such as enforced isolation from the community, temporary loss of the privileges of citizenship (the right to vote, to leave the country, to drive a car, etc.), community service, house arrest and reparation or reimbursement for the victim. For one example we can look to traditional aboriginal approaches to the administration of justice; to healing and sentencing circles and temporary banishment. Denver, Colorado provides us with another example. The courts there, like those in a number of American cities, experienced a 400 percent percent increase in nonviolent, drug-related cases in the decade from 1985 to 1995. In an attempt to cope with this, Denver began to experiment with a program of rehabilitation rather than incarceration: one which involves starting at the source of the problem—the offender's drug addiction—and dealing with that.

Two initial steps are already in the process of being adopted in some North American cities. They are the community policing and cleaning up of inner-city neighborhoods and the specific targeting of gangs by these stepped-up forces. Establishing drug-free and weapon-free schools is another imperative, as is a well-publicized change in the law dictating that adolescents who commit violent "adult" crimes be treated with appropriate recognition of the seriousness of the offense. Yet another necessity is an incentive system encouraging community-led provision of leisure-time activities designed and conducted with clear objectives for altering behavior. Dedicated religious leaders, local leaders of organized youth groups and neighborhood schoolteachers have proven to be more successful here than professional welfare workers introduced from the outside.

VIOLENT OFFENDERS

In the case of the resocialization of *violent* offenders, the most important requirement is a recognition by all concerned that *every aspect* of the prison experience must be carefully structured with the desired outcomes in mind. Clearly, the most dismaying current aspect of incarceration is the "prisonization" or unplanned peer socialization that sets in for every inmate upon arrival—in spite of the best efforts of those officially in charge. It is fruitless and apt to be grossly misleading to focus on formally organized therapy sessions, courses and workshops—to the exclusion of what *actually* goes on within the network of informal social interaction among prisoners and between prisoners and guards. This would be the case *even if* these attempts at education were operating from sound principles of learning, rather than from the scientifically unwarranted, and sociologically unsound, premises that too often prevail. Numerous studies have documented the fact that good intentions and ideological commitment may well be counterproductive in the prison environment. Most have concluded that treatment-oriented programs will be effective only to the degree that they deliberately foster identification with the goals of the larger community, rather than (as is too often the case) with those of the deviant subculture dominating the prison social system.

Sociologists as well as prison officials have been particularly damning of those well-intentioned workers and volunteers in penology who have so little understood the structure of inmate interaction—and their personal educative role within it—that they have allowed themselves to be maneuvered by prisoners into collaborating in their own neutralization. Their therapeutic or "people-changing" programs are exploited by inmates who quickly learn to use the system for their own ends; that is, for obtaining an easy ride inside and an early release. The individualistic orientation of many of these professionals and their helpers seems to render them unaware of the insidious prisonization process which has turned a majority of modern prison environments into virtual schools for crime. The situation is now so bad that prisoners are *far more likely* to become addicted to drugs, to be subjected to homosexual rape and to contract AIDS than is any other segment of the population. A 1996 study by Correctional Service Canada found that one in five prisoners reported having been physically assaulted by fellow prisoners, three in five claimed to have been the victims of rape, and 11 percent admitted to using illegal drugs while in prison. In general, studies indicate that too many of the social systems within prisons are controlled by the most ruthless of the inmates in the pursuit of their own corrupt ends, with guards often being forced to collaborate for their own safety.

PREPARING CITIZENS

It is no wonder that the prison system is failing to recognize and implement its major task of preparing inmates for responsible citizenship, for "political socialization" seems to have been increasingly ignored in modern democratic political systems in general. Quite the opposite is the case for authoritarian and totalitarian societies, however, and for those tribal groups maneuvering for separation from larger, territorially defined states. Typically, despots and demagogues are all too aware of the need to indoctrinate their citizens into attitudes of respect and loyalty to the regime and its symbols and icons, as well as into habits of obedience to the regime's laws and lawmakers. Liberal democrats, on the other hand, seem to imagine that good citizenship is innate; or that a love of freedom and equality will invariably unfold in the bosoms of all if the authority structures are kept sufficiently loose and if the regime avoids imposing its values. This is ironic as well as unfortunate for, of all the requirements of citizenship, those necessary for maintaining a democracy are by far the most demanding and least likely to be imbibed by osmosis or developed by chance.

The first concern of any political system has to be that of legitimacy. Do the citizens absorb and become attached to the goals of the system and to the official means employed to achieve these? Do they accept the authority structure as legitimate—including the authority of current incumbents of leadership positions? Are they respectful of the various political offices and of symbols of the collective such as the flag? Is there a potentially dangerous "cult of the leader," or is political legitimacy granted in a more abstract way to established political authority in general? All systems share this latter requirement. Democracies, which abjure coercion, are uniquely dependent on the voluntary acceptance of their legitimacy, an acceptance resting on the absence of cynicism and competing loyalties in the general population. This is why the role of politician in a democracy is such a sacred trust, and why dishonesty on the part of incumbents of office should be seen as almost the ultimate crime against the civic society.

Yet another issue is the set of attitudes, aptitudes and skills necessary for citizenship in the relevant system. Are the members concerned about the long-term welfare of the collective? Are they clear about the responsibilities and rights of citizenship? Are they familiar with the worthy characteristics of their own system; with how it works and how it compares to others? Do they perceive the individual citizen as powerful or powerless in instituting and guiding social change? It is on these matters that democracies differ from more authoritarian types of polities. There is an extensive list of qualities that are prerequisites for democratic citizenship. This includes a grasp of information about what is actually happening in the local community and the world at large, knowledge of economic and power relationships in general, a skeptical orientation and problem-solving skills. On the other hand, these same qualities may merely function as sources of trouble for authoritarian systems.

Obviously, socializing (or *indoctrinating*) young people with the objective of regime legitimacy in mind will be a vastly different undertaking from socializing (or *educating*) them in terms of the skills and knowledge requirements of participating citizenship. While an authoritarian political system will tend to emphasize the first objective only, maintaining a democracy requires some attention to both. Democracy makes special demands on citizens. It requires thoroughly educated people rather than merely well-indoctrinated ones, but it requires loyalty and commitment and respect for legitimate authority as well. Often we neglect one or the other of these objectives. Increasingly, we are neglecting both. It is time we realized that no democracy can long endure in the absence of an engaged, knowledgeable, inquiry-oriented, responsible and loyal citizenry, and that the development of these qualities cannot be left to Providence or fate. If democracies fail in this major objective of the second stage of socialization there may be, for them, no second chance.

REFERENCES

Adler, N. and Harrington, C., eds. *The Learning of Political Behavior*. Glenview, IL: Scott, Foresman, 1970.

Bumstead, D. C. "Freshman Socialization: The Influence of Social Class Background on the Adaptation of Students." *Human Relations* 28, 4 (1975): 387–406.

Clausen, John A., ed. *Socialization and Society*. Boston: Little, Brown, 1968.

Coulter, F. and Taft, R., "The Professional Socialization of Teachers as Social Assimilation." *Human Relations* 26, 6 (1973): 681–693.

Dager, E. Z. *Socialization*. Chicago, IL: Markham, 1971.

Dean, Jaros. *Socialization to Politics*. Melbourne, Australia: Thomas Nelson, 1973.

Hafferty, Frederic W. *Into the Valley: Death and the Socialization of Medical Students*. New Haven, CT: Yale University Press, 1991.

Hasselt, Van B. and Hersen, Michel. *Handbook of Social Development: A Lifespan Perspective*. New York, NY: Plenum Press, 1992.

Kelling, George L. and Coles, Catherine. *Fixing Broken Windows: Restoring Order and Reducing Crime in Our Communities*. New York, NY: Martin Kessler Books, 1996.

Langton, Kenneth P. *Political Socialization*. London, UK: Oxford University Press, 1969.

Leymann, Heinz. *Socialization and Learning at Work: A New Approach to the Learning Process in the Workplace and Society*. Brookfield, UK: Gower, 1989.

McCorckle, L. and Korn, R. "Resocialization within Walls." In *Readings in Criminology and Penology*, ed. D. Dressler. New York, NY: Columbia University Press, 1972.

Women's Advancement in Corporate and Professional Canada. Ottawa, ON: Conference Board of Canada, 1997.

CHAPTER 8

A Tale of Two Cultures: The Culture of Affluence and the Culture of Poverty

In previous chapters we discussed the faltering family in modern North American society. Clearly, the family as an institution has been weakened. However, we need to recognize that, regardless of the problems besetting it or the form it takes, some type of family will necessarily function as the unit of primary socialization if human society is to survive. As such, it will continue to play a powerful role in determining the world view and life chances of the individuals who are molded within it. For this reason it is essential to understand that decisive family-centered cultural traits do not emerge from nowhere. In this chapter we attempt to elaborate on how families are shaped to an extent seldom recognized by feedback from cultural forces beyond the common way of being and behaving shared by all citizens.

It is increasingly the case that, in modern industrial societies, these primary agents of socialization tend to reflect either the "culture of poverty" in which the particular family (or fragment of family) is mired, or its mirror image: that of the "culture of affluence" to which the family aspires. They will reflect other subcultural influences as well: influences crossing the lines of class and income, such as the ethnic group or "tribe" from which the family derives its ancestral roots. The latter will be examined in Chapter 9.

How can it be, one might ask, that the above sorts of distinctiveness are maintained when the mass media seem well on the way to producing a global culture of shared icons and expectations the world over? The answer resides in the hierarchical nature of cultural entities. We are shaped at one and the same time by a number of *levels of culture*. Cultures are like nesting systems, one within the other, from the subculture of the primary socializing unit (usually the family) to the all-encompassing culture of the international community—as filtered, in today's world, through television, radio, newspapers, telecommunications and the Internet. Between these two extremes we find several dynamic controlling systems of built-in limitations and opportunities, all of which are contributed to and transmitted by their members and, in turn, help to shape the values and beliefs of those who are exposed to them. In previous chapters we discussed the socializing function of the peer group, school and various community agencies, as well as the intrusive nature of the media.

CULTURES THAT ENCASE AND SHAPE THE FAMILY

There is also an influential culture originating in the give-and-take within the home. What the adult members of the family themselves bring to the socialization process in their role as caregivers and authority figures is uniquely effective and long lasting. At the same time, the values and ways of doing things modeled by these family members are powerfully affected by what happens to them outside the home. For example, the daily experience of the *losers* in an industrial society is very different from that of the *winners*. Families in which there have never been regular wage earners; families for whom welfare has become a way of life; families living in a crime-ridden ghetto whose adult members are in and out of jail; families trapped, for several generations, in the "underclass" of an industrial society: these are families that typically exhibit a particular variation on the culture of the country as a whole. We can describe this distinctive subculture as the "culture of poverty." On the other hand, those who have found a productive role in society, regardless of the size of their incomes, operate in a very different subcultural setting: the "culture of affluence." The fear of falling from the one subculture into the other places severe stresses on ordinary working people for whom the growing gap between their own take-home pay and that of the more powerful and privileged among them is reflected in the ever-increasing cost of life's necessities, or of what the values of their culture *define* as necessities.

THE CULTURE OF AFFLUENCE

Members of this culture in North America and throughout the world are not merely the well-to-do. The middle classes share in its values and expectations, as do the working poor. Only the underclass is set tragically apart, condemned to a way of life labeled presciently by the anthropologist Oscar Lewis as "the culture of poverty." The "culture of affluence," on the other hand, is produced by what we like to call *free enterprise* capitalism—combined with a generous approach to welfare-state "entitlements" based on the principle of universality. It represents an attempt to accommodate two essentially irreconcilable principles: the Enlightenment ideals of absolute freedom and absolute equality. These ideals are commonly expressed in the form of two disputable beliefs, one which we can term the "conservative myth," and the other the "liberal myth." According to the former, the chief characteristic of free-enterprise capitalism is an economy with a minimum of regulations or institutional limitations. The goal of *freedom* is thought to be achieved by this system in that its winners are assumed to have made their way to the top by competing successfully in an open market. This goal is justified by the premise that, if all citizens are free to pursue their own ends, the result will be the best possible social arrangements and personal benefits for everyone.

The second myth maintains that what is required for *equality* to be guaranteed is the equal availability of every governmental expenditure or program to all citizens—no matter what their circumstances. Accompanying this uncritical commitment to universality is a belief that money borrowed by government, especially from its own citizens, is subject to quite different economic laws than is debt incurred by individuals or businesses. A long succession of annual deficits poses no real problem, according to the liberal myth, because government can simply "assume" its own debt by "creating" the bonds needed for raising the desired funds. As one might expect of such an impossible combination of goals and expectations, a system created in terms of them cannot survive for long. In practice, no economy is ever really "free"; and costly universal programs administered by the state to rich and poor alike, and financed by borrowed funds, are more likely to diminish equality than to enhance it.

EXPLODING THE CONSERVATIVE MYTH

In the affluent cultures of most of the capitalist countries in the developed world there remain few traces of either the moral or economic principles associated with the original free-market theory of Adam Smith. Countless programs and arrangements that limit and alter the workings of the economy in all sorts of ways are omnipresent. What is worse, these structures appear to have evolved haphazardly, election by election, labor settlement by labor settlement, tax policy by tax policy, into their present forms. Every ongoing capitalist system (except for those ruled by some version of the Mafia) now exists within a specific institutional framework defined by a vast network of rules and regulations: regulations establishing protective tariffs, tax codes, subsidies to business and agriculture, labor relations, and so on. Few of these are *necessary* to capitalism; indeed, most are due to the contingencies of history, political expediency and cultural bias. Many now operate in a largely unrecognized way to favor oligopolistic control over open competition on a level playing field; and to favor some fortuitously placed groups over others, and certain fortunate individuals within each group over the majority of their colleagues. Notable among these arrangements is the tax system with all the special "loopholes," deductions and deferrals that have allowed it to become a political tool for the bribing of vocal interest groups. It is all part of the widespread custom of designing tax laws for numerous purposes other than as the most fair and simplest possible source of necessary governmental revenue.

This applies as well in the case of special treatment of pension-scheme savings up to a maximum far beyond what would be feasible for any country if, in fact, a majority of workers could afford to take advantage of the program. Such schemes can only endure if their benefits are *in practice*—if not in law—monopolized by those in the upper section of the income curve. Unfortunately, that is the way things tend to work out, for our increasingly unequal reward system virtually guarantees that the majority of the population will be unable to afford the savings that would allow them to benefit from such schemes. Similarly, a tax code which allows home-mortgage interest to be deductible from taxable income disproportionately favors upper-middle income and wealthy homeowners over those who cannot afford to enter the housing market. Long-term deferral of tax payments on relatively large amounts of income can also only serve to decrease the pool of potential government revenue while adding to the gap between winners and losers.

Perhaps the cruelest deficiency in the affluent culture's conservative myth is the absence of any effective means of controlling the social/ political power inevitably accompanying the accumulation of capital. While it is true that there is now an accelerating diffusion of investment capital—along with the potential for social control associated with it— this has not translated into authentically democratic decision making by shareholders. Major interests in most large corporations are no longer owned by wealthy, long-established families, but by the pension funds of professional and labor unions such as those representing teachers and other relatively well-paid workers. (For example, one in two Canadians now hold shares in banks, through RRSPs and pension funds.) As capital *ownership* becomes more widespread and difficult to discern, however, *information* concerning the deployment of capital increasingly becomes the source of power. This means that the influence of top-level corporation managers—with access to, and control of, that information— grows apace.

The capital-dependent and knowledge-intensive nature of the new technologies is furthering a movement in industrial societies toward the creation of two impermeable classes: the knowledgeable "winners" and the "losers" with no access to the information highway. The resulting social inequality is contributing to numerous social problems. Efforts by national governments to reduce these by means of the tax system—or even to levy progressive taxes designed specifically to redistribute a grossly unfair distribution of income—seem doomed to fail. There are two obvious reasons for this failure, both rooted in the basic principles of learning discussed in Chapter 4. In the first place, those who wield the greatest political influence are the very people likely to be most adversely affected by the necessary restrictions and changes. Second, however difficult the task might prove to be, it would be more viable to build incentives into an economy that would function to distribute rewards relatively fairly in the first place than to reinforce gross disparities in income and then to take away from people what they believe to be rightfully theirs to invest and profit from as they wish.

The relatively disadvantaged situation of families with young children today offers an example of the confused goals and lack of evaluation characteristic of government policy concerning this crucial institution. In societies such as the American and Canadian ones we find a complex network of well-established economic incentives for people to live as married couples: special pension arrangements and rules governing inheritance, tax deductions and medical plan benefits. The only morally justifiable and rational objective of this kind of legislated unfairness would seem to be that which follows from the traditional assumption that marriage is about creating *families*—families operating in their institutional role of procreation and primary socialization. It is this crucial *childrearing* function that has direct implications for the future welfare of society, and it is that—and *only* that—which requires support from the rest of us. If we were not foregoing so much potential tax revenue, and squandering so much in needless subsidies to childless couples, there might be more funds available for furthering *legitimate* social goals such as making life easier for young working parents and providing better child care and teaching better parenting skills. It could be argued that, instead of engaging in fruitless and divisive arguments about whether the government-subsidized category of *marriage* should be enlarged to include unions between same-sex couples, bachelor brothers and sisters, and so on, a rational social policy would focus only on *families* currently engaged in the nurturing and socializing of dependent children, and confine all tax-funded subsidies, pension benefits and exemptions to these culturally critical entities.

A similar point could be made concerning institutionalized support for those groups of workers who are obviously not currently disadvantaged relative to other members of society. Perhaps it is time to ask why any professional association or union should be granted legal protection from the consequences of withholding their services *over the issues of salary levels or job security* for those of their members whose income is already several times that of the national median. The time may have come, as well, to ask who really benefited from the corporate takeovers of the 1980s and the ruthless downsizing of the 1990s—both combined with massive increases in managerial salaries. Other questions that could be raised have to do with our deeply embedded cultural prejudices regarding the relative "worth" of various social roles: biases that fundamentally influence who gets what in the competitive capitalistic enterprise. Does our current custom of assigning "brain-work" four or five times the remuneration of "brawn-work" really result from the unfettered operation of a free market?

Also relevant is the issue of the extent to which we, as a society, should be rewarding the mere accident of being in the right place at the right time. Why should the incentives—even *within* the same vocation or profession—be so grossly stacked in favor of the few who manage to clamber over their colleagues to the top? Why do we not pour scorn on the habit of giving bonuses for "superior performance" in corporations where there is no corresponding system in place for linking penalties to grievous failures? We might also ask why a few "top" professionals and business managers (and the winners in the lottery of movie, sport and television stardom in general) are rewarded by incomes grossly disproportional to what one might legitimately assume to be their fair share of the Gross Domestic Product (GDP). Why is stardom valued so much more highly than long-term dedication to the job at hand? All these customs which our culture presupposes us to accept so unquestioningly are expensive and counterproductive in the long run. They render the service provided by the group in question unnecessarily costly to society, while furthering an unhealthy winner/loser mentality rather than one of pride in rising efficiency and effectiveness in achieving institutional goals.

We cannot ignore the way the media reinforce the notion that *winning*—rather than excellence of output or devotion to service—is the ultimate achievement in the culture of affluence. Nor can we overlook the fact that schools and universities have functioned to guarantee family privilege across the generations and to perpetuate cultural biases dictating beliefs about the relative value of social roles. Those jobs requiring the most knowledge of the type provided by higher education tend to be the ones aimed at, and eventually filled, by the offspring of the most successful previous products of the system. These are the very youngsters who, because of their family income and culture, have had an obvious head start in the race from infancy.

There is an unacknowledged assumption throughout the culture of affluence that, because the route to be navigated in order to reach these jobs is a lengthy, expensive and sometimes unnecessarily tortuous one, the rewards at the end of the road should be accordingly great. The certification provided by the schools inevitably becomes the only gate through which these most privileged positions can be reached. This gives the gatekeepers within the higher levels of the educational system an inordinate amount of power; and it is not surprising that they, too, demand to be rewarded with a corresponding degree of security, privilege and pay. The more scarce and highly paid the top jobs become the more ferocious is the competition to achieve them—and the more essential it is that those controlling the process are in reality the most suitable for their task.

If it were indeed the case that the selecting and sorting process carried on in this setting did an efficient and effective job of fitting abilities to roles we would not have too much cause to worry *except for one obvious fact*. Clearly, there would seem to be a moral problem involved in compounding nature's obvious inequalities, where the distribution of intelligence and appropriate parenting are concerned, by adding a grievous social injustice as well. The latter injustice is in the form of a large income gap between those who work with abstract knowledge, or in an administrative, professional or managerial capacity, and those whose work calls for other—and often even more demanding—skills. In other words, the creation of a meritocracy of intelligence, even an honest one, raises serious questions concerning fairness wherever the winners of the process are encouraged to expect a disproportionately large share of the total "pie" of a nation's production. A century ago the French sociologist Emile Durkheim concluded that a democracy cannot long endure if the services provided by all the various contributors to the economy are valued and rewarded in grossly unequal terms. That said, however, modern affluent cultures actually get the worst of both worlds, for they tend to evolve formal post-secondary systems that monopolize the selection process while failing abysmally to operate as true meritocracies in an increasingly elitist society.

The causes of this are many, a major culprit being the lack of objectivity and the dominance of fads and "bandwagons" in many of the academic fields outside of the exact sciences. This has created a situation where the incentives within humanities and social-science departments too often operate so as to reward the manipulators and conformers to the dominant ideology rather than the serious critical thinkers among the students and would-be instructors and contributors to journals. Another problem stems from the bureaucratic nature of schools and universities—with all the evils inherent in that form of organization. As noted in the preceding chapter, bureaucracies tend to encourage mediocrity, skill at manipulating people rather than ideas, empire building, an overweening demand for security of tenure, a reluctance to make judgments, an inability to finalize decisions and a lack of accountability: all of which combine to render them singularly resistant to adaptation in changing circumstances, and incapable of ensuring that the best people are actually in the driver's seat. These are not the characteristics most likely to ensure the integrity of a system so crucial to the welfare of society as a whole.

EXPLODING THE LIBERAL MYTH

The preceding remarks apply as well to that other myth of the affluent society: the ideal of universality of state-administered entitlements as a means of achieving equality. There are two serious problems with this ideal, both dictated by logic. The first is simply that, contrary to liberal dreams, universality has succeeded neither in reducing inequality nor *redistributing* income. Merely adding equals to unequals does not guarantee that the *relative* outcome is changed. What *is* changed, however, is the cost of all goods and services as well as that of government, and the funds available to those who are in real poverty. This applies resoundingly to the popular notion of government-supported higher education. It is only through the provision of generous scholarships and student loans based on need, with payback programs tied to subsequent income, that equality of opportunity is actually fostered. Subsidized tuition for all comers is clearly not the answer in the current situation. *Given the present reward structure* which favors the highly schooled to such a grossly disproportionate extent, that policy can only function to *increase* inequality. As things stand now, those sufficiently fortunate (or devious) to be able to succeed in colleges and universities are virtually guaranteed a lifetime of relative affluence. If tax moneys are taken from general revenue to subsidize their expensive schooling we are, in effect, transferring wealth from the working poor and lower-middle class (whose children are least likely to attend university) to the relatively well off. This applies to all entitlements that are in theory available to all but in practice monopolized by the most privileged families.

One needn't be an economist to conclude that, for every tax dollar that goes into subsidized services for middle- and upper-class people, there will be one less dollar available for services for the truly needy; and it should not require a doctorate in philosophy to recognize that the principle of universality is not the same thing as the principle of equalization. The problem with universality is that the amount of revenue taken from citizens in the form of taxes for all these pleasantly liberal enterprises must be increased at the same rate as the sum of the entitlements being paid out; or, alternatively, the government must borrow to make up the deficit. Predictably, politicians in the culture of affluence, with its pressures for instant gratification, have chosen the latter route.

When we analyze the situation in terms of evolutionary systems theory, it becomes evident that deficit financing sets in motion an adaptive feedback loop which is difficult to rein in or redirect. Indebting future generations by borrowing for popular social programs, to be delivered in the present, provides immediate rewards for both politician and voter; while the costs can be ignored except by those relatively few who are burdened by a long-term view.

The future has a distressing way of becoming the present, and the problems of profligacy tend to proliferate over time. Governments soon find themselves forced to borrow more from society's winners—paying them (along with foreign lenders) rising rates of interest as the debt grows—or, alternatively, to accept an ongoing devaluation of their currency. A rapidly accumulating debt renders any investment in government bonds increasingly risky, and the pay-off must be made correspondingly rewarding for those who can afford the risk. An inevitable consequence is that ever more of the tax dollar goes to pay interest on the public debt, while the cost of those services still offered by the cash-strapped government becomes ever greater. Both the cost of borrowing and the price of necessities for the working poor necessarily spiral. For example, in Canada in 1996, a full 35 percent of total federal tax revenue was required for debt servicing. This meant that the country's biggest federal spending program had actually become not welfare or job-training for the poor, but the approximately $48 billion annually paid in interest on the national debt. The only winners of such long-term irresponsibility in the name of universality are the savers and investors who generally prosper—or are at least able to maintain their advantage.

Even this no longer holds, however, if the debt-burdened government takes the easy way out demanded by those voters and advisors who have bought into the liberal myth, and attempts to solve its problems by arbitrarily lowering interest rates, thereby allowing galloping inflation to ravage the real incomes of savers and borrowers alike. A deliberate policy of debasing a country's currency by "printing money" in order to finance annual deficits—and to meet interest payments on the national debt—could be termed the ultimate immorality on the part of politicians. It betrays a fundamental social contract by destroying the lifetime savings of the country's most responsible and trusting citizens.

Typically, in the difficult economic times that inevitably follow the popular resort to inflation, jobs are cut by businesses deciding to "downsize" in order to cope with rising costs. In the process, large numbers of workers trying desperately to hang on at the bottom of the income pyramid are shaken off and propelled into the underclass. Another result of the squeeze is that older employees, including generously paid professors, medical specialists and corporation managers, are encouraged to retire ever earlier with inflated, indexed pensions and settlements so that their places can be taken by less costly workers. This creates additional pressure on government entitlements—especially as increased demands are made on large federally funded and government-subsidized pensions. At the same time, the total amount available for entitlements is falling precipitously because of the rising proportion of tax revenues needed to service the government's burgeoning debt. All the while, as the very real need of the losers in the race for entitlements is doubling and tripling, the shrinking pool of available resources continues to be doled out evenly to the increasingly wealthy winners and the increasingly poor losers—and all in the name of equality!

The role of consumer debt in creating losers is too often ignored. Those who follow their government's lead, and routinely borrow for consumption purposes, are usually in the bottom half of the income pyramid to begin with. As their debts spiral out of control, and personal bankruptcies hit record levels, many find themselves sliding down into the underclass and becoming the clients not of banks, but of pawnbrokers and the "loan sharks" of organized crime. The fact that credit-card debt by Canadian consumers increased over tenfold from 1979 to 1998, to $500 billion—as compared to $518 billion total annual income—should be a signal indicating trouble ahead for any society; and particularly one for whom the official myth upholds the goal of equality.

A major source of energy fueling the entire process and forcing up the cost of all services—particularly in the areas of law, engineering, financial management, higher education, medicine and dentistry—is the ever-expanding share of the "pie" demanded by that very professional and managerial class which is already far above the median in income. Decision-makers at all levels of government seem oblivious to the fact that their policies are reinforcing a zero-sum game: one in which the power and greed of the winners—especially the exclusive in-group of winners among the winners—is pushing the lower-middle class and working poor ever closer to the brink.

Inevitably, the time arrives when debt-ridden and desperate governments are forced by the specter of national bankruptcy to begin the task of eradicating annual budget deficits. Typically, this happens only when a nation's fiscal irresponsibility becomes obvious to its international lenders and trading partners; and to its own affluent citizens who are unlikely to let patriotism stand in the way of shedding their country's doubtful bonds. Profligate governments then find that they have no choice but to make large cuts in the funds available for all universal entitlements. Inevitably, the effect of such a move is extreme, due to rapidly expanding numbers of participants and the rising expectations of the over-sixty age cohort—particularly for health care and pensions. For example, by the time Canadian governments at both levels began the struggle to bring their deficits under control, finance-department pro-

jections indicated that only sixty-eight cents worth of programs and services were being provided for every tax dollar paid out.

As in the case of businesses and universities, when governments are
finally forced to economize they cut from the bottom and seldom from
the top (where the implementers of the cuts happen to reside); or, at
best, they once more blithely apply the principle of universality—slash-
ing indiscriminately from services to the needy and comfortable alike.
The cuts to the poor usually come first because there is less political risk
in that course, simply because people burdened by the culture of poverty
are notoriously reluctant voters. Thus, what has actually been accomplished by the principle of universality and its inevitable correlate—government borrowing-for-consumption—is the precise opposite of what
was intended. It is nothing less than provision of a continuous supply
of fresh fodder for the self-destructive culture of the underclass.

THE CULTURE OF POVERTY

If the culture of affluence is inherently unstable, much more so is the
culture of poverty to which it has given birth and which it helps to
perpetuate. We are referring here not to the *situation* of relative poverty
in which many members of our society have found themselves from time
to time, but to a *culture* of poverty existing within an encompassing culture of affluence. In North America during the Depression of the 1930s,
the majority of the population were actually poorer in terms of goods
and services than are many welfare-dependent individuals today. The
same applies to various small groups of the underprivileged in the decades before and after the Depression. They lacked running water, elec-
tricity, indoor toilets, radios, opportunities for post-elementary schooling
and all the labor-saving devices that even the most poverty-stricken
among us now take for granted—or at least expect as a basic right of
citizenship. But the major values and beliefs defining the world view of
the less-privileged classes were not essentially different from those of
more fortunate citizens. They believed that they belonged to the larger
society, and indeed they did. They had not opted out or rebelled against
its ideals; nor had they been ejected or discarded by it. They still played
a part in the operation of their schools, churches and local government;
that is, they had roles in their community other than that of welfare
recipient or hustler. They shared the propensity to save in order to get
ahead and provide for "a rainy day" which is a defining characteristic
of contributors to an economy. They retained a certain amount of am-
bition and a faith that, if they persisted, someday things would be better
for their children. They kept before those children images of cultural
heroes from other times and other places who had conquered adversity.
Perhaps most important, the children of these families were immersed

in a web of intense communication from the moment of birth: a web that has been shown to be crucial for normal language development.

There are still many such families. A 1997 study by Susan Mayer of the University of Chicago indicates that, even more than variations in family income, the presence or absence of certain family practices and values are decisive in determining which children do well in life. Clearly, it is the culture of those financially strapped families who manage to be successful—their stubborn commitment to the common culture shared with their fellow citizens—that sustains them and eventually lifts their offspring from the *situation* of poverty. But this is not the way things are today for those who are trapped in the *culture* of poverty.

A culture of poverty is, for the most part, unique to modern industrial society. It is a phenomenon that occurred previously only in places such as the London portrayed by Dickens and in North America possibly in small geographically remote enclaves such as the Appalachians, and perhaps a few isolated corners of the Canadian Maritimes. Also, in spite of dreams of restoring a long-lost tribal heritage, it has become the overriding cultural characteristic of many aboriginal reserves today.

Ironically—for the intention was quite different—the culture of poverty was given a great impetus by the countercultural revolution of the 1960s. This connection is due to the fact that the basis, and the distinguishing feature, of the way of living typical of today's underclass is a direct challenge to the operating value consensus of the containing society. The counterculture legitimized this kind of challenge for the privileged youths of the affluent society. In fact, a number of these youths of the 1960s slid down into the underclass and the drug culture that defined it for them, and remained there. Today's underprivileged, with much more reason for grievance, have learned the lesson well. Members of the poverty subculture are drawn together in their repudiation not only of the wider society's common core of values and norms but of the rule of law that affirms and sustains it—and that they perceive as not having worked for them.

In many ways the ideals sought by, and the habits reinforced within, the community of the underclass in modern urban centers are counter to those of society as a whole. Self-esteem is achieved in ways quite foreign to the social workers who attempt vainly to apply individualistic, psychologically based palliatives to the problems created by this culture. The members of the youth gangs in "crackland" are a case in point. These boys (and increasingly, girls) who stalk and control the streets are not lacking in confidence and pride in their prowess and relative success. Although they tend to be linguistically and conceptually crippled, other more primitive traits are superbly honed. They are emperors of all they survey, and they display the material possessions to prove and symbolize it. They also demand the subservience and respectful observances from their peers that are an emperor's due. They see themselves not as the system's casualties but as successful subversives and conquerors of that very system; for, above all else, the culture of poverty is a *revolutionary* counterculture.

The *imperialistic* nature of the culture of poverty needs to be understood as well. It has the potential to expand rapidly in its takeover of the inner cities, and to alter them in radical and frightening ways. And, as with a spreading bed of quicksand, those who become mired in this subculture find it almost impossible to extricate themselves. It is extremely seductive for young people for the same reasons that the counterculture of the 1960s attracted many of the brightest of that era. As an ultimate irony, its carriers have harnessed the profit-driven mass media—at least the *music* which is such a powerful revolutionary force for changing values and behavior and for cementing individuals into a cohesive group. The unwitting supporters and justifiers of the culture of poverty are the political and academic elites who preach cultural relativism and disparage "white European cultural imperialism" without any clear picture of the real-life nature of the alternative culture for which they are making their exaggerated claims of equality.

The role models for that culture as it *actually* functions are the rap stars with their message of violence and rebellion against all forms of established authority. They are also the fathers, uncles and older brothers who have spent time in prison and return with freshly honed skills and criminal attitudes to take up their places in the various rackets which constitute the underground economy of the community. The mores and customs of this culture are evolved within the underclass of the inner city and then spread by the media across geographic, political and subcultural boundaries to susceptible youth everywhere. For young initiates it is a totalitarian peer-group culture rooted in raw power and the notion that "might makes right." These have become the precepts dictating the way the underclass community is *actually* run and who is actually in charge, regardless of what the planners and would-be implementers of government programs imagine to be the case.

The welfare system, as it currently operates, is an integral and essential part of this culture in that it provides the steady source of income on which the sharks can feed. Too often the welfare system—not as it was intended, but as it has worked in practice—helps to reinforce the twisted values and norms of the underclass. An inability to defer gratification is the most marked characteristic of individuals who have been shaped by the culture of poverty. The welfare system, as it evolved, has served to enhance and perpetuate this. It has not functioned to reinforce the ability to think ahead, or a willingness to save money, marry and to get established in a home of some kind before having children—and subsequently to work in available low-wage jobs, if necessary, in order to care for them. Instead, the way payments are doled out tends to reward single-parent families led by females with a succession of temporary live-in partners. Having children out of wedlock is reinforced in countless ways, as is cheating the system. This does not necessarily mean that the young people who learn to behave in these ways are *consciously* making choices to do so, with the cash payments in mind. The reader of this book will be well aware by now that this is not the way that socialization works.

Nice guys—those who try to live according to the rules of civic society—invariably finish last in a community ruled by the culture of poverty. Again, it is not merely the *fact of being poor*, but the kind of life experience to which that poverty exposes and condemns one, that creates the problem. The underclass in a modern industrial society is not a nice world in which to find oneself trapped. The culture that defines it is an appalling source from which to ingest one's beliefs about the way things are and the way things should be. The child whose family tries to fight against the tide and teach contrasting values finds it virtually impossible to survive as a dissenter. Only by a miracle could a youngster emerge emotionally undamaged and spiritually whole from such an environment. But politicians will never eradicate that underclass or its culture simply by identifying and blaming its carriers and victims. Nor will the problem it poses be solved by removing all responsibility for their behavior from these same individuals and merely shouting blanket condemnations at the rest of society.

The culture of poverty is in significant ways the mirror image of the larger social environment with its culture of affluence. It is a Looking-Glass World in which the rules and reward systems of the containing culture have been turned inside out, with many of the underlying drives and goals being retained in different guise. The idea of "winner take all" that has come to dominate the culture of affluence is operative here as well, but the larger society's losers have here become the winners. The drive to consume beyond one's means and to accumulate debt recklessly with no thought of "paying the piper," and no intention of being around when "the chickens come home to roost," is common to the two cultural worlds—as well as to the managerial and professional elite, and governing bodies, of the country as a whole. In both subcultures we find a stacking of the deck to enhance the bargaining position of the most powerful. The tendency of the winners toward the accumulation and ostentatious consumption of their excessive gains is consistent throughout, as is their short-sighted greed and disregard for the rights of others.

The chief difference between the behaviors exhibited in the two worlds is that in the underclass all these self-serving propensities are nakedly displayed and, because there is no attempt to clothe them in positive ideals, there is little possibility that the young in such a culture will encounter alternative visions or better ways of being. Perhaps, as Hannah Arendt implied, a little hypocrisy is the price we pay for civilization. Another thing we need to understand about the culture of poverty is that it is profoundly *anti-civilization*. It destroys its young, and therefore is dependent on a continuous supply of new members from an exploding birthrate, and from the ongoing recruitment of romantic and gullible young people. Its beliefs and norms are not even those of the herd, for any herd of animals behaves in ways that protect and contribute to the survival of its progeny.

The culture of poverty dominating and perpetuating the underclass is inherently self-destructive. Its economy depends for its vitality and survival on the trafficking of drugs and sex and on various protection rackets, all activities which, in the long run, ravage those who participate in them at any and all levels. Children and women are particularly vulnerable, and tend to be exploited for the immediate gratification of the most powerful. The latter, to succeed by the rules of their subculture, must bury all feelings of empathy for the suffering of their victims. Loyalty to the gang and the demands of substance-dependency eventually supersede all family ties and feelings.

A cruel colonial history has rendered African Americans more vulnerable than other groups to the family breakdown that both precipitates and follows from entrapment in the underclass—and that trend has been accelerating for some time. At the beginning of the 1960s, 80 percent of children classified as black were born into intact families. Thirty-five years later the corresponding figure was only 28 percent. By the late 1990s, black women were over seven times as likely as non-blacks to be incarcerated, while the comparable ratio for black men was nine to one. From 1985 to 1993, the murder rate among black teenagers tripled to 30 percent of all perpetrators, although they made up only 1.2 percent of the population. Every year a far higher proportion of black people than white are victims of violence.

A large part of the explanation for all this is the fact that so many African Americans have become trapped in the underclass. The culture of poverty unique to the underclass encourages its carriers to foul their own nests. The family as a protective and sustaining enclave is inevitably the first casualty, for its requirements and responsibilities are in direct conflict with the rules governing the surrounding culture. Democracy is the second casualty, because the extreme cynicism concerning politicians and belief in conspiracies that are characteristic of mob psychology are endemic here among people of all ethnic backgrounds. The underclass creates—and, indeed requires—members who are nihilistic and sociopathic. It evolves a cultural climate combining the totalitarian rule of neighborhood thugs with an anarchy of interaction at the level of the street and home, a climate that renders the community, in the long run, unfit for human habitation.

DEFUSING THE WAR OF ALL AGAINST ALL

Both the conservative dream of free-enterprise capitalism and the liberal dream of a bottomless well of government funding for needy and affluent alike operate as powerful causal forces in the culture of modern industrial societies. If they were less prevalent or less mythical we might have evolved a more workable economic system: one in which the competition for roles was truly less fettered and the dice less loaded in favor of a relatively few winners, and the children of the winners. We might have recognized that the management of the private sector cannot be left to the short-sighted self-interest of the gamblers in the marketplace, any more than that of the public sector can be left to the *ad hoc* reactions of pressure politics. Without these myths, we might be able to devise an income system in which the share of the GDP going to any particular necessary social function would not be monopolized by the few who had made it to the very top of the heap. We might even discover that it is not beyond human ingenuity to institute disincentives to discourage the "star" or "winner take all" custom of rewarding people who have been propelled into uniquely favorable and exploitative positions.

An authentically competitive economy would respond adaptively to all the rewards and punishments actually influencing choices in any part of the system, and in any government program within it. Every position carries with it a bundle of incentives and disincentives—all those reinforcing consequences (both positive and negative) attendant on one's performance of the role. These include the following: (1) income (from wages or other sources); (2) degree and relative scarcity of the *actual* skills and aptitudes required coupled with the nature and cost of the necessary training or preparation; (3) social status or prestige associated with the role; (4) power to influence events and people; (5) security of tenure and pension, and of life, limb and general health; (6) degree of control over the duration and regularity of one's daily working hours and of the pattern of work and leisure time involved; (7) psychological esteem (or stress) contingent on an awareness of contributing to, and being responsible for, the common good; (8) degree of inherently rewarding intellectual or physical challenge; (9) special privileges or costs such as potential for public recognition (or castigation) and opportunity (or requirement) for extended travel and various subsidized benefits and holidays; and (10) perceived meaningfulness of the associated tasks.

If competition for roles in the economy was actually based on a free market with real equality of opportunity, we might discover that a position with many natural incentives *other than income* (such as power, prestige, freedom to determine priorities, and opportunities to be intellectually challenged) required a lower monetary incentive in order to attract sufficient applicants. Conversely, jobs fraught with danger and stress, while being traditionally disparaged by society, might go begging in the absence of the compensation of relatively high wages—*if potential workers really had a choice.* However, one of the difficulties to be resolved in establishing conditions for a workable incentive system at the economic level is that the reinforcements associated with various positions are often not readily alterable. Many are provided by the larger culture, and values do not change overnight. A position of power provides countless opportunities for the accumulation of wealth, and privileges invariably follow. In other cases, the operative reinforcements (both positive and negative) are integral to the nature of the role itself. Clearly, brain surgery is more stressful and demanding of the extensive education and specialized skills that attract public recognition—and appear to justify privilege—than is landscape painting. Fire-fighting and policing are inherently more dangerous and less influential and prestigious than is judging.

A second source of difficulty lies in the dynamic and contingent nature of both the economy and the educational or training organizations servicing it. Together, these constitute a complex system within which detailed, ideologically directed, large-scale planning is inherently unworkable. What is required, instead, is a pragmatic approach combining openness to feedback with continuous evaluation. There is an inevitable time lag between the recognition by job-seekers that their skills are no longer in short supply, and the possibility of a resulting systemic adjustment in incentives. The less bureaucratic the system, however, the more continuous will be the adjustment.

The point is that income is the most readily alterable factor in the mix, and it is this that would tend to be evened out in any *authentically* open competition for roles. This course would require a commitment to equality of opportunity for all to be educated according to their abilities and interests, with a job of some kind for all able-bodied adults at the end of their preparation. Inevitably, government would have an active role as the employer of last resort. Another requirement is that all current institutionalized obstacles to the occasionally necessary *downward* adjustment of salaries would have to be removed from the system: notably, the resistance of managers and professional organizations and unions to this sort of adaptive flexibility in the face of changing circumstances.

Such a program might even force us to confront the possibility that society would have to pay more for those who patrol the streets in the effort to protect the public—or for those who operate in the front lines of inner-city high schools and hospital emergency rooms—than for those who sit in the grandeur and authority of the courts, or administer the hospital, or manage the corporation or are free to follow their research interests in the security of the university. An understanding of all this might help to bring home to even the most privileged of the winners among us the size of the current gulf between our myth and our practice of an equality-based, free-enterprise economy.

THE TRAGEDY OF THE COMMONS

Garrett Hardin originated the concept of "the tragedy of the commons" in his 1977 book of the same name. He was referring to what tends to happen when a resource (such as a community pasture) is shared by all. It soon becomes apparent that the immediate advantages of limitless overuse are more readily discernible to the individual than is the group's need to maintain the sustainability of the resource for the longer-term benefit of everyone. This is a remarkably powerful concept which goes to the heart of our continuing failure to educate society's members in the terms discussed in Chapter 4. It explains what is occurring in a variety of situations today—not only in public places and the environment but in the case of welfare and government-supported health-insurance programs of all kinds. Most programs and facilities designed for the entire population and subsidized by government are vulnerable to this human tendency which, if not restrained and redirected in specifically planned ways, could be suicidal for the planet. It is the drive to achieve immediate gratification, and gain for self and family, at the expense of more abstract and long-term considerations having to do with conservation of natural resources and the public good.

The pressures promoting the destruction of the commons are operative in the culture of affluence as well as the culture of poverty. In both cases the readily available, immediate reinforcement of our individualistic drive for self-aggrandizement results in consequences that feed back to destroy all those public amenities and fundamental institutions crucial to the long-term survival of any group. An example of this is the tragedy overtaking the world's fish stocks. Governments see it as more politically advantageous to refuse to achieve or honor international and interstate agreements on measures for controlling the annual fish catch and protecting habitats than it is to do what is necessary to ensure a supply over the long term. Another example is the physical deterioration of public places such as parks and playgrounds, as they have been encroached upon by the homeless who are then followed by prostitutes and their pimps and johns—and then by the drug dealers and ruthless gangs. Such a takeover favors the invaders for the time being, until the level of violence drives out the truly needy, and those selling their bodies are no longer safe to ply their pitiful and demoralizing trade. There is no immediate gain for individuals among the productive classes to clean up the public places. It is easier and more immediately fruitful for them merely to avoid such areas and to provide their own children with private clubs and sports centers. The same thing has happened in the case of public schools and is contributing similarly to their deterioration.

The tragedy of the commons operates in more subtle ways as well. It applies to the use (and abuse) of universal public services of all kinds. Those physicians and dentists who insist on being overpaid while they over-prescribe, over-treat, cheat on their submitted bills and participate in insurance scams; patients who over-use expensive, subsidized facilities: all clearly benefit in the short run. But in the long term, government-funded services flounder because of exploding costs, and private insurance leaps out of the reach of ordinary lower-middle-class citizens. Similarly, it is clearly to the short-term career advantage of a politician to cater to the most vocal interest groups—the ones controlling the most votes—even though this prevents the government from making the difficult choices necessary for solving worsening problems. Another example is the way in which those journalists and talk-show hosts who exaggerate the failings of politicians, and are the most vocal in trashing reputations, are often rewarded by immediate boosts to their careers. But democracy is the victim of this mutually destructive downward spiral in civility and concern for the public good.

GENERATIONAL SHIFTS BETWEEN THE TWO CULTURES

To what extent are children born into our own North American culture of poverty condemned to remain within it? Or, conversely, what proportion of the children of the affluent fall into the underclass? This gets at the issue of social mobility, either up or down in the social structure. Another way of asking the question is "Just how open or closed is the new form of knowledge-based class system now beginning to characterize all modern industrial societies?"

Traditionally, immigrant societies such as those of the United States and Canada were relatively open in this sense. People with a great variety of abilities came to the new countries and worked at menial jobs, intending to save and get ahead. The society they entered was egalitarian compared to the situation today. The gap between those in the top third of the income pyramid and those in the bottom third was not as wide as it has since become, nor as it was in the aristocratic societies which most of the immigrants had left behind. It is true that there was a small group at the top in North America who were extremely wealthy but, for the most part, their wealth had been achieved in one or two generations and was being re-invested into expanding, job-producing business enterprises. Most could still brag of being "self-made" successes. So the dream of upward mobility for one's children seemed a not-impossible general cultural goal. During and after World War II the economy was growing rapidly and the need for superior-ability candidates for higher learning from among the working and lower-middle classes seemed limitless. The generational shift upwards was rapid and widespread and apparently dictated by the nature of things.

Throughout the 1950s and 1960s an expanding economy and university system ensured that there was plenty of "room at the top"—so much so that a large contingent of the children of the already-secure middle class felt free to drop out for the time being. For some that "time being" turned out to be the rest of their lives, and the drop they took was a free fall into the newly emerging underclass. Little in their privileged backgrounds had prepared them for the bitter knowledge that the culture of poverty, like a lobster trap, is easier to drift into than ever to escape.

Countless others have ended in the same place in the decades since, merely because they had to begin their struggle too close to the bottom and with too many cards stacked against them. This forces us to ask why it is that the school has not operated for the children of the underclass as it has usually done for the children of immigrants—even those newcomers who have had to cope with learning a second language. Why has that same educational system not been the means by which youngsters raised in the culture of poverty are helped to overcome the disadvantages imposed by their home environments and to achieve more than their parents did?

The answer is that many immigrant families are caught in a *situation* of poverty in their new homeland but not in the *culture* of poverty. Their family subculture predisposes them to define themselves in terms of the goals and professed ideals of the larger society and they tend to progress accordingly. In addition, people who choose the difficult route of pulling up stakes and moving to a new country are likely to be highly ambitious and generously endowed with the work ethic. They are similarly likely to pass on these qualities to their children through family socialization. What is happening to the children of the underclass is a very different story.

THE SCHOOL AS AN AGENT OF SOCIAL MOBILITY

The school system required to operate as the vehicle of social mobility in a democratic but only nominally egalitarian society has been assigned an impossible task. This is especially the case where there is a steepening income pyramid and a relatively impermeable underclass. In addition to educating, the school is expected to sort and select those who pass through it—ensuring equality of opportunity for all to achieve a role in life commensurate with their abilities and interests. Even if the society were egalitarian in fact as well as ideal, the task would be daunting.

The fact is that the *total desirability quotients* of roles in North American society (the sums of their associated incentives and disincentives) are very unequal and likely to remain so for the foreseeable future. As long as this situation of general social inequality holds, the school can function only in a strictly meritocratic role. It can attempt to operate as the most honest possible ladder of upward mobility for those destined to be designated the winners by our current cultural value system. It can also do its best to influence cultural values by emphasizing the importance to society of roles not presently highly rewarded in terms of power, prestige and special privilege—and by providing potential winners with experience working at the lower end of the income scale.

A meritocratic educational system is very susceptible to corruption because, in order to be valid and reliable, it must accomplish a distasteful and inherently anti-educational task. It demands a high attrition rate in the upper reaches of the schooling process so that the majority are selected out before reaching the top of the university ladder leading to high-status professional and executive positions. Otherwise, there is likely to be a large number of unemployed or underemployed graduates. This often requires a periodic artificial narrowing of the gates, in response to the perception of a surplus of supply that might put pressures on the incomes of the previous generation of winners. All this means that, if the most intelligent lower-status youngsters are to progress by means of schooling, almost as many individuals must be propelled down from the status of their parents as are being helped to climb up. Exceptions occur only in the case of revolutionary technological breakthroughs and periods of extraordinarily rapid growth of the economy, and in situations where the birthrates of high and low socioeconomic families differ markedly.

The difficulty for any school system in a non-egalitarian meritocracy is that it cannot do very much to alter the social structure. It can only determine which individuals will climb to the top of it; and the more that its resources are devoted to this task the less able it is to focus on what should be its primary goal: providing *effective* equality of opportunity for intellectual and social development to all comers.

An even more serious problem is currently looming for the school in its service to society in North America. We now have a large and growing contingent of children entering the system who have been raised entirely within the culture of poverty. Many of these children have been so spiritually, intellectually and even organically crippled by their pre- and post-natal experiences that there is little that the busy classroom teacher can do for them. All imaginable forms of grievous harm have been imposed upon them before their birth by self-indulgent smokers and drinkers and drug-addicted parents, and by abusive and neglectful caregivers in the years that followed. This problem is spiraling in gravity and pervasiveness. We have not even begun to cope with all its ramifications, much less seek out and treat the causes of it.

This brings us back once more to the issue of unfortunate outsiders existing in the midst of the affluent society: those purveyors and victims of the culture of poverty that is steadily encroaching on the walls that the rest of us have attempted to build around our privileged enclaves. A society burdened with a non-communicating dual culture of affluent "knows" and alienated "know-nots" is inherently unstable and vulnerable to encroaching chaos and violence. No democracy can afford to ignore the worrisome potential posed by the existence of two such hostile solitudes.

REFERENCES

Bradley, Harriet. *Fractured Identities: Changing Patterns of Inequality*. Cambridge, MA: Polity Press, 1996.

Canadian Department of Finance. *Economic Reference Tables*. Ottawa, ON: Statistics Canada, 1995.

Canadian Department of Industry. *Employment Earnings and Hours*. Ottawa, ON: Statistics Canada, 1997.

Charvet, John. *A Critique of Freedom and Equality*. New York, NY: Cambridge University Press, 1981.

Dalphin, John. *The Persistence of Social Inequality in America*. Cambridge, MA: Schenckman, 1981.

Hardin, Garrett. *The Tragedy of the Commons*. San Francisco, CA: W. H. Freeman, 1977.

Herrnstein, Richard and Murray, C. *The Bell Curve*. New York, NY: The Free Press, 1994.

Hutcheon, Pat Duffy. "Abandoning the Liberal Quest?" *Perspectives on Political Science* 23, 4 (1994): 174–177.

———. "Obscuring the Message and Killing the Messenger: The Bell Curve." *Perspectives on Political Science* 25, 1 (1996): 15–18.

Itzkoff, Seymour W. *The Road to Equality: Evolution and Social Reality*. Westport, CT: Praeger, 1992.

Jencks, Christopher et al. *Inequality: An Assessment of the Effect of Family and Schooling in America*. New York, NY: Basic Books, 1972.

Lasch, Christopher. *The Revolt of the Elites and the Betrayal of Democracy*. New York, NY: W. W. Norton, 1995.

Lewis, Oscar. *Anthropological Essays*. New York, NY: Random House, 1946.

McAll, Christopher. *Class, Ethnicity, and Social Inequality*. Montreal, PQ: Queens–McGill University Press, 1990.

Richards, John. *Retooling the Welfare State*. Toronto, ON: C.D. Howe Institute, 1998.

Tavris, Carol. *The Mismeasure of Woman*. New York, NY: Simon and Schuster, 1992.

Westergaard, John H. *Who Gets What? The Hardening of Class Inequality in the Late Twentieth Century*. Cambridge, MA: Polity Press, 1995.

CHAPTER 9

A Culture of Pluralism
or a Culture of Tribalism?

The two class-dominated worlds described in the previous chapter are not the only subcultural systems that shape and limit views and behaviors in North America. Another influential representational world stems from the urge for clan survival buried deep within us all. It is the troubling culture of tribalism which is threatening to overwhelm pluralist societies almost everywhere in the world today. Einstein viewed tribal nationalism as a disease of cultures frozen in a stage of infancy or adolescence. He described it as the measles of civilization; and, like a measles epidemic, he said, it can erupt and ravage almost anywhere.

Today we are witnessing a troubling re-emergence of tribalism in many guises. In this chapter we will examine the biological and cultural origins of the phenomenon and argue that, although its causes are many, tribalism is greatly encouraged by a general lack of knowledge concerning evolution. Too many people are unaware that, while the tribal urges existing to some degree in all of us have their basis in our biological programming, they are given expression by our culture. The genetic component of tribal behavior is rooted in the "kin selection" common to all higher animals and discussed in previous chapters. The cultural component is usually the overriding one, however, and it is another matter entirely. Culture is programmed by experience and—in the symbolic form by which we typically define it—is unique to humans. It is an indication of the depth and prevalence of ignorance concerning biology and evolutionary theory that the majority of the population in North America continues to attribute cultural differences to the genes, and to support or oppose tribal pretensions on those terms. In fact, the very concept of "black culture"—so popular today—reinforces this misunderstanding, implying as it does that culture is determined by the color of one's skin.

APPLYING THE EVOLUTIONARY SYSTEMS MODEL

At the root of these confusions is a failure to comprehend three major aspects of the all-encompassing process of biological and cultural evolution. The first is its hierarchical nature, dictating that different units of analysis and laws of relationship are required for analyzing different levels or systems within the process—regardless of the fact that some form of selective feedback operates throughout. The second is that genetic, psychological and cultural aspects of evolution are inextricably intertwined—to the extent that attempts to isolate the influence of nature from that of nurture in any complex behavior are likely to fail. The third is that the group, as such, is not an evolutionarily meaningful entity.

The concept of hierarchy demands that all existence be viewed as evolution in progress, from the mechanistic causal relations at the physical level, to the "self-replicating" units generated eons ago by some particularly conducive chance arrangement of chemicals deep within the oceans of the earth's surface, to the phenotypes that began to function according to a new kind of causality. These were the first complex, dynamic, self-organizing feedback systems, in that their adaptive success within the environment was determined by the effects of the self-copying process that formed them. Richard Dawkins has explained how, once this phenotype threshold was passed, replicators had a means of surviving "by virtue of proxies, their consequences on the world" (Dawkins 1995: 153). This is the source of the contingent causality that replaced its mechanistic counterpart at the physical level. Dawkins surmises that replicator teams were the next step: one which subsequently allowed for the generation of simple cells and, ultimately, the eukaryotic cells of all living things—and the teaming-up of these. For our purposes, the next evolutionary-systems transition of significance was the emergence of the complex nervous system which gave rise to animal sentience and animal social life, all of which set the stage for the crucial transition into language that led to human self-consciousness.

Social science is concerned with three distinctive levels of interaction. The first of these is *the nervous system* which generates the sensorimotor responses to environmental stimuli studied by neuropsychologists. A knowledge of genes and their functioning—and of the molecular biology and chemistry basic to this—is necessary here, but it is the consequences of genetic programming for the human *organism* that provide the focus of study at this level. The second level of concern is with the nature of the self-conscious, believing, valuing and acting person. It is the *psychological system* resulting from the emergence of human communicative and conceptual capacities, and its focus is individual behaviors—whether overt (and thus directly observable) or covert, as in thought and language. It deals, as well, with the means by which these behaviors are acquired and sustained (or discouraged and eliminated) by surrounding contingencies. The third level is the *sociocultural system*: the world of collective ideas, arts, ideals and customs; and of ideologies and scientific theories and knowledge. It is also the world of technological tools—and of the social organizations which, if informed by reliable knowledge, gain the potential to function in a self-correcting feedback capacity as collective instruments of adaptive intelligence. The explosion of computer technology since the 1980s seems to have brought us to yet another transition point in cultural evolution: to the generation of a global digital culture with a capacity for asynchronous interactive feedback—the ramifications of which we can scarcely imagine, much less predict.

Just as our current cultural world emerged out of the possibilities generated by the organism's crossing of the critical language threshold, so, too, is the new digital culture a thoroughly natural product of precipitating conditions. All such levels of culture are the subjects of sociology and anthropology—and of the social psychology that attempts to study how all this comes together in the unifying concept of socialization. The latter process, through which the learner becomes a cultural being, demands some knowledge of how all three systems operate and affect one another. Edward O. Wilson has suggested the word "consilience" to describe the identification of explanations, such as those involved in socialization, that link together facts and conjectures across disciplines.

Social scientists now realize, as many failed to do in the past, that we cannot afford to ignore reliable findings about the systems of organic functioning out of which our psychological and cultural aptitudes evolved. Nor can we continue to spin theories that are inconsistent with that knowledge. However, this does not mean that explanations of psycho-sociocultural regularities can simply be reduced to those at the lower levels, as transcendentally inspired physicists and a few evolutionarily oriented "pop" psychologists demand. That road leads either to the dead-end of transcendental mysticism or back to genetic determinism: to the Social Darwinism that caused the revulsion against biology which has crippled social science for a century. The work of twentieth-century scholars such as Julian Huxley and Roger Sperry indicates that, on the contrary, the higher-level systems tend to exert control over those at lower levels of the evolutionary hierarchy. We need only be reminded of the power of culture discussed in Chapter 1.

Genetic determinism contradicts all that we know about socialization. It is also inconsistent with the second major implication of the evolutionary systems model: that all human behaviors are likely to be products of the complex, interactive feedback process described by Edward

O. Wilson as "gene-culture co-evolution," and illustrated throughout this book by the metaphor of the "triple helix." Nurture is inextricably intertwined with both the physical and social aspects of nature in the evolution of learned behaviors and components of culture. As was pointed out earlier, culture is indeed heritable, but not in the biological sense. Although rooted in the social behaviors arising from genetic evolution, culture is transmitted across the generations in the form of customs, artifacts, technology, ideas, ideals, ideologies, knowledge, written and recorded music and computer programs. Culture is both learned and contributed to (or forgotten and discarded) by individuals during the course of a single lifetime. It is Lamarckian in that it is acquired through experience rather than carried in the genes. This means that culture is subject to far more rapid cumulative change than is its biological counterpart.

However, there *are* similarities. Like the human species carrying them, idea systems (and the institutions to which they give rise) evolve in response to environmental contingencies. As with the phenotypic manifestations of genes, whether or not particular cultural components survive depends on the degree to which they enable their carriers to cope with the challenges of changing surroundings—including the evolved advantages of competitors. In both cases we have the operation of a vehicle of adaptation. At the psychological level the basic principle of reinforcement functions to select the *behaviors and beliefs* that are learned by individuals—just as it operates to select their collective *knowledge, ideals and customs* at the sociocultural level. At the biological level natural selection weeds out the maladaptive *individuals* before they can reproduce.

In neither situation is the *group* an evolutionarily meaningful entity, other than that it provides a protected space-and-time bound locale for the individuals within it, as well as the interactive context within which evolutionarily stable strategies can develop and function. These strategies are ways of relating to others that work most of the time to ensure the survival of the genes of most of those engaging in them. Such stabilized social patterns are carried from generation to generation as if they were genetically transmitted. Although it is the group context that makes this possible, the group, as such, does not evolve, either biologically or culturally.

Genes (as the crucial self-replicators) play the most basic role in biological evolution, for two reasons. Their copying errors (mutations) are the source of change; and the alterations in bodily architecture to which these give rise accumulate down the generations to the degree that they contribute to the successful reproduction of the organisms carrying them. Increasing complexity of the species results from this. In the analogous case of learning, it is the behaviors and beliefs of the individual that are selected by their consequences for furthering that person's capacity to adapt to challenges—or for gratifying the inner urge for power. Where culture is concerned it is the institutions—grounded in the ideologies, evolved scientific knowledge, technological imperatives, customs and ideals of those who perform roles within them and achieve their identity by means of them—that are selected by circumstances, refined and elaborated, and transmitted from generation to generation. The process does indeed affect the success of the group, "but group welfare is always a fortuitous consequence, not a primary drive" (Dawkins 1995: 122). This is an important understanding that may prevent the traditional tendency to group people in terms of so-called race or skin color or class and to predict the performance of individuals on the basis of average group scores of attributes such as intelligence. It may also prevent the newly popular practice of identifying individuals in terms of the values and beliefs of their ancestral group.

THE GENETIC AND SOCIAL ORIGINS OF "IN-GROUP" EXCLUSIVENESS

The defining feature of tribalism is this urge for "in-group" exclusiveness. We should understand that it is one of the most natural and pervasive of human behaviors. Studies of kin selection indicate that clannishness has a biological basis and is shared by all social animals. Furthermore, the social environment usually provides additional reinforcement—especially where humans are concerned. It requires only the smallest chance occurrence to set off a fragmenting social process that is extremely difficult to stem or redirect. It seems to be extraordinarily satisfying and ego-bolstering to establish an offending "other" and to define one's own group in opposing terms. But, whereas this ancient proclivity provided obvious benefits in pre-historic and earlier historic times, it is now a major threat to the survival of our species. In light of this, it might be argued that the wise course at the present time would be to seek every means available to *inhibit* rather than to *reinforce* our tribal urges.

In immigrant societies such as those of North America and Australia, a too-rapid intake—or a too-concentrated settlement—of newcomers may contribute to an accelerating tendency to define people by observable indicators of "race" or ethnic background such as skin color or religious dress. In the case of the newcomers themselves, it is understandable that they might emphasize tribal "belongingness" for reasons of security in a new and challenging set of circumstances. The ethnic group provides the bond of common experience without which empathy is impossible. It offers a closed community capable of enforcing familiar norms from the homeland. It is similarly not surprising that, as the pressures caused by rapid and unevenly dispersed immigration build, more and more of the native-born might also succumb to the call of the tribe: the longer-established European one. When this happens it is usually referred to as a "racist backlash."

There are also broader cultural/historical reasons why the issue of tribal identity is evoking such strong emotional responses in a number of countries at this particular time. Hannah Arendt, the political philosopher, noted that there was a resurgence of tribal nationalism in Europe during the early nineteenth century when old political borders and old national loyalties were disintegrating. The same phenomenon can be seen in Europe today with the fall of communism—and in Africa, with the liberation from colonialism that began in the 1960s. The accelerating move to globalization is no doubt part of the problem as well. Political instability, whatever the cause, is inevitably an important source of the attraction of tribalism. As federal and unitary nation states show signs of faltering, the resulting insecurity fuels the tendency to look inward for comfort and support—to the extended family and kinship group or clan. Given all this, as well as the confusion of values and lack of direction characteristic of modern industrial societies, it should not be surprising that many families are turning back for cultural nourishment to an older source of values and beliefs.

Also pertinent is the fact that the tribal myth exerts a strong romantic pull in the individual psyche. Many developments in modern industrialized society appear to be reinforcing this. Tribalism has long been associated with the tradition of Romanticism in Western cultures. Since the 1960s we have witnessed a wholesale turning back to nineteenth-century romantic idealism, combined with a distrust and rejection of science, among large segments of the academic elite. Even in the absence of socialization from this source, however, the call of the tribe is extraordinarily seductive. It is no less than the age-old urge to escape life's hard realities and join in an imagined "oneness" of blood and ancestral spirit. It answers the need to belong; to accept an authority capable of transcending and refuting both reason and the testimony of daily experience. It massages the ego and creates a tendency to blind obedience and mass hysteria. Dinesh d'Souza concludes, in *The End of Racism*, that we must fight it with every weapon available to a democracy, because not only is tribalism inherently destructive to the society at large, it destroys all moral capacity in the individual in-group member as well. As Glenn C. Loury reminds us in his 1995 book about race and responsibility in America, although the call of the tribe is seductive, it is ultimately a siren call.

THE SIREN CALL OF BLOOD AND BELIEF

Are there problems here for the future of the pluralist civic society and the modern liberal democratic state that has for so long defined and defended it? For a number of reasons there may be real cause for concern. To some extent the propensity to define individuals according to ties of "blood and belief" sets up a cultural evolutionary process that feeds on itself. It both requires and perpetuates the nursing of past grievances and in-group mythologies. Often ethnic and religious boundaries coincide, and this can make for an "us-them" world view with great power to command unquestioning commitment and to render more abstract national loyalties insignificant in comparison. And, to the degree that any particular group's celebrated (or abhorred) differences are explained biologically rather than culturally, we get a revival of racist ideologies. Thus, the process inevitably contributes not only to a dangerous weakening of national institutions, but to a flurry of demands for entitlements based on race. All this can readily spiral into a full-fledged force for tribal "sovereignty" or separation along ethnic lines, accompanied by a racist backlash on the part of the majority against all minority groups.

Sometimes the tribal myth can lead people trapped in the underclass to seek justification and blame for their predicament in a group history of exploitation by the establishment which controlled the country for centuries. They rightly conclude that their current situation is due more to that history than to individual life choices, but they are wrong in ignoring the very real socioeconomic and cultural factors involved. This applies to the condition of the Irish Catholics in Northern Ireland today, and to large numbers of North Americans of African background whose ancestors were brought over as slaves, and to the aboriginal populations. It is all too easy to move from the conclusion that racism was the original source of our problems to the idea that the only way to better our position today is through collective action on a racially defined basis.

Race is not really the appropriate word here, for we are all mongrels to some degree. The earliest evolved progenitors of the human race began to move out of Africa—and to evolve varying geographically specific adaptive traits—only about 100,000 years ago. Especially in North America, we are incredibly intertwined genetically, as is indicated by the extensive observable variations of pigmentation and facial features within the population. Archeological evidence now suggests that even our aboriginal ancestors came from different origins and arrived in successive waves over a period of at least 30,000 years.

"Racist" or "race-thinking" may still be useful terms, however, to denote the habit of classifying oneself and others according to skin color or other biologically inherited attributes, a habit that tribalism seems to encourage. If the racist way of behaving is undesirable, and the pluralist believes firmly that it is, surely it is undesirable wherever it occurs. It would seem that we should actively discourage it even when previously discriminated-against minorities engage in it, and especially when governments design policies in terms of it.

In spite of popular notions to the contrary, our differences, great as they may seem, are primarily *cultural* in origin and should be recognized as such. It is entirely possible that many who today define themselves as Latino or African or Native may have more in common with their fellows in the underclass—regardless of skin color or place of ancestral origin—than they have with affluent members of their own identifiable ethnic group. We should be aware that often what is viewed as racial discrimination is really discrimination of some other kind that has an *ethnically differential* impact because of the accidents of history and the cultural impediments that this history has provoked and perpetuated. For example, a policeman might have very rational, experience-based grounds for checking up on a group of dark-skinned youths eying parked cars on a quiet street in an American city, even though no crime has been observed. Similarly, job discrimination based on educational criteria could result quite legitimately in the relative underemployment of aboriginal and Jamaican Canadians, and the overemployment of those with Asian backgrounds. The solution is not to discard or subvert relevant selection criteria and standards, as some would demand, but to improve the qualifications of the individuals who lose out in the race for such jobs. The racist definition of social problems—employed by tribalists of all shades of skin—shifts attention away from all the very real cultural and economic causes and necessary solutions; and that may be the most damaging of all the consequences of our current rush to tribalism.

CULTURAL RELATIVISM AND MULTICULTURALISM

A perspective which has functioned to legitimize the new varieties of tribalism in modern industrialized societies is known as "cultural relativism." It is a non-negotiable ideology based on the premise that no particular cultural attribute or custom is better or worse than any other. Cultural relativism is associated with "moral relativism" (the belief that there are no universally applicable or objectively justifiable values) and subjectivism or "perspectivism." The latter are epistemological theories that deny the possibility of objective knowledge. Perspectivism places particular emphasis on the role of power relationships and linguistic constructs in the assertion and imposition of truth claims. Although this view has a certain surface plausibility, it is loaded with contradictions. Indeed, where human culture is concerned, relativists appear to exist in a strangely absolute world of Platonic "essences." It is almost as if each individual is viewed as a personification of some sort of immutable ideal culture, the intact preservation of which is the only insurance of the identity of that individual. It follows from such a premise that any challenge to an ancestral custom—or adverse judgment of it, or encouragement of adaptive change—is interpreted as a threat to the fundamental human dignity of the persons concerned.

The ideology of cultural relativism was to find its ultimate expression in the demands of the African-American activists in the United States and their white liberal civil rights supporters during the latter decades of the century. As in the case of all ideologies, the premise that no particular set of cultural beliefs and practices is in any sense better than any other had seldom been questioned or tested by its upholders and proselytizers. Many well-meaning people were both justifiably ashamed of the imperialism and slavery characterizing the past record of their own culture, and innocently unaware of the universal prevalence of such practices throughout history. For them a cultural relativism that subtly denigrated Western civilization simply felt too good not to be true. This held even more for the descendants of the victims of past abuses. Cultural relativism was also superbly suited to the movement for multiculturalism that had been effectively displacing that of biculturalism in Canada.

Because the Canadian case in some ways represents the extreme of what is being experienced by every pluralist democracy today, it may be enlightening to examine it in some detail. In 1971 the government of Pierre Trudeau—intending to promote tolerance of cultural diversity while at the same time making French-English biculturalism more widely acceptable—proclaimed a policy of multiculturalism. An Act to confirm the policy in law was finalized and became official only in 1988, during the tenure of the Brian Mulroney government. From the beginning, the principles and program objectives of multiculturalism were incompatible and confused. Cultural retention (undefined) was to be promoted, along with acquisition of one of the country's two official languages, together with encouragement of participation by minorities in Canadian society in order to ensure equality of opportunity for all. No priorities were established among these aims. It should have been obvious that, in the absence of clearly spelled-out restrictions on cultural retention on the part of incoming groups, the other objectives would be impossible to achieve. And, conversely, if the goals of a common language and integration were indeed emphasized, there would be no way to retain one's ethnic culture exactly as it had existed in the homeland, or (in the case of aboriginals) in some far-distant, romanticized past. Perhaps recognizing this, those working within the program (many of whom have a vested interest in preserving ethnic identification) have tended to focus on cultural retention for minority groups only and to ignore, or at least underplay, the principles fundamental to the Canadian civic society as a whole.

In effect, then, this legislation has provided financing for programs aimed at celebrating and maintaining ethnic-based *differences*. The sum of $26 million per year was devoted to the enterprise. Now, over ten years and some hundred million dollars later, the results of this well-intentioned act are being assessed. Critics of the program wonder whether, in an era of proliferating tribal nationalisms and worldwide demands for ethnic-based segregation, it is really necessary to reinforce such propensities with scarce tax dollars. To many, this seems inordinately perverse in light of the fact that the very existence of Canada is now being threatened from within by the demands for sovereignty of two of its founding groups—the Quebecois and the aboriginals—both of whom have come to feel increasingly relegated to the sidelines by the multiculturalists. On the other hand, the program's numerous vocal supporters argue with equal vehemence that there is an essentially unifying value in the formal expression of a collective willingness to respect and celebrate the multitude of subcultures brought to the country by successive waves of immigrants.

The debate being carried on today in Canada is not too different from that occurring in the United States and other countries with populations of varying backgrounds. Thus far, the American case is more often framed in terms of the need to ensure equality for African Americans—and of the "anti-Eurocentric" changes in educational curricula and the affirmative action presumed to be required for this—rather than the potential political separation of ethnic enclaves. However, what is apparent is a difference in emphasis only. The rising demands for independence in Hawaii, and the battles in Canadian universities over whether minorities should get special treatment and "proportional representation"—and whether the ideas of "dead white Western men" should continue to monopolize the agenda—are indications that the forces at work are common to both societies. In fact, Martin Loney has provided compelling evidence of the pervasiveness and increasingly adverse consequences of preferential hiring in Canada in his 1998 book, *The Pursuit of Division*.

Sometime during the late 1970s, multiculturalism began to edge out non-discriminatory integration as the political goal for which the tide of cultural relativism flowing from the universities provided the theoretical underpinnings. In the United States, African Americans were encouraged by many of their white liberal supporters and their new, increasingly militant leaders—such as Elijah Muhammed and his follower Louis Farrakhan—to turn from the struggle for racial equality and non-discrimination and integration marked out by Martin Luther King. They were told that the majority culture had nothing of particular worth to offer; that they would never really be free of the slavery-tainted past until they had returned to the culture of their ancestors, the culture of Africa. Farrakhan even claimed that whites must be recognized as the enemy, and Christianity as the chief cultural tool by means of which the black man has been exploited for centuries.

Although most black Americans rejected the explicitly racist position of Louis Farrakhan, a majority of liberals of all backgrounds swung to the support of race-based affirmative action programs. While this may appear contradictory, it is abundantly understandable in the context of multiculturalism and the premise of cultural relativism on which it is grounded. If one believes that there exists a "black culture" (as a distinctive way of life shaping the attitudes and mores of the dark-skinned population in the United States) and that it is of equal worth and workability to that represented by Western civilization as it evolved from its Ancient Classical heritage to the present modern universal scientific/technological culture, then two conclusions must follow. The first is that, *given* equality of opportunity, those defined by skin color as members of the black group will *in fact* come to be proportionately represented in every occupational level and institutional arena of society. The second is that, if this does not happen within a reasonable time, the fault must lie not in any cultural complex of values and habits that may have evolved out of the experience of slavery and subsequent entrapment in the underclass, but in a subtle persistence of systemic racism. The majority culture itself must be riddled with racist attitudes and practices. Affirmative action programs were therefore designed to put pressure on employers and educational administrators to make sure that "proportional representation" on the basis of race does indeed become a fact of American life. If this necessitates numerous race-based decisions and considerable discrimination *against* worthy individuals who happen to have the wrong skin color then so be it. The means may be regrettable, but it is all in the service of the greater good!

The problem is that, when the country's unifying symbols and traditions and standards of excellence are being trod underfoot, those whose commitment is to the national civic culture are made to feel like a threatened minority as well, and the entire country begins to dissolve into an aggregate of hostile camps. For example, nothing is more important to the American civic society than the tradition of the "melting pot," and of individual (rather than collective) rights in society; and of the evolving common language that makes it all possible. Of similar significance throughout the history of Canada has been a commitment to the "biculturalism" on which the nation was founded, as contrasted to multiculturalism. Riding roughshod over the very sentiments that comprise the glue so necessary for holding the entire society together, while showing ready deference to conflicting customs favored by each of the components, is not the way to ensure a happy integration of the old and new. It amounts to a dangerously reckless testing of the tolerance of "the silent majority," certain of whom may already feel themselves to be among the country's least fortunate.

The fear of being labeled racist stultifies honest debate about these issues. Neil Bissoondath, the Trinidadian-born Canadian novelist, said, "I think that white people can't really defend themselves against the excesses of multiculturalism any more. They are so easily cowed by charges of racism" (Bissoondath 1994b). Dinesh d'Souza made the same comment concerning the American scene in his book *The End of Racism*. Bissoondath, in *Selling Illusions: The Cult of Multiculturalism in Canada*, expressed the fear that the policy of official multiculturalism, far from promoting understanding and acceptance, has instead divided citizens by underscoring differences. One could add that, in the process, the policy may have communicated the dangerously false idea (premised on the ideology of cultural relativism) that it is inappropriate to criticize and make judgments about any aspect of an immigrant or minority culture. All too often people are branded racist merely for critically assessing particular cultural practices.

If we continue in our present direction, long-established white-skinned settlers may feel impelled to join the tribal dance as well—and the group they form is likely to be a powerful and ugly one. We already have the phenomenon of an exploding, home-bred Nazi movement in many countries. The desire of separatists in Quebec to identify those citizens of French ancestry as a "people" is a manifestation of this same tribal urge. Stephen Carter, in his book *Reflections of an Affirmative Action Baby*, quotes Anthony Appiah on this point, "Talk of 'race' is particularly distressing," Appiah noted, "for those of us who take culture seriously" (Carter 1991: 40). According to Appiah, wherever it is assumed that observable "racial" attributes are the causes of complex behaviors, what is actually occurring is the "biologizing" of what is really cultural; Social Darwinism, in other words.

The advantage of being able to discuss our problems in terms of culture rather than race is that culture is a human invention, and can be altered by humans so that it better serves the needs of the *total* group. Any policy that subordinates the culture of the country as a whole to those of its subgroups—and encourages ethnic or tribal identity at the expense of the identity of the national or world community—will be destructive for everyone in the long run. Michael Ignatieff, in *Blood and Belonging*, pointed out that "the only reliable antidote to ethnic nationalism turns out to be civic nationalism, because the only guarantee that ethnic groups will live side by side in peace is shared loyalty to a state strong enough, fair enough, equitable enough, to command their obedience" (Ignatieff 1993: 185). Ignatieff also noted that there is a close connection between belonging and violence. "The more strongly you feel the bonds of belonging to your own group," he said "the more hostile, the more violent will your feelings be to outsiders" (188). This accords with the sentiments of Charles Simic, the Yugoslavian poet, who wrote,

"Sooner or later our tribe always comes to ask us to agree to murder" (Simic 1993).

CULTURAL EVOLUTION *VERSUS* CULTURAL RELATIVISM

Someone once said, "Show me a cultural relativist in a plane thirty thousand feet up and I'll show you a hypocrite." Of course, certain cultural achievements are superior to others. Of course, we *must* make value judgments of other cultures, and of our own as well. It is our democratic responsibility to select from the pluralist seedbed those ideas and ways of behaving ("memes," as opposed to "genes") that seem to be the most effective in allowing people to cope with life's challenges and contingencies. For example, the World Health Organization's successful global drive to eradicate polio by the year 2000 is but one of the many practical benefits of modern scientific culture. On the other hand, some memes should be selected out by the forces of reason and education. Some quite obviously cripple those who have been raised according to them, and prevent them from being mobile in either social or geographic terms. A few, like the genital mutilation known as female circumcision, are *literally* crippling. Some are like viruses, spreading in the form of epidemics of hatred. Some memes *are* better than others simply because they enable their carriers to adapt better and thus to live more rewarding lives. Some aspects of every subculture will therefore be discarded over time if the society is an open one, while others will not only survive but will invade other groups.

No culture succeeds by stagnating—neither the majority culture nor those brought to the host country by immigrants. No one can prevent cultural evolution, but we *can* apply the wisdom gained from past mistakes to affect the path of its development. Today, for many cultures such as the American and Canadian ones, that path is increasingly a cause for worry. By encouraging the "dance of the tribes," we may be undermining the very culture of pluralism that made it possible to welcome diverse subcultures in the first place. We may be on our way to replacing an admittedly imperfect and hard-won culture of pluralism with a tribalistic one. In the culture of tribalism, with its criterion of "race," no one is free *not* to join a tribe. There is no place for all those intercultural, inter-ethnic and interfaith families who have been lighting the torch of civilization for all to follow toward a truly integrated human world. These are the real pioneers of the new world order. Their essential message to the rest of us is that, at the level of the individual where it matters most, we are *all* different; and the least important of these differences are the surface attributes of skin and eye and lip. Only the culture of pluralism can accommodate this fundamental fact.

BENEFITS OF IMMIGRATION

One of the most worrying results of misguided multicultural programs is that they tend to create a backlash against immigration. This is beginning to happen in both the United States and Canada at the very time when signs of the successful integration of immigrants have never been more apparent in every walk of life, particularly in politics and economic entrepreneurship. But there is nothing new in this. Both countries have been mixed-race and intercultural societies from the very beginning: from the importation of African slaves by the French and British in the seventeenth century; to the intermarriage of Scottish fur traders and aboriginal women in the Canadian North in the eighteenth century; to the nineteenth-century influx of Chinese laborers in the era of railroad construction; to the flood of workers from Central and South America to the southwestern states, and the immigration of Asian business people and professionals in the current era.

To turn to a specific example, one of the most important contributions of the immigrant Asian community within North America has always been in the realm of morality. Increasingly, as welfare and health systems become overloaded, established citizens are looking to some of our subcultures for guidance. The cultural norm demanding respect for parents and a willingness to assume responsibility for them—along with the example of extended families living together and helping one another—is viewed by many as worthy of respect and emulation. The typical Asian reverence for education, frugality, teamwork and the work ethic are likewise virtues from which the entire country can benefit. Finally, the Asian cultural lack of tolerance for violent pornography and obscenity, and concern for maintaining a wholesome environment for children, might contain a wisdom that we can no longer afford to ignore. All this provides a gratifying example of how immigration can lead to a two-way process of cultural enrichment: one of *inter*culturalism rather than *mul*ticulturalism.

THE IMPERATIVES OF CULTURAL EVOLUTION

In the end, the aggregate of ethnic cultures envisioned by the American and Canadian multiculturalists inevitably drifts into a culture of tribalism necessarily incorporating all citizens: a culture in which there are no universal criteria or principles beyond the dictates of the tribe. That is what the "racist backlash" really means. To quote the anthropologist Robin Fox, "What the relativists never seemed to realize, however, was that their logic did not abolish ethnocentrism, it simply *extended* the privilege to *all* societies" (Fox 1989: 37). This is inevitable because the logical implications and imperatives of multiculturalism are very different from those of interculturalism. Indeed, they are opposites. Interculturalism seeks to promote the *breaking down* of in-group barriers, not their *building up*. Only in the case of multiculturalism do we aim for a multiplicity of relatively isolated, homogenous, *static* cultural enclaves of the type encouraged by current policy in North America. The goal of interculturalism offers the vision of one major culture with subcultural groups feeding into it and being, in turn, nourished by it. There is a crucial difference between the two models. The first situation emphasizes the intact transmission of traditional beliefs and customs, a pursuit resulting in resistance to change and intolerance of diversity both within and without the protected in-group. The second encourages the kind of cultural evolution that has been much more typical of the world's immigrant societies since their inception.

A successful pluralist culture is one that is continuously enriched and altered by innovation from within, and by the subcultures being carried into it by immigrants. Fruitful innovations are positively reinforced by general public support. This is why a backlash against immigration brought on by irresponsible government policies is harmful to the host societies as well as to those individuals seeking better opportunities. It remains the case, however, that the carriers of the pluralist culture are members of *only one* society in the institutions of which all members, old and new, participate and make their contributions. Granted, it is a society with a great deal of mobility: social, geographic and across subcultures; and like any society undergoing rapid change, it is susceptible to the chaos of wholesale cultural breakdown. For this reason, the continuity provided by its shared institutions—whether spiritual, economic, educational, judicial or political—is essential. A country's institutions reflect the core values and ideals comprising the cultural glue needed to hold its people together. This is why any weakening of the nation's central institutions and national standards of excellence, in a misplaced zeal for multiculturalism, poses a threat to all citizens.

In the absence of an integrated society, we have merely an aggregate of non-communicating ethnic cultural groups inhabiting a single geographic area in which there are few, if any, shared institutions. This makes it impossible to protect the long-term welfare of "the commons": all those shared resources and public places and basic services without which a society slides into barbarism. The various groups are, instead, isolated by the archaic boundaries of tribalism. Such boundaries are marked by blood lines, distinctive language preventing effective "out-group" communication (particularly by the less privileged members), a romanticized heritage of grievances against neighboring groups and immutable religious beliefs and rituals. In the tribal situation *collective* rights are seen to be paramount, the distinction between public and private is lost and cultural relativism is the order of the day. It is an article of faith that no one has the right to make judgments about the worth of any aspect of a group's culture—whether or not these impose obvious physical harm and psychological disadvantages on the individuals involved. There are no meaningful limitations at the societal level on the operation of cultural mores introduced to the country by incoming groups, even when these include obsolete gender and work roles. Freedom for the *individuals* within the group boundaries, however, is another matter entirely.

In fact, where multiculturalism is carried to its logical end, it is apparent that the two freedoms are antithetical. The more that freedom is granted to separate cultural enclaves to preserve an unchanging way of life in the public arena, the more the freedom of the individual within the enclave is restricted. There is therefore a world of difference between a pluralist culture within one integrated society and a collection of independent ethnically defined communities in uneasy geographic cohabitation. The integrated pluralist society emphasizes and values individuality, along with the shared civic language that makes possible a joint responsibility for the commons. The tribal enclave, on the other hand, is concerned with transmitting its culture intact to succeeding generations, and with barring the intrusion of outside influences. The first situation represents a social reality out of which dreams are made; the second is the stuff of Balkan nightmares.

A useful metaphor for the entrance of immigrant subcultures to the larger cultural flow of pluralism is a mountain river joined and enriched by numerous streams as it carves its way toward the sea. The situation implied by many of the proponents of multiculturalism is something else entirely. It brings to mind a landscape of stagnant pools on a volcanic plain: pools that periodically erupt into jets of steam and molten debris. This is the vision of tribalism with its inevitable intergroup warfare.

There is a potential for tribalism wherever multiculturalism is taken to mean what the term actually implies: the preservation of a multiplicity of isolated, static, sovereign cultures within one geographic area. Perhaps the most telling indictment of this vision is that it cannot work; for cultures are rivers of interactive life—and like life itself, they must evolve or die. The richest source of evolutionary adaptation and change for human culture is the disciplined pursuit of knowledge. Indeed, science is the only human endeavor with a self-correcting mechanism at its very core. Another source of innovation is internationally recognized art. Aesthetic productions become powerful shapers of the values and habits that promote adaptive change. The third great source of revitalization for any country is the periodic entry of immigrants bringing with them new ways of doing things. All three of these vital sources of cultural adaptation are in jeopardy wherever tribalism reigns.

The image of a mountain river can help us to understand the concept of a pluralist, immigrant culture: the way of life of a society which is continuously being enriched by new, tested knowledge and imaginative imagery, and by new members as they interact with those whose ancestors came before. But this enrichment requires open communication and the casting off of old tribal grievances and hatreds, along with unworkable attitudes and life styles. (This is why a *common language* is so essential.) It demands that only the most fruitful and workable of the cultural attributes from the diverse homelands survive in the new. That cannot happen where the tribal dance predominates: a dance reinforcing, and establishing as sacred writ, every traditional ritual and custom.

It cannot happen because an evolving pluralist culture requires interaction and mutual respect and a willingness to learn on the part of newcomer and established citizen alike. Building fences hurts both groups, because cultural isolation brings stagnation and racist backlash, and it brings the danger of wholesale cultural breakdown for the separated group whenever the fences are breached. This danger is very real today for many aboriginal communities. All groups—especially the well-established, successful ones—have to experience those who are more vulnerable, or who have more recently arrived, as people with something of value to offer. In the same vein, newcomers to countries like the United States, Australia and Canada must recognize and respect the previous existence of a powerful, ongoing culture: that river into which they are carrying their offerings and from which they have much to gain.

Always the key to a vibrant, evolving culture is the *interaction* required for the functioning of dynamic self-organizing systems. This implies a cross-fertilization of the new with the great flow of ideas and customs that constitute the civic culture. The only government policy that can work over the long term is one that is aimed at integrating newcomers into the society which they have chosen to enter; just as any workable policy must be aimed at reclaiming and integrating members of the underclass. A prior understanding and subsequent insistence that the official language of the country (or province, in the case of Quebec) be spoken in public places, and that children learn it before they enter school, is a prerequisite for peaceful cultural evolution. More than any one thing, it would appear that the inability or refusal of some newcomers to use the common language of the host culture is responsible for the backlash against immigration now appearing in North America. Increasing numbers of citizens are now saying that the laws of a country should not function to perpetuate linguistic and ethnic divisions any more than they should function in the service of an unjust class system. In particular, they are questioning the use of tax revenues for reinforcing "us-them" divisions. Above all, many would maintain, an integrated society requires that all of its members learn to communicate in the official language(s) of work and government.

This does not mean enforced *assimilation*. Dinesh d'Souza (and Hannah Arendt long before) emphasized the necessity for maintaining a distinction between the public and private spheres. In private life members of every group should be encouraged to practice, and to share with neighbors, those family customs and arts and religious rituals that contribute to the richness of the unique personal identity being offered to the cultural mix of the country as a whole. In the community and workplace the sharing is bound to be a two-way street. This is the way that cultural evolution occurs at the grassroots level. But in the public sphere—in the nation's schools and where government legislation and the justice system are concerned—the maintenance of a civic society requires people to function as citizens of one integrated political and national social system.

There is indeed a precious core of values defining the pluralist culture of host countries such as the United States, Canada and Australia. That core has many parts. It comprises those ideals and principles underlying our democratic institutions: the responsible parliamentary (or the representative presidential) system of government; the secret ballot; equality before the law; freedom to express ideas; the American insistence on separation of church and state; freedom of spiritual or philosophical belief; the concept of collective responsibility for the weak and vulnerable; the commitment to internationalism and global peace; respect for the rule of law and for scientific inquiry; and tolerance of diversity. Such freedoms are not unlimited, however. Newcomers need to be aware that although *ideas* are unrestricted, there are certain *behaviors* which will not be tolerated, regardless of whether or not these involve customs sanctioned by religion. They should understand that no pluralist democracy can allow political activists to mask themselves in the garb and ritual of religion in order to subvert either their home governments or that of their host country. They should also be aware that, while the use of religious observances to celebrate one's family culture is encouraged, it is not acceptable to use these to keep alive old tribal grievances and intergroup hatreds.

It has been argued that, because many long-time members of the majority culture have never fully achieved their aspirations, they have no right to demand adherence by newcomers—or by an established minority such as African Americans, in the case of the United States. But the fact that a culture's core of values does indeed represent ideals rather than the exact nature of current reality does not undermine the validity of those values or their significance in shaping the society's past and present and directing its future. It was the dream of an *authentic* pluralist culture that inspired Martin Luther King in his battle for civil rights for those Americans who had descended from slaves. Likewise, most newcomers to the United States and Canada have chosen to immigrate precisely *because* of their perceptions of what the pluralist culture represents.

Most immigrants (and, certainly, most refugees) do not want a replica of what they left behind. Least of all do they desire a re-playing in a new setting of the old religious conflicts, caste rules and blood feuds that they were trying to escape. In the end, the best reason of all for refusing to support policies aimed at reinforcing tribal pretensions is that—except for a few vocal romantics in every camp—most people who understand the concept simply do not want a culture of tribalism.

INCOMPATIBLE DEMANDS ON THE SCHOOL

The educational systems of North America are increasingly being asked to respond to the siren call of the tribe. For example, during the 1990s in the province of British Columbia, the media heralded a move to establish non-public schools based on lines drawn by ethnicity and religion. Indeed by 1997, the sum of $125 million was being spent annually by the provincial government for subsidizing the new "independent" schools. This amounted to almost $2,800 per student. Attendees of these schools, when interviewed, told of "learning who I am"—and parents repeated the statement like a mantra. Many of these same parents were themselves well integrated *precisely because* of having had the opportunity (which they now denied to their offspring) for common, public schooling. Nowhere in the publicized objectives of these separate schools was there mention of "learning to be a Canadian citizen"; but even if there were, it would be difficult to accomplish such a goal in this new situation of legislated educational apartheid. One would think that, if we have learned anything about how to build a pluralist civic society, it is that children must have early and continuous opportunity to communicate across subcultures. It appears that Canadians are now busily setting up official obstacles to prevent this.

In the United States, educational apartheid is of the unofficial variety most often manifested at the post-secondary level by fragmentation into peer-group activities and special-studies areas defined in terms of skin color or gender. Whatever form it takes, the long-term consequences of moving in this direction could be devastating, chiefly because the role of the school in a culture of tribalism is very different from its role in a pluralist culture. In a culture of tribalism it is first and foremost the servant of the tribe. Its role is to transmit the cultural heritage as intact as possible from generation to generation. This includes the mother tongue and traditional forms of art and artisanship—as well as the beliefs expressed by these symbolic systems concerning the "good" and the "real" which the group members hold to be true. Imitative skill, memory and obedience are the most treasured characteristics in this type of educational system. The curriculum is selected with the intent that any information superfluous to this objective, or in conflict with it, not be accessible to the learner. The students are not exposed to the ideals, norms or customs of other cultures unless it cannot possibly be prevented and, wherever this is the case, the presentation is given in the form of an inoculation. Habits of thought such as a willingness to sit quietly and memorize stories, verses, series of numbers and multiplication tables, and to repeat them in unison, are developed early in a culture of tribalism. Curiosity is not encouraged.

Where the school operates as the servant of a pluralist society, the objectives are not so clear-cut. The overall goal must be to provide youthful learners with the tools to cope with change, both global and local, and to visualize and judge possibilities and test alternative means of achieving these. As well as in-depth knowledge of the history and current features of the world's major cultures, the student will need to develop the scientific approach to knowing and the moral-reasoning capacities for making wise judgments. The latter are crucial prerequisites for citizenship in a democratic society and for benefiting from—and contributing to—a culture of pluralism.

More specific objectives are: (1) development of *self*-discipline as opposed to discipline imposed from without; (2) reinforcement of curiosity and of an eagerness to engage in age-appropriate, trial-and-error behaviors; (3) provision of sufficient in-depth comprehension of broad, universal systems of knowledge to arm individuals with the conceptual tools for organizing, assessing and interpreting incoming information; and (4) encouragement of imagination, empathy and wisdom through opportunities to experience the consequences of choices. Clearly, a culture of pluralism demands different approaches from the rote teaching and learning that may have been workable in previous times and in relatively isolated, stable tribal environments.

What we must ask of our schools would be difficult *even if* our demands were coherent and represented a general societal consensus; but, because of the confusion about whether we want a culture of tribalism or a culture of pluralism, we have placed our educators in an impossible position. The school and university systems in the modern industrial society are being torn between two conflicting cultural goals and, consequently, are doomed to fail at both. It is time that we gave up the dangerous ideology of cultural relativism and recognized that not all beliefs and ways of doing things are equally worthy of transmission and perpetuation. We have to decide whether we want to prepare our youth primarily as transmitters of obsolete traditions or as builders of a universal culture and wise participants in the directing of its evolution. Tribal or ethnic cultures can survive intact in today's world only if their members are indoctrinated early and exclusively into the doctrines and customs of the in-group and kept isolated from contamination from without. Such individuals will grow up to be true believers in "us" and intolerant, distrusting enemies of "them." Their ultimate rewards will stem from unquestioning submission to established authority. Conversely, the widely knowledgeable, skeptical thinker will thrive in a culture of pluralism, while contributing happily to its capacity to adapt to changing environmental conditions. This same person will be the dangerous heretic in the culture of tribalism and may well end up experiencing some modern version of burning at the stake.

Ultimately, the culture of tribalism is self-defeating for its members. So long as only a relatively few enclaves live according to its norms they can maintain their isolation and distinctiveness by benefiting from the technological advances and the tolerant acceptance of diversity characterizing the containing culture of pluralism. But the call of the tribe is contagious, and as it spreads throughout the society that well of tolerance dries up, along with the artistic and scientific sources of adaptive technology and innovation. This is just another way of saying that, in today's world, the culture of tribalism is evolutionarily unstable. In the final analysis, it provides no means of responding to change other than with the age-old mechanism of intermittent tribal warfare.

In countless ways we are indeed the creatures of the environmental circumstances that shaped our species. The urge to respond in tribal ways is deeply embedded in all of us, simply because it contributed to clan survival in primitive times. But times have changed. The demands and challenges of survival have been reversed. It is now imperative that humankind evolve a more appropriate cultural response: one capable of overriding and inhibiting tribalism. At this juncture in human history, the tribal dance can only contribute to destruction over the long term. We need not continue to be victimized by it, now that environmental conditions have changed. Our fate is in our own hands.

REFERENCES

Almond, Gabriel and Verba, S. *The Civic Culture*. Princeton, NJ: Princeton University Press, 1963.

Arendt, Hannah. *The Origins of Totalitarianism*. New York, NY: Harcourt, Brace and World, 1951.

Bernstein, Richard. *Dictatorship of Virtue: Multiculturalism and the Battle for America's Future*. New York, NY: The Free Press, 1994.

Bissoondath, Neil. *Selling Illusions: The Cult of Multiculturalism in Canada*. Toronto, ON: Penguin Books, 1994a.

———. "Hoping to Heal Canada's Intellectual Sickness." *The Globe and Mail*, October 10, 1994b, p. A1.

———, ed. *If You Love This Country: Fifteen Voices for a Unified Canada*. Toronto, ON: Penguin Books, 1995.

Cardozo, Andrew and Musto, Louis, eds. *The Battle over Multiculturalism*. Ottawa, ON: Pearson-Shoyama Institute, 1997.

Carter, Stephen. *Reflections of an Affirmative Action Baby*. New York, NY: Basic Books, 1991.

Cohen, Y. A. *Man in Adaptation: The Biosocial Background*. Chicago, IL: Aldine Press, 1974.

Dawkins, Richard. *River Out of Eden: A Darwinian View of Life*. New York, NY: Basic Books, 1995.

Donald, Leland. *Aboriginal Slavery on the Northwest Coast of North America*. Berkeley, CA: University of California Press, 1998.

D'Souza, Dinesh. *The End of Racism*. New York, NY: The Free Press, 1995.

Ellis, John M. *Literature Lost: Social Agendas and the Corruption of the Humanities*. New Haven, CT: Yale University Press, 1997.

Fox, Robin. *The Search for Society: Quest for a Biosocial Science and Morality*. New Brunswick, NJ: Rutgers University Press, 1989.

Hutcheon, Pat Duffy. 1994. "Is There a Dark Side to Multiculturalism?" *Humanist in Canada* (Summer 1994): 26–29.

Ignatieff, Michael. *Blood and Belonging: Journeys into the New Nationalism*. Toronto, ON: Penguin Books Canada, 1993.

Keefer, Michael. *Lunar Perspectives: Field Notes from the Culture Wars*. Toronto, ON: Anansi, 1996.

Loney, Martin. *The Pursuit of Division: Race, Gender and Preferential Hiring in Canada*. Montreal: McGill–Queens University Press, 1998.

Loury, Glenn. *One by One from the Inside Out: Race and Responsibility in America*. New York, NY: The Free Press, 1995.

Simic, Charles. "Elegy from a Spider's Web." *The Globe and Mail*, November 13, 1993, p. D2.

Sperry, Roger. "Mind, Brain and Humanist Values." In *New Views of the Nature of Man*, ed. John Platt. Chicago, IL: University of Chicago Press, 1965, pp. 71–92.

Wilson, Edward O. *Consilience: The Unity of Knowledge*. New York, NY: Alfred A. Knopf, 1998.

CHAPTER 10

The Culture of Fantasy: Gullible Victims and the Spinners of Delusion

Along with the hostile solitudes of the cultures of poverty and affluence, and the incompatible cultures of tribalism and pluralism, there exists yet another system of ideas and customs affecting how people operate from day to day. We are all immersed to some extent in what we can call "the culture of fantasy": a way of being that is fed by the human propensity for creating an imaginary world to provide a cushion against the harshness of the surroundings. From our earliest beginnings, the need to render impinging circumstances in some way controllable drove our primitive forebears to explain their daily experience. For this crucial task they used those terms available to their conceptual framework and reasoning capacity which appeared most capable of generating an illusion of security. Much of what we now recognize as fantasy was the only conceptual world known to early humans. It should not be too surprising that, regardless of their proven lack of efficacy and reliability, these ancient interpretations continue to beckon and gratify many of us. When we consider our innate suggestibility, coupled with the fact that even the content of our dreams and private hallucinations reflects these deeply embedded cultural beliefs, we can even better understand their pervasiveness. Nonetheless, when "the culture of fantasy" threatens to cripple the reasoning capacity of the *majority* of the population, it is time to look for the source of the problem in the socialization process to which our children are currently exposed.

How is it, we might ask, that in this so-called Age of Science so many people seem to be attracted to astrology, psychic healing, fortune telling, searching out sea monsters and UFOs, communing with the dead, joining cults, engaging in therapeutic touch and mystical incantations of all kinds, achieving "oneness" with the universe by walking on fire, and so on and on? How can we explain the fact that the bookstore sections devoted to the occult are often much larger than those housing philosophy or the social sciences? How does it happen that so many highly schooled young people are willing to follow totalitarian political or religious gurus? How can we explain phenomena such as middle-class tourists swarming to casinos and the poor lining up to buy lotto tickets? What causes so many people to live out their lives dreaming of instant wealth, or convincing others to join some "get rich quick" scheme? How can we avoid the paradoxical conclusion that our much-lauded, media-driven explosion of information seems to be rendering the general public ever more ignorant and more vulnerable to delusion? What makes people want to explain their experience in terms of mysterious forces lurking within, or impinging from without? What accounts for the widespread resistance to readily available *natural* explanations for apparent anomalies—and to the recognition that no actions can occur in isolation from predictable natural consequences? What, indeed, causes so many of us to be so gullible?

Over the centuries, professional hucksters like P. T. Barnum have said it very well. "There's one born every minute" is the catch phrase referring to the seemingly endless supply of "suckers" in every society. Thoughtful and concerned people have long agonized over the prevalence of gullibility in the population at large and the corresponding persistence of that particular form of amoral cynicism which provides a ready vulture for every potential victim. "How," people have asked, "can the very same culture produce two such contrasting personality types?" "Pop" psychologists tend to respond to such queries with various sets of dichotomies. "There are two kinds of people," some are fond of saying, "The exploiters and those who willingly assume the role of victim." Others prefer the labels of "controller" *versus* "enabler," and so on and on.

But, as was pointed out in a previous chapter, labeling people in terms of "types" does not *explain* anything—unless one really believes that children are fated from birth to belong to one category or the other. It does not define the problem in terms that identify possible causes and point the way to a solution. In fact, the very persistence of this practice of labeling tells us far more about the culture in question, and the socialization undergone by those who accept the practice as valid, than it does about the problem being faced. The question that should be posed is "How does a similar process of socialization produce both the social predators and the 'sitting ducks' who seem such easy prey?" We might also ask how this affects the general culture which, in turn, feeds back to shape us all. In what precise ways has this ongoing feedback cycle of socialization failed in the case of *both* the gullible victims and the spinners of delusion? Could it be that there is a common cause for what can only be defined as a symbiotic relationship?

People are gullible to the extent that they are easily *satisfied* by the explanations coming from those who set out to persuade them. They neither demand nor feel comfortable with explanations that identify observable cause-and-effect connections: connections amenable to some sort of public procedure of verification. In fact, there are some who seem not to think logically and skeptically at all. To think in terms of cause-and-effect relations, and observable evidence for these, is to be equipped with a "built-in doubter": Isaac Asimov's concept of an internal barometer for assessing the probable reliability of propositions about reality. It means that curiosity is not quelled by explanations relying merely upon magic; or upon popular New Age versions of animism; or upon esoteric exercises in semantics; or upon appeals to fellow feeling and attributed motivations; or upon traditional mythology or utopian ideology. It means that one has been fortunate enough to have been socialized in such a way that curiosity is aroused rather than satisfied by the above types of explanations, because none of these provide answers to the question of "How could that possibly have come to be?" And only answers to questions of that particular type will lead to the understanding of cause-and-effect relationships that results in reliable knowledge.

ANSWERS THAT STIMULATE CURIOSITY AND
ANSWERS THAT SUPPRESS IT

In Chapter 4 we discussed the instinctive urges (apparently shared by all animals) that energize infant behavior. The one most relevant to the problem being examined here is the urge to control the circumstances impinging from without. This is the all-important source of curiosity, the need to *know* or to seek explanations that arouse emotional as well as intellectual satisfaction. In the normal course of development such satisfaction comes through the resolution of some previously sensed contradiction between current intuitions—built up from past experience—and new sensory inputs: a contradiction manifested in the feeling of "cognitive dissonance." This is our necessary energy source in the ongoing search for more effective means of controlling the results of actions. We can only achieve such control to the extent that we have gained some awareness (however dimly perceived) of the effects of our actions as these feed back upon us. In other words, the tension or curiosity produced by the unsatiated urge to control such effects is the spur that forces learners to keep trying until something *works*. It propels them into their environment to encounter new stimuli which, in turn, activate new learned responses. To the extent that a response is positively reinforced by its consequences, it is repeated in other circumstances until satisfaction is no longer forthcoming. As language is developed, *questioning* becomes an additional instrument for exploring the physical and social surroundings. The process is thus not only ongoing and interactive but, because of system feedback, has the potential to be cumulative and increasingly powerful.

Questions demand answers, but not all answers are equally *satisfying* to the questioner. Our *emotional needs* as well as our intellectual capacities are implicated in this. At different stages in our cognitive development different types of explanations appear to operate as reinforcers. In *The Copernican Revolution*, Thomas Kuhn noted that explanations are the foundation stones for imaginative conceptual schemes which define not only the pursuit of knowledge, but the very way people perceive and experience reality. In a 1970 book called simply *Explanations*, Gwynn Nettler coined the term "explainway" to describe the way in which different cultures—and variously educated people within the same culture, and sometimes even the same person in varying circumstances—can find quite different types of explanations satisfying. Clearly, previous socialization and level of learning have a powerful impact on the process by which human curiosity is both fueled and reinforced.

If we think of curiosity as the engine of intellectual growth, we can readily understand that the way in which adult agents of socialization respond to the child's questioning is critical. At every stage of development certain kinds of responses will activate the engine while others will turn it off. Thus it is that the opportunities provided for safe exploration of the physical and social environment, and the explanations provided for the discoveries that the child finds puzzling, will either encourage further intellectual development or will tend to stultify and cripple it. Chapter 5 dealt with the way in which appropriate socialization results in the gradual development of the mature *conscience* capable of operating as an internal standard for distinguishing right from wrong. So, too, is it possible to provide the child with a "built-in doubter."

In Chapter 5 we also discussed the connections between morality and cognitive development. The health of the vital engine of curiosity is related in a similar manner not only to cognition but to the emotions as well, in a complex, three-way relationship of cause and effect. (Again, the "triple helix.") Curiosity stimulates intellectual growth and is, in turn, further stimulated by that growth—to the degree that it is energized rather than lulled by the experience of contradiction and dissonance. But curiosity is reinforced in different ways, according to the level of emotional development. If socializing agents are to respond effectively and constructively to children's discoveries and questions—so that their primitive scientific endeavors are encouraged rather than inhibited—it is essential that they understand how those children develop *both* emotionally and intellectually.

It seems clear that there exist distinctive patterns of intuitive response and conscious belief—and distinctive ways in which emotional needs are gratified—which are characteristic of children at particular stages of intellectual development. But these emotional needs requiring satisfaction are not unique to children in their various stages of growing up. Certain cultural influences can cause needs appropriate to earlier or more primitive phases of development to be carried over into adulthood, where they will continue to determine which types of explanations will be *experienced* as satisfactory and which will not.

Because curiosity is actually satisfied and reinforced quite differently at these various levels of cognitive functioning, different explainways are demanded in the normal course of events. If age-appropriate answers are not provided, or if those that have proven rewarding in the past are repeated long after the child should have outgrown that stage, then curiosity may be permanently crippled. Such children are frozen or trapped into a way of interpreting experience that makes them easily deluded by self and others—and many remain in this mode throughout their lives.

These typical explainways have been described in various terms, but for our purposes we will refer to them as (1) the magical, (2) the tautological, (3) the projective, (4) the ideological, and (5) the conjectural, or cause-and-effect modes. This does not necessarily mean that conceptual/ emotional development follows a rigid pattern, with all children managing to navigate each of them successfully at the same age and proceeding to operate consistently within the most recently achieved level. Nor do most grown-ups necessarily function in all aspects of their lives within the most advanced mode—regardless of whether they have mastered the intellectual tools required for accomplishing this. In fact, our previous socialization can make it appear that different circumstances demand different explainways. Even the most mystically inclined among us is usually content to rely on cause-and-effect when shopping for a new car, while conjectural thinkers can lapse into mysticism when explaining the source of their own artistic genius. As in the case of moral development, the relevant cognitive level is *necessary* for a corresponding advance from one explainway to another. However, it is by no means *sufficient to ensure it*.

THE MAGIC MODE

In what Piaget called the *sensorimotor* stage of cognitive development, the infant's view of the surroundings can be viewed as "magical." Things happen in an undifferentiated physical/social fantasy world because all-powerful adults or unknowable entities can make them happen. All is mysterious and arbitrary. A major task of the caregiver is to provide the experiences that will move children toward a more effective way of interpreting the world. They need to learn that the toy dropped over the side of the high chair does not automatically reappear on the tray, and that crying does not inevitably make Mummy or Daddy materialize. Where the magic mode persists as the child becomes older, the dominant belief will continue to involve non-material influences capable of being humanly controlled by obscure rituals. Our cultural myths of the tooth fairy, Santa Claus and the Easter Bunny come to mind—and the reluctance of some parents and children to question the effects of these or to relinquish them. Some cultures encourage magical interpretations of experience to such an extent that the mode remains the prevailing one throughout adulthood. In fact, it has been found that certain tribal groups impose magical explainways so powerfully that youngsters actually *regress* in this sense as they experience their culture's "rites of passage" in the process of leaving adolescence behind. Even within modern scientific cultures there are many who live out their lives in a conceptual world defined in magical terms.

Those operating according to this mode are *satisfied* by magical explanations. In other words, their curiosity is readily quelled by pronouncements from self-styled propitiators or manipulators of the "unknowable" forces of nature. They are positively reinforced by involvement in almost any sort of ritualistic activity deemed meaningful by an authority figure. That figure may be the guru leading a popular cult, a psychic, a therapist, a faith healer, a political demagogue; or possibly a clan warlord or proselytizer of tribal nationalism or race hatred. It may simply be the latest high-pressure salesperson to appear at the doorstep. Another possibility is that the individual in question may have graduated to the role of authoritarian leader or shrewd manipulator, rather than the follower or "mark." Those in the magic mode do not expect anything to make sense in terms of their own immediate experience; therefore they lose the capacity to be energized by feelings of dissonance. They have learned to accept ambiguity and contradiction as "the way of the world." They are content to "feel the mystery" and pray for a miracle. In other cases, curiosity becomes harnessed to the drive to manipulate *people* in the service of the actor's immediate ego needs—rather than to control *objects* and the *consequences of action*. In this way are shaped some of the more extreme of the spinners of delusion, along with their ultimate victims.

THE TAUTOLOGICAL MODE

Not too far beyond the magic mode is what we can call the "tautological" way of explaining things. As we learned in Chapter 5, the most significant features of the *pre-operational* stage of development (usually beginning at about the age of two) are egocentrism and language acquisition. Egocentrism encourages a self-centered way of being in the world, while the rapid onset of language requires and produces a repetitious, definitional approach to everything encountered. The explainway which seems to be demanded by children operating at this level of development is that which satisfies the urge for the security which comes from being able to *name* everything; and to feel that all these named entities have no purpose other than to serve one's needs .

The most telling example of an adult body frozen into the response pattern of childhood egocentrism is the character of "Mr. Bean" so familiar to television audiences today. Mr. Bean operates in a closed little world of his own making, and is oblivious to other people except as objects in the environment, presumably put there solely either to enhance or impede his own intended actions. He is utterly incapable of feeling empathy for other "selves." He exhibits the overweening self-centeredness of young children, which limits understanding to a process of discovering how external things impinge upon them. Everything is still arbitrary to the egocentric child, and answers phrased in terms of regularities will not be effective in quelling curiosity at this stage. For the nursery-school child, the landscape can seem quite naturally to be peopled with spirits, demons, fairies and ghosts, all of which are concerned in some way with responding to the whims of the "self." Planetary objects, animals and plants in the surroundings are viewed in the same way—as are the humans who intrude into the private domain of the egocentric little person. Their sole function is viewed as the satisfaction of the child's felt needs. Answers that do not take this natural egocentrism into account tend not to satisfy the child in question.

Something else of critical importance is happening at the same time. The child's imitative capacities are instigating a rapid soaking-up of symbols from the communication occurring within the family and neighborhood and on the television. Increasingly, children progressing through this developmental stage want to know the *names* of things. They are endeavoring to dissect and map their hitherto amorphous world. Their questions reveal the need to categorize and label every event and, to the extent that this is occurring, responses offering and repeating names and simple definitions are required in order to provide emotional and intellectual satisfaction. Positive reinforcement at this stage demands not only the quelling of curiosity but satiation of the need for security. Labels and definitions, viewed as unchanging units of an otherwise arbitrary reality, satisfy the all-important desire for certainty.

When pre-school children continuously ask "why?" they are not seeking cause-and-effect explanations. They want answers expressed as simple tautologies and assurances concerning how the matter in question will affect them. They will be satisfied only with "The tooth fairy is a magical person who pays money for your teeth," or "The tooth fairy leaves money because she likes you" or "Santa comes down the chimney because he knows you have been good." Authority remains all-important in the *pre-operational* scheme of things. Only knowledgeable adults can render ghosts and fairies and bearded Christmas gnomes personally helpful and harmless; and only they can pronounce over and over the names and symbolic meanings of events and objects.

THE PROJECTIVE MODE

During the early part of the *concrete-operational* stage of development (at about the age of seven) the great breakthrough in conceptualization has to do with perspective. Children learn to view things from perspectives other than their own. This enables them to understand the operation and functional utility of rules. The idea that rules ensure fair play can very easily be made a feature of the family and school culture of these children. All rules—even those governing the external world—tend to be interpreted by children of this age in terms of fairness. A teacher once reported the comment of one such pupil concerning the law of gravity: "It means no fair if you jump up and don't come back down," the child said.

Another critical breakthrough occurs at this stage where conditions are conducive to it. It is now possible for the development of empathy to proceed apace—providing, of course, that the socialization process provides the appropriate experiences. The type of explanation most likely to satisfy curiosity in the *concrete-operational* phase is what can be termed "projective." For the first time, there is a strong tendency to look for what causes things to happen. However, "causes" are viewed here as the essentially hidden *motivations* of the actors rather than in terms of observable events preceding the action, or the consequences that followed previous choices. Intentions are everything for these children. "I didn't mean to do it" is thought to excuse any transgression; unanticipated consequences are "not my fault."

One of the fruitful side-effects of this intellectual breakthrough is the capacity to recognize an element of randomness, or of accident and coincidence (as distinct from magical arbitrariness) in human affairs. The earlier explanatory modes are antithetical to this necessary concept. The scientist David Suzuki tells of having arrived at the territory of a primitive tribe in the Amazon at precisely the same time that someone in the village became ill. The newcomers were immediately thought to have caused the illness for, according to the primitive way of thinking, coincidence equals causality in the form of a solicited response from some immanent force. There is nothing unusual in this, for causal connections are inevitably built upon that intuitive association of simultaneously occurring events which David Hume rightly assumed to be the basis of the reasoning process in all higher animals and humans. However, for the pre-school child—as with the Amazonian native—an occult power in the control of a human authority figure is the interpretation given for this natural mental association of simultaneous events. No other type of explanation can possibly bring satisfaction. Everything that happens is viewed as the result of arbitrarily accessed, mysterious forces; therefore when bad things happen to people someone or something must be blamed for manipulating or encouraging these forces.

Another culture, another historical era, and the explanations become less fraught with magic and more definitional and egocentric. The appearance of the newcomers and the unexpected illness and death were both "meant to be." It was in the nature of things that the individual would move on to another sphere at that particular time and under those particular circumstances. The advent of strangers had been arranged for the sole purpose of marking that departure.

Once humans achieve the *concrete-operational* stage, however, they are capable of moving a step beyond both magical and tautological explanations. While their natural anthropocentrism continues to attribute human purpose to their physical surroundings and encourages them to ignore any possible role of chance *in the world at large*, they now tend to overemphasize it where the immediate consequences *of human actions* are concerned. Because things do not always happen as they intend, they actually experience the occurrence of accidents in connection with their own behavior. This makes it easy for them to accept the operation of chance at that level. But the concept of coincidence in their natural surroundings remains beyond their grasp. The new situation is the psychological source of primitive dualism; it encourages a sense that the realm of human relationships is isolated from physical reality—and essentially irrational—because things often do not come about as desired. At the same time, the physical world is still being perceived as "planned" and ordered for some unfathomable "purpose;" and therefore essentially rational. In fact, children operating in the projective explainway are natural teleological dualists. They will inquire about why we have mosquitoes or spiders, demanding an answer in terms of their purpose in the engineered scheme of things. When asked a question such as "How do clouds form?" a child at this developmental stage responded "They just know how they're supposed to do it." Cause is understood as reason, and reason equals anthropocentric purpose projected by the child into the non-human world.

Clearly, a primitive notion of cause and effect is emerging at this stage of intellectual development. But it can be comprehended only in concrete, personal terms. "Cause" is limited to "purpose." It relates to motives or intentions as the actor experiences them directly, as with some mysterious transcendental Purpose in the world at large. The person operating in the projective mode "takes everything personally." Ideas cannot be separated from the person communicating them. A teacher who gives a student a bad mark must hate her, according to the student. Cause and effect is understood solely in terms of purposeful rationality, and is recognized as applying only to external, physical events. At a more sophisticated level, science is limited to the study of non-human phenomena, with a complex taxonomy deductively derived from axiomatic "truths" substituting for open-ended empirical inquiry into the nature of things.

An enlightening example of this mode of explanation is Aristotle's theory of motion. The fact that it prevailed for over fifteen centuries tells us a good deal about the barriers to scientific progress created by the dominant explainways of Medieval Europe. Aristotle had taught that earthly bodies fall because of a desire on their part to approach as near to the center of the universe as possible. Because of his enduring influence, the accepted explanation for why heavenly bodies revolve around the earth in an orderly fashion was that it is in their nature to do so. This explanation quelled curiosity and stifled scientific inquiry in astronomy until compellingly refuted in the seventeenth century by the cumulative breakthroughs of Copernicus, Kepler and Galileo.

In the realm of human activity, on the other hand, things are seen by the projective thinker to be much less predictable in terms of subjective desires. If events can happen otherwise than as an actor intended that they should, then something quite foreign to causation *as the concrete-operational individual understands it* must be in control of human affairs, something that marks them off irrevocably from the physical. This is why people operating in this explainway tend to feel that they are not responsible for the results of their actions as long as they meant well. Intentions are everything. All of life is seen as equally a gamble. Warnings about the long-term effects of substance abuse and poor nutrition and reckless sexual behavior tend to fall on deaf ears. "Cause" is equated with purposeful "reason" in this mode; and reason is understood intuitively only as after-the-fact rationalization in terms of the actor's motivation. The individual feels that where there is no discernible motive there can be no cause and effect. Curiosity about the event is satisfied solely to the degree that rationalization in terms of motive is possible.

Something else is occurring here as well. While operating in the previous tautological mode, most children have become habituated to the reification of abstract ideas. This means that the constructs symbolizing these entities have been given an existence of their own in concrete terms—quite apart from any observable indicators of their presence—and firmly housed as explanatory "motives" within the makeup of human beings. This tendency is very difficult to eradicate, and often continues throughout the *concrete-operational* phase and beyond. It is reinforced by the propensity of adult caregivers to answer questions with abstractions having no reference points in the child's immediate experience. There is no more apt example of this explanatory mode as applied to human behavior than Freudian psychoanalysis and the curious theories of Carl Jung. The history of these movements, along with that of the Scholasticism based on Aristotle's teachings, clearly demonstrates how such reified constructs—when firmly embedded in the culture—can function as obstacles to the ongoing search for knowledge.

With the emerging recognition of the role of chance and coincidence in human affairs, the desire for certainty intensifies at this *concrete-operational* stage. This is why the myth is so readily grasped by older elementary-school children. Myths are stories which present a comprehensive purpose and plan for the world as experienced. They give meaning and provide comforting answers to every newly recognized fear and concern. At this age personal death becomes a real possibility for the first time. Because the self's annihilation is inconceivable to the self in question, the very concept cannot be viewed by people at this level of development other than in terms of the annihilation of the world as a whole. Human life can only be understood to have continuity if the individual can be presumed to survive death in some other form. Myths provide satisfaction here because of their traditional and unchangeable explanations for birth, death and other decisive events in the traditional human story. Among these are the "creation of life," "the purpose of life," the birth of figures defined by the group as divine, the origin of fire and other technologies and institutions. Mythological explanations respond to the individual's "why?" in the empathetic, purposive terms demanded by the question. They have a particular power because they tend to be expressed in terms of motives. The person inquiring about why giraffes have long necks would be frustrated and dissatisfied by a complex response in terms of natural selection. "Because they need them to feed on the leaves in the tops of the trees" is the kind of answer that satisfies. Such explanations imply a cosmic plan and teleological purpose, direction and end. All these are essentially human attributes which have been projected onto non-human nature. Because these have been defined as rational and causal in the personal sense, the world has been made abundantly comprehensible and satisfying to those habituated to the projective explainway.

Myths also provide objectives, context, bodies of beliefs and rituals and rallying cries for *groups*. This function is particularly meaningful for children of late-elementary school age. It is the age of group formation, group activity, herd behavior and peer-group pressure. The mythological explanation tends to be a communal explanation rather than an individualistic one. It appeals to people in the collective. In its positive form, this can encourage cooperation and rule-following. On the negative side, it can interfere with rule-*making* activity and can exacerbate the tendency for individuals at this level of development to indulge in coercive herd behavior and the most blatant kinds of cruelty. The myth defines the group Will, or consensus, and the group Will must be enforced!

THE IDEOLOGICAL MODE

The age of adolescence is critical for a number of reasons. One of the most important, but least recognized, is the fact that it marks a decisive turning point in the process of conceptualization. The latter begins to snowball in one or the other of two intellectual directions. Young people of this age either make the leap into what Piaget called the stage of *formal operations* or they remain at the *concrete-operational* level and become increasingly committed to the quest for certainty. Most of those who have developed the intellectual capacity for operating logically tend to be attracted to, and stimulated by, cause-and-effect thinking. They begin to develop rapidly beyond the need for certainty, as they increasingly find their rewards in the new-found power of inductive reason to order experience and direct open-ended inquiry into the nature of things.

For countless others, however, the quest for certainty—combined with the idealism and rebellion against authority typical of their age—moves them in the opposite direction. They are propelled into the "ideological" mode of interpreting their world. For the most part, these are the youths who still require the reassurance provided by magical, tautological or projective explanations, but who are ripe for a change in the *focus* of their beliefs. The ideologies to which they now turn as substitutes for traditional family myths continue to satisfy their need for certainty, but they serve other functions as well.

The ideological mode is in many ways merely the reverse of the mythological one, and it is no less projective. It operates in the service of a soon-to-be-attainable utopian future rather than a traditional past. This makes the ideological explainway particularly appealing to idealistic and impatient young people. Myths and ideologies both provide a comprehensive and meaningful story. However, it is a story grounded in feeling and *preference* rather than in the desire for testable knowledge. Both deal with "poetic truths" which refer not to how things actually are but to how things were in some golden past, or to how things will be in some perfect future. These are beliefs that strike a resonating chord in half-remembered sets of conditioned images and poorly understood abstractions within the psychological makeup of the adolescent. As tools for ordering reality they are extremely seductive because they usually contain interwoven elements of the magical, tautological and projective explainways. This means that they provide satisfaction on a number of levels. They arouse emotional commitment to a simple, one-factor cause; they prophesy an immutable future; they promote immediate action free of the need to assess consequences; they are grounded in *de facto* teleological thinking; the concepts defining them are abstract and accordingly non-testable; and they tend to be expressed in terms of attributed motivations and conspiracy theories.

In addition, ideologies are group-enhancing and group-based ways of believing. They reinforce the adolescent need for peer acceptance by appealing to, and promoting, "in-group" versus "out-group" sentiments. They encourage *cultus*; that is, an obsession with the "correct" rituals, postures and even clothing—all of which serve to define and isolate the group from outsiders. They also encourage an undiscriminating repetition of group-building slogans and of pejorative labels and name calling for any who would dare to express doubts or opposition. Indeed, *de facto* excommunication and ostracism is the likely reward for doubting the faith of the group. Ideologies satisfy those operating in the projective mode in that they are characterized by a preference on the part of their adherents for *argumenta ad hominem*: the habit of judging ideas by who said them, rather than on their merits. (Mao Tse-tung expressed the ultimate in this tendency when he exhorted his followers to support whatever the enemy opposes and oppose whatever the enemy supports.) All these ways of behaving provide an effective glue for holding the group together—and, for the adolescent, the group is crucial indeed.

Also decisive is the fact that most adolescents have been exposed to long years of the type of schooling that overemphasizes the tautological mode of explanation. How many educators reward memorization rather than reasoning and testing ideas against the evidence? This focus feeds a need for the kind of holistic frame of reference that only a closed tautological system like mathematics can provide. Ideology appeals to these holistic yearnings in that it invests the totality of life with a non-negotiable meaning.

At an age when patience is in short supply, and action is the order of the day, ideology provides easy answers to complex problems. It also offers the promise of escape from uncertain futures. It presents the possibility of avoiding the type of painstaking scholarship needed for any honest attempt at objectivity—and which, in turn, would require a commitment to cause-and-effect thinking. Not only does the ideological stance not recognize the quest for objectivity as desirable, it defines it as an unnecessary and impossible guideline and ideal. Small wonder, then, that many young people who are creative in their approach to ideas, but find the conditions of authentic scholarship too burdensome to bear, are among those most likely to be satisfied by the ideological explanation.

THE CONJECTURAL OR CAUSE-AND-EFFECT MODE

Clearly, not all of those who achieve the *formal-operational* stage of intellectual functioning manage to complete the transition to the "conjectural" mode of being in the world. The appeal of the earlier-acquired explainways remains uppermost for a large percentage of intellectually advanced individuals—even those in the so-called "hard" sciences. Many mature scientists compartmentalize their approach to life so that they respond conjecturally when operating in their own discipline while demanding magical, tautological or projective explanations in everyday situations. On the other hand, countless individuals without the advantage of any higher education live out their lives in a common-sense world of cause-and-effect.

If induction into a scientific community is neither necessary nor sufficient to guarantee a conjectural conceptual stance, what, then, *are* its indicators? First and foremost is a commitment to the universality of cause and effect. The habitual response of the conjectural thinker is to seek out the causal connections for any event, and to feel unsatisfied in the absence of evidence concerning these. "How?" rather than "why?" is the question asked.

Second, as the term indicates, the stance is hypothetical and tentative. It is driven not by the need for certainty but by an attitude of respect for truth and for objectivity in the search for it. That drive launches conjectural thinkers upon an open-ended journey, a journey that rapidly becomes far more rewarding than any certain arrival could ever be. It is an attitude described by Hannah Arendt as a curious passion, largely unknown outside of Western civilization, for intellectual integrity at any price. This stands in stark contrast to the ideological passion for certainty at any price.

Third, the conjectural mode has to do with an insistence on explanation based upon experienced connections between act and consequence. These are non-tautological regularities open to public test and falsification. Generalizations built upon them are the foundation stones for explanations that deal with cause and effect. The object of such an explanation is to cite an empirical rule of which the thing to be explained is an instance. Furthermore, whereas ideological explanations tend to be couched in tautological terms that render them immune to disproof, conjectures are the exact opposite. They specify the empirical conditions under which they are presumed to hold and the precise and observable results to be expected if, indeed, the conjecture is reliable. This means that a commitment to cause-and-effect thinking encourages the habit of being satisfied only by the promise of objectivity—or the possibility of some form of "intersubjective" checking—rather than by appeals to the subjectivity implicit in special interests, intuition and emotions. It also ensures that the explanations found satisfying by people in this interpretive explainway are only those that can be expressed with simplicity and clarity.

Fourth, the cause-and-effect mode both encourages and depends upon the ability to abide with selected aspects of reality, and with the identification of relations among these. This means it requires and promotes analytical ability. Synthesis is also central. However, that process is viewed as an *activity*—not as the reception of an intact image of some pre-existing "holistic" unity. The synthesis common to the conjectural explainway is found in a creative reorganization of parts rather than in the mystic's dream of immediate and perfect immersion in the whole. For the person who thinks in terms of cause and effect, it is the units and their interrelationships that define the whole. On the other hand, for the "holistic" thinker operating in the ideological mode, the whole invariably determines the nature of the parts to such a degree that it cannot be understood at all in terms of those parts.

A fifth point involves a peculiar sensitivity to the instrumental function of language, a sensitivity that inevitably accompanies the cause-and-effect orientation. For the person who sees the world in this way, linguistic constructs are understood as humanly created and continuously evolving conceptual tools for the ordering and testing of experience. They are not held to represent unchanging particles of reality, or feeling states, to be explored as ends in themselves. Neither Socrates' rhetorical question "What is Justice?" nor Freud's "Oedipus complex" makes sense to cause-and-effect thinkers. For them, symbols and the concepts they represent are not equated with the underlying reality that is being structured and defined. The conjectural thinker is a philosophical "nominalist" rather than an "essentialist." The nominalist stance ensures that the person operating in this mode will not be satisfied with definitions and reified abstractions which, although masquerading as explanations, actually impede the inquiry process.

Lastly, those who have learned to demand cause-and-effect explanations are seen to possess a number of identifiable characteristics. They are people who readily recognize general principles and are capable of applying them to a variety of current or imagined future circumstances. They are able to propose workable solutions for problems, to predict probable consequences of projected programs, and to evaluate the actual consequences of these in terms of the original guiding principles. This is really what is meant by being freed from the concrete and immediate and from the static imperatives of the past. Altogether, these attributes constitute the final piece of equipment for the "built-in doubter."

IMPLICATIONS FOR SOCIALIZATION

An appropriate socialization process will always be aimed at encouraging the individual concerned to move beyond the current level of conceptual development, until, ultimately, the conjectural mode of interpreting experience becomes habitual. There is no better way to accomplish this than by understanding the role played by explainways as both indicators and facilitators of learning. The knowledgeable parent, caregiver or teacher will begin by "taking the role of the other." This requires an ability to recognize the mode in which the learner currently operates, and to build on that—with the aim of encouraging a gradual development to more effective levels of functioning. The magical world of the infant poses few problems, for stimulating contingencies in normal family surroundings are usually enough to initiate a natural progression onward and upward. A regression into infantile explainways in later years is another matter, however. For example, it appears today that many young people have become mired in a strangely magical way of interpreting their world. This has made an increasing number of them vulnerable to cults. An overwhelming unmet need for certainty in an insecure environment may well be the driving force behind this. Direct attacks on their mystical beliefs will not be fruitful. Until such individuals are placed in contexts where they can experience directly the power of understanding simple cause-and-effect connections in the world around them—connections that contradict their magical "truths"—they are not likely to grow intellectually.

It is probable that the fault lies in the early socialization process undergone by these youths. The problem typically begins at the *pre-operational* stage of normal development. An adequate socialization process at this stage aims at doing more than merely satisfying curiosity and the need for certainty in personal and symbolic terms. It is directed, instead, toward moving the individual beyond reliance upon magical and tautological explainways. In the case of many of the pre-school children for whom these modes are normal, consistent interaction with peers is sufficient. This encourages a developing recognition of symbols as tools for reciprocal communication rather than as essential aspects of the surrounding environment. The result is that egocentrism gradually makes way for the first stirrings of that crucial capacity to take account of "the other" which is the prerequisite for cooperation.

At the same time, wise caregivers will emphasize the difference between the fantasy that allows us to assume that everything revolves around us and occurs for our benefit alone and the actuality that relegates us to the role of minor participant or observer. Granted, it is important to encourage imagination and the use of the rich store of imagery available to *pre-operational* children. Along with this, however, every effort should be made to develop the ability to distinguish between imagining and being. Accompanying all the other mental categories that they are building at an astounding rate must be a firm line between the child's magical world and that of empirical reality. Caregivers can begin by making sure that storybook characters such as Santa Claus—and sacred personalities viewed by the culture as objects of worship—are clearly distinguishable from those people and animals accessible to sensorimotor experience.

A significant problem can arise because of the tendency for children who are lodged in the tautological explainway to view words as absolute particles or "essences" of the real world, rather than as tools for mapping that world. They are natural Platonists in that their curiosity is readily satisfied by the presentation and repetition of a name for something and, later, by a definition. This means that the socializer has a responsibility to be as specific as possible. If the name to be learned has a concrete empirical referent the child should be given the opportunity to experience the actual object or event in the process of acquiring the symbol for it. (The schoolmaster in *Nicholas Nickelby* who said, "First they spells 'winder' and then they washes it," was not as misguided as Dickens made him out to be!) Abstract terms having no concrete referents *should not be taught* to pre-school children. Any memorization of "content-less" symbols such as words denoting complex ideas, or consecutive letters of the alphabet and extensive series of numbers, can often do more harm than good.

Much of what passes for religious education is particularly problematic here. Purely "ideal" definitions satisfy curiosity at this stage while, in fact, closing the doors of discovery and adding nothing to the child's authentic understanding of the world. For example, what could a four-year-old make of concepts like Heaven or Hell? Or that of reincarnation? Or of ideals like freedom and human dignity? Or emotional appeals for "good" behavior based on the disapproval of an absent Daddy or God (or both)? Or diatribes based on the child's presumed awareness of possible future consequences of "bad" behaviors? In fact, for the pre-school child, resorting to such explanations amounts merely to exercises in semantics. Usually, these verbal constructs obstruct learning because they contradict the child's personal sensorimotor experience and can therefore promote a lasting confusion and distrust of the senses. Although the child may well remember the words, these will not operate as effective mappings for ordering experience. As incomprehensible abstractions in the form of unrelated images, they may even crowd out subsequent learning. At the other extreme, if every instance of naughty or potentially dangerous behavior elicits a lengthy but incomprehensible cause-and-effect explanation from a concerned parent, something else is likely to happen. The sensations of pleasure and power generated in the child by that attentive response may serve to *reinforce* rather than discourage the behavior in question. In this process the habit of having one's curiosity satisfied with tautologies and exercises in semantics (rather than by experiencing meaningful sensory connections) becomes deeply, and sometimes irrevocably, ingrained.

Once children begin to function in the projective explanatory mode, however, the task of socializers is quite different. The major desired outcome of socialization in elementary school is that children become conscious of the connection between choices and actions, and of the consequences flowing from them. This is the understanding that will prepare them to move ultimately in the direction of further conceptual growth. It is the necessary grounding for the "built-in doubter." We have discussed the fact that a primitive concept of cause and effect is emerging at this stage, and that causation is at first understood intuitively as motive or purpose, with unanticipated consequences not being recognized as in any way connected to the preceding behaviors. This means that agents of socialization would be well-advised to use mythology in the form of fables and proverbial tales for driving home lessons about responsibility for the consequences of one's actions. Myths provide the concrete and personal settings necessary for beginning learnings about the universality of cause and effect, a goal not fully achievable until the *formal-operational* stage.

Myths are helpful in other ways as well. A primary concern at this stage is to prevent the formation of exclusive, bullying gangs. Needless to say, parents, teachers and youth leaders should be on guard against the tendency for herd behavior in their charges and work to turn it in constructive directions. The most effective inoculation against the virus of group-inspired scapegoating and bullying is the capacity to empathize with those under attack. The encouragement and reinforcement of the child's considerable potential for empathy with other animals and persons should be one of the major objectives of socialization for this age group. If cruelty is not discouraged in children when they reach this stage, and empathy for one's victims not encouraged, it may be too late. It is virtually impossible to compensate in subsequent years for the brutalization that results from this particular failure in socialization. Legends and myths of all kinds can be useful vehicles for developing empathy, and are particularly effective for children who tend to interpret their world intuitively in projective terms. *Virtuous heroes* are particularly necessary.

Myths can provide yet another means for instilling the roots of the "built-in doubter." Toward this end, a sound process of socialization requires a multiplicity of myths, fables, legends and parables from the world's cultures: myths which are often incompatible and divergent in their explanations of reality, but consistent and universal in terms of basic principles such as personal responsibility for the consequences of one's actions. The child is then forced to recognize that the stories ordering reality for various peoples throughout history represent differing *perspectives* on that very reality. The need to choose among competing stories can lead to a need to select; and the need to select can initiate a search for *criteria* for distinguishing those more likely to be true from the more blatantly false. Over time, as a result of such experiences, children gradually acquire the means to become more independent in their judgments about truth and falsehood. Similarly, with moral behavior and valuing, they learn to rely on a developing self-discipline and conscience rooted in the application of the universal ethical principles fundamental to all the selected mythologies—rather than on culturally specific precepts that may no longer be valid.

A potential problem with the mythological approach of *concrete-operational* children is that it can habituate them to ideological explanations in later life. However, those who become permanently trapped within the ideological explainway tend to be people who have not been exposed, during their middle childhood years, to myths emphasizing cultural pluralism. Rather than being equipped by their experience with a "built-in doubter," they have been initiated into only one story and one irrevocable "truth" about the shape of reality—and thereby inculcated with an insatiable desire for certainty. From that stage onward the adolescents concerned tend increasingly to feel comfortable only with those explanations expressed in the most absolute of terms. Often they live out their lives in fear and loathing of "foreign" points of view. In other cases, they become the followers of a guru with a new cult based on a new myth that seems to allow for even greater certainty than did their traditional one; or they mature into the self-deluders who lead cults or militant political movements.

An effective socialization process designed to move secondary-school students into the conjectural—rather than the ideological—mode would involve them in the following types of experience: (1) formal debates demanding logical argument and the orderly presentation and refutation of evidence; (2) assignments requiring students to identify the major issues dealt with in a publication and to assess these in terms of logic and supporting evidence; (3) research papers involving the posing of a thesis and the gathering of *all* relevant data; (4) assignments requiring students both to compare and contrast the positions of two or more thinkers on a number of issues; (5) papers or discussions aimed at identifying and enlarging areas of agreement between conflicting ideologies; (6) role playing (such as running parallel political campaigns) requiring individuals to assume ideological positions that directly contradict their own commitments and opinions, and to study these and argue them persuasively; (7) numerous exercises dealing with the identification of premises and implications and the recognition of logical contradictions and absurdities; and (8) assignments demanding the inferring of generalizations from empirical evidence, and the application of general principles to concrete situations. Most important, however, is the requirement that the educators and other socializers are themselves firmly ensconced in the conjectural way of being in the world. Unfortunately, as childhood socialization—and even a considerable amount of post-secondary student experience—renders ever more adults vulnerable to the seductions of ideology and mystical transcendentalism, this requirement is likely to be increasingly unmet.

THE EXPLANATIONS THAT SATISFY

The various interpretive modes or explainways discussed previously are not unique to children. They co-exist, in more or less sophisticated forms, within the adult population of every modern pluralist society. Prevailing modes may vary across cultures, and in different historical eras within the same culture. To an overwhelming extent, the kind of explanation that satisfies us is dictated by our cultural imperatives—and the socialization process implied by these and functioning both to preserve and alter them. Although genes are the source of our essential engine of curiosity, culture tends to establish its limits and to provide or withhold the fuel that fires it.

World views, and the conceptual frameworks housing them, interact within biological limitations in the context of environmental challenges to determine the very questions that can be asked as well as the answers that will be found satisfying. Once again we see the "triple helix" in action! All this would trap humanity in a vicious circularity were it not for the fact that ever-changing physical circumstances make it imperative for cultures either to adapt or die. Because of the exigencies of genetic-cultural co-evolution there have always been incentives for at least some of the people to socialize some of the children into independence and open-ended inquiry—rather than merely into dependence upon a non-adaptable tradition grounded in revealed authority. These are the fortunate children who, although not finding it necessary to rebel against all conventional wisdom, have been encouraged to develop the sound conscience and the "built-in doubter" that together make wise, independent judgment possible.

How is it possible for so many people to have grown up to be so gullible? For too long during their formative years their need for certainty was reinforced, and their curiosity lulled, by explanations which, by their very nature, were not subject to falsification. These are the people who never learned to respond to truth claims by requesting checkable evidence. In fact, such a response would now be foreign to their makeup and would produce discomfort rather than the satisfaction readily aroused by magical, tautological, projective or emotionally charged ideological appeals and explanations. What causes some people to turn into the frauds and charlatans who prey on others? They, too, are the products of a form of socialization that allows them to remain forever cut adrift from a recognition of the chains of cause and effect that operate in the world of actual experience. Very often these people have regressed into the magic mode. They constantly delude themselves into a belief in the "quick fix" and make their living by convincing others of the particular mirage that beckons for the moment; or they have become adept at the reification of abstract constructs and the semantic obfuscation typical of the more sophisticated forms of the tautological mode. Then there are those who, having become mired in the projective mode, may avoid accepting any responsibility for their actions because they believe that only intentions count, and that if their goal is defined as good by some religious or political leader, the means are irrelevant. Others may be frozen into the ideological mode and can readily convince themselves that, by defining reality as they wish it to be, they can make it so.

Most of us, when we attempt to plan and structure the socialization process (and thereby consciously set out to educate), conceive of our objectives in terms of the beliefs or faiths we wish to inculcate. But we should remember that lack of faith is seldom the problem for children. Faith is their natural condition. It is *doubt* that is in short supply. The ability to doubt rationally and wisely does not emerge naturally with maturation or even with intellectual development. It must be planned for, and carefully encouraged by a socialization process dedicated to the goal of making people less easily satisfied by explanations that lead nowhere. In the end, the only lasting cure for gullibility is an independent "built-in doubter" established step by step in the context of conceptual development. It is also our only hope for developing the wise and reasonable people needed to create and sustain a self-governing civic society.

HOPE FOR THE FUTURE

Julian Huxley once wrote that "All reality is evolution, in the perfectly proper sense that it is a one-way process in time; unitary, continuous, irreversible, self-transforming; and generating variety and novelty during its transformations" (Huxley 1957: 10). In this book we have examined adaptive systems at the most complex levels of the evolutionary hierarchy: those involved in the processes of individual learning, organizational change, and the transformation of culture. We have seen that we have developed as human beings out of a chance conjunction of the accumulated accidents of our biological history and the vicissitudes of a lifetime of social interaction—in the context of our current physical surroundings. We have seen how we are irrevocably shaped within the complex adaptive process described throughout this book as the "triple helix." This means that, as a social group, we are to a large extent the generators of the very circumstances that feed back to shape us. Our hope for the future lies in the fact that we have evolved intellectual and moral capacities capable of guiding the socialization process of our members in more rational ways than has happened in the past—and in directions more in keeping with the potential of the human spirit and the ideals of our common ethical traditions.

Human beings are not doomed to be forever helpless pawns of the cruel fates spawned by their own mindless activities. Our species can choose to take up the task that none but we can accomplish: the challenging task of developing citizens of good *character*. To be able to do this we must provide a containing *culture* with the potential to nourish a respect for individual diversity rather than to poison with tribal pretensions; to uplift by encouraging an appreciation of humanity's loftiest ideals and achievements rather than to degrade and corrupt by reinforcing the vilest of our impulses; and to enrich by fueling problem-solving capacities rather than to impoverish by reinforcing the need for magical, tautological, projective and ideological explanations.

The previous chapters have demonstrated how the character of the individual and the culture of the group are inextricably intertwined and interdependent. There is thus no issue of either/or: of whether we should begin with the individual or with the content of the culture of society at large. The battle to rebuild both character and culture must be engaged on all fronts—and with whatever influence we can muster. The evolutionary systems model implies that we must ask of every social program and every physical setting: "What have been the *consequences* of people's actions here, regardless of what was originally *intended*?" and "What values and behaviors are actually being reinforced?" and finally, "How can we *alter* the established ways of rewarding behavior so as to achieve more fulfilling and constructive ends for all concerned?"

Our problems have been a long time in the making and they will not be rapidly resolved. Because we are all implicated in the web of organic life and social interaction it will take all of us to redirect a process gone so sadly wrong. Just as we are all undergoing socialization from birth to death, so are we all affecting others. We are all socializers, irrevocably enmeshed in a web of dynamic, self-organizing feedback systems. We must all assume the responsibility to use the thread spun by our living to strengthen rather than weaken the social fabric and ecology. There is nothing easy about the course implied by the explanations in the preceding chapters. The objective throughout has been to avoid offering holistic responses to the unsustainable situation which we humans have created for ourselves and other forms of life. The first prerequisite is to comprehend the social origin and nature of our current dilemmas and to proceed from there. Conditions can be altered only one step at a time; therefore it is critical that each step be in the best possible direction. To ensure that our steps are neither wasted nor counterproductive, it is essential that we develop and use an authentically *scientific* social science, in combination with our new computer technologies, to predict and assess the consequences of every move. Above all, we should be reminded that every problem—no matter how complex or deeply rooted—begins not with commitment to certain answers but with the understanding and courage to ask the right questions.

REFERENCES

Armitage, Angus. *The World of Copernicus*. New York, NY: Mentor Books, 1956. (First pub. 1947.)

Asimov, Isaac. *As Far as Human Eye Can See*. New York, NY: Doubleday, 1987.

Barnes, Cynthia A. *Critical Thinking: Educational Imperative*. San Francisco, CA: Jossey-Bass, 1992.

Dewey, John. *The Quest for Certainty*. New York, NY: Capricorn Books, 1929.

Galanter, Marc. *Cults: Faith, Healing and Coercion*. New York, NY: Oxford University Press, 1989.

Gilivich, Thomas. *How We Know What Isn't So: The Fallibility of Human Reason in Everyday Life*. New York, NY: The Free Press, 1991.

Gross, Paul R. and Levitt, Norman. *Higher Superstition: The Academic Left and Its Quarrels with Science*. Baltimore, MD: The Johns Hopkins University Press, 1994.

Gross, Paul et al., eds. *The Flight from Science and Reason*. New York, NY: The New York Academy of Sciences. Dist. by Johns Hopkins University Press, Baltimore, 1996.

Huxley, Julian. *Evolution in Action*. New York, NY: Mentor Books, 1957.

Keiser, Thomas W. and Jacqueline L. Keiser. *The Anatomy of Illusion: Religious Cults and Destructive Persuasion*. Springfield, IL: Thomas, 1987.

Kuhn, Thomas. *The Copernican Revolution: Planetary Astronomy in the Development of Western Thought*. Cambridge, MA: Publication of President and Fellows of Harvard College, 1957.

King, Patricia M. and Kitchener, Karen Strohm. *Developing Reflective Judgment*. San Francisco, CA: Jossey-Bass, 1994.

Leahey, Thomas and Hardy, Grace Evans. *Psychology's Occult Doubles: Psychology and the Problem of Pseudoscience*. Chicago, IL: Nelson-Hall, 1983.

Nettler, Gwynn. *Explanations*. Toronto, ON: McGraw-Hill Book Company, 1970.

Noll, Richard. *The Jung Cult: Origins of a Charismatic Movement*. Princeton, NJ: Princeton University Press, 1994.

Popper, Karl. *The Open Society and Its Enemies*. Vols. 1 and 2. Princeton, NJ: Princeton University Press, 1962.

Sagan, Carl. *The Demon-Haunted World: Science as a Candle in the Dark*. New York, NY: Random House, 1996.

Schell, Jonathon. "The Uncertain Leviathan." *The Atlantic Monthly* (August 1996): 70–78.

Shermer, Michael. *Why People Believe Weird Things*. New York, NY: W. H. Freeman, 1997.

Talaska, Richard H. *Critical Reasoning in Contemporary Culture*. Albany, NY: State University of New York Press, 1992.

APPENDIX A

Guidelines for Moral Education

I. AIMS AND OBJECTIVES

The long-term aim of moral education is the development of human beings with empathy, a sound conscience and strong self-concept, and the ability to make wise value judgments. Achievement of this goal requires the development of at least ten essential virtues by means of (1) carefully selecting and organizing the experiences to which the child is exposed, and (2) modeling and reinforcing appropriate behavior. The following list could be debated, and no doubt could be added to or subtracted from. However, it would seem to represent the ethical core of the great world religions and philosophies, and to incorporate those attributes most necessary for individual fulfillment and group life. Individuals who learn to be virtuous in these terms will be sensitive to the needs and suffering of others, self-disciplined and self-assured. They will also be equipped to apply ethical principles to the problems of everyday life.

II. VIRTUES REQUIRING INCULCATION

1. *Compassion* (based on empathy and manifested in kindness and helpfulness)
2. *Honesty*
3. *Nonviolence* (involving a desire for peaceful relations with others, tolerance and a willingness and ability to employ compromise rather than coercion in conflict resolution)
4. *Perseverance* (requiring self-discipline and manifested in the ability to defer gratification and to work hard to achieve excellence)

5. *Responsibility*

6. *A Sense of Justice*

7. *Courage* (manifested in the desire to explore new situations rather than to withdraw, and in the habit of asking questions and demanding evidence, rather than merely following the pronouncements and dictates of powerful others)

8. *Respect for the Rule of Law*

9. *Respect for Life*

10. *Respect for Human Dignity*

These virtues cannot be placed into the learner by fiat, nor by preaching. They must be slowly and painstakingly developed over the years, from infancy on, through the provision of experiences suitable for each age level. It is neither possible nor desirable to designate before-the-fact the precise activities that could be planned for all children in every learning situation. Nonetheless, the age-appropriate "desired learning outcomes" on the following pages can provide guidance for parents and educators in the selection of essential experiences, and in the protection of the child from those which serve to distort and cripple moral development. A few suggestions as to fruitful approaches are also included.

III. SUGGESTED APPROACHES

A. Integration as the Necessary Premise

Moral education should not be perceived as an isolated "course" to be added to the curriculum. Rather, it implies a new way of teaching every subject. The virtues listed above should permeate the entire curriculum. Simply by operating in the role, every teacher is inevitably a moral (or immoral) role model. Therefore, all teachers must recognize their responsibility for developing moral values in the children who pass through their classes. The entire staff of teachers or leaders in a daycare facility or school or leisure-time organization who are working at each of the designated age levels are advised to form a planning group devoted to the attainment of the appropriate "desired learning outcomes." The group will meet to discuss, confirm and readjust these learning outcomes at regular intervals. They will also share their plans for utilizing the opportunities provided by their regular course materials and activities in order to achieve the required moral education, and share the results of their efforts as well. They will realize that the "desired learning outcomes" are cumulative and ongoing; that is, all those listed for previous levels will have to be continuously reinforced and expanded, in conjunction with the incorporation of the new. Evaluation will be constant and informal, with success or failure being reflected in the *behavior* of the children concerned—not in their verbalized responses.

B. Culture, Current Events and Daily Experience as Sources

Some school subjects lend themselves more readily to the task of moral development than do others. For example, storytelling and reading (and, subsequently, literature) are rich sources of the vicarious experience critical for developing the empathy underlying compassion. Fables, legends and the poetry of earlier times, as well as biographies of worthy human beings: all can provide priceless moral inspiration, if suitably presented. History is a mine of the past actions of humankind, for good and ill—including information about the moral precepts of the great world religions and philosophies. Sports activities offer invaluable practice in following rules, cooperating and demonstrating consideration for others. Finally, and perhaps most important, everyday experience in any home or classroom provides ample opportunity for driving home moral lessons if the parent or teacher is appropriately motivated and adequately prepared.

C. The Developmental Nature of Morality

Moral learning is integrally related to intellectual growth. In fact, at each level of development, a specific capacity to handle mental operations is necessary for the corresponding moral learning to occur. The "desired learning outcomes" for moral education listed in the following pages have taken this essential relationship into account. They are carefully planned to accord with the general developmental process of the average child at the relevant age levels. Teachers, parents and other moral leaders working in terms of these objectives will, of course, be aware that some children are more advanced intellectually than would be expected by their chronological age and others less so. However, we all need to be aware that intellectual maturity, in itself, guarantees nothing about morality. The total learning environment is crucial. While virtues are learned gradually from the experiences to which the child is exposed, the successful achievement of each level of moral development depends upon the prior achievement of a corresponding intellectual level.

D. Discrimination as the Key

The necessary limitations and *restrictions* to be placed on the experience of the children concerned are as significant for subsequent moral development as is what is selected for *inclusion* in that experience. Every source and activity available in the home or used in any school curriculum subject should be scrutinized carefully with the "desired learning outcomes" for moral education in mind. For purposes of moral development, only those experiences of listening, reading, viewing (and otherwise participating), which provide opportunities for learning *desirable* values—that is, the virtues—should be accessible in early childhood environments and educational settings. This is not a question of censorship. It is, rather, a question of discrimination in favor of making available to the children during their brief but precious time in our care, the *best possible* experiences in terms of our immediate and long-term objectives.

IV. DESIRED LEARNING OUTCOMES

A. Early Childhood (approximately aged 3 and under)

1. Compassion

(a) To learn that animals and other people feel the same hurt (from pinches and rough handling) that one does oneself.

(b) To learn to recognize the rights and needs of other children in play situations.

2. Honesty

(a) To learn what it means to pretend.

(b) To learn how to tell about what has actually happened.

3. Nonviolence

(a) To learn not to strike or bite others.

(b) To learn that screaming and kicking do not result in attentive and loving responses.

4. Perseverance

(a) To learn to sit quietly and look at pictures, or listen to short stories and songs or poems.

(b) To learn to complete simple tasks with building blocks and puzzles.

5. Responsibility

(a) To learn where toys are kept.

(b) To learn to replace at least a few of the toys after play.

6. A Sense of Justice

(a) To learn what it means to possess toys and to share them with others.

(b) To learn to share the time and attention of the parent or caregiver and to take turns.

7. Courage

(a) To learn to explore unfamiliar spaces.
(b) To learn to be away from family members for brief periods.

8. Respect for the Rule of Law

(a) To learn to accept *physical* limits such as hot stoves, light switches, and busy streets.
(b) To learn to accept *social* limits as established by caregivers concerning matters like sleeping times and eating habits as well as toilet training.

9. Respect for Life

(a) To learn to distinguish between living things that need special care and toys that do not.
(b) To learn that living things can get sick or be hurt.

10. Respect for Human Dignity

(a) To learn to feel loved and wanted.
(b) To learn to offer and accept expressions of love.

B. Nursery School or Kindergarten-aged Children (aged approximately 4 and 5)

1. Compassion

(a) To learn that others feel pain, sorrow, humiliation, fear and happiness as one does oneself.
(b) To learn to recognize the kinds of actions that can hurt people and make them sad.

2. Honesty

(a) To learn to distinguish between fantasy and reality.
(b) To learn to describe real-life experiences clearly and precisely.

3. Nonviolence

(a) To learn that it is not possible to have one's own way all the time.
(b) To learn that people can disagree without fighting.

4. Perseverance

(a) To learn to sit quietly during the telling or reading of relatively long poems and stories, and to listen patiently to the contributions of other children.
(b) To learn to complete whatever simple tasks one has chosen to begin.

5. Responsibility

(a) To learn to help tidy up after eating or play time.
(b) To learn to put away one's own toys and outdoor clothes.

6. A Sense of Justice

(a) To learn to distinguish between greedy ownership and generous sharing of possessions.
(b) To learn that some children have less than others, and some children have more, but that does not make them either better or worse than oneself.

7. Courage

(a) To learn that it is not necessary to wear the same clothes as or to look and talk like everyone else.
(b) To learn to speak up when someone is being bullied and to refuse to take part.

8. Respect for the Rule of Law

(a) To learn to behave according to the specific rules spelled out by the parent or teacher.
(b) To learn to behave according to a set of rules about "good" behavior in general, as contrasted to "bad" behavior.

9. Respect for Life

(a) To learn to appreciate the beauty and importance of a variety of living plants and animals.
(b) To learn about the helplessness and needs of babies, kittens, puppies and other pets and the role of human and other animal families in protecting and nurturing their young.

10. Respect for Human Dignity

(a) To learn that no one should be made to feel ugly, unimportant or stupid, or be excluded when children are being "chosen" for games.
(b) To learn that we feel good or bad as a result of what we do, and because of what others do, and that others may also feel good or bad because of our actions.

C. Primary-School Children (aged approximately 6 to 8)

1. Compassion

(a) To learn to "stand in the shoes" of people in other times and places, and to imagine their feelings.
(b) To learn to see oneself through the eyes of others.

2. Honesty

(a) To learn that if one acquires the habit of lying, no one will listen when one is telling the truth.

(b) To learn that lies hurt the liar more than the one lied to, for every lie demands more lies to cover up the previous ones.

3. Nonviolence

(a) To learn that shouting and name calling lead to violence, and must be curtailed if the chain reaction to violence is to be avoided.

(b) To learn that any form of "ganging up" on individuals is taboo.

4. Perseverance

(a) To learn to stick to assigned tasks until they are completed, even though others may have finished faster.

(b) To learn that careless work is not acceptable.

5. Responsibility

(a) To learn that it is never possible to undo the hurtful or harmful things that one has said or done.

(b) To acquire the habit of punctuality, both in avoiding late arrival at school, and in being where one is supposed to be at the appointed time.

6. A Sense of Justice

(a) To learn that people differ in abilities, and that we can share our skills with others just as we share our belongings.

(b) To learn that one must never allow others to take the blame for what one has done, nor must one ever take credit for what another has accomplished.

7. Courage

(a) To learn to stand up against one's friends if they are abusing some child or animal.

(b) To learn to refuse to break the rules, even if one's friends are all breaking them.

8. Respect for the Rule of Law

(a) To understand that rules are necessary in games, or any other setting, in order to prevent cheating and to ensure an equal chance, and the maximum of freedom, for all players.

(b) To understand that rules are made by human beings in order to make it possible for people to live together in peace and order; and to protect the "commons" or public places.

9. Respect for Life

(a) To learn how all living things are born, undergo changes as they develop, and eventually grow old and die.

(b) To learn how all living things depend on one another in some way, and that plants and animals depend in a special way on humans.

10. Respect for Human Dignity

(a) To learn to appreciate and accept differences in people, including their diverse appearances and ways of doing things, and of celebrating special occasions.

(b) To learn that it is acceptable to doubt the religious or traditional beliefs of others and *vice-versa*, but that it is not acceptable to make fun of what others believe, or to abuse them because of their beliefs and rituals.

D. Middle Elementary-School Children (aged approximately 9 and 10)

1. Compassion

(a) To learn that kindness toward others will likely result in their being kind in return.

(b) To learn that helpfulness toward others makes for a generally helpful family, classroom and community—all of which feeds back in the form of help for oneself in times of need.

2. Honesty

(a) To learn to respond to what one's conscience is indicating about a proposed action—such as cheating in games or tests—even though that action cannot be seen or known by others.

(b) To learn to keep promises, and to understand that one's word is a bond connecting friends and society. To understand that people who cannot be trusted to do what they have contracted to do lose all credibility and dependability as companions in life.

3. Nonviolence

(a) To learn that fighting resolves nothing and that it is, instead, an obstacle to problem solving.

(b) To learn that the use of weapons to abuse any person or animal is taboo.

4. Perseverance

(a) To learn to work cooperatively and diligently on a group assignment, taking pride in the group's objective; and to postpone playtime, if necessary, until the objective is achieved.

(b) To learn to complete required tasks willingly and on time (whether at home or school) and to devote the extra time and effort necessary to achieve the feeling of "a job well done."

5. Responsibility

(a) To learn to take on the sole care of a pet or garden, and to accept the temporary care and teaching of some younger child or children.

(b) To learn that one's first responsibility is to maintain the health and soundness of one's own body—through exercise, nourishing food intake, and protection from harmful and addictive substances such as drugs, alcohol and cigarettes.

6. A Sense of Justice

(a) To learn to question unfairness whenever it is experienced or witnessed—especially when one's group refuses to welcome newcomers or any other child who seems different.

(b) To learn to appreciate all the privileges that one has, and to share these as much as possible with less fortunate friends, while understanding that one has no right to take the possessions of anyone else or to force anyone else to share.

7. Courage

(a) To learn to stand up to bullies, whether they are attacking others or oneself.

(b) To learn to express one's ideas in group situations, and to attempt to influence others through reasoned argument.

8. Respect for the Rule of Law

(a) To learn to be both leader and follower, as the circumstances require.

(b) To learn how to be a rule-maker and a rule-changer for one's group, as well as a rule-follower.

9. Respect for Life

(a) To appreciate the gift of life on earth and to work at acquiring only those habits that will protect and prolong that precious one-time-only gift.

(b) To appreciate that all of our daily choices have unavoidable consequences for our own lives, and for the lives of other living things.

10. Respect for Human Dignity

(a) To appreciate the past and current contributions of older people in the community—including parents, grandparents and teachers—and to respect their ideas and teachings.

(b) To appreciate the contributions of mentally and physically handicapped people, and to offer the kind of help that allows them to participate as much as possible in everyday activities.

E. Pre-adolescent Children (aged approximately 11 to 13)

1. Compassion

(a) To learn to be concerned and caring about people who are different, and even those who are distant from us.

(b) To become aware of how one is viewed and known by others and how one will be remembered by them.

2. Honesty

(a) To learn that one must not "bear false witness," nor deny culpability when rightfully accused.

(b) To learn to accept without complaint the consequences of one's own stupid or wrong-headed behavior without making excuses or blaming others.

3. Nonviolence

(a) To learn that violent acts create lasting resentment and anger in the victim, and guilt or increased insensitivity to suffering in the perpetrator.

(b) To learn that the use of violence makes for a family, school and community that are full of hate and dangerous for everybody—including the violent ones.

4. Perseverance

(a) To learn to save up one's allowance or earnings for future projects.

(b) To learn to work at difficult menial jobs for designated periods, without giving up when the going gets tough.

5. Responsibility

(a) To learn to take on a specified role in some sort of sports or special interest organization, or to acquire a specific skill, and to see it through.

(b) To learn to do one's part and take pride in keeping the home area, schoolyard and community free of refuse.

6. A Sense of Justice

(a) To appreciate the contributions of people who have devoted their lives to doing away with injustice.

(b) To understand that each individual should try to struggle against injustice wherever it is found.

7. *Courage*

(a) To learn to take a position that seems right according to one's conscience, even though it is unpopular with the peer group.

(b) To appreciate the heroic behavior of certain historical figures and their impact on civilization.

8. *Respect for the Rule of Law*

(a) To develop a willingness to apply the same rules of conduct to oneself as one would have applied to the conduct of others.

(b) To acquire the habit of obeying the law as well as awareness of the price to be paid for disobedience—by oneself and family as well as by society.

9. *Respect for Life*

(a) To appreciate how the lives of great moral leaders throughout history continue to provide inspiration for humankind.

(b) To learn to trust that it is possible for a person growing up today to achieve a life that is similarly meaningful and significant.

10. *Respect for Human Dignity*

(a) To understand that sex is not a competitive game of conquest to be played by adolescents but a precious type of relationship to be shared in maturity with the love of one's life.

(b) To learn, first and foremost, to respect oneself and to insist on that respect from friends.

F. Teen-aged Youth (aged approximately 14 to 19)

1. *Compassion*

(a) To learn to respond to signs of distress in the people with whom one interacts on a regular basis.

(b) To acquire the capacity to sympathize with the suffering of all people, everywhere, and to feel a desire to alleviate it.

2. *Honesty*

(a) To learn to distinguish between times when it is appropriate to express one's feelings openly and those times when it is better for all concerned that they remain private.

(b) To learn to distinguish between those situations in which integrity requires that one should voice an honest opinion, and those situations in which polite dissimulation may be called for.

3. Nonviolence

(a) To understand that the viewing of violent images in the mass media can make people less sensitive to the suffering of others.

(b) To understand how playing violent games and watching violent behavior can create an addiction to violence as entertainment, and to brutal behavior as a means of getting what one wants.

4. Perseverance

(a) To aspire to excellence in all that one does.

(b) To acquire the capacity to defer immediate gratification in the pursuit of long-term goals.

5. Responsibility

(a) To learn to accept personal responsibility for punctuality in the meeting of deadlines in leisure-time, work and academic activities.

(b) To understand that, if one is to enjoy the rights and benefits of membership in society, one must be willing to contribute to the welfare of the social group.

6. A Sense of Justice

(a) To understand that social injustice is a function of the degree of inequality in income, power, prestige and privilege existing within a society; and that it can be decreased only by attacking unwarranted disparities in the reward system, as well as discrimination on the basis of irrelevant criteria, wherever these occur.

(b) To understand that civic injustice has to do with a lack of equality in the application of the law, and that it can be decreased only by strengthening the rule of law as opposed to nepotism and other kinds of political favoritism.

7. Courage

(a) To acquire the ability to withstand the pressures of the peer group—or the current media-inspired fad—in the interest of the greater good.

(b) To develop a commitment to making and expressing independent value judgments, in the light of the evidence, and with one's own long-term goals in mind.

8. Respect for the Rule of Law

(a) To understand the relationships and distinctions among moral precepts, the rules of conduct in particular organizations, cultural mores, ethical principles and the law.

(b) To learn that the law must be respected at all times and that, if one should decide to attempt to change an outmoded law by disobeying it (rather than by working for improved legislation) one must do so in a nonviolent, public manner and be prepared to accept the consequences.

9. Respect for Life

(a) To understand the principle of "reverence for life" and to begin to work out one's personal application of the principle to complex modern issues such as birth control, capital punishment, the request for assisted suicides and the problem of overpopulation.

(b) To understand the relationship of the human species to the total "web of life."

10. Respect for Human Dignity

(a) To refuse to participate in any way in the spread of ideas or the use of terminology hateful or injurious to any individual or group.

(b) To refuse to support any product of an artist or mass medium that degrades human beings—either through passive viewing or consuming the goods or services of advertisers who sponsor these products.

Annotated Bibliography of Research on the Effects of Media Portrayals of Violence and Pornography on Human Development

INTRODUCTION

Professionals are becoming increasingly concerned about the growing spiral of violence throughout Western society and the effects of the increasingly violent and pornographic nature of our mass media offerings on this trend. Unfortunately, although this destructive relationship has been documented and understood by social scientists for some time, it seems that the general public is still largely unaware of the peril in which our addiction to such entertainment has placed our children and entire culture.

The reason for this dangerous state of affairs would seem to be fourfold: (1) a dismaying misunderstanding of the nature of human development is deeply embedded in the ideology of our culture, causing most people to reject modern scientific knowledge about the social sources of beliefs and values and, consequently, about the appalling power of the media as agents of socialization; (2) social scientists, in reporting their findings, tend to publish only in academic journals and in language not readily understood by the public; (3) the commercial and competitive nature of our electronic media networks make them difficult to harness to constructive rather than destructive social purposes; and (4) the "red herring" of censorship is accepted thoughtlessly, and brandished by a powerful and articulate coalition of civil libertarians and media pundits, whenever the question of media irresponsibility is raised. The following bibliography of research on the issue, annotated as simply and clearly as possible, is a response to this problem. The hope is that it will enable concerned parents and other responsible citizens to begin to understand what we have been allowing to happen to our society and to the culture of humanity.

ANNOTATED BIBLIOGRAPHY

1. Allen, Mike et al. "Exposure to Pornography and Acceptance of Rape Myths." *Journal of Communications* 45, 1 (Winter, 1995): 5–26. This meta-analysis of 24 studies with 4,268 subjects was aimed at discovering whether there is an association between exposure to pornography and acceptance of rape myths (such as the belief that women harbor an unconscious desire to be raped, or that they implicitly "ask for it" by wearing certain clothes or placing themselves in certain situations). In the case of research employing experimental methodology, compelling evidence was found for just such an association.
2. Andison, F. Scott. "TV Violence and Viewer Aggression: A Cumulation of Study Results." *Public Opinion Quarterly* 41 (1977): 314–331. Tabulated here are 67 studies in which exposure to violent television and film portrayals and aggressiveness were measured. A large majority of the studies found an association between such exposure and aggressive behavior. This relationship held whether the aggressiveness was measured by degree of imitation of what was presented, willingness to hurt by electric-shock delivery or ratings by peers, or whether the subjects were nursery-school or college age.
3. Arms, Robert et al. "Effects on the Hostility of Spectators of Viewing Aggressive Sports." *Social Science Quarterly* 42 (September, 1979): 275–279. A random sample of males and females were exposed to three types of sporting events: (1) stylized aggression (professional wrestling); (2) realistic aggression (fighting in hockey); and (3) a competitive non-aggressive event (a swimming race) in a before and after research design. Support was indicated for an earlier finding of increased hostility in those viewing both the wrestling and the hockey, but not the swimming.
4. Atkin, Charles. "Effects of Realistic TV Violence vs. Fictional Violence on Aggression." *Journalism Quarterly* 60 (Winter, 1983): 615–621. To test the hypothesis that a violent scene will produce more aggressive responses in television viewers when part of a real newscast than when presented as a movie promotional clip, working-class and middle-class children were randomly assigned to watch one of three short programs. One program containing a 15-second segment with university students fighting was shown as news to 33 children; another 33 saw the same violent segment in the context of a fictional movie highlight; and a control group of 33 saw a neutral commercial. The hypothesis was supported. The theory that the viewing of aggressive behavior has a cathartic effect on the viewer was refuted.
5. Atkin, Charles et al. "Selective Exposure to Televised Violence." *Journal of Broadcasting* 23 (Winter, 1979): 5–13. In order to test the hypothesis that viewers have a tendency to select programs supportive of their own aggressive predispositions, 227 middle-elementary students were administered questionnaires designed to measure program-viewing frequencies. A follow-up study was conducted a year later. The selected content was assessed on an

aggression index, and the aggressive behavior of the children was also measured. It was found that aggressive children tended to watch aggressive programs, with an increase in both variables noted.

6. Bandura, A. et al. "Transmission of Aggression through Imitation of Aggressive Models." *Journal of Abnormal and Social Psychology* 63 (1961): 575–582. This is a pioneer study on the modeling of aggressive behavior. One-half of a group of pre-school children observed an adult playing quietly with toys; the other children saw the adult attack a Bobo doll—striking it with fists and a mallet, etc.—all accompanied by aggressive comments. Subsequently, the children's free play was rated by observers who did not know which children had been in which group. It was found that those who had been exposed to the aggressive model exhibited significantly more aggression than did the others, and that they imitated specific violent acts performed on the doll by the model.

7. Bandura, A. et al. "Imitation of Film Mediated Aggressive Models." *Journal of Abnormal and Social Psychology* 66 (1963): 3–11. In a replication of the preceding study, nursery-school children were exposed to a cartoon featuring an aggressive cat and to a human dressed as a cat who strikes a Bobo doll. The consistent response was found to be an imitation of the aggression. It was also found that, while a cartoon figure was less effective in the modeling of new aggressive responses than a real-life film character, it was equally effective in reducing children's inhibitions against assaulting their playmates.

8. Baran, P. "The Impact of the New Communications Media upon Social Values." *Law and Contemporary Problems* 34 (1969): 244–254. The author reminds us of the parallel between the relationship of the physical well-being of children to their food intake and that of their socio-psychological well-being to the inputs from community agencies providing their early experiences. He writes, "In our culture we tend almost completely to ignore the scope, effectiveness, and all-pervasive social conditioning that occurs for the younger recipient of the constant barrage of the mass media" (245). Baran concludes that the mass media may well be too powerful a socializing force to be left to chance.

9. Baran, S. et al. "Television Drama as a Facilitator of Pro-Social Behavior: The Waltons." *Journal of Broadcasting* 23 (Summer, 1979): 277–284. It was hypothesized that children viewing such a program would exhibit more cooperation than non-viewers. Three groups of primary-school children were studied: a control, an aggression-viewing group, and a group who viewed The Waltons. The follow-up comprised a game requiring cooperation. Immediate, direct and significant results were found in favor of the Waltons-viewing group.

10. Baron, L. and Straus, M. A. "Sexual Stratification, Pornography and Rape in the U. S." In *Pornography and Sexual Aggression*, ed. N. M. Malamuth and E. Donnerstein, pp. 185–209. New York, NY: Academic Press, 1984. This is a macrosociological (or demographic) study initiated by the fact that the reported incidence of rape in the United States has increased 200 percent since 1960. Three hypotheses were posed: (1) the lower the status of women in a state the higher the rape rate; (2) the higher the readership of pornography in a state the higher the rape rate; and (3) the higher the rate of non-sexual violent crime the higher the rape rate in the state. The authors noted ex-

tremely large state-to-state differences in rape rates, consistent over a 20-year period. Measures of the three variables were obtained and indexed and multiple regression analysis was applied. Hypothesis 1 was not supported— in fact, when other factors were controlled, a significant *negative* correlation was shown. In the case of hypothesis 2, the mass circulation of "porn" magazines was found to be highly associated with increased reported incidence of rape. This correlation persisted despite control for possible confounding variables and was confirmed when the study was replicated the following year. Hypothesis 3 was also supported.

11. Barrison, David et al. "Developmental Changes in How Children Understand Television." *Social Behavior and Personality* 10, 2 (1982): 133–144. Measures were obtained from a sample of 60 children aged 5 to 14 and 20 adults on their spontaneous reconstructions of television scenes and responses to a series of questions on the thoughts and feelings of particular characters. It was found that the younger the viewer the more likely he or she was to structure the content in terms of overt descriptive features, action, or literal repetition of bits of dialogue. The older subjects tended to consider motives and plot.

12. Beaulieu, Lucien A. "Media, Violence and the Family: A Canadian View." In *Family Violence*, ed. J. M. Eekelaar and S. N. Katz, pp. 58–68. Toronto, ON: Butterworths, 1978. In this article, an Ontario Provincial Court judge assesses the impact of the mass media on the promotion, legitimization and reinforcement of violence in the home. He notes the surprising absence of attention to this issue in the literature on family violence. He then explains how the media contribute to known causal factors in violence, such as the frustration syndrome, social alienation, the authoritarian personality, the compulsive masculinity syndrome and male aggression stereotypes. He also discusses the media's direct contribution to violence, in that they stimulate aggression in the recipient, teach criminal technique, and teach norms favoring violence by: (1) promoting violent role models; (2) routinely portraying violence as the normal method of conflict resolution; (3) legitimizing the use of violence by showing "good guys" resorting to it; (4) presenting violence as an acceptable outlet for emotions; (5) portraying violence as an appropriate and effective means to achieve desired ends; (6) showing violence as a standard technique of social control; and (7) teaching that violence is a means to success in sports. He attacks the "pernicious myth" of catharsis, showing it to have been refuted by a compelling body of evidence, and concludes by recommending some sort of accountability mechanism for the media.

13. Belson, W. *Television Violence and the Adolescent Boy*. Westmead, UK: Saxon House, Teakfield, Ltd., 1978. In a comprehensive study a random sample of 1,650 London boys aged 13 to 16 were assessed as to nature and number of violent acts committed over the previous six months and the degree and frequency of violence in the television programs viewed over the previous 12 years. A detailed analysis related type and quantity of violent activity and type and quantity of television violence viewed. A significant positive correlation was found except in the case of cartoons and violence in comedy, science fiction and sport.

14. Berkowitz, Leonard. "Some Effects of Thoughts on Anti- and Pro-social Influences on Media Events: A Cognitive-Neoassociationist Analysis." *Psycho-*

logical Bulletin 95 (May, 1984): 410–427. This article explains how media messages can give the audience ideas that may then be translated into behavior. Evidence indicates that depictions activate thoughts that are semantically related to the observed event. This may result in exaggerated notions of the prevalence of the observed behavior in real life, and lead to an indifference to it. The author examines a variety of factors that can affect the likelihood that the activated thoughts will kindle related behavior. These include the ideas that the observers already have, their interpretation of the appropriateness of these ideas, the probability and moral justification of the acts, the nature of the available targets, and whether the depicted incident is defined as real or fictional. The context of the viewing and what the viewer brings to the situation are crucial. Many viewers will not repeat what has been seen. However, the author suggests that, if even only 1 in 100,000 does so, this adds up to a great deal of needlessly initiated violence.

15. Berkowitz. Leonard. "Situational Influences on Reactions to Observed Violence." *Journal of Social Issues* 42 (1986): 93–106. Situational factors influencing the effects of viewing violent television and movies are discussed. These comprise specifics such as the presence of others, nature of available targets, things operating as retrieval cues, viewer interpretations of whether what was viewed was real or fictional and the viewers' focus of attention. The author argues that research should no longer deal merely with the issue of *how much* effect is exerted by violent media portrayals, but with the *conditions* under which effects are either heightened or lessened.

16. Berkowitz, Leonard and Rawlings, E. "Effects of Film Violence on Inhibitions against Subsequent Aggression." *Journal of Abnormal and Social Psychology* 66 (1963): 405–412. Two groups were exposed to the same violent film. The first group were introduced to it in such a way that the violence could be justified, while the second group saw it without the justifying introduction. The first group subsequently showed more aggression than did the second group. This would seem to indicate that justifications for violence, such as are common in films where the "good guys" triumph, can have a disinhibiting effect on the viewer.

17. Bogart, L. "Warning: The Surgeon General Has Determined that TV Violence Is Moderately Dangerous to Your Child's Health." *Public Opinion Quarterly* 36 (1973): 491–521. This article discusses the summary of research in Volume 2 of the 1972 U.S. Surgeon General's Report. The author reviews the evidence in the volume and relates it to 54 earlier experimental studies, all indicating that violent programs produce significantly more emotional arousal in young children than do nonviolent programs. He also refers to Volume 3 of the same report which states "there is clearly a preponderance of evidence in these studies to support the conclusion that adolescent aggressiveness and the viewing of violent TV programs are associated."

18. Bredemeir, Brenda J. and Shields, D. L. "Values and Violence in Sports Today." *Psychology Today* (October, 1985): 23–25, 28, 29, 32. The authors ask, "Does maturity of athletes' moral reasoning influence their aggressive behavior? What are the unique characteristics of sport morality and how does this 'game reasoning' influence the perceived legitimacy of aggression?"(23) They conclude that players (and viewers) seem to accept a kind of suspension

of ordinary morality, within the setting of the game, so long as the "legitimate violence" does not result in permanent injury. Questions are then raised
about the social consequences of an apparently increasing tendency to trans-
plant this game morality into other arenas of life.

19. Brown, M. H. et al. "Young Children's Perception of the Reality of Televi-
    sion." *Contemporary Education* 50 (Spring, 1979): 129–133. A group of 162
    grade-one children were measured by Piagetian techniques as to their
    cognitive developmental level, and then assessed regarding their ability to
    distinguish between reality and fantasy on TV. Those who had achieved the
    "concrete-operational" level were found to be able to make this distinction
    to a much greater degree than could the less cognitively mature children.
    (Most first-grade children are just beginning to achieve this level.)

20. Bryan, J. H. and Schwartz, T. "Effects of Film Material upon Children's Be-
    havior." *Psychological Bulletin* 75, 1 (1971): 50–59. The authors examine the
    role of violent movies in increasing violence in children, claiming that ag-
    gressive behavior is associated with judgments pertaining to the aggressor,
    so that "the aggressive hero who verbalizes socially sanctioned norms may
    well be teaching the observer how to be brutal and what to verbalize in order
    to justify brutality."

21. Bushman, Brad J. et al. "Role of Cognitive-emotional Mediators and Individ-
    ual Differences on the Effects of Media Violence on Aggression." *Journal of
    Personality and Social Psychology* 58 (January, 1990): 156–163. Two experiments
    were conducted to test the hypothesis that the observation of media violence
    elicits thoughts and emotional responses related to aggression. In experiment
    1, a highly violent videotape elicited more aggressive cognitions than did a
    less violent one. In experiment 2, aggressive cognitions increased with level
    of violence viewed. Self-reported hostility and systolic blood pressure both
    rose with the level of violence portrayed. The subjects who reported feeling
    the most hostile were those who had been identified as relatively susceptible
    emotionally and most inclined to brood about past grievances.

22. Cairns, Ed et al. "Young Children's Awareness of Violence in Northern Ire-
    land: The Influence of Irish Television in N. Ireland and Scotland." *The British
    Journal of Social and Clinical Psychology* 19 (February, 1980): 3–6. Two studies
    were conducted. In the first, 20 children from London and 20 from a town
    in Northern Ireland that has been free of violence were asked to make up
    stories in response to pictures of derelict houses and crashed trains. More of
    the Irish than London children mentioned bombs and fighting. In the second
    study, children from a relatively quiet part of Northern Ireland were com-
    pared with children from two separate areas in Scotland—only one of which
    receives Irish television. Both groups of children who viewed Irish television
    differed from the control group in tending toward explanations citing human
    aggression.

23. Canton, Joanne and Nathanson, Amy I. "Predictors of Children's Interest in
    Violent Television Programs." *Journal of Broadcasting and Electronic Media* 41,
    2 (1997): 155. A random sample of 285 parents of children in kindergarten,
    second, fourth and sixth grades was interviewed about their children's view-
    ing habits. It was found that children's attraction to classic cartoons (those
    featuring violence for its own sake) decreases with age. Males are more at-

tracted to cartoons demonstrating retributive violence but that, too, decreases with age. There was a significant positive correlation between children's aggression and their interest in justice-restoring genres.

24. Cantor, Muriel and Orwant, Jack. "Differential Effects of TV Violence on Girls and Boys." *Studies in Communications* 1 (1980): 63–83. These authors reanalyzed the findings of 14 studies from the 1972 Surgeon General's Report, controlling for gender, and found that boys and girls seem to learn differently from television and are influenced to behave aggressively in different ways.

25. Chaffee, Steven et al. "Defending the Indefensible." *Society* 21 (September/October, 1984): 30–35. This is a response to the arguments put forth by the ABC network to the National Institute for Mental Health Report on Media Violence in the United States. "The ABC argument is scientifically indefensible . . . it is only the latest example of unwarranted resistance to the clear policy implications of overwhelming scientific evidence. The renewed attempt to evade, undermine and discredit the work of hundreds of scientists . . . and to shape the course of public discussion by selective attention and misrepresentation is unworthy of an industry that professes—and is licenced—to serve the public interest" (31).

26. Cline, V. B. et al. "Desensitization of Children to Television Violence." *Journal of Personality and Social Psychology* 27 (1973): 360–365. Two groups of boys were studied, one comprising "heavy viewers" and the other, "light viewers." Both were exposed to a violent film scene, with their galvanic skin response and blood volume plus amplitude being recorded before and during the viewing. Emotional arousal during the violent scene was less for the hardened viewers than for the others, while the before-viewing measures were similar.

27. Cohen, A. and Adoni, H. "Children's Fear Responses to Real-Life Violence on Television: The Case of the 1973 Middle East War." *Communications* 6, 1 (1980): 81–93. A group of 96 Israeli schoolchildren were shown six film clips of soldiers either in tranquil settings or in combat. Their facial expressions were videotaped and they were questioned after each showing. No differences in fearfulness were found on the basis of age or socioeconomic status, but girls were more fearful than boys. Fear responses were greatest when sounds were included.

28. Collins, W. A. "The Developing Child as a Viewer." *Journal of Communication* 25 (Autumn, 1975): 35–44. Like the following study, this one set out to examine possible mediating effects of age-related differences in the comprehension and evaluation of television programs. Aggressive segments separated by commercials were found to affect grade 3 and grade 6 children differently. The younger children who saw the aggressive behavior in scenes separated from portrayals of the anti-social motives and punishing consequences associated with it showed greater tendencies toward interpersonal aggressive behavior than did their peers who saw the scenes without interruptions. Older children were not affected by the insertion of the commercials.

29. Collins, W. A. et al. "Observational Learning of Motives and Consequences for Television Aggression: A Developmental Study." *Child Development* 45 (1974): 799–802. In a comparison of the learning effects on older and younger

viewers of violent programs, it was found that younger children select information and images in an unpredictable way, in that they fail to use the dramatic framework to organize and understand the scenes presented, and make few inferences about motives, consequences or relationships.

30. Comstock, George. *Television in America*. London, UK: Sage, 1980. In discussing the effects of television violence on society, the author describes the phenomenon of "cultural contagion" whereby televised acts are copied in waves of violence or threats of violence across the country. He tells how, whenever the movie *Doomsday Flight* has been shown, there follows a rash of airline bomb threats. He notes the fact that criminals often report how they acquired ideas for violent attacks and other crimes from television (109). He claims that, despite the biased "loading" of the Surgeon General's Advisory Committee in favor of the networks, their report was forced to conclude by admitting that the convergence of findings from all types of scientific studies supported the hypothesis that violent programming increases the likelihood of aggressiveness among young viewers.

31. Court, John H. "Sex and Violence: A Ripple Effect." In *Pornography and Sexual Aggression*, ed. N. M. Malamuth and E. Donnerstein, pp. 143–172. New York, NY: Academic Press, 1984. The author reviews the literature and concludes that there is now a strong case for postulating a positive enhancement of sexually aggressive behavior after exposure to pornographic violence, and no adequate evidence for the formerly popular idea that a decline in such behavior might result. He is highly critical of the 1970 Report of the U.S. Commission on Obscenity and Pornography, claiming that it is obsolete (in that the nature of pornography has changed drastically since the 1950–1960s period from which its data were drawn, and that later statistics tell quite a different story) and biased (much research was omitted). He discusses the 59 percent increase in reported rapes in the United States from 1973 to 1980, in view of the probability of an even larger increase in unreported assaults. He then presents the findings of his own demographic study aimed at testing 8 propositions, as follows: (1) rape reports have increased wherever pornography laws have been liberalized (supported by recent statistics from the United States, Scandinavia, Britain and certain states of Australia); (2) areas where pornographic violence is not liberalized do not show a similar steep rise in rape reports (supported by statistics from Singapore, South Africa, Queensland and South Australia); (3) where restrictions have been adopted, rape reports have decreased (supported by statistics from Japan); (4) intermittent policy changes are reflected in rape report data (supported by statistics from Hawaii showing the effects of policy reversals in 1965, 1974 and 1977); (5) changed pornography laws are temporarily related to changed rape rates (supported by statistics from Britain and New Zealand); (6) the nature of the rape attack is changing, reflecting the increased perversion and violence of the pornography (supported by statistics in all countries studied showing increases in violence and indecent acts, and in the involvement of teenagers); (7) discrepant cases do not occur without adequate explanation (supported by discussion of the Far North—the discrepant case—showing the operation of other variables); and (8) the increase in rape reports does not parallel the increase in other violent crimes (here, the evidence is incon-

clusive). The author predicts that because more people (especially teenagers) are being exposed to more pornography than ever before and, because teenagers are particularly receptive, there will be a disastrous ripple effect over the next decade, spreading spiraling waves of sexual violence throughout society.

32. Cowan, Geoffrey. *See No Evil: The Backstage Battle over Sex and Violence on Television*. New York, NY: Simon and Schuster, 1979. The writer discusses how the competitive commercialism of the 3 large U.S. networks makes the possibility of harnessing this all-pervasive medium to social ends—or even making it somewhat more responsible—highly unlikely. "Television, some may argue, is too powerful a tool to be left to a process so crass and mindlessly competitive."(310)

33. Cramer, Phebe and Mechem, Melissa. "Violence in Children's Animated Television." *Journal of Applied Developmental Psychology* 3 (1982): 23–39. Pairs of cartoon episodes that did and did not meet the National Association of Broadcasters' Code for Violence were rated by college students and then by children, as to violent content. The results indicate that the code has been ineffective in reducing levels of violence.

34. Dahlgren, Peter. "Television in the Socialization Process: Structures and Programming of the Swedish Broadcasting Corporation." In *Television and Social Behavior*, Vol. 1, eds. George Comstock and Eli Rubenstein, pp. 533–546. Washington, DC: U.S. Government Printing Office, 1972. A content analysis of Swedish television was made for a week in May 1971. It was found that there was almost no violence. Another finding was that sensationalism in regard to sex is not indulged in, because it would be incompatible both with the goals and responsibilities of television as expressed in legislation and stated policies of the two channels involved.

35. Dee, Juliet Lushbough. "Media Accountability for Real-life Violence: A Case of Negligence or Free Speech?" *Journal of Communication* 37 (Spring, 1987): 106–138. This article presents a review of fifteen American court decisions in cases in which a child or young adult was the victim of violence claimed to have been induced by media presentations—from films to television to rock music. The decisions suggest that the courts in general have consistently refused to hold media organizations accountable for incitement to violence. The author's examination of these cases raises important questions about the applicability of First Amendment law to the issue of the media's accountability for the consequences of their actions. She notes that no congressional committee has ever contemplated major structural changes in U.S. broadcasting policy. Having everything to gain from reducing accountability for the negative effects of portrayals of violence, she says, the television industry has co-opted many research efforts by promoting studies by researchers who minimize such effects. She concludes that, in the long run, this testing of media accountability in the courts may yet be another in the long series of steps to find workable solutions to the problems of violence in American society.

36. Dominick, J.R. and Greenberg, B.S. "Attitudes toward Violence: The Interaction of TV, Family Attitudes and Social Class." In Comstock and Rubenstein, *Television and Social Behavior*, Vol. 3., 1971. The authors found a

significant relationship between frequency of exposure to violent television programs and attitudes toward the use of violence.

37. Dominick, J. R. et al. "Problem Solving in TV Shows Popular with Children: Assertion or Aggression." *Journalism Quarterly* 56, 3 (Autumn, 1979): 455–463. The 15 prime-time favorites and the 8 Saturday morning favorites of 6 to 11-year-olds were analyzed by trained coders who recorded each interpersonal problem occurring with the method by which it was resolved. Results indicated that, while the prime-time programs emphasized assertion and helping in problem solving, the Saturday morning ones had three times as many aggressive solutions.

38. Donahue, T. R. "Perceptions of Violent TV Newsfilm: An Experimental Comparison of Sex and Color Factors." *Journal of Broadcasting* 20, 2 (Spring, 1976): 185–195. It was found that females react more negatively than males to violence in a film and to lack of color.

39. Donnerstein, E. "Erotica and Human Aggression." In *Aggression: Theoretical and Empirical Reviews*, Vol. 2., ed. R. Geen and E. Donnerstein. New York, NY: Academic Press, 1983. It was found that non-pornographic films portraying aggression against women increased the level of male aggression against female victims, although to a lesser degree than aggressive pornographic films.

40. Donnerstein, E. and Berkowitz, L. "Victim Reactions in Aggressive-Erotic Films as a Factor in Violence against Women." *Journal of Personality and Social Psychology* 41 (1981): 710–724. Subjects in this study were placed in 2 groups, one of which was deliberately angered by a confederate, then both were exposed to 2 aggressive pornographic films—one having a negative ending, and one showing a positive ending (victim portrayed as having enjoyed the assaults). Aggression was increased only for the angered group after the first film, but for both groups after the second film.

41. Donnerstein, Edward and Linz, Daniel. "Sexual Violence in the Media: A Warning." *Psychology Today* 18 (January, 1984): 14–15. Researchers have shown that exposure to even a few minutes of sexually violent pornography can lead to anti-social attitudes and behavior. It can influence viewers' acceptance of rape myths (women like it), increase the willingness of males to commit rape, increase aggressive behavior to females in a laboratory setting, and decrease sensitivity to the consequences of rape and the plight of the victims. They conclude that this strongly documented possibility of habituation to sex and violence has significance social consequences. The authors describe a study in which male subjects were randomly assigned to an experimental and a control group. In the experimental group the men watched 10 hours per day of commercially released films depicting sexual assault: some X-rated and others R-rated. As viewing progressed, the men rated themselves as increasingly less repulsed, depressed and anxious concerning what they saw. Clearly, they were becoming desensitized to the violence. They reported fewer personally offensive scenes as time went on. On the last day they rated the films as significantly less debasing and degrading of women, and more humorous and enjoyable, and they claimed a general willingness to watch more of such films. Both the experimental group and the control group were then shown a rape trial. The victim was rated as signif-

icantly more worthless and her injuries significantly less severe by those in the experimental group than in the group who had not been exposed to the diet of sexually violent films.

42. Donnerstein, Edward et al. "Mass Media, Sexual Violence and Male Viewers: Current Theory and Research." *The American Behavioral Scientist* 29 (May/ June, 1986): 601–618. The authors survey and analyze available research on aggressive pornography as well as that on non-pornographic media images of violence against women and on nonviolent pornography. They also look for the major focus of recent research and the type of material that provokes the most negative reactions. They found that, in many aggressive porno- graphic depictions, victims are portrayed as secretly desiring the assault and experiencing sexual pleasure. They conclude that the bulk of the findings demonstrate that a non-rapist population will evidence increased sexual arousal at media depictions of violent rape. Other common findings are that exposures to sexually explicit rape in which the victim shows "positive" reaction tend to produce decreased sensitivity to rape, and that the viewing of sexually aggressive films significantly increases male (but not female) ac- ceptance of interpersonal violence and rape. The bulk of the evidence also suggests that violence against women need not occur in pornographic or sexually explicit contexts in order for it to negatively affect viewing males. The authors suggest that if callous attitudes about rape are indeed learned, then they can be unlearned. Finally, they conclude that the evidence is now quite compelling that long-term exposure to even nonviolent pornography may cause male and female subjects to (1) become more tolerant of bizarre and violent forms of pornography, (2) become less supportive of sexual equality and (3) become more lenient about punishment for rapists.

43. Downing, Leo and Bynum, Jack. "Substantiated Reports of Child Abuse and Neglect." *Free Inquiry in Creative Sociology* 10, 2 (November, 1982): 197–201, 206. This statistical study attempted to assess the premise that child abuse occurs at levels far above those indicated by reported cases. The validity of inferences about the incidence of such abuse in the entire population, based on number of reported cases, was assessed by examining large populations of child abusers. National demographic statistics were used. Variables ex- amined were type of substantiation, initial report source, perpetrator-victim relationship, educational level, sex, ethnicity and family income of abuser, characteristics of abused children and medical treatment required. Over the years examined, reported cases nearly doubled in number, with only minimal changes in proportional distribution of the assessed variables. This suggests that reported cases are indeed a valid sample of all cases—that is, the actual incidence of child abuse in the population doubled during the 1970s.

44. Drabman, R. S. and Thomas, M. H. "Does Media Violence Increase Children's Tolerance of Real Life Aggression?" *Developmental Psychology* 10, 3 (1974): 418–421. The authors report an intriguing study designed to assess the effects of viewing filmed violence on youngsters' subsequent readiness to report to an authority figure a potentially harmful fight among very young children for whom they have been made responsible. The data indicate a significant relationship between level of violence allowed among the children being

cared for and the immediately previous exposure of their "sitters" to film aggression.

45. Ellis, G. T. and Sekyra, F. "The Effect of Cartoons on the Behavior of First-Grade Children." *Journal of Psychology* 81 (1972): 37–43. Children who watched an animated football game for only five minutes subsequently exhibited significantly more aggression in a classroom setting than did those who either viewed a neutral film or participated in a discussion.

46. Eron, Leonard D. "Intervention to Mitigate the Psychological Effects of Media Violence in Aggressive Behavior." *The Journal of Social Issues* 42 (Fall, 1986): 155–169. The author concludes that interventions combining both cognitive and behavioral approaches are the most effective. He acknowledges that a major difficulty encountered by all attempts to undo the effects of media violence is the intractability of aggression, once it has been established early in life as a habitual problem-solving mode. It is devastatingly resistant to change.

47. Eron, Leonard D. et al. "Does Television Violence Cause Aggression?" *American Psychologist* 27 (1972): 253–263. This is a landmark longitudinal study of 427 teenagers who had been assessed in 1960 on (1) degree of aggression exhibited, and (2) various potential predictors of aggression such as preference for watching violent television, IQ, social status, mobility aspirations, religious practice, ethnicity and parental disharmony. In the early (grade 3) phase, a significant positive correlation was found between boys' preference for violent programs and peer-rated aggression. In the grade 13 phase, the correlation between early preference for violent programs and aggression was even more significant. In neither case was it true for females. The researchers conclude that, for boys, the single most plausible causal hypothesis (taking into account all of the variables studied) is that a preference for watching violent television in grade 3 contributes to the development of persistent aggressive habits.

48. Eron, Leonard D. et al. "Age Trends in the Development of Aggression, Sex-typing and Related Television Habits." *Developmental Psychology* 19 (1983): 71–77. A three-year longitudinal study of elementary school children assessed the following variables: aggression, frequency of television viewing, extent of violence viewed, judged realism of programs viewed, and preference for sex-typed activities. The data support the hypothesis that there is a sensitive period (age 8 to 10) when television can be especially influential.

49. Estap, R. and Macdonald, P. "How Prime-Time Crime Evolved on TV, 1976–1981." *Journalism Quarterly* 60, 2 (Summer, 1983): 293–300. It was found that in this five-year period the proportion of televised programming devoted to crime drama increased steadily until it came to constitute the bulk of prime-time viewing. To evaluate these changes, crime programs during three seasons were sampled. The two most frequently portrayed crimes, murder and robbery, were examined, and the findings as to suspects and victims were compared with official records for actual crimes. Media portrayals were found to differ markedly from real-life crime.

50. Eysenck, H. J. *Psychology Is about People.* New York, NY: The Library Press, 1972. The author suggests that, like certain drugs, "some of the products of the mass media are harmful" (332). He argues that our approach to research

has been backwards—that the onus of proof is not on the public, but on those who provide a suspect service.

51. Eysenck, H. J. "Sex, Violence and the Media: Where Do We Stand Now?" In *Pornography and Sexual Aggression*, ed. N. M. Malamuth and E. Donnerstein, pp. 305–318. New York, NY: Academic Press, 1984. The author refers to the British Williams Committee that studied the problem. "I can testify to the absence of psychologists on that committee and the obsessional tendency of members to protect themselves from any contamination or contact with scientific laws relevant to the topic" (306). And, regarding the U.S. Commission on Obscenity and Pornography, "What they have to say in their report shows little understanding of scientific methodology as portrayed by modern philosophers of science" (309). He concludes, "There is now very little doubt (1) that the portrayal of sex and violence in the media does have important effects on at least some people; (2) that it is possible to formulate general theories that explain the findings and that, indeed, have predicted most of them; and (3) that those results present problems for society that go far beyond the realm of social psychology" (317).

52. Eysenck, H. J. and Nibs, H. *Sex, Violence and the Media*. London, UK: Sector, 1978. This book presents an excellent overview of the evidence, discussed in terms of theory. The authors conclude that there is to date ample evidence that media violence increases viewer aggression and may also increase viewer sexual libido. Their recommendations are as follows: (1) Makers of films and television programs, producers of theater plays and others involved in the portrayal of violence must be required to assume more social responsibility for their cultural products. (They ask why incitement to violence against *all* the vulnerable members of society is not at least as serious as incitement to hatred against particular ethnic groups. (2) The type of control suggested for violence should also apply to the portrayal of perverted sexual behavior, with the content being judged according to the prevailing tone of the presentation. (3) Absurd suggestions for censorship should cease, as they only serve to create a libertarian backlash against necessary control measures. (4) We should stop regarding the struggle for such controls as a battle between left and right (extreme libertarianism is representative of *neither* the political left nor right).

53. Feilitzen, C. V. and Linne, O. "Identifying with Television Characters." *Journal of Communication* 25, 4 (Autumn, 1975): 51–55. The authors present a review of the findings of Scandinavian researchers on children's identification with television characters. The presumption is made that when children lack positive relations with parents and peers they tend to seek models in the world of the mass media. The studies reviewed found that young children tend to identify with characters similar to themselves, while older children (8 to 12) express wishful identification and appear to learn moral norms from their viewing.

54. Feshbach, S. and Singer, R. D. *Television and Aggression: An Experimental Field Study*. San Francisco, CA: Jossey-Bass, 1981. This book contains a report of an early field study that is often used to support the catharsis theory. Boys in private schools and boys' homes were divided into two groups and restricted to a diet of either violent or neutral television for six weeks (the

Untouchables vs. Lassie). Naturally occurring aggressive behavior was recorded each day by houseparents and teachers. It was found that there was a
cumulative trend for the violent television group in each situation to become
less aggressive, and the neutral group to become more so. However, the problems with this research are twofold: (1) anyone familiar with boys could guess
that the resentment of the group not allowed to watch their favorite program for
six weeks might aggravate aggression in such a closed institution (and do the
opposite for the favored boys), and (2) the recorders knew to which group each
boy belonged and were all committed to the catharsis theory.

55. Fowles, B. R. "A Child and His Television Set: What Is the Nature of the
Relationship?" *Education and Urban Society* (November, 1977): 89–102. According to the findings of developmental research, to a child of 4, if something can occur in the imagination, it can occur in fact. So, in merging fact
and fantasy, television manages to objectify the thought processes of the
"pre-operational" child. This increases the chance that the child will attend
to and internalize the material presented. However, television cannot provide
the child with the feedback about his own linguistic production that is necessary for language growth, nor can the interactions on the intellectual plane
that it can offer replace interactions on the social plane.

56. Friedrich, L. K. and Stern, A. H. "Aggressive and Prosocial Television Programs and the Natural Behavior of Pre-school Children." *Monograms of the
Society for Research in Child Development*. Serial No. 151, 1973. Children aged
3 to 5 were divided into three groups, each of which was exposed to a specific
kind of program for a period of four weeks. The "violence" group watched
Batman and Superman; the "prosocial" group watched Mr. Rogers' Neighborhood, and the "control" group watched neutral films. Naturalistic observations of aggression, prosocial interpersonal behavior and self-regulation
were made for three weeks prior to exposure, four weeks during the treatment period, and for two weeks following. It was found that, for previously
aggressive children, exposure to the violent television maintained their assaultive behavior, while the aggressive children in the prosocial and control
groups showed a significant decrease in aggression. The violence group
scored significantly lower than the other two groups on tolerance of delay.

57. Geen, R. G. "Some Effects of Observing Violence upon the Behavior of the
Observer." In *Progress in Experimental Personality Research*, Vol. 8, ed. B.
Maher. New York, NY: Academic Press, 1978. This is a comprehensive re-
view of the evidence to date.

58. Geen, R. G. and Quantz, M. B. "The Catharsis of Aggression: An Evaluation
of a Hypothesis." In *Advances in Experimental Social Psychology*, Vol. 10, ed.
L. Berkowitz. New York, NY: Academic Press, 1977. The authors conclude
this exhaustive review by suggesting that what little evidence there is for
catharsis can be re-interpreted in terms of inhibitions against aggression
caused by the research procedures used: when such inhibitions have been
minimized the opposite of catharsis occurs.

59. Geen, Russell G. and Thomas, Susan L. "The Immediate Effects of Media
Violence on Behavior." *Journal of Social Issues* 42 (Fall, 1986): 7–27. The authors summarize and analyze a multitude of research findings from a cognitive-neoassociationist perspective. They begin with laboratory experiments

on short-term effects, and interpret the findings in terms of *modeling, cognitive cueing, arousal* and *realism*. Concerning the significance of *modeling*, the evidence indicates that those children who have previously seen aggressive acts display more aggression after viewing violence than do others who have not been so subjected—especially when the modeled aggression was unrestrained. It also suggests that specific sets of motor responses are imitated and that degree of punishment versus rewarding of models makes a significant difference—as do the actions and attitudes revealed by adult viewers. As to *cognitive cues*, the authors conclude that subsequent observer-aggression is increased when the viewed violence is closely linked to the observer's potential victims through some shared characteristic. Another conclusion from the reviewed studies is that a high level of *arousal* will lower inhibitions and activate latent aggressive tendencies. Much of the evidence also indicates that there is a relationship between sexual arousal and increased aggression following the viewing of erotic films. Where *realism* is concerned, the findings overwhelmingly show that violence presented in realistic circumstances and justified morally by the story line results in more aggressive responses than does violence which is obviously fictional in character. Finally, the authors suggest that the majority of field experiments have been so poorly controlled that the results are ambiguous and meaningless. Long-term natural studies, on the other hand, have produced results that tend to support experimental work and these are recommended as the most fruitful approach for the future.

60. Gelles, R. J. "Violence in the Family: A Review of Research in the Seventies." *Journal of Marriage and the Family* 42, 4 (November, 1980a): 873–885. The author concludes that this was a decade in which domestic violence became increasingly visible, apparently having become an extensive phenomenon, not explainable solely by psychological factors or income.

61. Gelles, R. J. "A Profile of Violence toward Children in the United States." In *Child Abuse: An Agenda for Action*, ed. George Gerbner et al. New York, NY: Oxford University Press, 1980b. The widespread extent and growth of violence toward children is discussed. Reference is made to David Gil's 1968 survey of officially reported and validated cases which yielded 6,000. In 1976 the American Humane Society documented 26,438 cases, 14,115 of which had been proven valid. In 1977, Saad Nagi's survey of agencies produced an estimate of 167,000 annual reports of child abuse and 91,000 cases unreported. At the date of publication, the National Centre of Child Abuse estimated 250,000 a year.

62. Gerbner, G. and Gross, L. "The Scary World of Television." *Psychology Today* (April, 1976a): 41–45, 89. It was found that heavy viewers see the real world as more dangerous than do light viewers; they are less trustful of others and more fearful of urban living than are those who watch little television. Those under 30 seem to be more highly influenced by television than are older viewers.

63. Gerbner, G. and Gross, L. "The Violence Profile." *Journal of Communication* 26 (1976b): 173–199. The authors describe their ongoing research project aimed at making annual comparable assessments of the degree of violence in the electronic media. They discuss their "Violence Index" and "Cultural

Indicators"—the latter designed to measure conceptions of reality as they change over time. They make the case for studying television as a force for enculturation (or socialization) rather than merely a selectively used medium for entertainment and information. They discuss the far-reaching consequences of living in a symbolic world ruled largely by violence. "Fear . . . may be an even more critical residue . . . than aggression. Expectations of violence or passivity in the face of injustice may be consequences of even greater concern"(179).

64. Gerbner, G. et al. "TV Violence Profile No. 8: The Highlights." *Journal of Communication* 27, 2 (Spring, 1977):171–180. This summary of the fall 1976 television season shows a record rise in violent content. Overall violence was found to have increased uniformly in all categories of dramatic programming, on all three commercial networks, to a level exceeding that found 10 years before. For example, nine out of 10 prime-time programs contained violence; 75 percent of all characters were involved in violence, and violent episodes occurred at the rate of 9.5 an hour.

65. Gerbner, G. et al. "The Demonstration of Power: Violence Profile No. 10." *Journal of Communication* 29 (1979): 177–196 The authors report that the index for 1978 showed an increase in violence in children's weekend and late evening programs, but a decrease in violence during the family hour. They describe the measures that make up the index as follows: (1) percent of one complete week's programs containing violence; (2) two times the rate of violent incidents per program; (3) two times the rate of violent incidents per hour; (4) percent of characters involved in violence; and (5) percent of characters involved in killing. "The most significant and recurring conclusion of our long-range study is that one correlate of TV viewing is a heightened . . . sense of danger and risk in a mean and selfish world" (196).

66. Gerbner, G. et al. "The Mainstreaming of America: Violence Profile No. 11." *Journal of Communication* 30, 3 (Summer, 1980): 10–29. This violence profile summarizes trends in the amount and nature of violence on television since 1967–1968 (the family hour again becoming more violent) and reports two major theoretical conclusions concerning the media's social consequences. One of these is the understanding that the outlooks of heavy viewers in otherwise disparate subgroups in society converge into a homogeneous "mainstream." The second concerns a phenomenon called "resonance" which implies that special life circumstances creating a perceived congruence between a person's everyday reality and television messages can render those messages highly salient.

67. Goldsen, R. K. "Assembly-line Violence, Picture Tube Guns." *The Cornell Journal of Social Relations* 11, 1 (Spring, 1976): 39–45. The author reflects on the fact that, although governmental bodies have tried to curb the power of a few private companies to saturate our environment with violence, they have not succeeded. From time to time, it has been scientifically documented and officially declared that the prevailing programming practices: (1) incite to delinquency and crime, and (2) cause mental disorder on the scale of a public health menace. Still, the people and their governments in Western democracies seem to be powerless to change these destructive policies.

68. Greenberg, B. S. "British Children and Televised Violence." *Public Opinion*

Quarterly 38, 4 (1975): 531–547. The author tells us that the BBC analyzed its own program content and that of independent UK channels and American television. They found that fully half of all programs contained one or more major acts of violence, and that close to 100 percent of cartoons and 90 percent of all films shown in both countries contained violence in some form. He also reports on his own 1972 study of British schoolchildren. He found a significant relationship between watching violent programs and behaving aggressively, with the relationship being slightest for Westerns and highest where contemporary or futuristic settings were involved.

69. Gunter, B. and Furnham, A. "Perceptions of Television Violence: Effects of Program Genre and Type of Violence on Viewers' Judgments of Violent Portrayals." *The British Journal of Social Psychology* 23, 2 (June, 1984): 155–164. This study attempted to examine the mediating effects of program type and physical form of violence on viewers' perceptions of TV violence. Forty subjects viewed violent scenes from four different types of programs and then viewed four different kinds of violence. Both the fictional setting and the physical form of the violence as well as the aggressive predispositions of the viewer were found to affect perceptions significantly.

70. Gurevitch, M. "The Structure and Content of Television Broadcasting in Four Countries." In *Television and Social Behavior*, Vol. 1, ed. George Comstock and Eli Rubenstein, pp. 374–385. Washington, DC: U.S. Government Printing Office, 1972. The data from studies of Swedish, Israeli, American and British television were compared. Cartoons in the United States and United Kingdom were found to be almost totally violent. The American programs led in the amount of violence shown.

71. Hapkiewicz, W. G. "Children's Reactions to Cartoon Violence." *Journal of Clinical Child Psychology* (Spring, 1979): 8, 30–34. The author begins by stating the general conclusion of the extensive research on the effects of TV violence on behavior, that viewing violence *increases* violent behavior in the viewer. He then expresses three concerns about cartoons: (1) their disinhibition effects; (2) the fact that the incidence of violence in them is three times that of the average adult show; and (3) the fact that they are viewed extensively by very young children. He reviews 10 studies of the effects of cartoon violence and notes that their findings are somewhat discrepant. After examining these and attempting to assess and explain them, the author concludes that cartoon violence affects children differently, depending upon developmental level (ability to distinguish between reality and fiction and to connect cause and effect), gender, previous experience of violence, predisposition toward aggression, and socioeconomic status. He recommends moving toward more complex studies of the nature of the well-documented relationship between viewing television violence and aggressive behavior.

72. Hapkiewicz, W. G. and Roden, A. H. "The Effect of Aggressive Cartoons on Children's Interpersonal Play." *Child Development* 42 (1971): 1583–1585. This laboratory study exposed a group of 6- to 8-year-old children to a Woody Woodpecker film, while a second group, randomly matched with the first group on the basis of gender, saw a neutral film. Following the exposure, they were all involved in an exercise eliciting either sharing or assaulting strategies. Those who had viewed the violent cartoon used sharing strategies

less than did those who had not seen it. A third group was exposed to a film segment portraying real-life violent characters (*The Three Stooges*). The children who had seen this revealed significantly more assaultive behavior toward peers than did members of either of the other two viewing groups.

73. Hapkiewicz, W. G. and Stone, R. D. "The Effect of Realistic vs. Imaginary Aggressive Models on Children's Interpersonal Play." *Child Development Journal* 4 (1974): 37–44. This is a follow-up study to the preceding one. This time a violent Mickey Mouse cartoon was used. No difference was noticed in aggressive behavior in subsequent play of the control and treatment group. But, as in the previous study, children who viewed *The Three Stooges* exhibited significantly more assaultive behavior than did the others.

74. Harrell, W. A. "Verbal Aggressiveness in Spectators of Professional Hockey Games: The Effects of Tolerance of Violence and Amount of Exposure to Hockey." *Human Relations* 34, 8 (August, 1981): 643–655. Interviews of 391 male spectators at 14 professional hockey games were conducted. Measures were taken of variable levels of hostility relative to (1) tolerance of violence in the game, (2) amount of previous exposure to hockey, and (3) time of interview (whether at the beginning, during or after the game). Levels of hostility were found to be higher in those already tolerant of violence and were found to increase as the game proceeded. The opposite held for those intolerant of violence.

75. Hartnagel, T. F. et al. "Television Violence and Violent Behavior." *Social Forces* 54, 2 (December, 1975): 341–351. This study attempted to examine the nature of the relationship between television violence and aggressive behavior. Favorite programs of a large group of high school students were coded as to degree of violent content, and the students interviewed. It was found that adolescents who favored violent shows and who saw the violence as effective tended to be more aggressive in their own behavior.

76. Hearold, Susan L. "Meta-analysis of the Effects of Television on Social Behavior." Doctoral Dissertation. University of Colorado, 1979. This is a statistical analysis of 230 experiments and surveys documenting the relationship between filmed violence and aggressiveness and between prosocial programs and prosocial behavior. Altogether, it is based on the study of more than 100,000 individuals. The analysis focused on degree of relationships, and extracted 1,043 combinations of varying film exposure and behavior. Each permitted the comparison of persons differing in exposure. The degree to which the behavior differed in association with media exposure was assessed by calculating, in each instance, a measure representing the difference in behavior accompanying a difference in exposure. The findings showed that exposure to anti-social portrayals was positively associated with anti-social behavior and negatively associated with prosocial behavior.

77. Hicks, D. J. "Short and Long-term Retention of Affectively Varied Modeled Behavior." *Psychonomic Science* 11 (1968): 369–370. A group of 60 preschoolers were exposed to an eight-minute film of someone hitting a plastic doll, and to a neutral film. Imitation of the aggressive act was found to occur whether the model was an adult or a peer, male or female. Imitation of the same remembered act was still apparent when the children were tested six months later.

78. Horn, Jack C. "Fan Violence: Fighting the Injustice of It All." *Psychology Today* (October, 1985): 30–31. The author states that fan violence seems to be increasing (giving a number of examples of deaths and injuries caused by it in recent months), whereas it was seldom heard of in the past. He points out that people watching an aggressive sport tend to become more aggressive themselves. He reminds athletes that they are role models, and that it is up to them to eliminate fights, tantrums and prolonged arm-waving arguments over decisions, as such activities provoke violence in fans.

79. Huesmann, L. Rowell et al. "Television Violence and Aggression: The Causal Effect Remains." *American Psychologist* 28 (1973): 617–620. Having been challenged by researchers for the networks, the authors have re-checked their data and methodology, carefully answered criticisms and, after adding up all the other evidence available, reiterate their previous conclusion (presented to the Commission) that the most plausible hypothesis to explain all these findings is that early exposure to television violence has a causal influence on aggression in males.

80. Huesmann, L. Rowell et al. "Mitigating the Imitation of Aggressive Behaviors by Changing Children's Attitudes about Media Violence." *Journal of Personality and Social Psychology* 44 (1983): 899–910. A group of grade 1 and grade 3 children selected because of their high exposure to media violence were divided into an experimental and a control group. Over the course of two years the experimental subjects were exposed to treatments designed to reduce the likelihood of their imitating the aggressive behaviors they were witnessing. By the end of the second year the experimental group were rated as less aggressive by their peers, and the relationship between television viewing and aggression was diminished for them, but not for the control group which had not had the treatments.

81. Huesmann, L. Rowell et al. "Media Violence and Anti-social Behavior: An Overview." *The Journal of Social Issues* 42 (Fall, 1986): 1–6. This is an overview of research and a response to those who continue to maintain (against this large body of evidence to the contrary) that the data are inconclusive. The authors consider that two factors are important in perpetuating the minority viewpoint. The first is the propensity of different reviewers to concentrate on different types of studies. The authors suggest that field studies should be seen as supplements to well-controlled laboratory research—not as a substitute for it. Second, they recognize that the differing theoretical orientations of the researchers get in the way and obfuscate results. For example, the developmental-learning theory model *explains* the observed connections between media viewing of violence and aggressive behavior, while many competing models do not, and therefore those researchers who operate in terms of the latter have trouble interpreting the findings in an understandable way. The authors go on to elaborate how the developmental-learning theory model sheds light on the way in which violent media portrayals provide an aggressive script which the child stores in the memory for subsequent acting out, and the way in which such viewing changes attitudes which manifest themselves in behavior at a much later date—and eventually, in habits that persist and resist change. Within this model, research is organized into stud-

ies dealing with immediate effects and those dealing with cumulative long-term effects of exposure to violence.

82. Huesmann, Leonard Rowell. "Psychological Processes Promoting the Relationship between Exposure to Media Violence and Aggressive Behavior by the Viewer." *Journal of Social Issues* 42 (Fall, 1986): 125–139. The author argues that individual differences in the effectiveness of media violence on aggression are primarily the result of a cumulative learning process during childhood. Aggressive scripts are learned gradually, and environmental cues trigger these. Intervening variables either mitigate or exacerbate these reciprocal effects. However, television-viewing habits of early childhood correlate positively with adult criminality independently of other factors. The evidence concerning media violence and the knowledge about how children learn both indicate that intervention should focus on the pre-adolescent years.

83. Huston-Stein, A. et al. "The Effects of TV Action and Violence on Children's Social Behavior." *Journal of Genetic Psychology* 138 (1981): 183–191. This study attempted to examine the independent effects of action and violence in television programs on children's attention and social behavior, by investigating a group of 66 pre-schoolers. It was found that, when action was controlled, there were no differences in attention as a function of violence. Clearly, it is the action that arouses and retains attention. Imaginative and fantasy play was greatest for those in the low action/low violence group; least for those in the high action/high violence group; and in between for the high action/low violence group.

84. Iwao, Sumiko et al. "Japanese and U.S. Media: Some Cross-cultural Insights into TV Violence." *Journal of Communication* 31, 2 (Spring, 1981): 28–36. The content of one week's evening programs on five Tokyo television channels was analyzed. Those produced in Japan were compared with those imported from the United States. The amount of violence in both types was about equal, but its treatment significantly different. Japanese programs emphasized the suffering of the victims, while the American ones did not.

85. Josephson, Wendy L. "Television Violence: A Review of the Effects on Children of Different Ages." Ottawa: Canadian Heritage, 1995. This is a comprehensive review of the subject, formulated from a Canadian point of view.

86. Joy, L. A. et al. "Television and Children's Aggressive Behavior." In *The Impact of Television: A Natural Experiment in Three Communities*, ed. T. M. Williams. New York, NY: Academic Press, 1986. Elementary-school children were studied in three small communities in British Columbia. The communities were similar in size, and in average level of income, education, and occupation—but with one difference: "Notel" had no television, "Unitel" had one CBC channel, and "Multitel" received four channels. The second phase of the study was conducted two years later, after "Notel" had access to CBC television. Observations were recorded of verbal and physical aggression, with peer and teacher ratings being obtained as well. The findings indicate that "Notel" children increased in aggressive behavior following the introduction of television into their community. Increases were observed for both sexes and for all age levels, of a magnitude not found in the children of "Unitel" and "Multitel," although those had grown in aggressiveness as well.

87. Klein, B. D. and Lemaire, A. "The Effect of Television on Children Aged Less

than Six Years, with Reference to an Experiment in a School Environment." *Neuropsychiatrie de L'Enfance et de Adolescence* 29, 3 (March, 1981): 141–146. Three types of broadcasts (news, a commercial, and a children's show) were shown to French nursery-school children. Before and after assessments were made of level of cognitive and ego development. For all types of broadcasts, the effects were shown to be profound. The authors conclude that these findings reveal a need for extremely careful screening of programs by adults.

88. Kniveton, B. H. "The Effect of Rehearsal Delay on Long-term Imitation of Filmed Aggression." *British Journal of Psychology* 64 (1973): 259–265. A sample of grade-one boys was exposed to a film in which aggression was modeled. Imitation was found to have occurred whether they were tested immediately or one week later, and remnants of the modeled behavior were still retained up to five months later.

89. Kunkel, Dale et al. "Measuring Television Violence: The Importance of Context." *Journal of Broadcasting and Electronic Media* 39 (Spring, 1995): 284–291. The goal of the project described by the authors (PAT) is "to distinguish portrayals of violence most likely to contribute to effects generally considered to be anti-social or harmful from portrayals that may be less problematic." The measured violence is divided into three categories: credible threats to harm, aggressive behaviors and the harmful consequences flowing from these. Violent incidents are analyzed in terms of interaction between the perpetrator (P), the act (A) and a target (T). This same PAT framework is used for tracking and reporting on media-portrayed incidents and then ascertaining from *contextual* information which situations are most harmful to the viewer. The project began with the 1994–1995 viewing year, and was planned to continue for the following three seasons. The first findings, indicating the crucial importance of context, were to be reported in 1996.

90. Kutschinsky, B. "Towards an Explanation of the Decrease in Registered Sex Crimes in Copenhagen." *Technical Report of the Commission on Obscenity and Pornography*, Vol. 7. Washington, DC: U.S. Government Printing Office, 1971. The author attempted to discover whether a decline in reported sex crimes following the liberation of obscenity laws in Denmark was due to a change in public attitudes (which could be expected to have altered due to increased exposure to pornography). He interviewed a random sample of citizens, asking if they were more or less likely than ten years before, to consider various acts as crimes, and whether or not they had changed their minds recently over the seriousness of sex crimes. The findings indicated that the Danish people have become much more permissive, especially of such activities as "peeping Tomism," exhibitionism and indecent interference: precisely those crimes which statistics indicate to have decreased during the 1960s. The author concludes that, because figures for more serious crimes, such as rape, reveal no such reduction, what has been happening is an increasing acceptance by the public of behavior that would formerly have been defined as deviant.

91. Lefkowitz, Monroe M. et al. *Growing Up to Be Violent: A Longitudinal Study of the Development of Aggression.* Toronto, ON: Pergamon Press, 1977. This is the final report of a longitudinal study of the development of aggression from ages 8 to 18. A large sample of the least aggressive of a larger group of

children who had been tested a decade before on exposure to, and preference for, violent television and on aggressive propensities were studied once more. It was found that exposure to, and preference for, violent television programs in grade 3 is more strongly related to aggression at age 18 than it is at age 8.

92. Leifer, A. D. and Roberts, D. F. "Children's Responses to Television Violence." In *Television and Social Behavior*, Vol. 2. Washington, DC: U.S. Government Printing Office, 1972. An experimental group of children of various ages from 3 to 18 were exposed to a violent program while a control group viewed one that was neutral. They were then presented with descriptions of day-to-day conflict situations and asked to select one from among four possible responses (illustrated by stick figures). Those who had viewed the violence were more likely to select the more aggressive of the responses to the conflict situation.

93. Lester, David. "Media Violence and Suicide and Homicide Rates." Part 1. *Perceptual and Motor Skills* 69 (December, 1989): 894. The National Coalition on television violence has rated the 10 best-selling books each year from 1933 to 1984 for the amount of violence portrayed. The average rating for each year was correlated with the suicide and homicide rate for the following year. The films of 19 nations in 1987 were also rated for their violent content. In each case there was found to be a positive (although not statistically significant) correlation.

94. Leyens, J. P. et al. "Effects of Movie Violence on Aggression in a Field Setting as a Function of Group Dominance and Cohesion." *Journal of Personality and Social Psychology* 32 (1975): 346–360. Two groups of boys attending a private residential school in Belgium were exposed to contrasting sets of films. One group saw five violent movies, one on each of five consecutive evenings, while the other group saw five nonviolent films. Subsequent observation of the boys' behavior as they went about their normal activities indicated that those exposed to the violent films showed an increase in aggression; in contrast, the other group showed no such behavior change.

95. Liebert, R. M. and Baron, R. A. "Some Immediate Effects of Television Violence on Children's Behavior." *Developmental Psychology* 6 (1972): 469–475. Kindergarten children were exposed to either a violent sequence from The Untouchables or a nonviolent but exciting sports scene. A box with both a "hurt" and a "help" button was introduced to them as part of a game in which another child could be either helped to turn a handle or hindered because the handle would become so hot it would hurt his hand. The violence-viewing group was found to be significantly more uninhibited in pressing the "hurt" button.

96. Liebert, R. M. et al. *The Early Window: Effects of Television on Children and Youth*. Toronto, ON: Pergamon Press, 1973. The authors reported that, from 1952 to 1964, there was a 90 percent increase in the number of violent incidents shown on television. They estimated that by the early 1970s the average child between the ages of 5 and 15 had witnessed the violent destruction of 13,400 people in his own home. They claimed that "the best documented fact about TV is that it is violent" (23). They concluded, "It behooves us, in a world at the brink of disaster, to harness television's potential to contrib-

ute to our society in ways which we deem more desirable. All of us must bear the responsibility for what is being taught on TV" (70).

97. Linz, Daniel et al. "The Effects of Multiple Exposure to Filmed Violence against Women." *Journal of Communication* 34, 3 (Summer, 1984): 130–147. The effect of the filmed portrayal of brutality against women on male viewers was examined by having 12 adult males watch five commercially released R-rated films which were both erotic and violent, and ended with the killing of the female victim. They were shown a videotaped re-enactment of a rape trial both before and after the film viewing, and tested as to affective responses to the victim. Results demonstrate that, not only does repeated exposure to filmed sexual violence desensitize viewers to the violence and increase their enjoyment of the portrayals over time, but it decreases their ability to empathize with a female victim in real-life context.

98. Linz, Daniel et al. "Issues Bearing on the Legal Regulation of Violent and Sexually Violent Media." *The Journal of Social Issues* 42, 3 (1986): 171–193. The authors discuss legal responses to the problem of media violence and the implicit conflict between attempts to legislate solutions and the First Amendment in the American constitution. They recognize that applying social-scientific findings to legal policy is difficult. They identify the central issue as "Are we prepared as a society to deprive all persons, or even some persons, of the right to view forms of violent material if only a small percentage of these individuals will become criminally violent?" They say that the Canadian approach (unlike the American) attempts to balance the rights of women (and children?) with the traditional rights to freedom of speech.

99. Linz, Daniel et al. "Sexual Violence in the Mass Media: Logical Solutions, Warnings and Mitigation through Education." *Journal of Social Issues* 48 (Spring, 1992): 145–171. The authors explore and compare the probable efficacy of (1) legal restrictions, (2) informational labeling and (3) formal education as means of dealing with the problem. They conclude that it is premature to advocate legal restrictions; that labeling is not viable due to the prevailing assumption that such ratings should be based on what parents find offensive rather than on what research has shown to be the most harmful; and that education is therefore the only viable option at present. After presenting a review of the literature, they propose that an educational program focus on (1) what types of information are most effective in altering attitudes toward violence; (2) what type of format is best for presenting this; (3) the most effective sources of such socialization; and (4) the degree to which social-psychological factors effect long-term change in attitudes. The goal of all this would be an easily administered educational program for delivery to schools.

100. Linz, Daniel et al. "Sex and Violence in Slasher Films: A Reinterpretation." *Journal of Broadcasting and Electronic Media* 38 (Spring, 1994): 243–246. A previous study by Molitor and Sapolsky found that 44 percent of innocent victims killed in slasher films were female while 56 percent were male. The conclusion from this was that such films do not single out women as victims. However, Linz and his colleagues say that the former study failed to *compare these figures with those for movies in general.* Indeed, slasher films brutalize women twice as often as do other x-rated films. The rate appears

even greater when compared to television violence in general. Nancy Signorielli, professor of communications at the University of Delaware—and
collaborator on the Annenburg Cultural Indicators Project—has provided a
gender breakdown for characters killed in prime-time television programs.
From 1969 to 1988 there were 4,453 major characters portrayed, and of these,
180 met violent deaths. Of the latter, 83 percent were male and only 17
percent were female. Linz et al. maintain that Molifor and Sapolsky also
ignore the huge difference in treatment of females and males in slasher
films. According to the figures reported, there were 5 hours of portrayals
of women enduring extreme fear compared to only one hour for males.
Furthermore, sex and violence were paired a substantial amount of the time.

101. Lovass, O. I. "Effect of Exposure to Symbolic Aggression on Aggressive
Behavior." *Child Development* 32 (1961): 37–44. Three experiments were conducted with pre-school children, to discover whether viewing violent cartoons would increase their tendency to play with aggressive toys. No
significant effects were noted until after the third exposure; then a tendency
to select aggressive play became marked.

102. Lovibond, S. H. "Effects of Media Stressing Crime and Violence upon Children's Attitudes." *Social Problems* 15 (1967): 91–100. The author surveys the
Australian research and reports that a preference for programs featuring
violent crime and violence increases with rates of viewing. He expresses
concern about the effects of mass media violence on value systems and
world views and concludes that, although high levels of exposure to violence do not necessarily cause violent behavior, they are likely to result in
a decreased readiness "to oppose delinquent behavior and the associated
system of ideas, and . . . to take humanitarian principled action when the
situation demands it"(98).

103. McAuley, Clark et al. "More Aggressive Cartoons Are Funnier." *Journal of
Personality and Social Psychology* 44, 4 (April, 1983): 817–823. A positive correlation ranging from .49 to .90 was found between viewers' assessment of
a cartoon as humorous and the degree of aggression portrayed in it. This
held across six studies involving six different sets of cartoons and six different groups of subjects, including children and adults, people of both high
and low socioeconomic status, national as compared to foreign-born, and
females as well as compared to males.

104. Maccoby, E. E. "Effects of the Mass Media." In *Review of Child Development
Research*, Vol. 1, ed. L. W. and M. L. Hoffman, pp. 323–348. New York, NY:
Russell Sage Foundation, 1966. Following a comprehensive survey of the
literature, the writers conclude that "the existing evidence seems to indicate
that, over a normal population of children, with a normal range of pre-
existing aggressive emotion, the effect of aggression in films is to *arouse*
rather than discharge or inhibit aggressive impulses"(336).

105. McIntyre, J. J. and Teevan, J. J., Jr. "Television Violence and Deviant Behavior." In *Television and Social Behavior*, Vol. 3, pp. 383–435. Washington, DC:
U.S. Government Printing Press, 1972. The authors studied 2,300 high school
students. Each listed four favorite programs. These were rated as to violence. Measures of deviant behavior of the subjects were taken, using five
scales of deviance. Attitudes toward violence were also assessed. It was

found that those who preferred violent programs were significantly more likely to approve of teenage and adult violence. The relationship between program preference and deviant behavior was positive and significant on all five deviant variables.

106. "Major Crime in Canada." Compiled from *Crime Statistics*, 1960, 1976, 1986, 1991, 1996 and 1998. Ottawa, ON: Statistics Canada, Queen's Printer. Whether or not the connection is a direct, causal one, the statistics reveal a steeply rising rate of violent crime among Canadian youth, coincident with over three decades of steadily accelerating television violence. Figures from 1960 and earlier are not comparable with contemporary ones, as the Uniform Crime Reporting system now used throughout North America was not employed then. We *can*, however, compare per capita *rates* of criminal offenses. In 1959 there were 274 per 100,000 Canadians; in 1985 there were 8,574—approximately 30 times more. In 1974, 6.3 out of 100 offenses were violent; in 1985, 9 out of 100; in 1991, 10 out of 100. From 1974 to 1985 the following increases in crime involving *young* offenders occurred: homicide—38 percent; attempted murder—25 percent; and sexual assault—225 percent. From 1984 to 1991 the rate of violent sexual assault almost doubled and from 1986 to 1994 the rate of youths charged with violent crime more than doubled. Although the homicide rate in the United States has been historically 3 to 4 times higher than in Canada, this difference is diminishing. From 1993 to 1996 the total number of youths indicted for violent offenses decreased in Canada, but this coincided with a corresponding decrease in the population of the relevant age group and an increase in the brutal and purposeless nature of the assaults. In 1995 the violent-crime rate for youth was 1,000 per 100,000 youth population.

107. Malamuth, Neil M. "Erotica, Aggression and Perceived Appropriateness." Paper presented to the 86th Annual Convention of the American Psychological Association, Toronto, ON, 1978. Three groups of male subjects were exposed to three different treatments: group 1 to aggressive porn, group 2 to non-aggressive porn and group 3 to neutral stimuli. Following exposure, all were insulted by a female confederate and placed in a natural-appearing situation where they could aggress against her *via* ostensible delivery of electric shocks. Half were given a disinhibiting communication to read; the others, a message designed to make them sensitive to aggressive delivery of the shocks. No significant difference in aggression was found following the inhibiting message. The highest level of aggression was in group 1. After the disinhibiting message aggression increased, even in group 3.

108. Malamuth, Neil M. "Rape Fantasies as a Function of Exposure to Violent Sexual Stimuli." *Archives of Sexual Behavior* 10 (1981): 33–47. Subjects were presented with two versions of a slide-audio show: rape, or mutually consenting sex. All were then exposed to the same audio description of a rape incident. Later, in the same session, they were asked to create their own sexual fantasies and then record them. Content analysis of these showed that the group exposed to the rape scene created more aggressive fantasies than did the others.

109. Malamuth, Neil M. "Factors Associated with Rape as Predictors of Labo-

ratory Aggression against Women." *Journal of Personality and Social Psychology* 45 (1983): 432–442. This is a two-phase study. Male college students were assessed as to general proclivity to rape, and to Rape Myth Acceptance and Acceptance of Interpersonal Sexual Violence (RMA and AIV). Several days later they were placed in a situation where an opportunity for aggression toward a female confederate in an experiment was possible. It was found that the measures in the first phase successfully predicted aggressive behavior in the second phase.

110. Malamuth, Neil M. "The Mass Media and Aggression against Women: Research Findings and Prevention." In *Handbook of Research on Pornography and Sexual Assault*, ed. A. Burgess. New York, NY: Garland, 1985. This is a compilation of evidence documenting the implication of the media in the growth of violence against women in American society. The author ends with suggestions for tackling the problem, such as (1) the political-economic approach: either cooperative consultation with the media industry or pressure-confrontation, and (2) the educational approach, both direct and indirect.

111. Malamuth, Neil M. and Briere, John. "Sexual Violence in the Media: Indirect Effects on Aggression against Women." *The Journal of Social Issues* 42 (Fall, 1986): 75–92. These authors reviewed and analyzed available research in terms of the hypothesis that certain cultural factors (including the mass media) interact with individual variables to affect peoples' thought patterns and responses in the direction of aggression. They found that two streams of current findings can be explained in this way: (1) those documenting connections between exposure to sexually violent media and the development of cognitive patterns supportive of violence against women; and (2) those finding connections between such patterns of thinking and anti-social behavior in laboratory and naturalistic settings. They conclude that films with positive images of violent heroes can also affect the belief systems of youths in lasting ways.

112. Malamuth, Neil M. and Check, J. V. P. "The Effects of Mass Media Exposure on Acceptance of Violence against Women: A Field Experiment." *Journal of Research in Personality* 15 (1981): 436–446. This study attempted to test the hypothesis that depictions of sexual aggression with positive consequences (the victim "really enjoys it") can affect social perceptions and attitudes. A group of 271 male and female university students were asked to participate in research supposedly focusing on movie ratings. Two films from the campus film program that showed sexual aggression with positive consequences were shown to the experimental group on two consecutive nights; a control group saw neutral films. Measures used were (1) the AIV scale (acceptance of interpersonal violence against women), (2) the RMA scale (rape myth acceptance) and (3) the ASB scale (belief in the inevitability of adversarial sexual relationships). Measures of these scales were embedded in a general survey administered to all students. The results indicated that films showing positive consequences of sex violence significantly increased levels of AIV and RMA for males but not for females.

113. Malamuth, Neil M. and Check, J. V. P. "Factors Related to Aggression against Women." Paper presented at the Annual Meeting of the Canadian

Psychological Association, Montreal, PQ, 1982. This describes a successful replication of the Malamuth (1981) study. The authors also tried to predict aggression on the basis of scales measuring attitudes (GAV—general acceptance of violence—and RMA and AIV—see above). They found that the RMA and AIV predict violence against women, but not the GAV. This means that males who measure high on general propensity toward violence are not necessarily sexually violent but those who believe in the rape myth, and accept violence against women, *are* likely to be.

114. Malamuth, Neil M. and Donnerstein, E. "The Effects of Aggressive-pornographic Mass Media Stimuli." In *Advances in Experimental Social Psychology*, Vol. 15, ed. L. Berkowitz, pp. 103–136. New York: Academic Press, 1982. This review of the research leads the authors to conclude that exposure to particular kinds of coercive erotic imagery can result in an increase in aggressive sexual fantasies, aggressive behavior, acceptance of anti-female attitudes, and male aggression against females.

115. Malamuth, Neil M. and Donnerstein, E. *Pornography and Sexual Aggression*. Orlando, FL: Academic Press, 1984. This book presents and integrates new and previously existing scientific research on the relationship between pornography and aggressive sexual behavior. Worldwide data are used to examine the correlation between the availability of pornography and the officially reported incidence of violent crimes against women. Of particular value is the chapter entitled "Aggressive Pornography: A More Direct Relationship" (63–81).

116. Malamuth, Neil M. and Spinner, B. "A Longitudinal Content Analysis of Sexual Violence in Best-selling Erotic Magazines." *The Journal of Sex Research* 16, 3 (1980): 226–237. The evidence presented here suggests that, over time, subjects become conditioned so that sexual arousal is associated with aggression toward the sex partner and can occur only in that context.

117. Malamuth, Neil M. et al. "Sexual Responsiveness of College Students to Rape Depictions: Inhibiting and Disinhibiting Effects." *Journal of Personality and Social Psychology* 38 (1980): 399–408. Depictions of the victim as secretly desiring or enjoying the assault are shown to be particularly disinhibiting to males. Also, such images tend to remain in the memory, affecting subsequent beliefs and attitudes.

118. Martin, L. J. "The Media's Role in International Terrorism." *Terrorism* 8, 2 (1985): 127–146. The relationship between the mass media and terrorism is investigated. The author concludes that it is symbiotic. Each exploits the other, for terrorism has no meaning without media coverage. A content analysis was conducted of how 70 terrorist reports were handled by the *Washington Post*, the *London Times*, the *Frankfurter Allgemeine Zeitung*, the *Jerusalem Post*, and the *Egyptian Gazette*. A rate of at least nine incidents a day was found. Except for the Egyptian paper, favoritism toward certain terrorists was evident.

119. Marton, J. and Acker, L. "Television-provoked Aggression: Effects of Gentle, Affection-like Training Prior to Exposure." *Child Study Journal* 12 (1981): 27–43. Effects upon subsequent play behavior of teaching pre-schoolers to be sensitive and affectionate were assessed. It was found that televised aggression did promote both imitative aggression and general aggression, but

that those children trained to be gentle exhibited less of the generalized aggression.

120. Messner, S. F. "Television Violence and Violent Crime: An Aggregate Analysis." *Social Problems* 33, 3 (February, 1986): 218–235. The findings here seem to be discrepant with the bulk of the evidence, in that this researcher found an inverse relationship between areas in the United States with the highest rates of viewing of violent television programs and areas reporting the highest rates of violent crime. However, (1) highest rates of viewing are most likely to be found in rural areas where competing activities are scarce rather than in the high-crime inner cities, and (2) one would expect a lag of perhaps a decade between high exposure to media violence as a child and subsequent violent criminal activity.

121. Molifor, F. and Sapolsky, Barry S. "Sex, Violence and Victimization in Slasher Films." *Journal of Broadcasting and Electronic Media* 37 (Spring, 1993): 233–242. The authors claim that a content analysis of slasher films made in 1980, 1985 and 1989 indicates that females are not featured more often than males as targets. They report that a significantly higher number of deaths and injuries were actually suffered by male characters. However, they admit that females were shown in terror for longer periods than were men. It was also noted that, although heavier amounts of violence appear in 1989 films than in previous ones, sex and violence are not commonly explicitly linked. (See a response to the conclusions of this article in Linz, Daniel et al., No. 100.)

122. Mustonen, Anu and Pulkkinen, Lea. "Television Violence: A Development of a Coding Scheme." *Journal of Broadcasting and Electronic Media* 41, 2 (1997): 68–183. These researchers offer a coding scheme for measuring and analyzing television violence in terms of (1) *attractiveness* (justification, glamorization and efficacy) and (2) *intensity* (seriousness, realism and dramatization). The aim is to develop better means of assessing the context in which violence is presented, and in replicating subsequent studies.

123. Oliver, Mary Beth. "Portrayals of Crime, Race and Aggression in Reality-based Police Shows: A Content Analysis." *Journal of Broadcasting and Electronic Media* 38 (Spring, 1994a): 179–182. It was found that violent crime is overrepresented in the programs, as is the percentage of crimes portrayed as solved. Whites are more likely to be shown as police. Blacks and Hispanics are more likely to be suspects and to be recipients of unarmed physical aggression by police. (It was not made clear whether or not this racial representation was disproportional to that of the population at large—or to that which holds in the population of actually charged perpetrators of crime in the society.) It was also found that the plots of these reality-based programs usually feature a restoration of justice, although this is often accomplished by means of aggressive behavior.

124. Oliver, Mary Beth. "Contributions of Sexual Portrayals to Viewers' Responses to Graphic Horror." *Journal of Broadcasting and Electronic Media* 38 (Winter, 1994b): 1–17. This is the report of an experiment in which the subjects were rated after viewing a 10-minute horror film that varied the gender of the victims as well as the amount of explicit sex portrayed. It was found that sexual scenes increased viewer enjoyment—particularly so for males

and for those subjects who had scored relatively high on measures of sexual permissiveness. For males, these sexual portrayals increased the perception that the film was frightening, and for all subjects, psychological arousal was increased during the sex scenes. The author concludes that, although these immediate responses may appear to be harmless, long-term exposure to such entertainment (interspersal of explicit sex and violent images) may well desensitize viewers to sexual violence.

125. Osborn, D. K. and Endsley, R. C. "Emotional Reactions of Young Children to TV Violence." *Child Development* 42 (1971): 321–325. The emotional arousal of pre-schoolers to three different TV exposures was assessed. That precipitated by cartoon violence was significantly greater than the reaction to either non-violent human images or non-violent cartoons.

126. Page, Stewart. "Reply to Mould and Duncan on Pornography Research." *American Psychologist* 46 (June, 1991): 652–653. This author disputes the claim that violence is decreasing in American society. He argues that justifiable fear of violence is an everyday fact of life for women. He points out that much of the current research on the effects of pornography and violence continues to confirm the Attorney General's Commission on Pornography final report of 1986.

127. Parke, R. D. et al. "Some Effects of Violent and Nonviolent Movies on the Behavior of Juvenile Delinquents." *Experimental Social Psychology* 10 (1977): 135–172. This is a report of three field experiments conducted in the United States and Belgium. Groups of adolescent boys in minimum security institutions were exposed to either violent or nonviolent films. Measures of aggressive behavior were made before, during and after the exposure. It was found that exposure to violent films increased aggressive behavior, and that the increase was greatest for boys already most predisposed to aggression. Evidence of a cumulative effect was found. Viewers of five violent movies in a week manifested more aggressive behavior than did the viewers of only one.

128. Pearl, David. "Violence and Aggression." *Society* 21, 6, 152 (September/October, 1984): 17–22. This is a review of research on the relation between television violence and aggression. The author notes that a causal relationship is suggested by most, but not all, of the data.

129. Phillips, D. P. "Suicide, Motor Vehicle Fatalities and the Mass Media." *American Journal of Sociology* 84 (1979): 1150–1174. The author claims that contemporary sociologists have virtually ignored the social effects of suggestion, modeling and imitation. His purpose in this study was to provide sociological evidence of social effects of suggestion on one form of adult violence: motor vehicle accidents. He began with the premise that this fifth leading cause of death in the United States likely has a suicide component. He examined tables of motor vehicle accidents from four states, and recorded their incidence following front-page suicide stories. He found a sharp and localized increase in single vehicle fatalities involving lone drivers in all four states immediately after (and only after) such suicide stories. Where the front-page story dealt with murder *and* suicide, there followed a significant upsurge in multiple vehicle accidents involving passenger deaths.

130. Phillips, D. P. "The Impact of Fictional Television Stories on U.S. Adult Fatalities: New Evidence on the Effect of the Mass Media on Violence." *American Journal of Sociology* 87, 6 (May, 1982a): 1340–1359. This study presents systematic evidence that violent, fictional television stories trigger imitative deaths and near-fatal accidents. Data from the U.S. National Center for Health Statistics show that suicides, motor vehicle deaths and non-fatal accidents all rise immediately following soap opera suicide stories. These increases apparently occur because soap-opera suicide stories trigger imitative suicide attempts, some of which are disguised as single-vehicle accidents.

131. Phillips, D. P. "The Behavioral Impact of Violence in the Mass Media: A Review of the Evidence from Laboratory and Non-laboratory Investigations." *Sociology and Social Research* 66, 4 (July, 1982b): 387–398. In a review of the literature on the impact of violent messages on the mass media, the author compares and assesses methodology and findings.

132. Phillips, D. P. and Hensley, J. "When Violence Is Rewarded or Punished: The Impact of Mass Media Stories on Homicide." *Journal of Communication* 34, 3 (Summer, 1984): 101–116. The authors examined daily homicide rates in the U.S. from 1973 to 1979 and discovered (1) after media stories about violence that is rewarded the homicide rate rises significantly, (2) after media stories about violence that is punished the homicide rate decreases briefly but significantly, and (3) after media stories about violence that is neither rewarded or punished the rate remains relatively stable. These findings represent the first attempt to examine the impact of capital punishment using daily homicide rates for a large population, and to compare the impact of various kinds of punishment for violence.

133. Pierce, R. L. "Child Pornography: A Hidden Dimension of Child Abuse." *Child Abuse and Neglect* 8 (1984): 940, 483–493. Child pornography in the United States is analyzed, based on a variety of previous works, as to the characteristics of the children involved, the number of victimized children, the effects on the children involved, legal issues and the responsibility of the helping professions. Involved children are usually young runaways who sell themselves to survive, but they can also be the pornographer's offspring or neighborhood children. Nationwide, it is estimated that from 300,000 to 600,000 are involved.

134. Potter, James W. and Warren, Ron. "Considering Policies to Protect Children from TV Violence." *Journal of Communications* 46, 4 (Autumn, 1996): 116–138. It is argued here that most current programs for protecting children from the destructive effects of television violence are doomed to fail. This is because proposed solutions such as blocking devices and industry-produced violence ratings are all based on inadequate definitions of violence. Most focus simply on the *frequency* of physically violent acts. The authors support the preceding hypothesis with a report on their analysis of the violent content of a composite of 28 nights of television programming, covering the time from 6:00 P.M. until midnight. The total sample comprised 168 hours of programming. The unit of analysis was an act of aggression, defined as any action serving to diminish someone in a physical, social or emotional manner. The victim could be a person, animal or society in gen-

eral. Eight categories of acts were recognized, as follows: serious assault, minor assault, harm to property, intimidation, deception, hostile remarks, societal harm and accidents. Context was also documented, in terms of whether the aggressor's intent and motive were portrayed, whether the act was rewarded, whether remorse was shown, whether there were observable consequences and whether the main appeal was to reason or the emotions. It was found that the majority of aggressive acts were presented as stemming from malicious intent and selfish motives, with the perpetrators showing remorse in fewer than 4 percent of instances. Violence occurring during the 7:00 P.M. time slot was associated with the lowest percentage of punishment or any other major adverse consequences, along with the highest proportion of emotion-based appeal. The majority of aggressive acts were found in sitcoms, reality-based programs and talk shows (over 50 per hour for each). The authors conclude that action to promote fundamental change in television programming must be taken at once by two groups: (a) the creators and producers of the material, and (b) parents and others responsible for the moral/social development of children. The final conclusion is that the only sound and workable solution is education for all partners on the critical role of the electronic media in human socialization.

135. Potter, James W. et al. "How Real Is the Portrayal of Aggression in Television Entertainment Programming?" *Journal of Broadcasting and Electronic Media* 39 (Fall, 1995): 496–516. The data base for this analysis is 3,844 acts of aggression found in a composite week of 100.5 hours of entertainment programming. The authors looked at "replicated reality" and "contextual reality" and the match between the two. They identified four factors as determinative of how violence affects viewers: realism (or the match between the context of the media portrayal and that of real life), perceived legitimacy of the act, type of violence perpetrated and consequences in terms of observable pain and suffering on the part of victims. They attempted to assess the media portrayals in terms of these factors. They found that these tended to be realistic in terms of the proportion of physical to other types of aggression shown, but unrealistic in that serious aggression was not associated with black and white perpetrators in proportion to what actually occurs in American society today. A much higher proportion of the perpetrators of violence in the United States are youthful blacks than is being portrayed in television. As for contextual factors, fewer than one in six acts are shown with major consequences, while two out of six are actually rewarded! The remaining 50 percent are *neither* rewarded nor punished in any way—that is, they are shown as if no consequences flowed from them at all. In the aggregate, television is signaling to viewers that almost all aggression is acceptable today, or at least, it does not matter. The authors note that *this violates the pattern of the morality play which has served a necessary moral purpose all through history.* They recognize a high probability that the context in which viewers are presented with the violence is contributing to the anti-social nature of television.

136. Potter, James W. et al. "Anti-social Acts in Reality Programming on Television." *The Journal of Broadcasting and Electronic Media* 41, 1 (1997): 69–89. The authors found that anti-social activity in non-fictional programming fail

to correspond to patterns in the real world. They also noted the cultural contingencies accompanying televised anti-social behavior as it is typically presented (such as low rates of punishment and absence of other negative consequences, as well as an overriding emphasis on intentions rather than results) and concluded that all this increases the likelihood of viewers being influenced by the behavior as presented.

137. Rabinovitch, M. S. et al. "Children's Violence Perception as a Function of Television Violence." *Television and Social Behavior*, Vol. 5. Washington, DC: U.S. Government Printing Office, 1972. Two groups of grade 6 children were exposed to television segments, one violent and the other neutral. Violent and neutral scenes were then flashed momentarily before them as they were involved in another activity. The members of the group exposed initially to the violent segment were less likely than the others to notice the violent scenes.

138. Rachman, S. "Sexual Fetishism: An Experimental Analogue." *Psychological Record* 16 (1966): 293–296. This researcher set out to create a "boot fetish" by classical conditioning. Slides of sexually provocative females were shown to male students, and three who responded by an erection were selected for the subsequent study. A picture of black leather female boots was then shown to each subject immediately before one of the female pin-ups evoking the sexual response. This was repeated 18 times during each of the sessions. After several sessions each subject began to respond to the boots with erections. Then they were shown pictures of other female boots, and the sexual response persisted. (A procedure of "extinction" followed.) This has serious implications for the possible role of the media in influencing sexual preferences.

139. Rachman, S. and Hodgson, R. A. "Experimentally Induced Sexual Fetishism: Preference and Development." *Psychological Record* 18 (1968): 25–27. This is a replication of the previous study, with a control added. The results confirmed the earlier finding.

140. Roberts, D. F. and Bachen, C. M. "Mass Communication Effects." *Annual Review of Psychology* 32 (1981): 307–356. In reviewing the research, the authors discovered that the previous decade has witnessed a revival and considerable substantiation of the view that the mass media exert powerful influences on the way people perceive, think about, and ultimately act upon their world. They conclude that the findings documenting a relationship between viewing violent programs and behaving aggressively are the most compelling of all.

141. Robinson, J. P. and Bachman, J. G. "Television Viewing Habits and Aggression." In *Television and Social Behavior*, Vol. 3. Washington, DC: U.S. Government Printing Office, 1972. More than 1,500 adolescents were interviewed in depth for this study, concerning their television viewing habits. A violence-viewing index was computed, as well as measures of aggressive behavior. It was found that those who watched the most violence were significantly more aggressive and tended to prefer violent solutions to problems.

142. Rosenthal, Robert. "Media Violence and Anti-social Behavior and the Consequences of Small Effects." *Journal of Social Issues* 42 (Fall, 1986): 141–154.

The author has conducted a statistical analysis of current research findings and concludes that the issue of improving the prediction and control of anti-social behavior is not at all trivial in practical terms. He compares social science in this problem area today to meteorology in terms of the reliability of its findings and its ability to predict effects.

143. Rossiter, J. R. and Robertson, T. S. "Children's Television Viewing: An Examination of Parent-child Consensus." *Sociometry* 38, 3 (September, 1975): 308–326. This study attempted to discover the degree to which parents' reported perceptions of their children's viewing habits differed from the situation as described by the children themselves. Over 250 interviews of parents and their offspring were conducted. The results showed a consistent pattern of parental exaggeration. They claimed (1) lower viewing, (2) stricter rules governing viewing, (3) more shared viewing, (4) greater parent-child interaction concerning what was viewed and (5) lower susceptibility to commercials on the part of their children than was actually the case. The tendency to report an idealized situation increased with social class.

144. Rubenstein, E. "Television and Behavior: Research Conclusions of the 1982 National Institute of Mental Health Report and Their Policy Implications." *American Psychologist* 38 (1983a): 820–825. The author discusses this report: its general conclusion that television is a powerful influence on child development, and its specific conclusion that the convergence of evidence documenting a connection between televised violence and aggressive behavior is indeed overwhelming. He comments on the accurate press comments on this report, as compared to their biased coverage of the 1972 one, and on the outburst of denials from the networks, accompanied by attempts to discredit the scientists.

145. Rubenstein, E. "Televised Violence: Approaches to Prevention and Control." *Prevention in the Human Sciences* 2 (1983b): 7–18. The author discusses the fact that, although research since 1972 has documented the adverse effect on the viewer of televised violence, the situation continues to worsen. He claims that all efforts to reduce the level of violence will be of no avail until there is active collaboration by the industry.

146. Rule, Brendan Gail and Ferguson, Tamara. "The Effects of Media Violence on Attitudes, Emotions and Cognitions." *Journal of Social Issues* 42 (Fall, 1986): 29–50. This is a survey of research findings. The authors' conclusions are (1) heavy viewing of violence is related to favorable attitudes toward, and increased tolerance of, aggression; (2) the *context* in which the violence is presented is extremely important; (3) the actual message gleaned depends on the viewer's cognitive-skill level; (4) repeated exposure to violence may reduce psychological arousal (sensitivity); and (5) there is a need for more replicated research.

147. Sapolsky, B. S. "Arousal, Affect and the Aggression-moderating Effect of Erotica." In *Pornography and Sexual Aggression,* ed. N. M. Malamuth and E. Donnerstein, pp. 85–113. New York: Academic Press, 1984. In reviewing and summarizing the findings of research on the effects of aggressive pornography, this writer says that the evidence strongly suggests that films portraying rape are not only non-cathartic, but are potent generators of negative feelings.

148. Segal, Alan. "Censorship, Social Control and Socialization." *British Journal of Sociology* 21 (March, 1970): 63–74. This article concludes that there is a need for some form of effective censorship of harmful excess in the mass media, " not merely to protect society from depravity and brutality, but . . . to protect something more basic of which pornography and violence are simply subversive: namely, certain notions of human dignity."

149. Seiden, Richard and Freitas, R. P. "Shifting Patterns of Deadly Violence." *Suicide and Life-threatening Behavior* 10, 4 (Winter, 1980): 195–209. We are told that, while the total suicide rate in the United States has varied little in the previous decade, this figure masks a dramatic shift in the risk of suicide by age. A reduction of suicide at older ages has been matched by an unprecedented increase in both suicide and homicide at younger ages. For example, the youthful suicide rate has increased by more than 80 percent; the total death rate from violent aggression for those aged 15–24 has increased by 82 percent; and the number of youths arrested for criminal homicide has increased by 64 percent.

150. Sheehan, P. "Age Trends and the Correlates of Children's Television Viewing." *Australian Journal of Psychology* 35 (1983): 417–431. Early elementary-school children were tested in a longitudinal study. Boys showed a significant relationship between television viewing variables and aggressive behavior.

151. Shemberg, K. M. et al. "Aggression-Machine Performance and Rated Aggression." *Journal of Experimental Research in Personality* 3 (1968): 117–119. Because many studies aimed at assessing the relationship between media violence and aggression employ the "aggression machine" (administration of electric shocks in the guise of some game or test), a check on the validity of that method would seem to be important. Children were rated as to high or low aggressiveness by two counselors who knew them well (working separately). When given the opportunity, the "high aggression" group administered significantly higher shocks than did the "low aggression" children.

152. Siegal, A. E. "Film Mediated Fantasy Aggression and Strength of Aggressive Drive." *Child Development* 27 (1956): 365–378. In this study the teacher was asked to pair pre-school children for observation purposes. All viewed both a violent and a non-violent cartoon one week apart, with the order of viewing being reversed for the second week. No significant cartoon effects were found on measures of aggression during free play, but there were more signs of anxiety during the viewing of the violent cartoon.

153. Signorielli, Nancy et al. "Violence on Television: The Cultural Indicators Project." *Journal of Broadcasting and Electronic Media* 39 (Spring, 1995): 278–283. According to the authors, "the proliferation of new channels and new delivery systems only makes symbolic violence more pervasive, more normal and more invisible." In this article they describe the Cultural Indicators Project by means of which regular, periodic and consistent readings of levels of media violence have been taken since 1967–1968 to provide data for a study by the National Commission on the Causes and Prevention of Violence. The project deals with "message system (or content) analysis" and "cultivation analysis " or consequences. They define a violent portrayal as one involving "the overt expression of physical force . . . compelling action

against one's will on pain of being hurt or killed," or the act of hurting or killing. They measure prevalence, rate and role of such violence in media offerings. Their data base is 3,000 programs and 35,000 characters. This project is the only ongoing research since 1967 with the capacity to trace trends on the role of violence in television drama. It provides the baseline and backdrop against which all future measures of violence must be compared.

154. Singer, Jerome L. and Singer, Dorothy G. *Television, Imagination and Aggression: A Study of Pre-schoolers.* Hillsdale, NJ: L. Erlbaum Associates, 1981. The relevant chapters here are Chapter 5, "Television Viewing and Aggression" and Chapter 6, "Family Interviews: Home Lifestyle, TV Viewing, and Aggression" (96–132). The authors report in detail on their own study which they claim is the first attempt to follow pre-school children over an extended time period (from ages 3 to 4). They found a causal link between violent content and aggressive behavior, with the more aggressive children having wrested control of the television set from their parents. They comment, "How many parents might willingly introduce into their homes two neighborhood toughs who would daily demonstrate for their children fighting and violence as a way of resolving problems? . . . [Yet] regular exposure of children to this medium may be serving much the same effect"(97).

155. Singer, Jerome L. and Singer, Dorothy G. "Family Experiences and Television Viewing as Predictors of Childrens' Imagination, Restlessness and Aggression." *Journal of Social Issues* 42 (Fall, 1986): 107–124. This study reviews the research dealing with the influence of television on the imagination, activity and aggressiveness of pre-schoolers and primary-school children. The authors conclude that watching television trains children to "take the easy way" and simply to keep on watching ever more of the same thing. Those parents who are themselves the products of heavy viewing from childhood on, who (perhaps consequently) lack other interests, and who do not establish rules about viewing provide a home atmosphere that puts their children at risk of dysphoria (generalized feelings of anxiety and discontent—sometimes described by the children as being "bored").

156. Somers, Anne R. "Violence, Television and the Health of American Youth." *The New England Journal of Medicine* 294, 15, 8 (April, 1976): 811–817. Violence on television is reviewed with respect to America's youthful "culture of violence" (for example, arrests for robbery and murder increased 300 percent for children under the age of 16 from 1964 to 1973). An examination of the research evidence on the media's impact on the young reveals that (1) "real-life" violence is portrayed, (2) these portrayals are universally available, (3) pre-schoolers watch for seven to eight hours a day, (4) low-income children spend even more time in front of the television, and (5) this within-the-home medium imposes vicarious experience and psychological conditioning on children at a crucial developmental learning stage.

157. Sparks, Glenn G. and Ogles, Robert M. "The Difference Between Fear of Victimization and the Probability of Being Victimized: Implications for Cultivation." *Journal of Broadcasting and Electronic Media* 34 (Summer, 1990): 351–358. This random sample survey discovered that measures for the two concepts (identified in the title) were not highly correlated. Amount of tel-

evision viewing *was* positively correlated with fear of violence, but not related to probability of being victimized.

158. Sprafkin, J. N. et al. "Effects of a Pro-social Televised Example on Children's
     Helping." *Journal of Experimental Child Psychology* 20 (1975): 119–126. Grade
     one children were divided into three television-viewing groups for this
     study, with one group watching a Lassie episode that featured helping, and
     the other two, either a Brady Bunch comedy or a neutral Lassie episode.
     They were then involved in a game in which they were competing for
     prizes. At the same time they were given earphones and asked to summon
     help by pressing a button if they heard barking from some puppies being
     cared for by the experimenter. Those who had viewed the prosocial episode
     were found to be much more willing to sacrifice their prizes by pushing the
     "help" button persistently when they heard distressed puppy noises.

159. Steuer, F. B. et al. "Television Aggression and the Interpersonal Aggression
     of Pre-school Children." *Journal of Experimental Child Psychology* 11 (1971):
     442–447. In this study, pre-schoolers were exposed to 11 daily sessions of
     10 minutes each of either (1) violent films containing human and animated
     cartoon characters, or (2) nonviolent television. Free play with peers was
     then observed. Those in group 1 tended to be more assaultive. The differ-
     ence between the two groups on this was significant and increased over
     time.

160. Thomas, M. H. and Drabman, R. S. "Toleration of Real-Life Aggression as
     a Function of Exposure to Televised Violence and Age of Subject." *Merrill-
     Palmer Quarterly* 21 (1975): 227–232. This was a replication of the Drabman
     and Thomas (1974) study in which older children who had just seen a vi-
     olent televised detective movie were slower to summon help when younger
     children in their care began fighting than were a control group who had
     seen an equally exciting nonviolent film. The finding did not hold for chil-
     dren younger than age 7.

161. Thomas, M. H. et al. "Desensitization to Portrayals of Real-Life Aggression
     as a Function of Exposure to Televised Violence." *Journal of Personality and
     Social Psychology* 35 (1977): 450–458. Two experiments were conducted to
     discover whether being exposed previously to a violent episode on film
     would affect emotional response to real violence. Children were studied in
     one experiment; college students in the other. Emotionality was measured
     by changes in skin resistance. It was found in both cases that subjects who
     had previously viewed the violent drama were less aroused by real violence
     than were those who had seen a control film.

162. Turner, Charles W. et al. "Naturalistic Studies of the Long-term Effects of
     Television Violence." *Journal of Social Issues* 42 (Fall, 1986): 51–73. This is a
     summary of the research findings to date. The authors conclude that most
     of the evidence supports the hypothesis that television produces a long-
     term increase in aggressive behavior in boys, while the evidence of the effect
     on girls is still inconclusive. They consider that some inconsistency in the
     findings is due to different time intervals and analytical methods employed
     by different researchers. They suggest that there is a pressing need for sen-
     sitive, valid and reliable measures of the *cumulative* effects, and of the psy-

chological variables that may be moderating (or otherwise altering) these effects.

163. Walters, R. H. et al. "Enhancement of Punitive Behavior by Audio-visual Displays." *Science* 136 (1962): 812–813. This was a replication of the landmark Buss study in which subjects were shown a violent episode, and their aggressiveness measured before and after, in comparison with a control group that had seen a neutral film. All were asked to administer an electric shock to another whenever a mistake was made in a learning task (after having been told by an "expert" that it was an aid to learning). As in the case of the original study, those who had been exposed to the violent film were significantly more likely than the control group to use the shock technique aggressively.

164. Weaver, James. "Perceived Vulnerability to Crime." *Journal of Broadcasting and Electronic Media* 30 (Spring, 1986): 141–158. A small sample was studied to identify factors affecting the documented relationship between television viewing and perception of personal vulnerability to crime. It was found that the strength and direction of the association was contingent on (a) the viewer's previous experience, (b) the type of program watched (crime or non-crime) and (c) the context in which the violence was presented.

165. Weiss, W. "Effects of the Mass Media of Communication." In *Handbook of Social Psychology*, ed. G. Lindzey and E. Aronson, pp. 177–195. Reading, MA: Addison-Wesley, 1969. In this comprehensive review of the research, the author discusses the frequently cited argument that vicarious participation in aggression is cathartic (provides for a harmless release of inhibited emotions). He concludes that there is little evidence to support such a conclusion, and much that specifically refutes it.

166. Wells, W. D. "Television and Aggression: A Replication of an Experimental Field Study." Unpublished Manuscript, Graduate School of Business, University of Chicago, 1973. This is an attempt to replicate the findings of the early field study described in Feshbach and Singer (1981), which *had seemed* to support the catharsis theory. Boys in 10 residential schools were restricted to either violent or neutral television for seven weeks. A baseline assessment of aggressiveness was made, and the two groups were matched on this variable. Unlike the earlier study, a distinction was made between physical and verbal aggression. Another difference was that those who assessed aggressiveness after the viewing period were not told to which group the boys had belonged. This time, the findings did not confirm the catharsis theory, for, although it was found that the neutral television group measured higher on verbal aggression (many complaints about having to watch "this lousy tame" show), the viewers of violent programs ranked significantly higher on physical aggression.

167. West, S. G. et al. "The Effect of Viewing Physical Aggression on Verbal Aggression in Delinquent Girls." Unpublished Manuscript, Florida State University, 1975. Female delinquents were given a puzzle to solve while a confederate of the experimenter made insulting remarks to them about their stupidity. Following the viewing of either a violent or a neutral film, the puzzle-solving roles were reversed, with the subject, in each case, asked to comment on the performance of the confederate. Judges rated the degree of

aggression expressed. The girls who had seen the violent film were the more verbally aggressive.

168. Williams, Tannis. "How and What Do Children Learn from Television?" *Human Communication Research* 7, 2 (Winter, 1981): 180–192. This is a review and synthesis of the research and theory dealing with children's learning from television. The profound power of the medium as a source of learning is recognized. The author comments that "given the high levels of both physical and verbal aggression on TV, the fact that aggression in children's TV is increasing, and the fact that aggression tends to be portrayed with high levels of action, which is itself attractive to children, TV may well teach aggressive behavior best of all."

169. Wilson, Barbara J. "Applying Social Science Research to Film Rating: A Shift from Offensiveness to Harmful Effects." *Journal of Broadcasting and Electronic Media* 34 (Fall, 1990): 443–468. The author identifies four assumptions underlying the current rating system used by the Motion Picture Association of America (MPAA) and shows how these assumptions are inconsistent with the actual impact of media portrayals on young viewers, as documented by science. She offers a more appropriate alternative system based on findings showing non-explicit sexual content has a very limited effect. This is because (1) children between the ages of 2 and 12 are unlikely to comprehend the references and (2) it appears that such references have little adverse effect on adolescents. On the other hand, movies portraying rape and other sexually violent images consistently produce anti-social effects in laboratory settings. In addition, the research on adults has consistently shown that exposure to violence against women that is either juxtaposed with mildly erotic scenes results in callousness toward the female victims. Even stronger and more adverse effects would be expected in the case of younger viewers.

170. Wilson, W. and Hunter, H. "Movie-Inspired Violence." *Psychological Reports* 53, 2 (October, 1983): 435–441. This is a study of 58 incidences of violence which were alleged to have been inspired by movies from 1970 to 1982. One particular movie, *The Deer Hunter*, seems to have been most harmful, although *The Taxi Driver* and *The Exorcist* were also cited by murderers as having inspired them.

171. Wood, Michael. "The Iconography of Violence." *New Society* 42, 784 (October, 1977): 66–68. This is a study of the growing trend toward graphic displays of violence and the apparent attempt by all forms of the mass media to present violence as viable and acceptable entertainment.

172. Wood, Wendy et al. "Effects of Media Violence on Viewers' Aggression." *Psychological Bulletin* 109 (May, 1991): 371–383. This is a review and analysis of research to date. In the reviewed experiments, children or adolescents were exposed to violent and control representations, and their post-exposure behavior was coded for aggressiveness during subsequent spontaneous social interaction. The evidence is compelling that exposure to media violence significantly enhances aggressive behavior in general, but the effect is not uniform for all viewers. Marginally stronger relations were obtained in those studies using a cross-section of the normal population of children (as compared to the emotionally disturbed) and in those conducted

in laboratory settings *versus* other contexts. These findings illustrate the causal relations between media exposures and *naturally occurring aggression*. The authors emphasize that these findings cannot be dismissed as merely representing artificial experimental constructions because they show enhanced aggressiveness in subsequent interactions with strangers, classmates and friends, in normal situations.

173. Zigler, E. and Child, I. L. "Socialization." In *The Handbook of Social Psychology*, Vol. 3, 2nd ed., ed. G. Lindzey and E. Aronson. Cambridge, MA: Addison-Wesley, 1969. The authors note that "Comparison of societies, or groups within societies, has repeatedly suggested that overt aggression is higher, and guilt about it is lower, in groups that value and reward aggression than in groups that devalue and punish it" (352).

174. Zillman, D. and Bryant, J. "Pornography, Sexual Callousness, and the Trivialization of Rape." *Journal of Communication* 32, 4 (Autumn, 1982): 10–21. This study attempted to assess the consequences of massive, longitudinal exposure to pornography on perception of contemporary sexual behavior, and on attitudes toward women and to rape. For six weeks, 80 males and 80 females were exposed to hard-core pornography in either massive, intermediate, or nil quantities. Assessments were made two weeks after final exposure. It was found that massive exposure produced a trivialization of rape and diminished support for women's causes in *both* sexes. In the males, it resulted as well in the following: perceptions of hypersexuality throughout society; more favorable attitudes toward pornography; increased sex callousness toward women; and evidence of addiction.

175. Zillman, D. et al. "The Effect of Erotica Featuring Sadomasochism and Bestiality on Motivated Inter-male Aggression." *Personality and Social Psychology* 7 (1981): 153–159. In this study, 40 male undergraduates were provoked by a peer, and then exposed to either (1) relatively non-arousing, pleasant erotica (pin-ups), (2) arousing, displeasing and non-aggressive erotica (bestiality), (3) arousing, displeasing and aggressive erotica (sadomasochism), or (4) not exposed to erotica. They were then all provided with a legitimate opportunity to retaliate against an annoyer, who had performed a routine technique in the experiment so as to inflict pain unnecessarily. No difference in aggressiveness was found between groups 2 and 3, but groups 1 and 4 were significantly less aggressive than those who had been exposed to the depictions of bestiality and sadomasochism. It is concluded that, regardless of the violence involved, sexual stimuli portraying deviant behavior facilitates intermale aggression.

Index

About the Author

PAT DUFFY HUTCHEON is a writer, sociologist, and educator with broad experience both in teaching at all levels of the public school and university system and in policy-oriented research. Now retired, she taught courses in the sociology of education and early childhood education at the University of Regina and the University of British Columbia, as well as serving as a research advisor to the Health Promotion Branch of the Canadian Department of Health and Welfare and as a director of the Vanier Institute of the Family. Among her earlier publications are *A Sociology of Canadian Education* and *Leaving the Cave: Evolutionary Naturalism in Social-Scientific Thought*.

ISBN 0-275-96381-0

HARDCOVER BAR CODE